Investing By The Numbers

Jarrod W. Wilcox, Ph.D., CFA

Published by Frank J. Fabozzi Associates

Editorial consultant: Megan Orem
Cover designer: Scott C. Riether

ISBN: 1-883249-54-6

Printed in the United States of America

Foreword

During the last half of the 20th Century, human affairs have been transformed by the development of the computer. No field has been altered more radically than the practice of investing. As Jarrod Wilcox puts it, quoting a "speculator of 75 years ago: 'Observation, experience, memory, and mathematics — these are what the successful trader must depend on....' How much keener would be his faculties today, when electronic computers have marvelously expanded his ability to do mathematics and to rely on memory over many years! How much broader would be his powers of observation!"

Computing power by itself would have had little effect on investing without the astonishing development of mathematical finance theory and financial econometrics over the same period. From the mean-variance analysis of Markowitz in the early 1950s, through the development of the Capital Asset Pricing Model in the 1960s and option pricing theory in the 1970s, to the statistical analyses of time-series and cross-sectional patterns in asset returns that have characterized research in the 1980s and 1990s, and the recent incorporation of psychological insights in behavioral finance, intellectual advances have stimulated innovation throughout the financial world.

Despite the importance of these developments, surprisingly few people have a broad understanding of their meaning. The determined and mathematically prepared reader can find much of the story in textbooks of finance theory and econometrics; the historical evolution is better summarized by popular books such as Peter Bernstein's *Capital Ideas* or Burt Malkiel's *Random Walk Down Wall Street*. But neither kind of book conveys the "folk wisdom" of experienced professionals. Where do standard theories work well, and where do they fail? What are the pitfalls in applying textbook statistical methods to financial data? What is the proper role of human judgement in quantitative analysis? These are the questions Jarrod Wilcox sets out to address.

The author has 30 years of experience in academia, consulting, and asset management. He brings this experience to bear in an effective mix of simple mathematics, data analysis, historical anecdote, and practical advice. He has important things to say, and he says them in a personal, readable style. Any reader interested in the application of financial theory or statistical methods to investment decision-making will find valuable insights in this book.

John Y. Campbell
Otto Eckstein Professor of Applied Economics
Harvard University

About the Author

Jarrod Wilcox, Ph.D., CFA, is Director of Currency and Overseas Products at PanAgora Asset Management, having previously been both Director of Research and Director of Global Equities at that firm. Earlier he served as Director of International Equity at Batterymarch Financial Management and as chief investment officer at Colonial Management Associates. Jarrod was educated at M.I.T., where he also was a member of the faculty at the Sloan School of Management. He has published articles on many aspects of investing.

He writes: "I was always fascinated by the markets, beginning with a limited partnership I started as soon as I could legally trade Sadly, it took me decades to harness that enthusiasm with the right blend of quantitative tools and street experience to make it productive. This book is aimed at the ambitious younger quant who wants to accelerate that process."

Acknowledgment

I wish to thank Frank Fabozzi, for his patience and encouragement, and my colleagues at PanAgora Asset Management for their dialogue, secretarial assistance, and data for examples. Credit for this book's completion should go to Linda Wilcox, for cheerful willingness to share a year's worth of evenings and weekends.

Jarrod Wilcox
Boston, Mass.

Table of Contents

Foreword iii

About the Author iv

Acknowledgment iv

Part I. Motivation and Context

1. Purpose, Scope, and Plan 1
2. Why Quantitative? 9

Part II. The Market Ecology

3. Finance at the Crossroads — The Santa Fe Experiments 29
4. Feedback Structure, Indexing, and Active Investing 45

Part III. Conceptual Tools

5. St. Markowitz, or Single-Period Investing 77
6. Many-Period Investing 91
7. Options and Their Dynamic Equivalents 107
8. The CAPM and Its Descendants 125
9. Behavioral Finance 145
10. Trading Costs and Taxes 159
11. The Dynamic Market of Individuals 175

Part IV. Quantitative Skills

12. Valuation Models 185
13. Technical Heuristics 205
14. Econometric Modeling of Market Imperfections 219
15. Risk Assessment and Portfolio Construction 249
16. Performance Analysis 261

Part V. Practical Examples

17. U.S. Stocks 275
18. International Diversification 289
19. Emerging Markets 301
20. Currency, The Hidden Side of Equity 311

Part VI. Future Investing by the Numbers

21. Neural Nets and Genetic Algorithms 329
Index 343

Chapter 1

Purpose, Scope, and Plan

*Some books are to be tasted, others to be swallowed, and
some few to be chewed and digested.*
Francis Bacon, *Essays, "Of Studies" (1597–1625)*

I am a quantitative investor, yet I believe that the larger part of investing can never
be a science. Investors who use mathematical tools can be very well rewarded.
Too often, though, investors with quantitative backgrounds suffer more than their
share of disappointments. They often learn to live with an expectation of being
average. If you want to invest in a more scientific way to get better results in the
stock markets, but avoid that fate, this book is for you. On the other hand, this
book is also for me, the author. Between us, it is a kind of joint enterprise to see if
I can communicate the best use of objective, numeric disciplines in the very subjective world of shifting market values.

This is not a textbook, but a travel guide. With such a book, you hope at
first read to determine where you will have the best experience. Sometimes,
though, you will have to visit the site to really appreciate the description. Then a
rereading may give you a better idea of what the guide means in similar contexts.
So it is here. I will cover 20 useful places on the investment landscape after this
introduction. I'll try to make each understandable and practical. Still, though, you
will get the greatest rewards only if you come back and re-read sections after seeing similar material dealt with elsewhere or after intervals of your investing
adventures.

Let me give you an example of what not to do. In the early 1960s as a
college undergraduate I read all the books on investing I could find in the M.I.T.
libraries. Among them were descriptions of methods used by chartists, people
who tried to make money using charts of price action during the 1930s and earlier.
Among their tools were moving average methods for determining trends and specific heuristics for buying and selling when a trend broke out of a well-established
price range. However, my inclinations were more in the direction of analysis of
fundamental factors influencing company profits. I was also influenced by the
more science-oriented environment set by my professors. Franco Modigliani convinced me in his finance class that the market was rational. Paul Cootner taught
the investments course. He had just edited an influential book, *The Random Character of Stock Market Prices*, that suggested markets were highly efficient in
incorporating new information.[1] And so I discarded chartist methods.

---

[1] Paul H. Cootner (ed.), *The Random Character of Stock Market Prices* (Cambridge, Mass.: M.I.T. Press
1964).

An embarrassing number of years later, after I had gotten a Ph.D. in management, taught at M.I.T., been a management consultant for eight years, and been a portfolio manager for more than a decade, I read *Market Wizards*, Jack Schwager's excellent series of interviews with very successful traders.[2] Such adages as "cut your losses and let your profits run," combined with admonitions to follow the trend, then made more sense to me. I could relate stop loss orders to producing positively skewed results through dynamic hedging. Betting on the trend was an approach supported by recent evidence that positive analyst earnings estimate revisions were followed by excess stock returns for weeks. But still I made no systematic use of the insights from charting. Finally, several years later, when circumstances forced me to become more expert in short-term currency trading, I began serious econometric investigation of chartist methods. Only then was I able to integrate these ideas into my investment practice.

The point of the example is that until I made a determined effort to test chartist approaches, I got no value from the valid knowledge in the material I had read. The lesson is not to take this book on faith, but to go out and test its suggestions, and to come back and read it with new context.

PURPOSE

You can benefit from this book if you have already invested in stocks, find *The Wall Street Journal* or *The Financial Times* interesting reading, and enjoy applying logic and mathematics to daily life. Still, this guide is not a primer; it is meant to share a perspective with those who seek to earn their living through investing.

To use skillfully the various quantitative tools for investing in stocks, while avoiding the pitfalls, you will have learned well:

1. How a stock market works and who populates it;
2. The dominant conceptual frameworks and empirical findings, not all taught in business schools;
3. The most important tools developed by both academics and practitioners; and
4. A knowledge of some of the special characteristics of each market.

This is the outline followed by the parts of the book after the introduction.

When you are done reading I believe you will have a good outline of successful behaviors that you can try for yourself.

---

[2] Jack D. Schwager, *Market Wizards: Interviews with Top Traders* (New York, N.Y.: New York Institute of Finance 1989).

SCOPE

The emphasis here is on investing in developed-market stocks, both U.S. and international. However, currency and emerging markets are also covered. I have experience in both; and clearly both properly belong in the kit of the professional investor. Derivative instrument descriptions are limited to the essential. Bonds are not covered, both because I have less personal experience with them and because the proper treatment of their embedded options is frequently complex. I have tested every idea and every quantitative tool described.

In most of the book, you are assumed able to invest without worrying overmuch about taxes. If you are not an institutional investor then perhaps you are investing your own tax-deferred savings, as in an IRA. The world of tax-sensitive investing requires a very different outlook. However, Chapter 10 does describe important strategies for improving after-tax returns. It is, of course, a good idea to defer gain realization. Somewhat surprisingly, it is also a good idea to initially invest in high diversifiable-risk securities that add value to the option presented by the choice of when to sell and pay capital gains taxes.

For each of the 20 topic areas to be covered, you will read both the dominant views among investors and my views on what appears to be a more sensible approach, with examples wherever practicable. This promise implies that I believe the dominant approaches to investing are ineffective.

Like most of us, my thinking is conditioned both by personal experience and by many business colleagues, teachers, and authors. However, it might be helpful to some readers to know of two who were most influential. Jay Forrester at M.I.T. taught me to look for nonlinear feedback systems, and to see ideas as structures that govern system behavior. Dean LeBaron of Batterymarch Financial Management taught me to view ideas as variables. As a contrarian, he showed me that investment decision rules are subject to the law of fashion — differentiation followed by imitation. In what follows, you will see the result.

PLAN

Chapter 2 completes the introduction of the book with an essay titled "Why Quantitative?" There is among professional investors a sharp divide: "quants" versus other market practitioners who claim a greater role for judgment on a case-by-case approach. We first note benefits of the scientific and engineering cultures that we can exploit when we use numbers to help us invest. Then in the second part, we discover the need for non-mathematical judgment created by economic instability, by investor learning, and by the ongoing supply of new inexperienced investors, all of which produce an ever-changing environment. The great number of securities and the complex and multiple causes of changes in values also points to endless variation in detail, which inhibits model-building and leaves many important factors unmeasured. Finally, I argue for synthesis of these different viewpoints.

Part II of the book lays out a market ecology. In Chapter 3, I first briefly outline a traditional theoretical finance-based understanding of the market, focusing on Markowitz mean-variance optimization and the equilibrium-based capital asset pricing model (CAPM). Economists are, of course, aware that these models do not capture important aspects of market behavior, but the necessary qualifications are too often minimized by the time these ideas reach the practical investor. I point out the main areas in which academic finance falls short of reality and the reasons you should take care in using it even for prescriptive purposes. Then I compare this convention with the richer view that arises from artificial-agent simulations of markets. Some of the best such experiments have been conducted under the auspices of the Santa Fe Institute.

Dynamic computer simulations, like simpler analytic theories such as the CAPM, are incomplete unless accompanied by empirical testing. However, even at the theoretical stage the work at the Santa Fe Institute clearly demonstrates plausible circumstances under which the market may never reach equilibrium. Chapter 4 provides perspective from another direction as to what is meant by market equilibrium and what determines whether it is reached. This is done using simple feedback ideas at a relatively aggregate level. We then use both these pictures to help explain the behaviors of investors who are "indexers" and various types of "active investors." I will assert that these investor types are most appropriate for markets near equilibrium and occasionally far from equilibrium, respectively.

In Part III, we return in a series of short chapters to the more detailed study of specific investment-related concepts. Although the treatment may be condensed and irreverent, the purpose is a thorough grounding in ideas you need to be a better investor.

Chapter 5 deals with "Saint Markowitz." Harry Markowitz, in his best-known role, tells us how to think about investment diversification looking out a single period. Sadly, constructing an efficient portfolio is not as simple as it first appears. Consequently we will need some heuristics to deal with uncertainty and complexity. Chapter 6 explores the less-well-known side of Markowitz as the practical investor interested in improving long-term returns. He showed how diversification can increase the mean expected rate of return. I will extend his analysis and show you the practical implications of investing for maximum sustained growth of capital.

Chapter 7 begins with the famous Black-Scholes-Merton option value model. We go on to explore the profound implication of the discovery that dynamic trading patterns replicate the effect of particular tradable options. The critical benefit here is to understand that your rules for active investing, regardless of whether they add to short-term average return, may produce either positively or negatively skewed return patterns. And these will affect long-term capital growth rates as well as your comfort and survival along the way.

Chapter 8 reviews briefly again the capital asset pricing model and its descendants. The CAPM is now over 30 years old but still resonating the articulate voice of Bill Sharpe. It and its descendants attempt to describe a market at various kinds of equilibrium, while assuming differences among investors to be incredibly restricted. Investors differ only in their attitudes toward risk, and not in their beliefs, their decision-rules, or their access to capital or markets. The descendant models include variations that better accommodate empirical findings. I offer a polemic against the CAPM-inspired practice of minimizing residual risk around a naively formulated market at equilibrium, and suggest better ways of motivating investment management performance.

Chapter 9 provides a different critique of CAPM, that offered by behavioral finance, an intrusion by psychologists into the pristine gardens of mathematical economics. By pointing to the imperfections of real-world investors, this subfield of research has performed a real service. Its descriptions of cognitive limitations and "irrational" behaviors offer possible explanations for many of the opportunities for adding to return faced by skilled active investors. However, they are a bit unsatisfying in that they don't tell us much about how a market composed of such flawed participants can be rather impressively efficient in processing information. After all, this is the lesson of Adam Smith and his model of the invisible hand.

Chapter 10 reintroduces the real-world stickiness of trading costs and capital gains taxes. In this context, great benefit attaches to longer-term planning. The existence of substantial capital gains taxes has a deep influence on rational investment strategy. Somewhat paradoxically, taxes discourage most transaction activity but encourage risk taking. The policies of the active investor in the taxable world will therefore be rather different from pension-fund active investors, who can afford to ignore taxes.

Chapter 11 presents a dynamic market of individuals buying and selling securities. It synthesizes the views so far discussed by showing their place within the larger framework of markets as ecologies discussed in Chapters 3 and 4. Here we finally come to appreciate the different roles in stock selection played by fundamental analysts, growth and value investors, momentum investors, and other market actors. The added complexity that keeps real stock markets in flux comes because these types are continually changing both the details of the way they behave and the investors who adhere to each type of investment policy.

In Part IV we turn from building concepts to another series of short chapters building skills with particular techniques. Chapter 12 appraises a variety of valuation models as tools for the fundamental investor. I will give special emphasis to the price-book/return on equity valuation model. I can claim some credit for it, but, more important, it has been adapted and used successfully by other investors for whom I have great respect. However, since no valuation model as it becomes widely used can retain its effectiveness as an active tool, you must be familiar with the pros and cons of a wide repertoire. It is also important to note that valuation models can be used to organize not only objective facts but also judgmental ratings on economic performance. They can be a bridge between the "quant" and the fundamental analyst.

Chapter 13 reviews technical trading. I will offer some opinions for separating the grain from the chaff. This chapter is also the place to analyze in some depth the principles that lie behind the informal judgmental rules and beliefs typical of traders generally thought to be successful.

The practitioner who has spent a career analyzing factors that signal higher average returns in particular circumstances has a good vantage point from which to read the parallel efforts of academics to uncover the same factors. In Chapter 14, I will comment on a variety of published papers purporting to show market inefficiencies. Together, we can explore examples of research on the small stock effect, low price-to-book, calendar effects, price momentum and reversal, and other denizens of the inefficiency zoo. Besides all the usual problems of statistical inference, attempting to exploit these apparent inefficiencies must cope with a kind of investment Heisenberg Principle of Uncertainty. Academic validation of market inefficiencies introduces the complication that investors are constantly reading such studies, trying out the implied rules, and obliterating the circumstances that created them.

Chapter 15 treats risk assessment. This has become a critical topic, not only for Markowitz diversification optimization but also for option valuation and overall disaster prevention. We will go beyond simply projecting past variances and covariances. Better techniques take into account both time-dependent models and the information offered by related securities. Without good statistical estimation, Markowitz portfolio optimization is probably the single most dangerous weapon in the armory of quantitative investing. Here, those who can not learn from history truly condemn themselves to repeat it.

Chapter 16 deals with performance measurement. I examine performance attribution approaches, which turn out to be old-fashioned standard cost accounting in disguise. Then I go on to more functional process control ideas.

Part V provides additional practical examples, as well as an opportunity for me to share some interesting material, in four different market contexts. Chapter 17 deals with U.S. large capitalization stocks, whose transactions make up one of the world's most efficient markets. Here I also offer some simple econometric studies of the possibility of timing the market.

Chapter 18 covers international diversification and the adjustments that need to be made in adapting American-style investing tools to other developed stock markets. There are controversies on the degree of diversification offered, on proper benchmarks, on the difficulties imposed by different standards of company reporting, and on many other topics. International exposure is addictive. Once you have tried it, it is difficult to confine yourself to a single country, even one as rich in possibility as the United States.

Emerging markets range from those in only somewhat less-developed countries like Greece, Mexico, and Taiwan to the lawlessness of the frontier. Chapter 19 shows you how to encapsulate this variety and return volatility into a more attractive package than do the conventional capitalization-weighted indices. I will also use this as a case study for more effective portfolio construction.

International diversification of stocks is greatly advantaged by at least a rudimentary knowledge of currency. In Chapter 20 I will describe the return characteristics of currencies and the basic ideas for hedging them passively or actively. I find currencies fascinating and profitable.

Finally, Part VI offers a bonus look at what seem destined to be important future approaches for investing by the numbers. Chapter 21 describes neural nets and genetic algorithms, two techniques for constructing non-linear decision models that mimic biological processes. This chapter is important to investors because quantitative tools are as subject to the law of fashion as any other aspect of active investing. They must continually be renewed and reinvigorated if they are to retain their effectiveness.

Chapter 2

Why Quantitative?

Science becomes dangerous only when it imagines that it has reached its goal.
George Bernard Shaw, The Doctor's Dilemma, Preface, "The Latest Theories" (1911)

I have worked both in firms specializing in quantitative investing and in those dominated by judgmental fundamental and technical analysis. The quantitative professionals, generally feeling they represent the forces of progress, often disparage the efforts of more judgmental practitioners as operating by guesswork. The other camp describes those who specialize in quantitative techniques as trying to drive based on what appears in their rearview mirrors. Sometimes the gulf between the two seems unbridgeable. The plan of this chapter is show the merits of quantitative investing, to compare them to the advantages of qualitative judgments, and then to argue that the two approaches may be integrated. My preference is for a quantitative system leavened by the yeast of qualitative judgments.

WHY BE A QUANTITATIVE INVESTOR?

There are two basic arguments for the use of quantitative methods in investing. The first is that such methods are helpful in reducing the distractions of emotions and the cognitive biases that interfere with making good investment decisions. The second is that they more efficiently extract cumulative knowledge from the environment. After we review these arguments, I will highlight two important examples of quantitative tools: *efficient diversification* and *econometric analysis* of *market inefficiencies*.

Human Nature Was Not Designed For Active Investing

One of the best books ever written about what used to be called "speculation" is *Reminiscences of A Stock Operator*. It was written by Edwin Lefevre, as supposedly told by Jesse Livermore, a famous speculator when the book was published in 1923. Here are some samples of his thinking:

> "I sometimes think that speculation must be an unnatural sort of business, because I find that the average speculator has arrayed against him his own nature. The weaknesses that all men are prone to are fatal to success in speculation — usually those very weaknesses that make him likable to his fellows...."

9

Or... "The speculator's chief enemies are always boring from within. It is inseparable from human nature to hope and to fear."

And further: "Observation, experience, memory and mathematics — these are what the successful trader must depend on.... He cannot bet on the unreasonable or on the unexpected, however strong his personal convictions may be...."

Note the priority given to conquering one's emotions and cognitive biases. Our preexisting mental equipment did not evolve for the stock market, a very recent environment where the normal rules of life do not apply.

In the stock market, we cannot depend on feelings of confidence in our information. Straightforward connections make little sense. For example, good companies often make poor investments, and vice versa. Good news is often the stimulus for a drop in prices. And unlike most other situations, here we can draw no comfort from like-minded peers. The typical organizational value given to consensus decision-making is turned topsy-turvy here, where big profits are available to those who successfully disagree with their fellows. The stock market is a hyper-competitive arena where the investment actions of others have already incorporated in prices most of what we know.

Its transactions are also far more liquid. In normal life, it's helpful that human nature tends to sustain past commitments. The market teaches you to expect random disappointment; but it also teaches, when confronted by real evidence, to change your mind quickly. The normal human tendency is for greater difficulty in selling than in buying. As when obsolete machinery causes the bankruptcy of a factory, difficulty in deciding to sell can cause investment portfolios to become choked with stale ideas.

A few professional traders say they have learned to conquer their emotions. They are able to observe a price movement dispassionately, without hoping that it will move one way or the other. For my part, when I see a move in the value of the yen that means millions of dollars of profits, I tend to think I am rather smart. It is very helpful to have a pre-existing strategy that governs what events will trigger either an exit or a further investment in the position, rather than rely on my inflated feelings of confidence. Even though I have been through investment ups and downs many times, I still am subject to more emotion than is good for accurate decision-making. For most of us mere mortals, quantitative models are what give us the discipline we need for investment success.

When we can crystallize our decision rules to the point that they can be carried out as a definite procedure, we bring our human natures under very useful control. One way to make sure this happens is to program our policies for computer implementation. We retain the right to decide when a rule might need changing. As a practical matter, though, the friction of doing so helps us to avoid daily distractions, and even to ride out storms of fear, hope, and greed.

The Advantage of the Scientific Method

The competitive nature of the stock market gives an overwhelming advantage to anyone who can gain new knowledge — not only in direct facts but also in better interpretation of the significance of facts. We need to learn how to learn. The revolution in Western knowledge that began to make itself felt in the 1600s was driven in large part by the invention of the *scientific method*. Careful documenting of measurements made possible formal testing of theoretical hypotheses. The publication of findings rather than hoarding of guild secrets made it possible for others to replicate results. The invention of special descriptive languages, increasingly mathematical, enabled surer and more accurate chains of reasoning. Together with a code of honest conduct, these changes enormously accelerated the rate at which new knowledge accumulates. The maintenance of a competitive edge in interpretation of investment facts is a race. Why not put the *scientific method* to work?

To do so, we have developed both a public science and a private science of investing. The public science is played on the stage of *The Journal of Finance* and more practitioner-oriented journals such as *The Journal of Portfolio Management* and *The Financial Analyst's Journal*. Techniques for optimal risk diversification, for example, are helpful no matter how many market participants use them. In contrast, knowledge of market relationships that could be used by investors aiming for above-average returns faces the challenge of surviving long enough to be useful in the face of widespread publication. When enough investors master each newly invented technique for achieving above-average results, that technique loses most of its value.

In the meantime, however, there remains a potential benefit to the fast-adopter who implements the latest results of financial science before these are fully incorporated in the market's prices. For example, there has gradually grown up a list of "anomalies" or predictable return patterns. The most famous anomalies have been a tendency for smaller stocks and for stocks of unsuccessful companies to have higher returns, particularly in January. Investors may take advantage of such "publicly revealed" anomalies only so long as they remain unpopular. Sometimes, however, the shelf-life of a well-known investment strategy may be prolonged by its successive application to additional arenas such as less developed or emerging markets.

Private science is the application of the parts of the scientific method that do not involve dissemination of knowledge to others outside one's firm. If sufficiently original, its findings may be useful for a long time. Private science is not so difficult as it used to be. We now have enormous statistical databases and the latest econometric modeling techniques to discover predictive relationships. We can also use computer simulations to better understand the behavior of our decision rules, both with real and realistic data. Making our ideas explicit allows them to be challenged and overthrown, whether simply by fresh data or by colleagues and junior associates. This can afford the investor greater protection against stale knowledge that no longer applies.

The growth of computational and memory resources through the arrival of computers plays a key role here. We earlier referred to the speculator of 75 years ago: "Observation, experience, memory and mathematics — these are what the successful trader must depend on...." How much keener would be his faculties today, when electronic computers have marvelously expanded his ability to do mathematics and to rely on memory over many years! How much broader would be his powers of observation! The development of global databases puts at his fingertips the prices, income statements and balance sheets of thousands of stocks in a score of different countries. He, or she, need not form investment policy based solely on the few investment events, such as the crash of October 1987, that are so striking that they fix themselves in memory.

To the public's benefit, not a few quantitative investors have adopted these advantages. Consequently, the bar is raised. The vaulter must jump higher than before to assure above-average results. Some techniques, however, are of lasting value. We will now introduce two basic tools for quantitative investing – the efficient portfolio and the econometric study of market inefficiencies. The examples shown illustrate only the basic ideas. We will build on them in later chapters.

Efficient Diversification

At the beginning of the 1950s, a young Ph.D. candidate at the University of Chicago recognized that investors typically diversified their wealth among collections of stocks, or portfolios, rather than put all their money into their favorite stock. He posited that it was risk, measured as expected return variance, that underlay this. His name was Harry Markowitz, and his dissertation and subsequent writings gave us a most important quantitative tool: the concept of an efficient portfolio and a plan for constructing it.[1] I will merely outline his idea here, but with concrete numbers.

Although Markowitz also thought in terms of long-run results, his basic model deals with but a single time interval. Over this interval, each stock has an expected percentage return and an expected statistical variance of percentage return. Each pair of stocks has an expected correlation of expected returns. The expected percentage return and variance of the portfolio are completely determined by these quantities and by the weight of each stock in the portfolio. The problem of constructing the portfolio with minimum return variance given each possible portfolio expected return is therefore well defined and not very difficult to solve. The collection of all such answers is called the *efficient frontier*. This is a list of portfolios. Each is the optimum that can be achieved given the inputs and some particular rate at which the investor is willing to take on additional variance to achieve greater expected return.

Markowitz posits that the rational investor will want such a portfolio because variance is a good indicator of near-term risk. Also, as he points out, the variance of percentage returns, along with the mean single-period percentage return, is an important determinant of expected long-run return. He also assumes the investor will be able to specify the required inputs. Let us show how this may be done with a simple

---

[1] Harry M. Markowitz, *Portfolio Selection* (New Haven, Conn.: Yale University Press, 1959).

example. To make it more interesting, suppose we are considering optimal portfolios of countries, putting aside the details of how this is to be achieved through representative baskets of stocks in each country. Our investment interval is one year, and we begin with index percentage returns for each of five countries as shown in Exhibit 1.

I will sketch out the calculations and thought process necessary. If you are handy with a spreadsheet you might build a simple "optimizer" yourself using these recipes plus the "solver" option in Microsoft's EXCEL or equivalent. Commercial versions that handle more assets and more problem features are more complicated, but they follow the same principles.

May I assume that you know how to calculate the means, standard deviations, and correlations shown in Exhibit 1? If not, you will benefit by referring to a text on basic statistics before proceeding.[2] If you are untrained in academic finance, you probably also need a more conventional viewpoint to appreciate the skeptical practitioner's perspective of this book.[3]

Exhibit 1: International Finance Corporation Indices
% Total Returns, Selected Countries

	Brazil	Greece	Malaysia	Mexico	Taiwan
1985	94.2	3.4	−14.3	18.4	10.4
1986	−24.6	52.2	11.9	97.2	49.3
1987	−63.1	152.2	0.9	−4.8	120.8
1988	125.6	-37.6	27.7	108.3	93.3
1989	39.9	80.2	44.0	73.4	100.0
1990	−65.7	104.1	−11.2	29.7	−50.9
1991	170.4	−19.2	12.1	106.8	−0.6
1992	0.3	−27.0	27.9	21.2	−26.6
1993	99.4	21.9	102.9	49.9	89.0
1994	69.8	2.0	−21.5	−40.6	22.5
1995	−20.2	10.	3.6	−26.0	−30.7
1996	34.5	5.1	24.5	17.8	37.4
Mean	38.4	29.0	17.4	37.6	34.5
Std. Dev.	75.6	57.4	33.2	50.3	56.9

Correlations:

	Brazil	Greece	Malaysia	Mexico	Taiwan
Brazil	1.00	−0.70	0.28	0.44	0.16
Greece	−0.70	1.00	−0.13	−0.17	0.30
Malaysia	0.28	−0.13	1.00	0.39	0.46
Mexico	0.44	−0.17	0.39	1.00	0.29
Taiwan	0.16	0.30	0.46	0.29	1.00

---

[2] Richard P. Runyon, Audrey Huber, and Kay A. Coleman, *Behavioral Statistics: The Core* (New York: McGraw-Hill, 1994). Many other introductory statistics texts would be adequate substitutes. Though this one is not targeted at business, it is particularly clear.

[3] My favorite academic text is William F. Sharpe, Gordon J. Alexander, and Jeffery V. Bailey, *Investments: Fifth Edition* (Englewood Cliffs, NJ: Prentice Hall, 1995). Those who want to see Sharpe's more recent instructional material on the Internet may wish to visit http://www-sharpe.stanford.edu/. As of November, 1997 this also contained a sample algorithm for portfolio optimization in MATLAB.

Exhibit 2: Expected Covariance Matrix of Returns

	Brazil	Greece	Malaysia	Mexico	Taiwan
Brazil	5,713	-3,024	713	1,669	685
Greece	-3,024	3,295	-238	-504	983
Malaysia	713	-238	1,103	653	877
Mexico	1,669	-504	653	2,529	831
Taiwan	685	983	877	831	3,238

The estimated risk of a portfolio is based on the weights for each stock combined with the expected covariance matrix of their returns. Each element of the matrix represents a pair of stocks, stock i and stock j. Each is calculated by multiplying the standard deviation of the ith return by the standard deviation of the jth return and then by the correlation between the two stocks. The covariance matrix, shown as squared percentage returns, comprises Exhibit 2.

To estimate the variance of the portfolio return, you matrix-multiply the row vector of country weights, expressed as a decimal fraction, times the covariance matrix and then times the column vector of weights.

Matrix multiplication sounds complicated but is not. The shortest way to demonstrate is by example. Suppose we want to multiply matrix A by matrix B. Let

$$A = \begin{bmatrix} a_{11} & a_{12} \\ a_{21} & a_{22} \end{bmatrix} \text{ and } B = \begin{bmatrix} b_{11} & b_{12} \\ b_{21} & b_{22} \end{bmatrix}$$

If $C = AB$ then

$$C = \begin{bmatrix} c_{11} & c_{12} \\ c_{21} & c_{22} \end{bmatrix}$$

where $c_{11} = a_{11}b_{11} + a_{12}b_{21}$ and so on.

Note that the number of rows in the first matrix must be equal to the number of columns in the second. Also, it is not generally true that $AB = BA$. The transpose of a matrix A is constructed by exchanging its rows and columns, and is labeled A'. If a matrix X has only a single column, it is called a column vector. Its transpose X' is a *row vector* with the same number of elements.

If our country weights are a row vector X' and our covariance matrix is V, then the variance of the resulting portfolio is given by $X'VX$. Let's calculate this expression for our emerging market example.

Suppose we wish to use past risk as our estimate of future risk. We want to know the risk of a portfolio whose weights are 0.2 Brazil, 0.1 Greece, 0.4 Malaysia, 0.2 Mexico, and 0.1 Taiwan. Then the result of our first multiplication is [0.2 0.1 0.4 0.2 0.1] times our covariance matrix, giving [1528 -373 778 1133 1076]. When this resulting row vector is multiplied by the final column matrix of weights, the result is a variance of 914. The square root of the variance is the standard deviation, 30.2% in our illustration. This is a bit lower than the estimated risk for Malaysia alone, and far lower than the risks of the other four countries. If the mean returns expected for the other countries are greater, then we should expect the portfolio defined by our proposed weights to be an investment superior to Malaysia alone.

It may not be a good idea to project past risks exactly, and it is usually even worse to project past returns. The reasons will become obvious in later chapters of this book. However, as an example, let us expect the historical mean single-period returns for Brazil of 38%, 29% for Greece, and so on. Then,

$$R = [38\ 29\ 17\ 38\ 34]$$

We note that the sum of the fractional weights must be one. Suppose we wish to exclude negative weights (going short). Then we can only obtain portfolio expected returns between 17% and 38%. For each portfolio return r in that interval, it is possible through well-defined iterative procedures to determine the set of portfolio weights X to any desired precision such that

$X'VX$ is a minimum subject to the constraint $X'R = r$

This portfolio comprises a single point on the efficient frontier. For this example, the estimated minimum risk portfolio has weights [0.24 0.39 0.35 0.01 0]. That is, 24% will be in Brazil, 39% in Greece, 35% in Malaysia, 1% in Mexico, and nothing in Taiwan. Exhibit 3 defines several points along the efficient frontier given our assumptions. The portfolio you would select as optimum along that frontier depends on the amount of additional risk you are willing to incur to gain additional expected return.

This is a very interesting and potentially profitable analysis. We see that the minimum risk portfolio has an expected return (27%) far higher than that of the single country with least risk (Malaysia's 17%). Its risk, expressed as standard deviation of return, is also lower than for that country alone (22% versus 33%). At this conservative end of the risk-tolerance spectrum, a great deal of attention is given to Greece, because its negative return correlation with several of the other countries makes it attractive as a diversifier. Mexico, whose risk appears to be more correlated with other countries, affords less diversification. It is not selected unless we give little weight to risk and more to added return. Finally, Taiwan, which has a decent return but positive correlations with all other countries, is not selected.

Exhibit 3: Approximate Efficient Frontier

	Conservative					Aggressive
Brazil	0.24	0.28	0.31	0.34	0.26	0.18
Greece	0.39	0.43	0.46	0.48	0.24	0.00
Malaysia	0.35	0.23	0.11	0.00	0.00	0.00
Mexico	0.01	0.06	0.11	0.18	0.50	0.82
Taiwan	0.00	0.00	0.00	0.00	0.00	0.00
Mean Return	27.2	29.3	31.5	33.7	35.8	38.0
Std. Deviation	21.7	22.1	23.3	25.1	33.8	48.8

Markowitz diversification analysis is often misapplied. Nevertheless, when used correctly it is of great practical benefit, of aid in both passive and active investing. It has also been a crucial building block for theorizing about the market as a whole. If the market should ever come to a static equilibrium, that point is likely to be determined by the collective activities of investors following Harry Markowitz's advice.

Identifying Market Inefficiencies

I have in my possession a book by G. A. Drew, published in 1941 and titled *New Methods for Profit in the Stock Market*.[4] I bought it for 50 cents in the basement shop of a now defunct used-bookstore in Boston. It describes as old-fashioned the tape-reading methods of the prior several generations of speculators. It regards as fruitless the amassing of careful fundamental statistics on coal and iron production, railroad traffic, and the like, used during the 1920s to forecast the market. It refers to point and figure charts as being 30 years old. Also, of course, the Dow Theory was already old hat in 1941. Newer methods based on moving averages, divergence curves, odd-lot indexes, buying power, contrary opinion, and even the Elliot wave theory are described. Reading this slim volume makes it immediately apparent that intelligent people have been at the business of trying to forecast stock prices a long time.

To paraphrase a more recent academic, the job of the stock market is to make understandable economic events into random numbers. Obviously that is what an efficient market must do — as soon as a pattern is predictable, speculators who discern it will take advantage of it and change its nature. Yet hope springs eternal.

Since the rise of econometrics about the time *New Methods for Profit in the Stock Market* was written, many respectable seekers after market imperfections have used statistical regression techniques. We will introduce them here in the context of identifying the so-called small-stock effect and the book-to-price effect, or unsuccessful company effect, in the U.S. market. The theory is that most investors identify the prospects of the stock with the current success of the company. Before beginning, however, it is worthwhile noting what Drew, the bemused chronicler of 50 years ago, had to say about all such methods.

> "As a matter of fact, it is possible to take almost any series of changing figures and, by suiting various statistical adjustments to the known facts, arrive at something approximating what would have been a 'forecast' of the stock market."

Even if the methods are more rigorous, and eschew what we know today as "data mining":

> "The inherent danger of all such economic barometers is that when used as rigid formulae, they may be applicable to one period, but not in another."

---

[4] Garfield Albee Drew, *New Methods for Profit in the Stock Market* (Boston: The Metcalf Press, 1941).

Finally, for those who do not consider many decades in modeling the market:

> "Those who ... compare [today's conditions] only with the periods that they may have known as "normal", are neglecting the lessons of history."

Now let's look at our example. When I joined Batterymarch Financial Management in 1980, it was enjoying a wonderful run of stock market success under Dean LeBaron's leadership. Much of that success was based on using newly available computer-readable information to screen among smaller stocks than considered by competitors. Much was based on applying what were termed "value-oriented criteria." That is, stocks were bought with some combination of high dividend yields, low price-earnings ratios, and low price/book ratios. This last was particularly controversial, because low price-to-equity book values were found among generally unpopular, unsuccessful companies. This approach fit my personal outlook. It seemed that its success would go on for a long time because human nature and institutional decision-making constraints tends to favor large, successful companies, making bargains of the stocks Batterymarch was buying.

The ferociously competitive nature of investment research sometimes leads to it to run well ahead of academic research. It was only in 1992 that a leading academic proponent of the market's efficiency, Eugene Fama, published with Kenneth French in the *Journal of Finance* an article on these factors that shook academics.[5] In that article, Fama and French convincingly presented what would be a surprising puzzle in the context of a perfectly arbitraged market. Apparently it had been possible for a long time to earn very substantial extra returns by investing in stocks with small market capitalizations and stocks with high book-to-price ratios (low price-to-book) ratios.

We will use ordinary least-squares (OLS) regression to confirm this evidence of market inefficiency. We can pretend that we do so without being stimulated by reading a publication, but rather as part of our private science investment research.

First, what is OLS regression? Using the matrix notation of the preceding section, suppose we wish to predict a vector Y of return observations and that we are willing to assume that the Y are determined by an array of independent facts X such that

$Y = XB + u$, where u is a vector of random disturbances.

In other words, except for unpredictable random disturbances or errors, the Y are completely predictable by the independent variables $X1$, $X2$ ...., the column vectors making up X, using a single linear relationship composed of weight coefficients that are the elements in B.

---

[5] Eugene F. Fama and Kenneth R. French, "The Cross Section of Expected Stock Returns," *Journal of Finance* (June 1992), pp. 427-465.

In our practical example, we will hypothesize that stock returns are predictable from the prior period's price-to-book ratio and market capitalization. We use values of the natural log of price-to-book and natural log of market capitalization (price times number of shares) because the logarithmic transformation will make the highly positively skewed distributions of price-to-book and market capitalization more symmetric.[6] We will use data from the *Value Line Survey* for over 1,000 stocks over a 20-year period. Our job is to estimate a set of coefficients or regression weights B for these two factors X that best predict Y, the returns. We also want to test how likely are the estimated B given the null hypothesis that the true B were zero.

We will not dwell on the calculations here. Fortunately, the mathematical method for computing the relevant information is incorporated in all commercial statistics packages for use on computers. Under certain assumptions, the OLS will provide the best estimate of the coefficients B and thus of the effects of log price-to-book and log market capitalization. The first assumption is that X have more rows (observations) than columns (predictors). Then we assume that the elements of u each have mean zero and a constant variance. Finally, we posit that no element of u can be predicted from the others or from the elements of X. As these assumptions are relaxed, the procedures for estimating the elements of B get more complicated; here we stay with simple OLS. Another way of stating the problem is to find the B that minimizes the sum of the squared disturbances (residuals) $u'u$. Hence the name "least-squares estimates." This gives the same answer. The resulting estimates of B will be unbiased and will have the smallest mean squared errors versus the true B of any linear estimator. If the disturbances also have a "normal" probability distribution, the estimates will be the best possible.

Commercial statistics packages also provide measures that indicate how good the estimates are. Typically, these assume the normal distribution for the u disturbances. The "t-statistics" measure the probability that each measured coefficient could have been observed if the true coefficient were zero. An "F-statistic" measures the probability that the true vector B has zero in each element given the B estimate observed. Because these statistics applied to OLS regression results are reasonably robust even when normality and the OLS assumptions are not precisely satisfied, OLS is a practical quantitative tool for investigating market imperfections. We will look at some of its problems in a later chapter; for now, let's see what it shows us.

First we will pool all observations in our database: about 180,000 monthly returns from over 1,000 U.S. stocks over a 20-year period ending in early 1997. Second, we will transform the data by subtracting the mean value in each period from each of the variables. This allows us to separate the pure cross-sectional effect Fama and French reported. Exhibit 4 shows a simple OLS regression.[7]

---

[6] We will use natural logs, powers of the mathematical constant e, 2.718.

[7] The results were generated using the STATA 5 statistics package. (*STATA 5 Users Guide*, Stata Corporation, College Station, Texas, 1997.)

Exhibit 4: Excess Future Return Versus Excess Log P/B and Size

Number of observations = 179,958
F(2,179955) = 391.15
Prob > F = 0.0000
R-squared = 0.0043
Adjusted R-squared = 0.0043
Root MSE = 10.701

Source	Sum of Squares	Degrees of F	Mean Square
Model	89,575.47	2	44,787.74
Residual	20,605,084.91	5	114.50
Total	20,694,660.42	7	115.00

	Coefficient	Standard Error	t-value	P>|t|	[95% Conf. Interval]	
Log of price-to-book	−0.1331149	0.0386868	−3.441	0.001	−0.2089402	−0.0572897
Log of market cap	−0.5276335	0.0193409	−27.281	0.000	−0.5655412	−0.4897259
Constant	0.0015087	0.0252249	0.060	0.952	−0.0479315	0.050949

There are 179,958 observations. If we increase the natural log of price-to-book by one, or multiply price-to-book by 2.718 (the value of e), the average return in the subsequent month is 13 basis points (0.13%) lower. If we multiply market capitalization by 2.718, the average return per month is 53 basis points lower. These are big effects! It looks as if Fama and French were right. The t-statistics for each effect (−3.4 and −27.3) appear significant. Of course, there is a high degree of disturbance around the effects. We know this because the R-squared, the percentage of the total variance of return explained by the model, is only 0.43%. Fama and French highlighted these effects by constructing portfolios of similarly rated stocks; diversification within each of the portfolios damps out much of the random noise surrounding them.

I cannot resist showing off one trick that sheds a rather different light on the relationship of the size effect to the low price-to-book effect. Note that the log of market capitalization is just the sum of the log of price-to-book and the log of book. That is, some of the so-called size effect is really the impact of the pricing multiple. Exhibit 5 rearranges the contents of the two variables. It is immediately apparent that the unsuccessful company effect captured by low price-to-book is much more important than we saw before. We see in Exhibit 5 that multiplying price-to-book by 2.718, when we account for both places price-to-book plays a role, appears to be associated with a reduction in return of 66 basis points per month, or about 8% a year!

Of course, the evidence will not prove nearly so compelling on further investigation. The requirements of the OLS model are not precisely satisfied in reality. For example, the 179,958 observations do not really have independent disturbances, and so on. Also, in this example we make no allowances for variations in the effects over time, or within the sample. If we did, we would see that the effects are strongest for smaller stocks least available to large institutional investors. We would also see that the market capitalization effects among the largest half of the sample have tended to diminish over time. Unfortunately, further investigation would disclose that a disturbing portion of the price-to-book effect is found in outlier observations that may reflect problems in the data. Finally, we make no allowance for survival — that is, stocks that were small and got smaller tended to fall out of the database and are subsequently unavailable for study. Consequently, we know the sample is at least a little biased — commonly referred to as *survivorship bias*.

However, our study has a very practical use. Provided we have access to a large database of return observations, we can with a simple model narrow the field for more refined quantitative methods or even case-by-case judgmental analysis.

THE ARGUMENT FOR JUDGMENTAL INVESTING

Investors operating with less scientific methods can flourish if they do well those things that those using quantitative models do not. There are many useful areas for investment judgment where quantitative models never become practicable, and others where extensive misuse of quantitative models creates opportunities.

What would we say, if our vantage point is early 1997, will be the result on stock values of the beginning of European Monetary Union, scheduled at this writing for January 1999? We cannot do a statistical regression of similar cases because there are not enough cases of similar type to form a meaningful statistical sample. In such cases, the judgmental fundamental analyst who can reason by analogy and investigate a myriad of details about this case will have an advantage.

Exhibit 5: Accounting for Valuation Within Market Capitalization

Number of observations	= 179,958
$F_{(2, 179955)}$	= 391.10
Prob > F	= 0.0000
R-squared	= 0.0043
Adjusted R-squared	= 0.0043
Root MSE	= 10.701

Source	Sum of Squares	Degrees of F	Mean Square
Model	89563.58	2	44781.79
Residual	20605096.82	5	114.50
Total	20694660.42	7	115.00

	Coefficient	Standard Error	t-value	P>|t|	[95% Conf. Interval]	
Log of price-to-book	−0.6607222	0.0415053	−15.919	0.000	−0.7420717	−0.5793727
Log of book value	−0.5276008	0.019341	−27.279	0.000	−0.5655087	−0.4896928
Constant	−0.0030895	0.0252243	−0.122	0.903	−0.0525286	0.0463497

Consider also the impact of new technology such as the appearance of high bandwidth Internet access. Most of us may be thinking in terms of the effect on entertainment or telephony. However, perhaps it will turn out that the big effect is on setting up efficient markets, such as that for professional employment, where today the markets are very imperfect. Even if there have been some broadly similar instances, the most crucial variables may simply not be measured and recorded in a way conducive to future quantitative analysis. These variables may deal with scope of application, the barriers to entry, future economies of scale, and so on,

These first two points concerned lack of data sufficient for scientific method. Judgmental analysis may also have an advantage where there is plenty of data but the systems involved do not lend themselves to simple mathematical models. Very broadly, this is true of the market as a whole. Our quantitative models of the market are usually based on extremely simplified assumptions. For example, the quantitative model may assume that all participants have similar access to data, or similar ways of interpreting it, and that the market has already come to equilibrium. In a more complicated world, where investors change their minds based simply on the actions of other investors, the judgmental investor may have useful heuristics that could not be justified with the available mathematics.

Instability of system structure of all kinds is a very significant obstacle to quantitative methods. The partial chaos created provides a friendly environment for intelligent speculation based on intuition, analogy, collection of unusual data, and a complex view of the system. The investor group, as we noted, keeps changing its criteria as it reacts to new economic trends, to prior investor behavior, and to the endless injections of fresh, naive investors. The judgmental investor also has an advantage whenever investing opportunities are sufficiently different from the average case on which a policy is founded that they deserve special treatment as an exception.

New computer technology can assist the judgmental investor at least as much as it does the quantitative investor. The available information for the judgmental analyst has multiplied many-fold through the arrival of the Internet. You can now read English-language articles published around the world without leaving your desk. You can sense waves of public, and therefore of investment, opinion without having it filtered through as many layers of interpretation as before. It is likely that the Internet has amplified the power of shrewd judgmental analysts at least as much as the earlier advent of computer-readable financial databases increased the power of quantitative analysis.

Another advantage for judgmental analysts in a mostly non-scientific organizational world is that their reasoning and conclusions are much easier for most people to follow. The security analyst who says that Russian investments are too risky to hold in any amount because the rule of law has not yet been established in Russia may be making a questionable statement. But his or her argument, based on common sense, is liable to be more persuasive to most people than the demonstrable quantitative fact that diversified portfolios of frontier-like economies have superior risk and return characteristics. Belief in the latter requires specialized training and experience that most people do not share.

Being able to keep judgmental analysis more private than can a quantitative investor may also be an important advantage, provided the investor is adept. Lack of full disclosure may reduce argument and allow for greater originality within investment organizations. After all, the ideas that make up the consensus tend to be already priced into the market. Disagreement and originality, although they can be profitable, may not be popular within an investing organization. Further, an unannounced chain of reasoning makes it easier for the investor to change his or her mind as circumstances change. Quantitative models are often rather sticky. They usually depend on much history, and if made public they are easier targets for critics who think that you as an investor should not change your approach. For example, suppose you are hired as a value-oriented manager, but as you learn more and the market evolves you begin to pay attention to price momentum. That this deserves question is perfectly understandable, but nevertheless it exacts a cost on investors using explicit quantitative models that judgmental portfolio managers and analysts may not have to pay.

Finally, judgmental analysts may earn a living simply exploiting the mistakes of maladroit quantitative managers. Like judgmental analysis, quantitative analysis may be done well or poorly. When it is done poorly, it offers opportunities to others. Here are some typical quantitative blunders:

1. Econometric modeling based on periods too short to show a full range of behaviors;
2. Over-fitting limited data with a model that works mainly by coincidence;
4. Assuming that standard statistical tests are valid when the assumptions on which they are based are not met;
5. Assuming static relationships which are in fact extremely dynamic;
6. Believing that the world has a certain simple structural form simply because that form is mathematically tractable;
7. Assuming that problems may be divided that may need treatment as an integrated whole, for example in not linking the problems of forecasting and portfolio construction (trading costs, short-selling restrictions and risk preferences);
8. Implementing a strategy that will theoretically work well long-term but is unlikely to survive long-term because it implies substantial contiguous periods of short-term poor performance.

An Example

Here is an example of free-form judgmental analysis. In February 1997, I accepted an opportunity to give a talk on the effects of the possible European currency union. At that time, it was still quite controversial whether this event would occur. There was extensive political disagreement whether it should go forward, which countries would be included, and when it might happen. No broad consensus had formed on its likely consequences if it did take place.

I began searching references on this topic in newspapers, magazines, governmental agency reports, and commentaries from brokers and banks in Europe. What I was looking for were little-known facts and, regarding well-known facts, logical inferences that were not widely held, if held at all. What I wanted to avoid were consensus statements where I could add no value as a speaker. Since these are exactly the tactics required for intelligent investing, I submit the result as a typical example of what may be termed strategic judgmental analysis.

I quickly became convinced that European monetary integration would go forward. The reason was that it was only the latest in a series of similar integrating steps European leaders had taken periodically ever since World War II. The political will existed to overcome economic and social pain for two basic reasons: (1) to reduce the threat of European war, and (2) to restore European preeminence in the economic arena. Further, this strategy was succeeding, as evidenced by a gradually growing share of European equities as a percentage of the total world equity market. I reasoned that the key European leaders, despite public posturing, would not give up what seemed to be a successful and deeply motivated strategy.

Second, there was the issue of when it would take place. This was intertwined with the issue of which countries would be included. German leaders were insisting that the Italians, thought to be rather profligate, could not be founding members. The Italians were equally determined to join, and were actually making excellent progress toward a more fiscally responsible governmental consensus. Although the public discussion of the formal Maastricht Treaty criteria for membership tended to focus on government deficits at 3% or lower, there were several additional criteria. It was obvious that Germany, the role model around which the treaty was originally created, could not formally meet all of them. This was particularly true for the criterion of governmental debt, which had to be below a certain level or *falling*, whereas German debt would clearly be over the limit and *rising*. Also, I found very few writers knew the mechanism by which the terms of the treaty could be modified. In that process, if the "Southern" countries — Italy, Spain, and Portugal — stuck together, they had veto power. Thus, Germany was in no position to effectively block Italian membership.

Since very few countries could actually meet the criteria, it seemed very likely that criteria would be fudged, and that renegotiation would have to include Italy. This process need not wait for countries to "qualify," and consequently I reasoned that the Treaty would go into effect on time as planned in January 1999.

The investment implications began to seem clear as well. Each round of further economic integration had tended to break down barriers to effective markets and business organization, which led to accelerated economic growth. Further progress meant that European equities were a somewhat better buy relative to other parts of the world than a strictly quantitative analysis would show. Of course the caveat was that this expectation was not already built into the consensus. And it was not! I reasoned this not only from average European equity valuations! The fact was that many intelligent and informed people were defensively arguing that the Euro would not go forward, or if it did, would be accompanied by dreadful consequences.

The analysis could be carried to more levels of detail. For example, the initial deregulation and integration would fall heaviest on the financial institutions of the region. Most immediately they were losing foreign exchange bid-ask spreads, an important source of profit for many large banks. Only a little further in the future it was clear that increased competition would result from removal of currency-related barriers. For example, there would be little excuse for the Dutch to insist that their pension funds be invested in Dutch bonds, etc. Such deregulation argues for consolidation, with most banks hard hit. Consequently, it would seem that the banking industry, an important part of the market, especially in protected markets such as Spain, should be under-weighted relative to positions resulting from purely quantitative analysis.

Additional value added could be created by bringing the analysis down to the company level, but this should suffice to show how different from econometric modeling is the judgmental mode of analysis.

SYNTHESIS

In this chapter we have laid out two polar opposites in making investment decisions. On the one hand, quantitatively model as much as possible, with consequent advantages in learning and greater discipline over emotions. On the other, judgmentally explore the fringes around the consensus for new ideas and facts, maximizing your ability to deal with a changing and varied environment. A combination of both approaches might be even more advantageous. A favorable synthesis will employ quantitative methods where they are most beneficial and use qualitative judgments for defining and going beyond those boundaries.

Of course, clearly one cannot eliminate judgment. It is always required in deciding what quantitative technique will be employed, where and for how long. Once that is done, however, the usual approach by quantitatively oriented investment firms is to try to diversify away the investment risks incurred by not carrying out the additional judgmental analysis possible. This usually means holding very large portfolios of different stocks. However, more and more investment firms are trying to integrate within one decision process both quantitative and judgmental inputs.

One way such integration may proceed is to provide a "score" based on quantitative research. The portfolio manager may use the score in combination with his or her own intuition and judgment or with that of research analysts. In unusual circumstances it may be overridden. The opposite way, which I prefer, is to build up a score from subjective ratings that can be an ingredient of predetermined weight in a quantitative procedure. Both approaches can work.

The scope for quantitative investing depends on the availability of data and of models. Contrary to the belief of many, it does not depend on accurate data. The data need only be, in combination with the model applied, sufficient to derive some value added. This can be done without great precision so long as it pertains to information that is not already well-priced in the market. What it does depend on is repetitive phenomena. Similar events must happen frequently enough to form a valid sample and frequently enough to justify the effort required to construct a model of what is likely to occur in those circumstances.

I have seen quantitative models successfully applied at the stock-picking level, at the country selection level, and at the asset class level, where stocks are compared with bonds at the global level of aggregation. The degree of decision disaggregation, not the level of market development, excludes quantitative decision-making. However, it is very helpful if new types of data become available, or new markets are opened to global investors, or new insights are developed, just as these events also offer opportunities to judgmental investors.

There is another direction for scope definition for the application of quantitative investment approaches that is critical — that of timeliness. That is where I will close the chapter — with the lesson that I have learned through sometimes painful experience on the proper time to apply a quantitative technique. To do so, I want to introduce one more key idea in this chapter. The concept is *fashion*. I do not take fashion as a frivolous topic but rather as representing a deeper understanding of the time-sensitivity of what we assume as objective social reality. What is fashion, really?

In clothing and art, fashion is the attempt by elites to differentiate from the masses, later imitated by the masses, and so on in endless cycle. It is a dynamic process in which a new style, for example Picasso's cubism or a particular style of dress, is first adopted by very few. Then it is adopted by increasing numbers until much of the relevant population has caught it. Then its further penetration gradually slows as fewer and fewer people are left who have not tried it. Fashion is the dynamic process that produces a history of styles.

If there were only one style replacing another, the dynamics would be exactly like a disease epidemic. That is, the growth rate of infected people would be proportional to the product of the people who already have the disease and the number of people who have not yet been exposed. It would produce an S-shaped "logistic" curve of penetration. Note, this is the same dynamic that has accompanied the adoption of major new technical innovations in history, for example the triumph of steam powered ships over sailing ships.

See how similar are the motivations of the fashion house and a company introducing a new product or even a scientist aiming for a Nobel prize! A successful attempt to be different is followed by imitators who become competitors. To stay ahead of the pack requires repeated innovation. The residue of fashion is a history of styles. The residue of entrepreneurs is an accepted industrial infrastructure. The residue of scientific pioneering is what we think of as science, which is a body of knowledge widely shared for making predictions.

Where does fashion begin and economic or scientific progress end? The process of creating new science or a new profitable business is very similar to fashion.

However, in the case of industrial or scientific innovation, the "old-fashioned," no longer useful to entrepreneurs or Nobel prize seekers, is of great use to the rest of us. This residue provides what may be regarded as long-term memory that gives a sense of progress and direction. That is, it is rare that the new business organization goes to a less efficient process for transforming inputs to outputs. It is also rare that science goes back to a model that produces poorer predictions of natural phenomena. The kind of fashion that we think of as frivolous differs primarily in that it has a shorter memory, so that it sometimes cycles back through styles seen in previous eras.

Now, let us return to the stock market. If the goal is more effective practice by all investors as a group, then there can be an investment science. But if the goal is to earn above average return at average risk, then we must be entrepreneurs, Nobel prize seekers, and fashion leaders. Quantitative methods for earning above-average returns do not stand apart from fashion. They are part of it. Active investment management can never be accepted science, because it is continually making obsolete its truths through the process of destructive imitation by other investors. Nothing we discover can be a permanent sinecure for earning excess profits. Successful quantitative investment is a reward for innovation, not eternal truth. Like fashion in dress, and unlike in industry and science, the residue of old-fashioned ways of earning excess investment returns may have negative value for late adopters. Not only will you not earn a Nobel prize for employing the ideas pioneered a decade earlier, you may fail to do as well as passive index funds.

Let me give you an example, which to protect the innocent, we will call Factor X. Factor X used to work exceptionally well in producing excess returns. However, it has been publicized in the *Journal of Finance* and more practitioner-oriented publications for about 15 years. Let us examine the evidence using our large sample from the Value Line database. Each month we calculate Factor X less the month's mean Factor X, together with next month's percentage return less that month's mean percentage return. These observations are pooled with others made in the same calendar year and an OLS regression is estimated for that year. Exhibit 6 shows the history of the regression coefficients so generated for two samples. The first includes all the stocks available in the database each month. The second includes only the larger stocks, those in the top half of the sample each month as ranked by market capitalization.

For the whole sample, about 500 stocks at the beginning, and rising to over 1,000 by the end, Factor X exhibits a reliably positive regression coefficient. The picture is very different when you examine the largest half of the sample. Within that group, there is a weaker effect that declines erratically over time. Beginning in the mid 1980s the mean averages near zero, with cyclical ups and downs. For the three years beginning in 1994, the effect was perverse. Quantitative firms relying on Factor X have been hurt. Will Factor X be useful in selecting among large stocks in the future? Possibly it will be from time to time. However, so long as it is well known it is unlikely to give the good results it did before the advent of publicity regarding its usefulness.

Exhibit 6: Regression Coefficients for Factor X

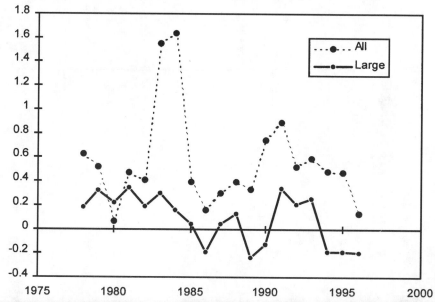

On a more distant scale, OLS regression of all commonly reported indicators will probably suffer the same fate, as more and more investors imitate the policies discovered by pioneer quantitative investors. As that happens, we will need new sources of data, and more advanced modeling methods, to retain an advantage.

Chapter 3

Finance at the Crossroads — The Santa Fe Experiments

[Science is] a series of peaceful interludes punctuated by intellectually violent revolutions.
Thomas Kuhn, *The Structure of Scientific Revolutions (1962)*

The purpose of this chapter is to begin to characterize the ecology of the stock market — who inhabits it and how does it work. Theoretical finance has offered a rigorous and mathematically idealized starting point in answer. We should salute its inventors. But we want to keep awake a more varied and realistic perception of the investment world. We also want to introduce a radically different theoretical approach to characterizing investors and markets: that of bottom-up computer simulations.

THE REAL WORLD

To begin, consider the following true-to-life cast of investors:

Gino, a barber originally from Italy, invested badly in a small high-tech company recommended by a good customer just before the market crash in 1987. For a decade after that, he did not invest in stocks, putting his savings into fixed income instruments. Then, with the U.S. stock market having risen to around three times book value, Gino invested a good portion of his savings in a single stock, General Electric, because it was generally agreed to be a solid growth company. He plans to hold it long term.

George sold out his small software company a decade ago, Since then he feels he has done very well with a selection of special situations and growth stocks. He is a good customer of discount brokerage houses and a frequent trader.

Mary is an institutional portfolio manager. She uses a "value-oriented" investment approach. She would like to buy some small growth stocks but doesn't want to hurt her style's clear definition, necessary to attract new customers.

Her friend Eleanor is a portfolio manager at the same firm. She really doesn't care about absolute return volatility. She manages money to

29

beat a benchmark, with the only risk that is important being tracking error versus the benchmark. The risk attached to the benchmark itself is considered irrelevant.

John runs a personal holding company so large he has a stable of professional money managers. However, most of the family's portfolio is locked in at today's prices because of long-term unrealized gains that would be taxed heavily if the stocks were sold. As a result the portfolio is heavily biased toward a few giant holdings that are selling at high valuations.

Aunt Sylvia is retired and has only a few stocks, all utilities. She would never sell them unless they dropped their dividends.

Michael runs a small-stock mutual fund. Although he tries to stay within the bounds of the law, he likes to buy a big position in a small company and then talk enthusiastically about the stock to acquaintances. Michael also has to worry when he trades because he can easily move prices 10% in the stocks in which he usually invests.

Helmut is a day-trader. He trades in stocks, commodities, and anything with volatility in which he can specialize to gain a good feel for the market.

Bill believes strongly in social causes. All his savings are invested in a mutual fund that uses social responsibility as a key investment criterion.

Everyone on the list, from Gino to Bill, owns more U.S. stocks in proportion to their market value than foreign stocks in proportion to their market value.

As we go through the assumptions made in the development of mathematical models of investing and the resulting market conditions, we will return to these individuals. The wonder is not that finance predicts so little about the real world. The wonder is that in the face of this variety of investor motive and procedure, theoretical finance can predict anything at all.

FOR WHAT PURPOSE THEORY?

Theories help us make predictions about the real world. What kinds of predictions about investors and markets could we be interested in?

If we are part of government, we might be interested in the kinds of market that could develop given a certain legal and regulatory structure. For example, we might want to know whether insider trading prohibitions should be relaxed in such a way to allow investment analysts to do a better job of investigation.

Given existing market structures, and our individual personalities and life situations, we could be interested in whether investing a certain way would make us happy. We might be more specific and ask what investing policies are most likely to lead to the highest expected growth rate in wealth. As a professional money manager, we might ask the question of what investment policy would lead to greatest success in running our investment advisory business.

We see that the kind of theory we need depends on what we want to do with it. Our needs are broad. However, conventional theoretical finance merely shows us how to maximize an owner-investor utility based on expected wealth and its variance measured at a single point in time. It then also logically derives what kind of market would result if a group of very similar, very rational investors all acted this way. In this manner, it gives us some idea of the context within which we must seek our larger goals.

THE INVESTOR VERSUS THEORETICAL FINANCE

To understand what theoretical finance is now, it is helpful to know from whence it comes. Perhaps the best place to start is with classical microeconomics as developed before World War II. Micro-economists had managed to construct several empirically testable theorems about consumer choice, markets, and pricing based on a minimal foundation. They assumed merely that the consumer could rank-order bundles of goods in terms of preference. For convenience, each bundle could be thought of as having a certain utility, but this utility was ordinal, with no measure of distance between utilities of bundles.

At the same time, however, John Von Neumann was developing his theory of games, which he published with Oskar Morgenstern as *Theory of Games and Economic Behavior*.[1] Their book dealt with situations where probabilities could be estimated and where opponents' motives and capabilities were known. As a preliminary, Von Neumann and Morgenstern worked out axioms for a new kind of utility theory that would deal with bundles of risky outcomes, or lotteries. In it, preferences were determined by utilities derived in such a way that the utility for a lottery was equal to the statistical expectation of the utility of its possible outcomes. Conversely, the decision-maker should be indifferent between a certain outcome and some lottery between a more preferred outcome and a less preferred outcome. This equivalence in utility established a metric that placed the middle-preferred outcome at a specific distance from the two bracketing outcomes, the distances determined by their relative probabilities. So we see that the kind of utility required for microeconomics in finance became a cardinal measure like a yardstick rather than an ordinal ranking.

A few years later the statistician L.J. Savage showed that a kind of subjective probability, in theory assessed operationally, could be substituted for probabilities based on objective frequencies within the game-theoretic framework.[2] However, whether one uses frequency-based or subjective probabilities to assess the utility of risky lotteries, the degree of rationality and self-knowledge required

---

[1] John von Neumann and Oskar Morgenstern, *Theory of Games and Economic Behavior* (Princeton, NJ: Princeton University Press, 1944).

of the decision-maker is far higher than assumed in classical microeconomics. The cardinal utility metric so-created does have very nice properties if you care to theorize using the tools of calculus to find mathematical optima.

Exhibit 1 shows how this utility defined by probabilities works in the simple case where there is only one objectively measured attribute, Attribute X. The vertical scale shows U, the utility. The decision-maker always maximizes U in choosing among available outcomes. Point A is an event achieved with certainty. Points B and C are two events possible with equal odds under a lottery D. The U value of D is the expected utility of B and C. Point E is the certainty equivalent to the utility of lottery D.

The curvature of the utility function of X reflects the degree of risk aversion by the decision-maker. The greater the curvature, the greater the discount given to lottery D relative to original point A, and the greater the discount in Attribute X from that of A in order to obtain a certainty equivalent E. Also note that the wider the dispersion between B and C around A, the more the curvature has a chance to come into play, and the greater the loss of utility. Thus, the aversion to a particular lottery is a function both of the risk aversion characteristic of the decision-maker, and the risk inherent in the lottery. Note also that the statistical standard deviation of the outcomes B and C making up lottery D is a kind of rough measure of the distance between them on Attribute X.

Exhibit 1: Utility and Risk Aversion

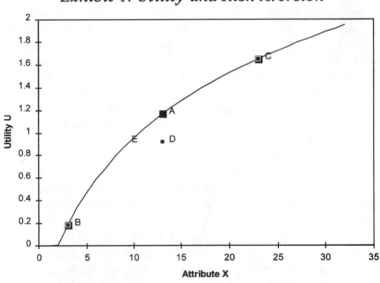

[2] Luce and Raiffa provided a reasonably accessible description of game theory and early forms of statistical decision-making by what is now called the Bayesian approach. See R. Duncan Luce and Howard Raiffa, *Games and Decisions, Introduction and Critical Survey 2nd Edition* (New York: John Wiley & Sons, 1958).

For an investment problem, Attribute X conventionally would be viewed as the terminal wealth, or more often, as the period return.

In Harry Markowitz's first article in the *Journal of Finance* in 1952, he relied on this framework for dealing with utility of lotteries in his approach for building a diversified portfolio.[3] We are all indebted to him for the first rigorous characterization of portfolio theory. Having said that, we should recognize that there is much further to go. Let us see why.

His proposed utility is simply a linear function depending positively on expected mean end-of-period wealth and negatively on the expected variance of that wealth. We briefly described his framework in Chapter 2. Remember, Markowitz considers only mean portfolio return, the variance of portfolio return, and the rate at which the investor is willing to accept additional variance for additional return. His idealized investor first forms the portfolio that minimizes portfolio risk for every attainable expected return given the stocks under consideration. This set is his efficient frontier. The required calculation is quite sophisticated, the equivalent of solving what mathematicians call a quadratic programming problem. After performing it, the investor chooses the portfolio that maximizes his or her explicit objective function, trading off expected return against portfolio risk measured by variance.

We see that Markowitz's investor is intelligent, self-aware, very good with numbers, and exceptionally focused on the single problem of increasing wealth. Fortunately, you and I, as expert quantitative investors, are willing to take on this task, although we will see more of the challenges in a later chapter. However, the Markowitz framework is quite inadequate as description of what most investors do.

None of our friends, from Gino to Bill, matches his description. Even though Markowitz himself did not claim that the framework was an accurate description, this lack creates a potential problem. For theories for the behavior of a market as a whole usually do assume the Markowitz optimizing framework for its participants.

Even as a prescriptive model, the Markowitz model is rather demanding in its requirements and narrow in its application as policy. Let us go through some of the problems real investors might have with it. These can be broadly categorized as (1) bounded knowledge and computational capacity, (2) inseparability of related decisions, and (3) inadequacy of the utility framework. More, some quandaries involve more than one category.

Bounded Knowledge and Computational Capacity

The first Markowitz requirement is that the investor have a well-defined set of alternatives. For most investors there is necessarily a boundary, even if fuzzy, beyond which stocks are not considered for analysis. Stocks must pass one or more attribute screens before they are ever deeply analyzed. For example, stocks must have a certain combination of size, information availability, and so on. Most stocks for most investors are too unknown to consider fully at reasonable cost. This problem bears to some degree on all investors, but it is most insoluble for small inves-

---

[3] Harry M. Markowitz, *Portfolio Selection* (New Haven, Conn.: Yale University Press, 1959).

tors like Gino, who invests only in a single company that he has heard about from customers, and Aunt Sylvia, who knows little but the relative safety of utilities.

Next, the investor has to know the stock's expected return and expected risk. Even if one is satisfied with subjective estimates for return and risk, including the correlations necessary to calculate portfolio risk, this is not a trivial task. The errors made in estimating these quantities may be so great that the resulting portfolio will have a worse risk-return tradeoff in *ex post* terms than a randomly selected portfolio. Again, this problem exists for all investors, because the Markowitz framework has no room for uncertainty as to probabilities. But it is most severe for investors with a limited experience base against which to judge the extent of their own knowledge. For example, even though George is a successful special situation investor, he may have too little experience to understand that his risk estimates can be more accurate than his mean return estimates, and what to do about different degrees of uncertainty.

A third problem in defining utility is to know the shape of one's own utility curve. Who can say how they will react to a large loss or gain until it has been experienced? How will Helmut react to losing 80% of his trading capital if that has never happened before? How certain can he be of the curvature of his utility for wealth? The assessment of personal utility is also subject to day-to-day inconsistencies based on both financial situation and mood.

Inseparability of Related Decisions

Perhaps with help from a superbly-equipped investment advisor, Gino the barber, George the amateur hot-stock investor, Aunt Sylvia the dividend buyer, and Helmut the day-trader are candidates to try out the theory as given at this point. At least Gino and Aunt Sylvia would probably gain from more diversification. It is not entirely clear whether Helmut and George would benefit. All the others would have more substantial difficulties.

Markowitz assumes that the expected return is independent of the amount invested. This is clearly not true for Michael, because he gets part of his return through possibly illegal, and certainly unethical, manipulations of the price after he has bought the stock. Should we have a theory that works for manipulators? Perhaps not. But independence of amount invested and return is also not true when we consider Helmut the day-trader, if we are willing to think about multiple investment periods. His ability to make money trading a particular stock is highly dependent on personal familiarity. To over-diversify would be to lose that edge.

Couldn't the same thing be true to some degree of every investor whose expertise is in-depth analysis of particular companies? In part, this issue arises from multiple periods. But also it arises because Markowitz has left out of the decision framework the budget constraint linking the portfolio with the cost of obtaining further information. Even if probabilistic wealth were the sole basis of utility, the Markowitz framework only deals with half the problem. That is, it is constrained by the presumption that expected risk and return are given. This might trouble George if he were made aware of it. He invests in active investment research through paying relatively high brokerage commissions for research advice. It might also trouble Helmut even beyond the issue of specialization. He sometimes enters trades just to smoke out what kind of liquidity is present on the other side.

In many cases, the adequacy of dividing a stream of investments through time into separate intervals, each with its own mean-variance optimization, is not a bad assumption. It is a worthwhile simplification for pension fund asset allocation studies where the time horizon for each optimization is several years and the expected return is justifiably assumed relatively insensitive to the assets deployed in each category. Yet, we see that Michael, who deals with relatively large investments in small companies, has to be very concerned about trading costs. Unfortunately, simply subtracting buying and selling trading costs from expected returns is an over-simplification. One needs to know over how many periods they may be amortized. And this cannot be known until the portfolio construction problem is solved repetitively. Anyone with high trading costs and a short time horizon has such problems.

So far we have implicitly gone along with the assumption of utility based on end-of-period wealth. But sometimes that assumption is severely flawed.

Adequacy of Utility Framework

Mary, the value-oriented manager, is an agent hired by other agents, far removed from the owners of the funds she manages. She will not necessarily be rewarded if she earns better returns by owning stocks outside the conservatively-priced type necessary to give her fund a focused marketing image. As an agent, she is likely to aim for a mixture of benefits: some for the fund's shareholders, some for her firm, and some for herself. Her associate Eleanor, who is also an agent, has similar issues, as does Michael the small-stock fund manager. That is, their solutions as agents will necessarily involve attributes not contemplated in the Markowitz framework.

Eleanor also illustrates a very important specialized problem of agents in the investment world. As an agent, she has defined risk along an entirely different dimension. Rather than dispersion of returns, she views as the pertinent risk dispersion of the difference between her fund's returns and a benchmark return. Other managers may define their own risk as dispersion from the median return rank attained by fund managers within a particular style-based competitive universe. These distortions in risk measure will lead to quite different solutions from those envisioned by Markowitz.

Similarly, Bill knows what he wants, but it is not only money. He wants to own companies that have certain social characteristics. John, who runs a taxable entity for his family, is concerned with after-tax returns, but these are difficult to define at the end of a period unless all the stocks are liquidated and the taxes paid. He may also have to be concerned with a "fair" split between dividends and capital gains, because the younger members of the family have a greater financial interest in increasing the size of the principal, Both Bill and John can use the Markowitz framework only if it is heavily modified. And their solutions will look very different from those of many other investors.

Combining Inseparability and Utility

Let us go on to consider jointly time division and the shape of the utility curve. Did I forget to tell you that George invests on 50% margin? What if the overall expected portfolio variance is reasonable but there is a small chance that the whole portfolio will decline by 50% before the end of the period to be analyzed? George cannot meet a margin call. As we will see in a later chapter, the long-term result of taking even a small risk of going bankrupt each period is that you will eventually fail with certainty. In practical terms, George should not take the position that Markowitz single-period analysis suggests in such cases. We will study this case further in a later chapter on capital growth theory.

I have used Markowitz mean-variance optimization as a foil to force the recognition of substantial differences in investor types. Now I invite you to explore another pillar of theoretical finance as a foil to force recognition of the way investors interact in the marketplace.

THE MARKET VERSUS THEORETICAL FINANCE

Theoretical finance models the market almost solely as though it were in equilibrium. This is because the academic roots of the field are in microeconomics. The classic paradigm in that field is based on two insights: (1) what you observe frequently probably is in, or near, equilibrium, and (2) what makes equilibrium points calculable is that the actors are maximizing something. Both focus attention on those aspects of reality that may be easily modeled mathematically. Sometimes this is advantageous. Let us see what theoretical finance has to offer as a description of the market.

The central model of the market, still very influential after more than 30 years of criticism and adaptation, is the capital asset pricing model (CAPM). It describes a point of short-term equilibrium of market prices and expected returns. Although he is not the sole author, William Sharpe is the best known and has provided the greatest impetus.[4] His critical assumption is that the market is composed of many participants, each of whom is a maximizer considering a single-period investment choice in the Markowitz mean-variance framework. The investors are identical in every respect, including estimated expected return and variance, except in their tolerances for risk. Homogeneity of investor types provides the mathematical symmetry that along with maximization makes the equilibrium point calculable. His second critical assumption is that there is an additional risk-free asset that may be freely borrowed or lent at a fixed rate of interest.

The CAPM assumes that information flow is instantaneous across investors. It assumes that investors all have the same investment horizon and all have

---

[4] William F. Sharpe, "Capital Asset Prices: A Theory of Market Equilibrium Under Conditions of Risk," *Journal of Finance* (September 1964), pp. 425-442.

equal access to all securities in the market. There are no taxes, transaction costs, preference changes nor changing availability of security returns contemplated. (More recent contributions to the paradigm are a bit more expansive with respect to these last two assumptions.)

Exhibit 2 illustrates this. The curved line is an initial hypothetical efficient frontier, drawn at a level appropriate for a high-risk, high-return economy. Every investor faces the identical efficient frontier. The straight line is the new efficient frontier that can be reached by including a riskless interest-bearing asset in the mix. To the left of the point of tangency the investor may lend at 6%. To the right, the investor may borrow at 6% and buy more stock. Note that in the diagram the horizontal axis is in terms of the standard deviation of return rather than the variance of return. This convention allows the set of mixtures of a particular stock portfolio and varying amounts of cash to fall on a straight line.

Note, first, that the curve will be tangent to straight lines drawn from 0% risk and 6% return only at only point A. This represents the only portfolio of risky securities any investor will want to hold, since it is the only one (excepting the degenerate case of two perfectly correlated securities) that allows one to fall on the straight line, that line being otherwise uniformly of greater utility than the curved risky-securities-only efficient frontier. Consequently at equilibrium point A must be the market as a whole. Second, the slope of the straight line sets the return price for incremental portfolio risk. Arbitrage among securities then forces the marginal expected return per unit of contribution to portfolio risk to be the same across all securities. Security risk that is uncorrelated with market risk will not be rewarded.

Exhibit 2: Hypothetical CAPM Efficient Frontier

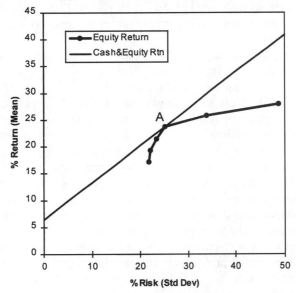

CAPM thus reaches two descriptive conclusions. First, the market of risky securities as a capitalization-weighted whole is efficient in the Markowitz sense of best expected mean return for a given expected variance. Second, the expected return for an individual security is the risk-free rate plus a linear function of the market's expected excess return. The slope of that relationship, "beta," is the expected regression coefficient of the security's excess return on the market's excess return. It measures what is called systematic risk.

To the extent the descriptions are accurate, they provide a context for further prescription radically simplifying Markowitz. Equity investors should simply buy index funds that attempt to replicate the performance of the market as a whole. And many people have done just that We have a new investor type, reputed to account for well over 25% of the U.S. stock market, the passive investor who is undisturbed by news or emotions with regard to the superiority of one stock over another. These people represent less competition for the active investor, but they may also represent a less exploitable source of profits than was the public of 100 years ago. In the United States, index funds based on the Standard & Poor's 500 appear to have enjoyed performance slightly better than those of the average professionally managed institutional fund. However as we move to a global perspective, capitalization-weighted market efficiency becomes quite doubtful.

It is hard to see why any investor in the CAPM world should care how securities are priced, since presumably the rational investor simply invests in already efficient index funds. Nevertheless, if someone is foolhardy enough to care to try to beat the market, the CAPM would suggest as fair value a price consistent with the stock's expected beta. Perturbations from that price would be opportunities for active investors. Regretfully, CAPM is consistent with the fact that over long periods risky stocks have higher returns than bonds, but has been of very little use in predicting average profitabilities of stocks with different systematic risk or market beta.

It is easy to see that the CAPM adds its own unrealistic assumptions to those already made by Markowitz. Most of its implications are far from empirically supported. Yet its prediction of the market as offering an efficient portfolio is not so far from the truth as we might expect given its assumptions. Just as a yardstick is the asymptotic result of more and more rank order distance comparisons, so, too, can an efficient market result from the combination of many different partial price and value comparisons made by heterogeneous investors of bounded rationality. The question is under what conditions and to what degree.

I can still remember from 30 years ago a comment from a wonderful professor who went on to his own well-deserved Nobel prize. Paraphrasing, he said that even if his theorems described more rational investors than yet existed, still, his teachings would make them more so in the future. Although this is one way to make a descriptive theory fit the facts, the business school mechanism hasn't gone far enough to obviate the problems in making the theoretical finance description of the market fit the facts.

When we think back to our lineup of investors, several are obvious candidates for index funds, beginning with Gino and Aunt Sylvia. But many investors have goals that are incompatible with that course. Not only are they not now the investors described in the CAPM, holding only index funds, but they never will be. A picture of the market that encompassed multiple investment periods, that allowed investors of bounded rationality to have differentiating ideas, would offer more useful guidance for professional investors.

Perhaps better answers may be found by leaving mathematically-tractable calculus and turning to computer simulation. Certainly, this can produce a richer picture of the market, one derived from aggregations of rules for behavior and learning at the investor level. Rather than rational optimization, we can consider frequency of survival; rather than symmetry of investors, we will allow differences, and we will not force equilibrium unless it arises naturally.

STOCK MARKET SIMULATIONS USING ARTIFICIAL AGENTS

Social Science through Simulation

The following quotation from *Growing Artificial Societies: Social Science From the Bottom Up*, written by Epstein and Axtell and published in 1997, captures exactly the spirit of my critique of theoretical finance.[5]

> "The social sciences are hard because certain kinds of controlled experimentation are hard. In particular, it is difficult to test hypotheses concerning the relationship of individual behaviors to macroscopic regularities....Another fundamental concern of most social scientists is that the rational actor — perfectly informed individual with infinite computing capacity who maximizes a fixed (nonevolving) exogenous utility function — bears little resemblance to a human being....Relatedly, it is standard practice in the social sciences to suppress real world agent heterogeneity in model building....While such models can offer powerful insights, they 'filter out' all consequences of heterogeneity....Finally, it is fair to say that, by and large, social science, especially game theory and general equilibrium theory, has been preoccupied with static equilibria, and has essentially ignored time dynamics."

Epstein and Axtell begin by simulating "ants" who live on a computer-generated grid by foraging for randomly appearing sugar in competition with one another. They add rules of behavior and structure characteristic of social systems one at a time and observe what happens. Each ant has its own characteristics. Very

---

[5] Joshua M. Epstein and Robert Axtell, *Growing Artificial Societies, Social Science from the Bottom Up* (Cambridge, Mass.: The M.I.T. Press, 1996).

simple individual structures and behavior rules lead to complex social results in terms of migration, carrying capacity, income inequality distributions similar to those found in human societies, organized wars between tribes, and so on. When a second commodity, "spice," is added and trade allowed, they observe fundamental determinants of pricing behavior. Trading increases the environmental carrying capacity but it also increases income inequality. In their example, if agents live forever, and under sufficiently stable and independent commodity production conditions, decentralized prices may settle down to an equilibrium, even though all trading is done on a decentralized basis by agents of very limited cognitive capacity, and with no central market or auctioneer.

Under other conditions, however, episodic production activities and population growth dynamics may constantly modify the underlying abundance and scarcity of the commodities. Even if production and consumption instabilities are not dominant, when both trading and reproduction are allowed, the continual entry of inexperienced agents into the process causes much more extensive perturbations around such equilibrium prices. And when agent's preferences between sugar and spice are allowed to change in response to their neighbor's preferences, the trading volume goes up and prices assume a pattern similar to a random walk. The role of changing preferences, either because of imitation or of the arrival of naïve participants, in encouraging market price fluctuations is striking.

The analogy with stock market trading is apt. Obviously there is an underlying potential for dynamic behavior caused by classic business cycle behavior in the labor and product markets. But the equity markets can be quite unstable even when the business cycle is relatively calm. When particular modes of behavior sweep the investor population, they can cause imbalances that set up their reversal. For example, one can be caught up in a mania for intangible growth (spice) at any price. If everyone joins together in this, prices will go too far. Then the "ants" concerned with tangible bargains (sugar) have a better chance of increasing wealth (surviving). But their rules may not recognize growth appropriately. And so the oscillation continues.

When investors are also short-lived they do not readily arrive at the equivalent of an estimate of fair value that takes into account a balance. Long-lived surviving investors tend to develop rules based on fair value that could be used to anticipate the ultimate equilibrium price and thus damp down the oscillation. If we want to find markets far from equilibrium we should look for fads sweeping inexperienced investors. Consider emerging stock markets like China, or even Korea and Malaysia, as examples. Or consider even the U.S. stock market at a time when a period of prosperity has brought forth statements by reputable economists that we are in a "new era."

Epstein and Axtell are interested in a broad range of interrelated social phenomena. For a deeper and more specialized look at stock market behavior, let us turn to a remarkable series of experiments being conducted under the auspices of the Santa Fe Institute.

The Artificial Stock Market

The Santa Fe Institute is not the only place where interesting stock market simulations have been carried out, but it is perhaps the best known. Founded in 1984 by a group of outstanding scientists from diverse fields, it focuses on interdisciplinary research. It emphasizes the highly non-linear relationships that make up what it refers to as "complexity." Here is how its Internet web site (www.santafe.edu) described its program of stock market simulations in late 1997.

"It is difficult to sort the work into traditional academic categories in an environment as fluid as the SFI. Because some of the questions being asked here are new and cross many academic disciplines, scientists often find it challenging even to define the concepts they are studying. But it is safe to say that the SFI studies tend to follow living and non-living agents and groups of agents as they emerge, as they organize themselves into complex communities and networks, and as they adapt, evolve and learn. The processes of emerging, organizing and evolving often are inseparable; in a way the three are merely different filters through which we view the dynamics of complex systems.

.... Traditional economic theory suggests that markets remain in equilibrium as economic agents display rational behavior in anticipating changes in supply and demand. Yet the stock market generates a type of volatility that does not match the rational expectations model. How does this behavior emerge? W. Brian Arthur and a team of SFI researchers have developed an artificial model of the stock market. Analysis of the model over the past year indicates that the stock market converges to one of two attractors — one corresponding to the equilibria posited in conventional theory and the other exhibiting the more volatile qualities observed in the real stock market. The researchers determined that conventional behavior is observed when individual agents have slow rates of learning about conditions affecting the market. But when learning is rapid, the artificial stock market behaves in the more volatile manner.

The stock market model project typifies the multidisciplinary, multigenerational approach that the Institute strives to encourage. In addition to economist Arthur, the team comprised Blake LeBaron, economist from the University of Wisconsin; John Holland, computer scientist from the University of Michigan; Richard Palmer, physicist from Duke University; and Brandon Weber, an undergraduate intern from Bard College."

The goals of this work appear to involve reproducing various phenomena of real markets as they emerge from the simulation of relatively simple artificial intelligence agents. The authors of the representative paper note that if we allow different agents to have different expectations in a market, and if we acknowledge uncertainty in knowledge about the expectations of other investors, we introduce infinite regress.[6] The payoff to me depends on my expectations regarding your behavior, which in turn should, but may not be, based on expectations of my behavior, which is possibly anticipating your behavior.... Well, you get the idea. This creates a fundamental difficulty in deducing an equilibrium point for the next move. The investor may have some idea about equilibrium, but he or she will in general be forced to rely on induction for what investing rules work best. That is, each investor becomes an econometrician in miniature.

The authors create a market model for one stock with a fixed number of shares, with the alternative being a risk-free interest-bearing deposit. There are 25 investor agents. Each is controlled by a Holland classifier system. This is a series of *if condition X, then forecast Y* statements of varying specificity based on varying descriptive attributes. Typically the attributes may be classified as *technical*, such as buy more if the price is above the 5-period moving average, or *fundamental*, such buy more if price times interest rate divided by dividend is less than 0.5. The most accurate of a bank of such rules in each investor's repertoire are called on for use, with accuracy updated each period based on a mean squared error criterion for forecast return. At much wider intervals, new replacement return forecast rules are formed from quasi-random combinations of pre-existing relatively accurate rules, plus a bit of mutation. This is done by representing each rule as a string of zeros and ones, or bits, that comprise a kind of genetic code that can be altered either through swapping partial strings with other successful rules or by randomly flipping bits from zero to one or vice versa. That is, the rules are updated through a genetic algorithm. The agents also forecast risk, though the authors do not specify that forecast algorithm. Demand quantities are formed based on expected return in excess of what could be earned risk free, divided by a risk tolerance parameter times estimated variance. Prices are adjusted to clear the market.

The driving force is a dividend level that can move up and down in an auto-regressive scheme driven by random noise with a normal statistical distribution. For example, the dividend rate next period is equal to a constant central tendency plus 95% of the difference between the dividend last period and the constant, all plus a deviation generated randomly from a normal statistical distribution.

The reported simulations are started with random rules and run for thousands of periods. The authors find that two kinds of market behavior regimes can

---

[6] W.B. Arthur, J.H. Holland, B. LeBaron, R. Palmer, and R. Tayler, "Asset Pricing Under Endogenous Expectations in an Artificial Stock Market," in W. B. Arthur, S. Durlauf, and D. Lane (eds.),*The Economy as an Evolving Complex System II* (Reading, MA: Addison-Wesley, 1997).

emerge, depending on how frequently the genetic algorithm is called into play to search for better investment rules.[7]

When genetic learning is very slow, after a while trading dies down to a relatively low level and prices, though subject to continued small random disturbances, are near those predicted by a rational expectations hypothesis based on the theoretical equilibrium predictable from the noise in the dividends and the risk tolerance of the investors. So we see it is possible to arrive at a solution which we imagine close to CAPM without having to specify that all investors begin with the same expectations. As a matter of fact, they can learn the long-run equilibrium expectations because the system is relatively stable, and as they do so, it can become more stable.

On the other hand, with faster genetic learning, a much richer set of dynamic behavior emerges from the feedback systems involved. These reproduce many of the stylized facts about markets that econometricians have verified but which the CAPM cannot explain, as well as some that practitioners have suspected, but academicians have not yet verified.

Here are some examples the authors report:

1. Even though the dividend disturbances (from the economy) are normally distributed, stock returns exhibit considerable kurtosis, or fat tails.
2. Trading volume is high.
3. Price volatility is amplified far beyond that directly attributable to dividend volatility.
4. Technical rules for earning profits become profitable.
5. Fundamental rules for earning profits become profitable.
6. Sub-populations of investor agents specializing in these two investment styles, technical and fundamental, tend to be rewarded by one another's behavior at irregular intervals, and mutually encourage one another.
7. The market self-organizes around essentially random combinations of events, so that the same combinations of market attributes tend to stimulate patterns of organized behavior in a self-sustaining way, once established. In different simulation runs, different attribute combinations serve this role.
8. The market exhibits periods of turbulence followed by periods of quiescence. Both trading volume and return volatility are separately predictable based on recent behavior. Activity is clustered because of changes in rule dominance cascading among investors.
9. Volatility and trading volume are strongly correlated.

---

[7] A much faster, though less radical, type of fine-tuning learning takes place in both regimes through the accuracy update that determines the frequency with which existing rules are called into action.

10. Increased trading volume can have a secondary inhibiting effect on next period's volatility, though this may be masked by simultaneous volume and volatility clustering tendencies.
11. There may be no tendency for the system to come to equilibrium.

It is remarkable that the Santa Fe results showed the same striking dependence on speed of learning as a source of instability as did the simpler and less specialized work of Epstein and Axtell. The key impact of heterogeneity of investor types is not so much disagreement in a single period as it is the potential for complex behavior over extended periods as different investor groups learn in opposition to one another. This suggests that theoretical finance can no longer treat the fiction of homogeneity of investor expectations as a mere mathematical simplification in determining the price equilibrium point. Rather it is the interaction of differences in viewpoint, what we might call fashions in thinking, that is the principal driver, along with variations in economic prosperity, of trading behavior. This is a principal food from which the active investor draws nourishment.

This chapter's title is "Finance at the Crossroads — The Santa Fe Experiments." It would appear that several years of experiments with dynamic simulation models of heterogeneous agents with bounded rationality have produced as many useful insights for the serious investor about market behavior as several decades of work in conventional theoretical finance. This is not to say that it has produced a body of empirical knowledge of markets comparable to that amassed by financial econometricians. Nor do I mean to imply that economists operating in other fields have not begun to use dynamic models, although they have not much come to grips with the problem of heterogeneity. But the sub-field of theoretical finance has not kept up and needs to move on. As a micro-economist might say, the human capital invested in classic equilibrium models of finance has reached a point of diminishing returns.

Chapter 4

Feedback Structure, Indexing, and Active Investing

*Sir, he was dull in company, dull in his closet, dull every-
where. He was dull in a new way, and that made many
people think him great.*
Samuel Johnson, *Quoted in:* James Boswell, Life of
Samuel Johnson (1791)

Investing in a representative index of the entire market of available risky securities, as advised by the CAPM, is typically a good strategy. A similarly passive strategy is to avoid market timing. That is, do not move in or out of cash based on changing expectations for stock market return. This rule does not have the sanction of the CAPM, but it is a good strategy if you assume the market is efficiently priced and that long-term equity return expectations change little. These two similar rules may not be truly optimum, they may be dull, but for most savers, in most situations, they are a good practical solution. For the investor seeking to add value, however, they can be only a starting point.

Fundamentally, the index solution and the no-market timing solution rely on the market being in equilibrium. Thus, we study the conditions under which markets are likely to be in equilibrium, when there will be mild departures from it, and when equilibrium may be only a distant possibility. Why study aggregate market dynamic equilibrium? Study it because the cross-sectional equilibrium envisioned by the CAPM and its indexing adherents is much less plausible if the market as a whole is in dynamic disequilibrium with cash. Neither stocks nor investors are truly homogeneous; if they are in motion it is much more difficult to achieve cross-sectional equilibrium.

In this chapter, we focus on the market as a whole, gradually assembling a concrete picture of the dynamic roles played by different types of investment thinking. We will do this by building a model of the market, piece by piece. In the process we will gain a better understanding of the principal types of investment strategies, an understanding that has many analogies in the world of cross-stock decision-making. At the same time, we will gain an appreciation of the challenges and opportunities facing investors who try to time the market as a whole.

Exhibit 1: Cumulative Return for IBM

WILL THE REAL MARKET EQUILIBRIUM STAND UP?

If by equilibrium we mean a constant price level or even a constant rate of return, it is clear from inspection of stock market price histories that returns never come to equilibrium. Exhibit 1 illustrates this with a history of International Business Machines (IBM). We sum each month's dividends and price increases and divide by the starting price to produce a percentage return. Then we compound and add a starting base of 100% to provide a wealth index. A constant equilibrium return would show a smooth upward-sloping line.

The equilibrium contemplated by finance theorists is less ambitious. It is merely statistical in nature. In this equilibrium we might mean that a rational observer with no information other than past returns might choose to abandon forecasting the ups and downs of particular periods. He or she could then assign the same statistical mean forecast to the excess return over cash in each period. This is a form of the random walk theory that swept the field of finance in the early 1960s.[1] A sophisticated analysis of the data presented in Exhibit 1 would show a slight tendency for good and poor returns to cluster, but that is a refinement. (Even such modest opportunities vanish through averaging when we plot the returns of a capitalization-weighted market index such as the Standard & Poor's 500.)

---

[1] See Paul H. Cootner (ed.), *The Random Character of Stock Market Prices* (Cambridge, Mass.: The M.I.T. Press, 1964).

Exhibit 2: Distribution of Correlations of Return with Prior Month's Return
May 1977 Through February 1997, Large Sample of Value Line Stocks

Observations	238
Sum of Wgt.	238
Mean	−0.0029
Standard Deviation	0.111
Variance	0.0124
Skewness	−0.671
Kurtosis	4.767

	Correlation	
Percentiles		Smallest
1%	−0.38	−0.44
5%	−0.22	−0.40
10%	−0.17	−0.37
25%	−0.08	−0.37
50%	−0.02	
		Largest
75%	0.04	0.18
90%	0.10	0.26
95%	0.14	0.27
99%	0.26	0.27

Source: Value Line

If we mean by equilibrium that a rational investor might settle for identical expected returns *across* stocks, that is not a bad first approximation as well. Of course it does not quite conform to the CAPM's postulated linear relationship with systematic risk. On the whole, the cross-sectional relative returns of stocks in one month are very little correlated with those of the next month.

Exhibit 2 provides a statistical distribution of such correlations, each calculated in one of 237 pairs of adjacent months. The mean is −0.029, a slight reversal effect. Other empirical research suggests that in the United States, at least, correlations of returns calculated over longer intervals, say a year, are slightly positive. For very long periods, say five years, the correlations turn negative again. But for every interval over which we calculate returns, the correlations between adjacent intervals remain small.

Given these approximate phenomena, a rational investor might well choose to index rather than to pick stocks, and might also ignore the possibility of a changing expected return differential between stocks and cash.

Still, a common expected return variable, though it might correspond as a first approximation to the returns that the market forms, is not a good assumption. It is a shortcut that goes against daily observation of how people form expectations. Investors seem to form expectations based on experience, with more recent experience given greater weight. Also, the specific indicators different individuals use vary wildly. Most investors have very different short-term return expectations for different stocks — thinking some will go up and others down, which is highly inconsistent with CAPM assumptions.

Empirical investigation also suggests that investors tend to respond negatively to price increases after a long period of stable prices with fluctuations within a range, but positively when they follow an apparent upward trend.[2] This behavior is clearly destabilizing. Someday we will have a theoretical model that shows how a relatively efficient and not entirely unstable market can arise from the interactions of such varied investor behaviors. We will take some small steps in this direction as we go on in this chapter.

It is vital to understand that the statistical characteristics of returns arise as a result of market interactions rather than of a single super-informed, super-rational investor type. We are then in a better position to appreciate those times when opposing forces are off balance and the market is in disequilibrium. These are opportunities for the active investor.

So far we have discussed only the issue of expectations. The market's equilibrium depends on an interrelated web, not only of expectations, but also risk preferences, prices, and holdings. Each of these responds to changes in both the other market components and external factors. These include additional changes in the way investors interpret economic events, changes in the capital available to investors with different outlooks, and changes in risk tolerances reflecting economic events. An important external disruption is the periodic arrival of entirely new and inexperienced investor groups, as when extended prosperity leads a large group of bond investors to enter the stock market for the first time.

Given all these disturbances, a practical view of market equilibrium must include the forces that arise after a disturbance. These may lead to a stable outcome, to oscillations that die out quickly, or to subsequent behavior that bears little connection to the disturbance that initially triggered it.

It would take another whole book to construct a full-fledged market model. Here we will have to do without formal modeling of trading stocks among the different types of investment viewpoints. We will not show how investor types fluctuate in their market buying power based on experience and recruitment. We will not even illustrate the impact of market action on risk expectations and thus on subsequent market action.

In this chapter we can only introduce the major types of investment thinking and the strategies appropriate to each. We will begin with a single-stock market consisting of a single type of dynamic expectation formation. Then we define and illustrate several additional of investor behavior. Along the way, we will see how such a mixed group can still interact to form a relatively stable and effective market.

---

[2] See Jay Bradford De Long, Andrei Shleifer, Lawrence H. Summers, and Robert J. Waldmann. "Positive Feedback Investment Strategies and Destabilizing Rational Speculation," *Journal of Finance* (June 1990), pp. 379-395.

Perhaps it is not too far-fetched to think of different types of investors as different species filling different ecological niches, with diversity operating to produce a relatively efficient market in total. Rather than the efficient use of energy and materials formed by the predator-prey food web, we will see an efficient use of information by both cooperating and competing investor types.

The technical device employed in this chapter is to use aggregate feedback systems. These incorporate a minimum of heterogeneity in investor viewpoint. Such a perspective is intermediate between static equilibrium models and the full richness of evolutionary agent simulations. The advantage is that we can capture a surprising variety of insights on investors and markets in a relatively simple model.

POSITIVE AND NEGATIVE FEEDBACK

In 1961, Jay Forrester, a professor at MIT applying to management problems techniques he had learned as an electrical engineer, published *Industrial Dynamics*.[3] He recognized that networks of information flowing through decision points and delays were directly analogous to feedback systems he had worked with in designing servomechanism controls. The same principles could be used to analyze and correct problems in both. We will use my interpretation of his insight to better explain the kind of dynamic near-equilibrium typically reached by the stock market and its participants.

First, what is a *feedback system*? It is a set of causal links that loop. That is, changes in A causes changes in B, which cause changes in C, and so on. The causal links must loop back, so that changes in C cause further changes in A.

If changes in A result in consequences that eventually cause further changes in the same direction in A, we say that there is a *positive feedback loop*. A positive feedback loop can be operating in either of two directions. If an increase in A causes a further increase in A, we see growth. If a decrease in A causes further later decreases in A, we see decline or decay. For example, the money invested in a bank saving's account earns more interest. This causes more money to appear on the balance, which causes even more money to be earned the next period. Here is a second example in the other direction. A decline in business competitiveness causes decreased sales, which reduces the rate at which a company gains experience relative to its competitors, which causes further deterioration in competitiveness, further losses in sales, and so on.

If a change in A results in consequences that eventually cause changes in A in the opposite direction, we say that there is a *negative feedback loop*. Depending on their characteristics, negative feedback loops can either promote a gradual return to an equilibrium value or oscillations around it. Any oscillations may be *damped*, in which case the system will approach equilibrium through a series of overshoots and undershoots of declining magnitude. Alternatively, the oscillations

---

[3] Jay W. Forrester, *Industrial Dynamics* (Cambridge, Mass.: The M.I.T. Press, 1961).

can be *explosive*, leading to larger and larger swings until some other force outside the system comes into play.

A simple damped negative feedback loop of the first kind may occur for you while driving a car as you merge into a fast expressway from a slower street. As you sense a large gap between your speed and that of the ongoing traffic on the expressway, you press hard on the gas pedal. As your speed increases toward that of the traffic, you ease off until you blend in at the same rate of speed.

An example of damped oscillations may occur in the shower as you adjust the temperature of the water. Beginning with cold water, you turn up the volume of the hot water. Since there is a slightly delayed response, but you are a bit overeager, more hot water may build up in the pipe between your control and the water you feel than anticipated. This causes an overshoot of too-hot water. Then you turn the control too far in the opposite direction, but by a lesser degree, causing water to be a little too cool. You may need to make several adjustments in each direction before you are completely satisfied.

An example of an explosive oscillation could occur if you are driving on an icy road and the car starts to slide sideways left in response to a bump. You overcorrect a bit because at first the car does not seem to be responding. Then after an anxious delay, the car finally does respond. Unfortunately, it overshoots even after you stop turning the wheel, producing a swing to the right bigger than the one you began with on the left. You frantically correct this, producing a still bigger swerve to the left. A few such cycles and the car may hit the concrete barrier fence at the edge of the road.

Let's look more closely at what a feedback system does. Fundamentally, it conveys information in loops. For the moment, consider a system where changes operating along the path of causal links are sinusoidal waves of information. (See Exhibit 3.) That is, suppose they comprise a sinusoidal wave of given amplitude and period. As this sinusoidal signal passes through the component decision points and delays in a system, it is transformed. The wave may be attenuated or amplified; it may be pushed forward in time; it may even flip sign, pushing forward 180 degrees. Suppose in a firm, for example, that sales were to rise and fall in a sinusoidal pattern. An increase in sales results in falling inventory. Lower levels of inventory result in increased production. This happens, however, only with a delay. The delay results partly because inventory time-integrates sales, and partly because reporting is not instantaneous. Thus, the peak in production will occur substantially later in the cycle than the peak in sales. This delay should be seen as relative to the period of oscillation of the sinusoid disturbance under consideration. It constitutes a *phase shift* in the signal. Depending on the urgency with which inventory is corrected, the *amplification* of the production surge may be high or low. Since the production process requires time to operate and produces results with differing delays, it too will transform the sinusoidal signal, introducing further phase shift. Eventually there will be an increase in finished goods. If the phase shift, or delay relative to the period of the oscillation in sales, is sufficient, the increased product availability will hit inventory just as the down cycle in sales strikes. This unfortunate coincidence then causes a rapid buildup in inventory which will lead to overshoot. The stability of such an inventory-control negative feedback loop is governed by the relationships between the phase-shift and amplification induced by transformations of information as it goes around the loop. (The product of the amplification multiples going completely around the loop is called the loop's *gain.*) Most typically, time integration (or accumulation of results) and higher urgency, or amplification, lead to less stable systems.

Simple feedback systems are *linear.* That is, every variable in a feedback loop is influenced as a linear additive function of the other variables within the loop. Multiplication and division are with constants or parameters unaffected by the endogenous variables in the system. Such linear systems are relatively easy to understand because their output in response to a composite disturbance is simply the linear sum of their responses to the individual disturbance components. We take advantage of this property as follows. It can be shown mathematically that any signal pattern of finite amplitude and length can be decomposed into the sum of a series of sinusoids of decreasing period. We can calculate the phase shift and amplitude change of a sinusoid as it passes through each feedback loop component. Therefore, we can readily predict whether a linear negative feedback loop will be stable or oscillatory, and which frequencies of disturbance it will amplify. Negative feedback loops often amplify, or resonate with, periodic disturbances.

Exhibit 3: Component Impact on Information Signal

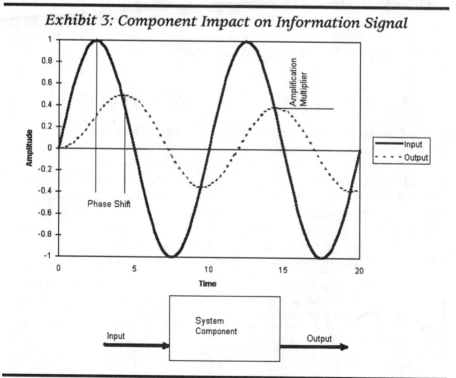

Feedback loops are usually combined to make a *complex feedback system*, such as a negative loop linked with a positive one. For example, in the stock market, if prices get too high, the implied return from dividends can get so low compared to interest rates that demand for stocks falls. This happens through a negative feedback loop. On the other hand, increases in prices can encourage some investors to think that capital gain returns will be high, thus causing an attempt to move more assets into stocks and further increasing prices. This positive feedback loop overlaps the negative loop and creates more complex behavior.

The story gets more complex. Even in the simple example of the swerving car on ice we described earlier, a non-linearity in the form of a concrete barrier intervened to stop further gains in amplitude of the oscillation. In the economic arena, the parameters that we used to multiply or divide our endogenous loop variables in the linear case are very frequently affected by the behavior of the variables in the loop. The resulting complex systems are *nonlinear*, and their behavior is less easy to generalize. For example, the same nonlinear feedback system can at different times be in an oscillatory mode, at times be stable, and at times undergo exponential growth. Nevertheless, we can often get fundamental insights into its behavior by focusing on the one or two loops that have the most power at particular points in time, perhaps approximating them with temporary linear equivalents. We begin with analysis and then move to simulation and sensitivity testing to changes in disturbances or system parameters.

These ideas will become much clearer with a practical example. Let's turn now to build the simplest feedback model of the market we can devise in which to embed the Markowitzian decision rules.

AGGREGATE MARKET FEEDBACK STRUCTURE[4]

Exhibit 4 is a diagram of the simplest feedback structure I have been able to devise for the market. It has one negative feedback loop, which adjusts market prices to disturbances in dividends relative to interest available from a risk-free security I will call "cash." The main feedback loop thus runs from Dividend Yield through Indicated Return through fraction of securities desired for stocks through Price and back again to Dividend Yield. It is, as we shall see, highly nonlinear. The variables that are part of this closed loop of relationships are *endogenous*. Other constants and variables are *exogenous* to this feedback system. The detail at the upper left in the exhibit is the apparatus necessary to construct an appropriate economic

---

[4] You can get a taste of the insights available from modeling market variables through feedback systems here simply by continuing to read and study the illustrations. However, if you wish to try some feedback modeling on your own, you might investigate two software packages that are specially constructed for this purpose. While the models shown here were written in *Vensim*, which has provided an inexpensive home use version, *Stella* is very highly recommended. (*Stella*, Stella Software, High Performance Systems, 45 Lyme Road, Suite 200, Hanover NH 03755. Internet: http//www.hps-inc.com/; *Vensim*, Ventana Systems, Inc. 149 Waverley Street, Belmont, MA 02178. Internet: http//www.vensim.com/.)

disturbance to the market system. It constructs random variation in "dividends" as a random walk in short-term mean dividends plus an instant further random variation. This simulates a business cycle of indeterminate amplitude and period. The dividends should be thought of as a proxy for all sorts of economic precursors of dividends. This loop functions to adjust prices to the approximate level of dividends so that expected returns come into equilibrium with interest rates.

The models shown here were written in *Vensim*. Here are general system parameters governing the length of the run and the accuracy with which difference equations simulate true continuous relationships.

Simulation Controls:

INITIAL TIME = 0
Units: Month
The initial time for the simulation.

Exhibit 4: The Simplest Market

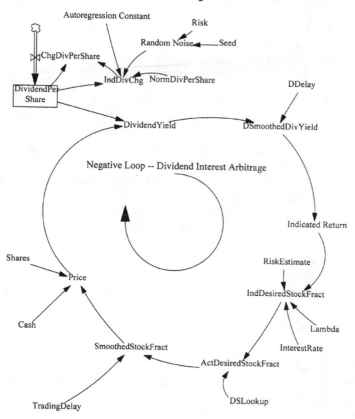

FINAL TIME = 240
Units: Month
The final time for the simulation.

TIME STEP = 0.25
Units: Month

The time step for the simulation. The smaller this number, the closer the time integration functions approximate to the continuous case.[5]

Exogenous Disturbance Through Dividends Per Share:

This material is exogenous to the system and simply produces periods of prosperity and recession in economic conditions. Dividends should be regarded as a generic indicator of company success.

Seed=0
Program parameter used to set sequence for random number generation.

Risk=0.015
Standard deviation of random noise variable. Produces this standard deviation disturbance of dividend every calculation, or four times a month, since the time step is 0.25.

Random Noise=(RANDOM UNIFORM(0,1,Seed)+RANDOM UNIFORM(0,1,Seed)+RANDOM UNIFORM(0,1,Seed)+RANDOM UNIFORM(0,1,Seed)+RANDOM UNIFORM(0,1,Seed)+RANDOM UNIFORM(0,1,Seed)+RANDOM UNIFORM(0,1,Seed)+RANDOM UNIFORM(0,1,Seed)+RANDOM UNIFORM(0,1,Seed)+RANDOM UNIFORM(0,1,Seed)+RANDOM UNIFORM(0,1,Seed)+RANDOM UNIFORM(0,1,Seed)-6)*Risk
Produces random numbers that are very nearly normally distributed, with a mean of 0 and a standard deviation of 1.

NormDivPerShare=1/12
Units: Dollars per Share per Month
The exogenous mean for dividends per share, here $1 per share per year. Actual dividends per share fluctuate randomly around this figure, driven by random noise, but tending to return because of autoregression below.

Autoregression Constant=20
Units: Months
Equivalent to a conventional autoregression coefficient of 0.95 for DividendPerShare.

---

[5] The cognoscenti might be interested to know that the numerical integration used here is simple Euler.

Exhibit 5: Exogenous Dividend Disturbance
Graph for Dividend Per Share

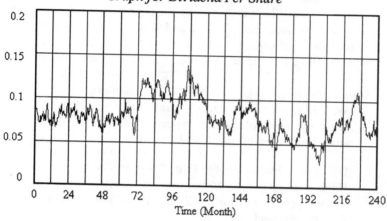

DividendPerShare : Current ————————— Dollars per Share per Month

---

IndDivChg=(NormDivPerShare-DividendPerShare)/Autoregression Constant + Random Noise
Units: Dollars per Share per Month per Month
This is the unconstrained change in dividend per share each month.

ChgDivPerShare=IF THEN ELSE(IndDivChg<−DividendPerShare,−DividendPerShare, IndDivChg)
Units: Dollars per Share per Month per Month
The actual change in dividend per share is constrained to keep the latter from going negative.

DividendPerShare= INTEG (ChgDivPerShare,NormDivPerShare)
Units: Dollars per Share per Month
The resulting dividend per share is the time integral of its change. It must have an initial value, which in this case is set equal to the normal dividend per share. Time integration is approximated by setting the stock at time t equal to the stock at time t-1 plus the time step (here, 0.25 months) times the sum of the flows. Note that we have not smoothed dividends here. In reality they are changed with a quarterly seasonality, and such real dividend changes are also much smoother than those pictured here. The reason these are more jagged is that they are intended to represent more generic economic information, which, like earnings and its antecedents, might change with much higher frequency and amplitude than dividends.

Now let's look at the resulting exogenous disturbance in Exhibit 5.

The typical dividend per share is 0.0833 Dollars per Share per Month, but over a 240 month or 20-year period it ranges from about 0.13 to 0.03. The implicit assumption made here is that all dividends are spent on consumption, as is interest. We do so to avoid complication and to focus attention on stability conditions rather than on growth. Now let us construct a market system that can respond to this disturbance, and as a byproduct achieve equilibrium stock return.

Negative Feedback Loop — Dividend Interest Arbitrage:

We will first create a prototype investor who simply expects future returns to be similar to the expected dividend yield. The latter is a smoothed version of past dividend yields.

DividendYield=DividendPerShare/Price
Units: Fraction per Month
The exogenously disturbed dividend per share is divided by price to form the dividend yield.

DDelay=60
Units: Months
How long must a dividend yield persist before it is perceived to be something worth generalizing to the future? Here we will model a perception delay as a first order exponential delay with a delay constant of 60 months. That is, our prototype investor is rather reluctant to change expectations.

DSmoothedDivYield=SMOOTHI(DividendYield,DDelay,0.007)
Units: Fraction per Month
Vensim's SMOOTHI function smoothes the input, in this case Dividend Yield, using the following internal device: DSmoothedDivYield=Level/ Ddelay, Level=INTEG(DividendYield-DSmoothedDivYield). The internal "Level" must be initialized, and here it is set to 0.007, close to what will turn out to be the equilibrium fractional dividend yield per month. Ddelay is a smoothing parameter. For a first-order delay (with one internal level), half a step-function disturbance will be reflected in the output after an interval equal to the smoothing delay. This kind of first order exponential delay is the most sensible all-purpose model of expectation formation I can imagine.

Indicated Return=DSmoothedDivYield
Units: Fraction per Month
For this first model, the total return forecast is simply the perceived long-term dividend yield. There is no long-term growth built into the system.

InterestRate=0.05/12
Units: Fraction per Month
This is the interest rate with which stocks must compete.

We assume a Markowitz type investor whose objective function is "expected return less lambda * variance of return/2." If this is true, we determine through elementary calculus that the optimal weight for stocks is equal to the following: expected stock return less the riskless interest rate, all divided by lambda times the estimate of return variance. Lambda may be thought of as the intolerance for risk, or the *price of risk*.

Lambda=1
Units: Fraction per Month per Risk Unit
In this model, all participants have the same risk preferences.

RiskEstimate=0.005
Units: Risk Units
The risk units here are in terms of variance in return on a monthly basis. The figure here is equivalent to an annual variance of 0.06, or a standard deviation of about 25% per year. This is more risky than the U.S. stock market of recent years, but of approximately the right order of magnitude. In this simple model, we are going to hold perceived risk constant to avoid additional complicated feedback

IndDesiredStockFract=(Indicated Return-InterestRate)/(RiskEstimate*Lambda)
Units: Fraction
Here is the investment decision resulting from Markowitz maximization. However, as it stands it is unsuitable for a model of the entire market, though it might work for some individual. This is because if stocks were a zero weight in the economy's portfolio, prices would go to zero, and if they were a negative weight, prices would go to negative numbers. Alternatively, as stock's fractional weight approached unity from below, prices would rise to infinity. We next make the model more realistic by assuming that there is a residual demand for both stocks and cash of 10%. That is, stocks will not be desired to be less than 10%, nor more than 90%, of the total portfolio. This might arise because of, on the one hand, the need for cash for liquidity and, on the other, the need for stock for corporate control. In purely mechanical terms, if we did not do this, the nonlinearities in the feedback loop would make it explosively unstable under big disturbances, even under otherwise plausible circumstances.

DSLookup([(0,0)(1,1)],
(0,0.1),(0.1,0.13),(0.2,0.21),(0.3,0.3),(0.7,0.7),(0.8,0.79),(0.9,0.87),(1,0.9))

Exhibit 6: Desired Stock Fraction Lookup Table

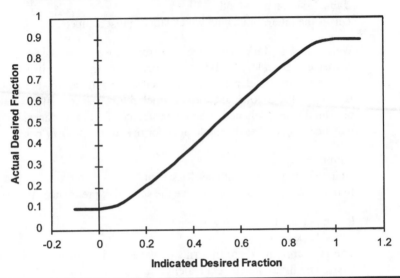

Exhibit 6 shows how Vensim's format, shown above, translates into a table function the desired non-linear relationship between Indicated and Actual Desired Stock Fraction.

ActDesiredStockFract=DSLookup (IndDesiredStockFract)
Units: Fraction
The actual desired stock fraction has its wings clipped by other realistic forces, operating according to the Markowitz — CAPM mode only in the wide central range.

TradingDelay=6
Units: Month
There is an additional delay after perceiving the indicated return before making actual trades. Observing the slow reaction of equity mutual fund sales to shifts in prosperity, I have put in a relatively long delay — 6 months. Again, the form of the delay is a first order exponential. This provides a response to sudden change that is strong at the beginning and then gradually tapers off. See the structure of Dsmoothed Div Yield for reference.

SmoothedStockFract= SMOOTHI(ActDesiredStockFract,TradingDelay,0.55)
Units: Fraction
The fraction of wealth put in stocks as opposed to cash. The initialized stock fraction is set at 0.55, close to equilibrium given our parameters. We will look at what controls this fraction shortly.

Cash=100
Units: Dollars
The size of the alternative riskless investment pool is taken as fixed by
the real economy. All the market can do, given that we have assumed
investors immediately spend their dividends and interest, is to adjust the
price of the stock market. It might be helpful to think in terms of Cash
equaling $100 *billion*. This would give a market the size of a medium-
sized country in Europe.

Shares=10
Units: Shares
Since we have aggregated all stock investors, they cannot reduce their
share holdings. Note that we have excluded the complication of corporations issuing more shares when prices are high and repurchasing them
when shares are low. For more realism, think of this as 10 *billion* shares.

Price=(Cash/Shares)*(SmoothedStockFract/(1−SmoothedStockFract))
Units: Dollars per Share
The price of a share in the market is highly non-linear as a function of
the desired stock fraction of wealth. When the fraction is low, the slope
of the price function is the Cash/Share ratio. When the fraction nears
one, the slope steepens to infinity. Suppose we divide the slope of price
to fraction by the underlying price, to get a relative change. Then we
would find that the implied relative change is highest at either fractional
extreme, and more modest in the middle. This is a recipe for system performance that will be more stable under modest disturbances but can
become extremely unstable under large disturbances.

EQUILIBRIUM CHARACTERISTICS OF BASE CASE

If disturbances to the dividend ceased and the system came to rest, what would be
the equilibrium price, equity return, and fraction of wealth represented by stocks?
I have set the example so that this equilibrium point is within the middle range;
indicated desired stock fractions are not clipped by constraints. The equilibrium
relationships that the system must satisfy are:

$$f = \frac{(r-i)}{L\sigma^2} \tag{1}$$

$$r = \frac{D}{P} \tag{2}$$

$$P = \left(\frac{C}{S}\right)\frac{f}{(1-f)} \tag{3}$$

where

f = ActDesiredStockFract
r = Indicated Return
i = InterestRate
L = Lambda (the price of risk)
σ^2 = RiskEstimate
D = DividendPerShare
P = Price
C = Cash
S = Shares

If we combine these equations by substitution, we can obtain quadratic equations in any of the three unknowns: f, r, or P. One of the most interesting permutations is a quadratic in the risk premium, shown as equation (4):

$$\left(\frac{C}{L\sigma^2}\right)(r-i)^2 + \left(\frac{DS+iC}{L\sigma^2}\right)(r-i) - DS = 0 \tag{4}$$

The positive solution is given in equation (5).

$$r-i = \sqrt{\left[\frac{(DS+iC)^2}{4C^2}\right] + \left[\frac{DSL\sigma^2}{C}\right]} - \frac{(DS+iC)}{2C} \tag{5}$$

The risk premium $r - i$ can be understood as the hypotenuse of a right triangle less one of its sides. The risk premium goes up as the other side, the square root of the right-hand term under the square root sign in equation (5), goes up. Whether the risk premium goes up more as the estimated risk variance or as the estimated risk standard deviation depends on the ratios of the two orthogonal sides of the triangle. You can also see that in this model the equity risk premium is an increasing function of the ratio of the dividend flow to the cash alternative, DS/C. Thus, not only equilibrium price, but also equilibrium return, go up with increasing economic "dividend."

The insight into the market's equilibrium risk premium one gets from equation (5) or similar models is not the same as one derives through the CAPM. CAPM describes under certain assumptions the relations we might expect between the risk premia for specific securities and that associated with the market as a whole. As a partial equilibrium model, it does not address the market risk premium directly. Our very simple model does take into account the additional factors necessary for global equilibrium, although within a very restricted framework.

Of course, keep in our mind that in our model Cash and the interest rate are fixed, or inelastic. In the real world, they obviously vary in part based on what happens to the stock market; this would require modifications to our formula.

With the parameters above, the equilibrium return, calculated using the quadratic formula for solving equation (4), is $r = 0.0069$, or about 8.3% per year, as compared to an annual interest rate of 5%. The fraction of wealth invested in stocks is 0.547, and the price per share is $12.07.

We can make some qualitative observations about the dynamic behavior of the loop before simulating its behavior. First, since it has two time integrations and a sign change, it is theoretically possible for it to phase shift a sinusoidal signal far enough to exhibit overshoot and oscillations. However, at most, these cycles will be damped. Second, the very unequal delays involved in smoothing dividend yield and in trading mean that any such oscillations will normally be very damped indeed. The system can only exhibit oscillation tendencies when the gain compensating the loss of signal strength going through the two unequal first order delays is very high.

Here is where the system's non-linearity comes in. The influences on gain going around the loop are lambda, the risk estimate and the current stock fraction. In this simple model, the first two are constant parameters uninfluenced by system operation. The system has more stability the higher the perceived risk and the higher the price of risk. This is intuitive because under these conditions stocks are not perceived as close substitutes for cash. However, by taking derivatives going around the loop, we discover that the link from f to P causes the gain multiple to be proportional to some constant times $1/(f(1-f))$. Thus, the system will be most stable when the stock fraction is 0.5 and least stable when large disturbances push it to extremes.

Beyond this, the long 60 month first-order delay in forming expectations about return should effectively smooth, or filter out, the jagged high frequency content of the simulated dividend disturbance. (Remember that "dividends" here proxy for all kinds of economic news, translated into dividend equivalents.) Second, the peaks and valleys that remain should be delayed from the point of original disturbance. Overall, the system should be reasonably stable given the dividend disturbance, and act to smooth and delay the disturbance signal. However, it will gradually respond to changes in the average dividend level to maintain a reasonably calm expected rate of return.

Exhibit 7 illustrates the system behavior over 20 years, when disturbed by the variations in dividend per share noted in Exhibit 5. If you compare Exhibits 5 and 7, you can also observe that the signal is not only smoothed but delayed about 12 months.

Now let's try to destabilize the system. We will lower the estimated risk from 0.005 to 0.002, without changing the external economic risk. This is equivalent to assuming that the standard deviation of returns is about 35% lower, not unlike what can be observed in practice in successive 5-year periods. Equilibrium prices will be higher, the fraction held in stocks will be higher, and indicated return will be lower. However, we will not change the initial conditions on the two delays. This will give the system a powerful one-time jolt, primarily because the initial indicated return will now be much higher than the new equilibrium. Finally, we will increase the trading delay from 6 months to 33 months, and decrease the dividend smoothing delay from 60 months to 33 months. This will maximize the similarity in the signal frequencies these two "filters" pass through without changing the overall total delay. Exhibit 8 shows the result.

Exhibit 7: Base Case Market Response
Graph for Price

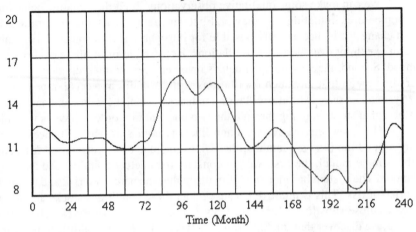

Price : Current ——————————————————— Dollars per Share

Exhibit 8: Base Case Reengineered for Instability
Graph for IndDesiredStockFract

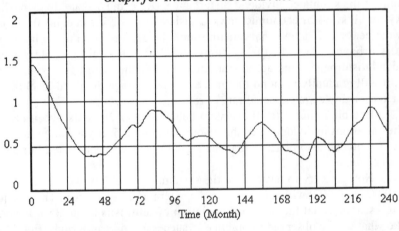

IndDesiredStockFract : Current ——————————————— Fraction

In this case we show the indicated stock fraction rather than the resulting price. It better illustrates the dynamics before the first price peak is clipped by the DSLookup table function that insures that actual stock fractions stay within the permitted range. Note that there is more high frequency content because we reduced the longest delay time of the dividend yield smoothing. However, the key point is the effect on stability.

Exhibit 9: Adding Momentum and Fundamental Investors

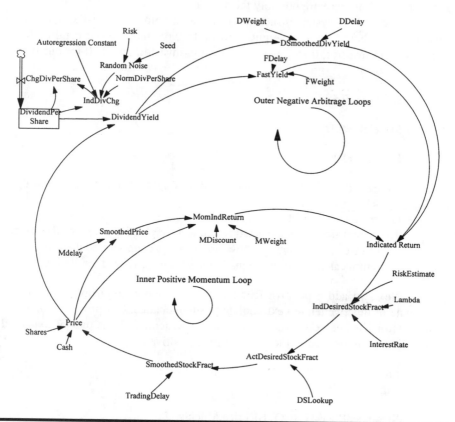

The initial condition imbalance results in an indicated stock fraction well above one. We see in Exhibit 8 a modest degree of overshoot, with the indicated stock fraction falling from its initial maximum to only 0.39 before eventually rising to a new equilibrium range centered on 0.61. The key point here is that the system as originally presented in Exhibit 7 is very stable. It has some potential for resonance to outside disturbances, but only under extreme situations.

We will now go back to the base case of Exhibit 7, but we will modify the system to have additional pathways for feedback. These will correspond to different types of investment thinking. This will give us a clearer understanding of the roles played in the market by several key types of investment styles.

Adding Momentum and Fundamental Investors

Exhibit 9 diagrams the additional structure. We add both a type of momentum investor and an investor with a much faster perception of reality whom we will label as a fundamental analyst. (We will get to growth and value investors in the next section.) There are several alternative structures we could have considered for each type, but these are possibly the simplest.

The revised system structure is indicated below. The last simulation of this section is based on this weighting: weight 0.65 given to our original long-term dividend investor, 0.15 for our momentum investor, and 0.20 for our fundamental analyst.

DWeight=0.65

MWeight=0.15

FWeight=0.20

IndicatedReturn=DSmoothedDivYield*DWeight+MomIndReturn*Mweight
　　+FastYield*FWeight
Units: Fraction per Month
The new structure for expected return is a weighted average for three types of investors. (Exhibit 9 shows the weights connected to their individual return calculations; this equation has been rearranged for clarity.)

Next we add a positive feedback loop of momentum investors. We all have some of this: we tend to extrapolate positive change. Our prototype momentum investor has been constructed to ignore dividend yield as part of expected return, to show more clearly the impact of the positive loop.

Mdelay=12
Units: Months

SmoothedPrice=SMOOTHI(Price,Mdelay,12)
Units: Dollars per Share
The base price against which current price is compared.

MDiscount=0.01
Units: Fraction
This is the fraction of the past increase that is projected into the future.

MomIndReturn=MDiscount*(1−SmoothedPrice/Price)
Units: Fraction per Month
The momentum investor smoothes price with a first-order exponential smoother having a 12-month delay constant. A fraction MDiscount of the price change implied by comparing Price to a 12-month SmoothedPrice is extrapolated into the future as a return on today's price. As we will see, even this apparently tiny degree of trend extrapolation, if uncompensated by other forces, seriously destabilizes the market system.

Exhibit 10: Base Case Plus 10% Momentum Players
Graph for Price

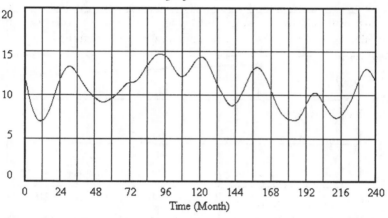

Price : Current ———————————————————— Dollars per Share

Here is the simple structure for our fundamental analyst, who is merely able to discern changes in the dividend yield much faster than our prototype long-term investor. Keep in mind this is intended to be analogous to looking at earnings antecedents and near current prices as opposed to waiting for smoothed dividends to appear.

FDelay=3
Units: Months
FastYield= SMOOTHI(DividendYield,FDelay,0.007)
Units: Fraction per Month

Now we will demonstrate the impact of these new investor types. Exhibit 10 shows what happens when we add a little momentum investing to our prototype long-term dividend investor, leaving the weight of the fast dividend, or fundamental analyst, at zero — that is, Dweight=0.90 and Mweight=0.10.

Because the positive momentum loop destabilizes the negative feedback loop, it enhances the tendency for the system to resonate, finding its own preferred oscillation. In this case the internal resonance corresponds to a period of about three years. The system no longer responds so much to the frequencies that happen to dominate the dividend disturbance signal. In this particular case, the net effect is to result in behavior that is more cyclical but that somewhat dampens the total range of behavior otherwise driven by the disturbance.

In comparison with the pure base case of Exhibit 7, the keen eye will also spot the existence of a transient difference at the beginning. This occurs because the relationships implied by the new loop, which ignores the dividend yield component of return, lowers the expected return and creates an imbalance with the initial values of smoothed stock fraction.

Exhibit 11: Base Case Plus 13% Momentum Players
Graph for Price

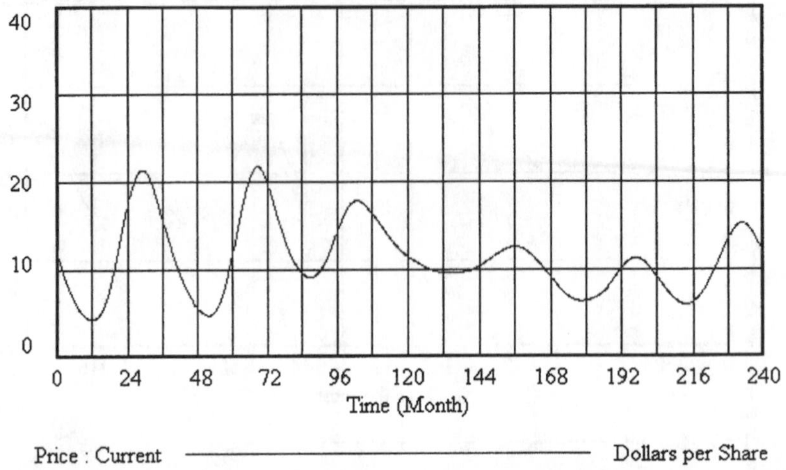

| Price : Current | ———————————————————— | Dollars per Share |

There is a precarious knife-edge boundary between local stability and large-scale oscillation as the weight given to momentum investing increases. Exhibit 11 shows the result of increasing it to 0.13, while decreasing the long-term dividend investor weight to 0.87. The positive feedback pushes returns to greater extremes, interacting with the nonlinear impact of desired stock fraction on price to produce much greater instability. At this point the external dividend disturbance impact has been greatly obscured. During the first 10 years, transient oscillations dominate. During the second decade, these have died down, and it is possible to see some steady state response to the external dividend disturbances, which, however, is greatly modified by the system.

Finally, we will increase the weight of the momentum investors just a bit more, to 0.15, decreasing the long-term dividend investor to 0.85. And we see an astounding transformation of behavior, resulting in Exhibit 12. Now the system explodes, coming to a limit cycle only because we have clipped the range of desired stock fraction to between 10% and 90% of wealth.

The initial transient becomes an explosive oscillation, accelerating as the fraction of stock desired begins to get very high, pushing up prices at ever faster rates. The second such oscillation reaches the boundaries of possible stock fraction, and the oscillations cannot expand farther. Note also that the period has increased to about 8 years. Sometimes we have seen such behavior in real markets, as with the Tulip Mania and the South Sea Bubble, where prices increased by orders of magnitude, and then fell back again. We may have seen a milder version in the runup of the Japanese stock market through 1989. However, we know that this usually does not happen, despite the very substantial fraction of the market's investors who can be observed in momentum investing. What could be stabilizing the market?

Exhibit 12: Base Case Plus 15% Momentum Players
Graph for Price

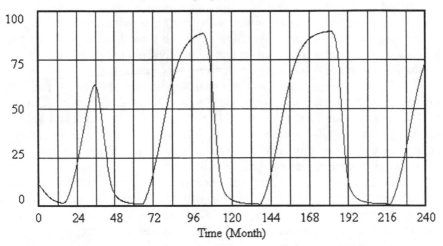

Price : Current ——————————————————— Dollars per Share

We will illustrate the stabilizing effect of speeding up the reaction to changes in dividend yield. Somewhat stretching common usage, we will call the more sensitive investors fundamental analysts. As we characterize them, they are represented simply by earlier knowledge of what is happening. Keep in mind, again, that although we are calling our disturbance dividends per share, it may be regarded very broadly as all kinds of foreseeable economic events. We are allowing our fundamental analysts to sense these with only a three month first order exponential delay, as compared to the 60 month smoothing delay applied by the long-term dividend yield investors. Moving an additional 0.20 weight from the long-term dividend investors to the fundamental analysts effectively stops momentum investing's impact dead in its tracks, as we see in Exhibit 13.

The quick response of fundamental investors to a change in yield counteracts the price trending reinforced by momentum investors before it can build up a head of steam. Compare Exhibit 13 to Exhibit 5 to see how closely the market now tracks dividends.

GROWTH AND VALUE INVESTORS

In everyday life, many of the investors most people call "fundamental" do not pay much attention to changes in the price factor, which is about as fundamental an ingredient as I can imagine. However, they may be very up-to-date on economic events. In our simulations we represent all economic information external to the market through "dividends." Only smoothed versions are available to investors. The less smoothed, the more this information maps into the signals growth investors attend. In practice, growth investors may focus on growth in earnings per share or on improved return on equity, with price coming into their decisions in a more limited way. I have represented this through smoothing price with a much longer smoothing delay than used separately for dividend per share, and only then combining the two to determine growth investor expected return.

Growth investors may be either stabilizing or destabilizing. If their price smoothing is slight relative to the periods of the external disturbance cycles, they will simply be less effective in stabilizing than the fundamental analysts described at the end of the preceding section. However, if their price smoothing is greater, that is if they pay very little attention to current pricing in reacting to changed fundamentals, they can be destabilizing.

Exhibit 14 shows the final complications to our model of the stock market — separate strands of expectation formation for growth and value investors. These are added to the mix of long-term dividend investors, momentum players and fundamental analysts that we have already assembled.

The incremental structure is detailed below.

DWeight=0.25
Units: Fraction
As we add new types of investors, we reduce the weight given to long-term dividend investors.

Exhibit 13: Base Case Plus 20% Fundamental, 15% Momentum
Graph for Price

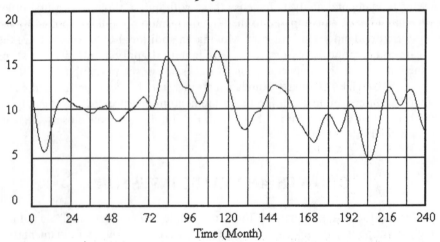

Price : Current ———————————————————————— Dollars per Share

Exhibit 14: Adding Growth and Value Investors

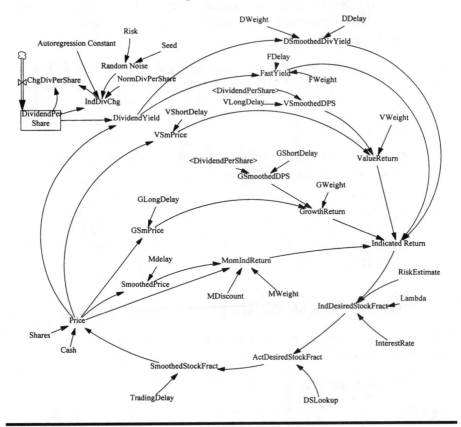

FWeight=0.12
Units: Fraction

GWeight=0.20
Units: Fraction

MWeight=0.13
Units: Fraction

VWeight=0.30
Units: Fraction

Indicated Return=
Dweight*DSmoothedDivYield + Mweight*MomIndReturn
+ Fweight*FastYield + Gweight*GrowthReturn + Vweight*ValueReturn
Units: Fraction per Month

We combine all the investors to form a weighted expected return. Again, there is a little artistic license used here. The actual structure in the diagram shows the weights before expected return is calculated, but the two models are equivalent.

Growth investors are represented by forming return expectations from a fast update on "dividends" and an insensitive update on price.

GShortDelay=4
Units: Months

GSmoothedDPS=SMOOTHI(DividendPerShare,GShortDelay,1/12)
Units: Dollars per Share per Month

GLongDelay=120
Units: Months

GSmPrice=SMOOTHI(Price,GLongDelay,12)
Units: Dollars per Share

GrowthReturn=GSmoothedDPS/GSmPrice
Units: Fraction per Month

Value investors are represented with an insensitive delay on "dividends" but a short delay in sensing price.

VLongDelay=120
Units: Months

VSmoothedDPS=SMOOTHI(DividendPerShare,VLongDelay,1/12)
Units: Dollars per Share per Month

VShortDelay=3
Units: Months
VSmPrice=SMOOTHI(Price,VShortDelay,12)
Units: Price per Share

ValueReturn=VSmoothedDPS/VSmPrice
Units: Fraction per Month

Exhibit 15 shows a reasonably stable system where the growth and value weights shown above have been returned to the long-term dividend yield Dweight. The momentum and fundamental (balanced, but fast) weights have been set at 0.13 and 0.12, respectively. This is our base case against which to view the impact of adding growth investors.

Exhibit 15: Base Plus 12% Fundamental, 13% Momentum
Graph for Price

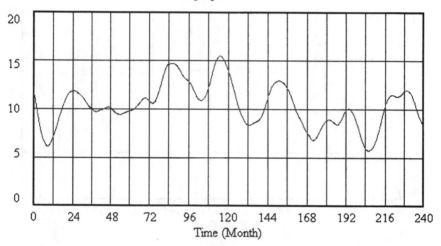

Price : Current ——————————————— Dollars per Share

Exhibit 16: Impact of Adding Growth Investors
Graph for Price

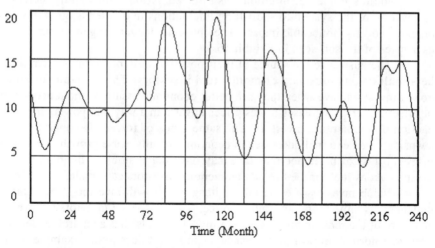

Price : Current ——————————————— Dollars per Share

In Exhibit 16 we see the impact of taking 0.20 weight from Dweight and putting it into our new class of growth investors. Their presence is highly destabilizing! This may at first seem nonintuitive, since all they did was to somewhat neglect price. Are not external disturbances from dividends neutral?

Exhibit 17: Value Investors Stabilize Growth Investor Impact
Graph for Price

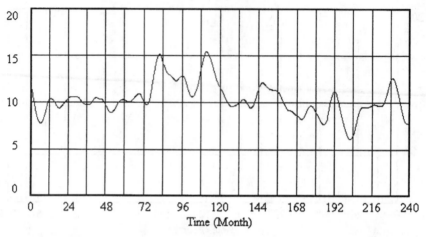

Price : Current ———————————————— Dollars per Share

If we performed another pair of simulations, with base case 100% long-term dividend and trial case 20% growth investor, 80% long-term dividend investor, we would see that our intuition was satisfied. Aside from slightly increasing the reaction of the system to short-term fluctuations in dividends, growth investors have no very noticeable impact. They pose no danger for generating internal resonances of the sort seen in Exhibit 16.

The answer to the source of their power to destabilize the system lies in the simultaneous presence of momentum investors! The demand for stocks growth investors have when they see better economic results without accounting for offsetting price increases forces prices upward in a way that powers increased reaction by momentum investors. The same kinds of forces also operate on the downside when external decreases in economic results cause growth investors to sell regardless of price declines that may have made stocks a bargain. Growth investors act as fuel for the fire that momentum investors can create.

Value investors are the mirror image of growth investors. They smooth fundamentals more than they smooth price. It is as if value investors believe that the nature of the random process generating "dividends" has a natural tendency to revert to a normal level of performance, as indeed it does in our example. I have represented value investors through smoothing dividends per share more than price in their expected return calculation.

Exhibit 17 shows the result of taking a further 0.3 weight from the long-term dividend yield investors and giving it to our value investor mentality. We see the system is again stable, with price movements largely synchronized with the dividend disturbances of Exhibit 5.

CONSEQUENCES

What have we learned about the market environment in this chapter?

First, we saw that to a first approximation, stock returns do behave as though a single type of rational investor might take expected returns as the same both across stocks and across time. This would argue for some kind of index investing as an appropriate strategy, perhaps not capitalization-weighted, combined with a policy of no market timing. However, we argued that the market's observed behavior cannot be determined in this way, because the process of expectation formation we see around us is very different. Our best hope of finding exploitable market imperfections is to model a process in which expectation formation of different types combine to produce familiar results.

We noted that if the market were out of balance with respect to cash, that is, dynamically out of balance, it would be more likely to be out of balance cross-sectionally as well. We then set off to construct, investor-type by investor-type, a market that incorporated very different types of expectation formation but was stable in its ability to absorb economic disturbances.

We discovered long-term dividend investors tended to smooth short-term economic disturbances but still responded to longer-wave disturbances. On balance, they were remarkably resistant to internally amplified instability. On the other hand, momentum investors, those who extrapolated past price changes, profoundly destabilized the system, setting up speculative boom and bust cycles. Growth investors, those who react quickly to changes in economic value but slowly to price, were not in themselves destabilizing but added to instability in the presence of momentum investors. We found that value investors, whom we defined as sensing economic changes very slowly but price changes very quickly, tended to stabilize both these groups. Finally, a group we called fundamental analysts who could sense both economic changes and price changes more quickly were also a stabilizing force.

Adding one more type of investor here would overburden the feedback structure diagram and unduly lengthen the chapter. However, I can briefly summarize what happens when indexer investors are added. Suppose we define indexers in this context where no individual stocks exist as being those passive investors who simply choose to continue the existing fraction of stocks to total wealth implied by market prices. That is, by not rebalancing with cash, they act as though their expected return on stocks fluctuated just enough to justify existing prices, without any consideration for the level of economic "dividends." If we were to substitute a 0.25 weight for this group for the long-term dividend investors in Exhibit 17, we would get almost identical results for the system as a whole. However, this is in the presence of a diverse group, including strong stabilizers such as the fundamental analysts and value investors. If, on the other hand, we were to eliminate the strong stabilizing forces in the system, we would still find that indexers contribute little to system instability by substituting for long-term dividend yield investors in isolation in moderate doses, but greatly contributed to instability when present in large doses. And like growth investors, indexers generate more instability in the presence of momentum investors. For example, a system of weight 0.1 momentum investors, 0.3 indexers, and 0.6 long-term dividend investors is wildly unstable.

What kind of strategies make money, and under what conditions? We will be returning to that topic in various ways in most of the remainder of this book. Because we did not simulate the results of trading among strategies in this chapter, we cannot be very definitive here. However, we can use what we did observe to make some intelligent guesses.

Long-term dividend investors resist change in their expectations for stock returns but generally act to stabilize the system. They hope to earn additional returns if economic changes are mean-reverting.

Fundamental analysts exploit long-term dividend investors by more rapid estimation of true returns.

Momentum investors can use the price-change signals generated by fundamental analysts to further exploit long-term dividend investors. However, momentum investing can easily turn into a losing strategy if positions cannot be reversed early enough because of a lack of takers on the other side. Fortunately for them, they may run into either growth investors or new indexing investors at that point, so long as the system is not too unstable.

Growth investors make money if through specialization in discovering growth signals they can get ahead of fundamental analysts. Sometimes they can exploit an over-abundance of value investors. Growth investors depend on prices having been already taken care of by other participants and benefit when the system is not too far from equilibrium.

Value investors make money if there are too many growth investors and momentum investors. They can also exploit mean reversion in economic benefits. They benefit from oscillations in prices, and so can win best, if intermittently, when systems are far from equilibrium, if they do not enter too early.

These types benefit from specialization. Value investors often buy stocks with low price/book ratios, and are adept at resisting social pressure from those who confuse good companies with good stocks. Growth investors seem more focused on sales, cash flow, and earnings as giving earlier signals of economic performance. Momentum investors are good at technical trading and at sensing changes in fashion. In this sense, growth and value investors are cooperative, in that they each specialize and so more effectively exploit the information habitat. Momentum investors are amplifiers, generating no information on their own but amplifying the effect of fundamental analysts.

There are also true noise traders — that is, those who make stock purchases and sales for reasons unconnected with either prices or economic dividends.

Indexers tend to be innocuous in small numbers but in large numbers are destabilizing. This is because they react to price moves in a way that is identical to an informed Markowitz investor who decides that expected returns have adjusted in the same direction. By themselves, they can generate no problems. But their characteristics can feed the efforts of momentum investors. This is a good strategy under two conditions — that better ones are not worth the effort because of intense competition, and that momentum and growth investors are not present in sufficient numbers to drive prices far from equilibrium. The first is true to a first approximation for many investors, but the second condition occasionally fails, even in a developed market such as the United States. Thus indexing is best when the market stays near equilibrium.

A final ideal type is the rotational investor, who can shift styles depending on the situation. He or she can go from growth to momentum to value investing as the system moves from under-reacting to new economic events, to chasing prices, and finally to correcting the overshoot. This is exceptionally challenging, because the skills for each specialty are quite different.

That's it, the principal market actors. In the rest of the book as we go through additional quantitative investment concepts, skills, and market examples, you will be able to relate them to the practices of these different investor types and to their likely success environments.

Chapter 5

St. Markowitz, or
Single-Period Investing

It is well for his peace that the saint goes to his martyrdom.
He is spared the sight of the horror of his harvest.
Oscar Wilde, *The Critic as Artist (1890)*

A little knowledge *is* a dangerous thing. Part III of this book is a series of mostly short chapters pursuing the basic concepts of investing in more depth. The best advice I ever heard about investing is, first, to know yourself, how your decisions react to changing circumstances, second, to learn to manage risk, and only third, to look for opportunities to add return. Ideally, the first topic in this book would be you, the reader. This topic is impractical here, although we will come back to the generic investor's decision-making biases in a later chapter on behavioral finance. But we can give the maxim its due by focusing on risk management concepts at the beginning before pursuing added return.

At my side as I write is a copy of Harry Markowitz's 1952 paper on "Portfolio Selection."[1] By the standards of more recent financial works filled with abstruse mathematics, it is remarkably accessible, relying mostly on logical argument and some simple geometrical diagrams. He argues that the observed phenomenon of portfolio diversification is an essential fact that must be explained by any theory of investing. He notes that this behavior can only be explained based on aversion to portfolio risk. He then shows us how by measuring risk as statistical variance we can construct portfolios that give better tradeoffs between return and risk.

Despite all the imperfections in applying his model that we saw at the beginning of Chapter 3, his method remains indispensable as a foundation for thinking about managing risk. Our goal is to know it well enough to know how to apply it best. (You may want to review the concrete introduction of it given in Exhibits 1, 2, and 3 in Chapter 2 before going on.)

Markowitz maps the real investment problem into a mathematical one by focusing on only a single investment time interval during which the investor is interested only in (1) expected portfolio return, (2) dispersion of estimates around that expectation represented by the expected variance of return, and (3) linear constraints on the weights of the securities in the portfolio.

---

[1] Harry M. Markowitz, "Portfolio Selection," *Journal of Finance* (1952), pp. 77-91.

In the compact matrix notation we introduced in Chapter 2, the job is to maximize the objective function below, subject to the constraints that follow it. Maximize by choosing X:

$$U = X'R - (\lambda/2)X'VX \tag{1}$$

Subject to:

$$\sum_i x_i = 1 \text{, and } x_i \geq 0 \text{ for all } i$$

where

    U = utility
    X = a column vector of weights for the securities under investigation
    R = a column vector of expected returns
    λ = a scalar (single number) representing intolerance for risk
    V = an array of expected covariances among the expected returns

Note that this formulation does not prevent one from some short selling, although it does assume that capital is consumed by so doing. An additional security with reversed expected returns and covariances can be used to represent each short position. Many later writers omitted the constraint that the individual security weights be non-negative, a deviation from the original Markowitz doctrine.

Equation (1) and its constraints is a *quadratic programming* problem. When V is a covariance matrix of stock returns, where no return can be precisely forecast from a combination of the others (a "positive definite square matrix"), the quadratic programming problem has the very convenient property that the objective function is guaranteed to have only one peak, which may be reached starting from any solution by simply going "up-hill." And although it can be solved by any of several mathematical techniques, such simple hill-climbing, step by step, will eventually arrive at the answer. At each step, one can find the direction of apparent greatest improvement (that is, which stock should be bought and which sold from the existing portfolio based on their relative contributions to portfolio risk and return), and then move in that direction. The step size is gradually decreased as progress in improving the objective function slows.

The Markowitz framework has been applied in many contexts. Among these are (1) two-asset tactical allocation between stocks and cash, (2) investment among from 5 to 20 asset classes, both in long-term asset allocation studies and in active country and currency selection, and (3) selection among hundreds, or even thousands, of stocks by quantitative equity managers. It has also been used with residual risk or "tracking error" relative to a benchmark substituted for standard deviation of return in managing both index funds and closely-controlled active funds. Finally, it has been used as a descriptive basis for theorizing about the market as a whole, as in the CAPM, the Santa Fe experiments described in Chapter 3 and the simulations you just saw in Chapter 4. Some of these applications have been very successful, others doubtful.

In this chapter we will deal only with the framework's best recognized practical problems and their solutions or workarounds. This will not be the more exhaustive list we saw in Chapter 3, but a shorter one of those that have received the most attention. It includes:

1. Limitations of variance as risk
2. Ignoring non-negativity constraints
3. Transaction costs
4. Large numbers of securities
5. Using statistical estimates as inputs.

LIMITATIONS OF VARIANCE AS RISK

In his 1959 book, Markowitz recognized the possible inadequacy of variance as a measure of risk, since investors object only to downside variation, and not upside variation.[2] He suggested the "semi-variance," calculated using only losses, as perhaps desirable but at the time impractical. In recent years this concept has gained in popularity, although not yet much in practical use, as it begins to seem more feasible. It would enable us to better handle investments with unusual risk characteristics such as puts and calls.

Despite the upside-downside symmetry of ordinary statistical variance, it is still our most available tool for managing risk. It has turned out to be a quite practical indicator in most investing situations, because ordinarily higher variance also implies higher apparent risk, and vice versa. Various studies have considered under what combined conditions of statistical return distribution and utility function shape maximizing the Markowitz objective function also maximizes expected utility. Ordinarily, the approximation is very good. On the other hand, problems do arise when portfolio returns may take on extreme variance relative to the wealth of the investor or when they may have large negative skew or kurtosis. Examples include gambling for high stakes, investing using leverage, and various strategies using derivative securities such as buying stocks and selling calls on them. Also, currency exchange rates can have substantial kurtosis of returns. In these cases, an analysis based on portfolio return variance will underestimate the effective risk.

These exceptional cases, which I label as examples of "edge" investing, often cause particular problems when the size of the possible losses approaches 80% to 90% in a single period. The investor's utility function curves radically downward as losses become large relative to total wealth. Fat-tailed return distributions can be particularly insidious, because the chance of a serious loss is too

---

[2] Harry M. Markowitz, *Portfolio Selection* (New Haven, Conn.: Yale University Press, 1959).

small to drive up variance, but too large in its consequences to ignore. In this situation a quadratic curve is a very poor approximation to utility. Consider a so-called conservative investor who bets everything he has on nearly "sure things," but with a tiny chance of losing. At any one turn the expected variance of return is small, because the squared 100% is multiplied by a very small probability. Yet the probability of eventually losing everything become very high as the game is repeated. The moral is not to hazard high proportions of your wealth in a single decision period. One partial solution to this "gambler's ruin" problem if we are dealing with liquid securities is to reduce the effective size of the bet by repeating the single-period Markowitz analysis more frequently. Then you can adjust the risk intolerance lambda to reflect changes in your wealth. However, high trading costs or sudden loss of market liquidity may sometimes make this workaround impractical.

We will be able to make some further conceptual progress in dealing with such cases through multiple-period analysis to be introduced in Chapter 6. However, if you think you may be "gambling," keep in mind that the assumption that variance is enough to describe loss of utility from risk may result in inadequate risk control in such cases.

IGNORING NON-NEGATIVITY CONSTRAINTS

In 1982, 30 years after publishing his original work on portfolio selection, Harry Markowitz served as President of the American Finance Association. His presidential address, published the next year in the *Journal of Finance*, was titled "Nonnegative or Not Nonnegative: A Question about CAPMs." In it he criticized the practice of using equation (1) in a form that lacked non-negativity constraints on individual positions. That is, the investor could take unlimited short positions, and offset those with unlimited long positions, while still staying within an overall budget equality constraint. He then went on to question the validity of those forms of the CAPM based on such an assumption. Why did he bother to use such an important occasion to make such an apparently obscure point?

The answer is that it is indeed a critical point in practice and possibly so in theory. Remember that Markowitz is not arguing against short sales but against unlimited commitments to them. As early enthusiasts for "optimized" portfolios posed the problem without non-negativity constraints, they noticed that they sometimes got very impractical answers. For example, large offsetting long-short portfolios were selected, such as several hundred percent leverage in each direction, which were rightly rejected by common-sense investors. The optimizer, as the algorithm to determine optimal portfolios was called, often came up with combined portfolios that were riskier than predicted. Second, two very similar securities, not just two diversified portfolios, would have opposite positions recommended, one very long and one very short. Such phenomena were difficult to explain to the unsophisticated "non-quants" even the first time they happened.

They became even more so when after very small changes in inputs the recommended allocation should be exactly reversed the next period. Many early converts to the new religion were embarrassed in this way. Consequently, going to the trouble of setting up short positions in the format Markowitz recommends is wise.

The constraints investors face in the real world on short-sales and leverage exist for good reasons; we will come back to this point shortly when we talk about statistical estimation. The statistical arguments for error in our estimates are so strong that even if we should find no legal or financing constraints on short-selling, we should impose them on ourselves. But in any case there is no doubt that such constraints exist as descriptive fact, although there are exceptions in the world of derivative securities where sometimes hope, greed, and gullibility overcome experience. Markowitz then went on to argue that if these non-negativity financing constraints were included, and if money could not be borrowed freely, then the CAPM could not hold, even if all investors thought alike. He suggested that in this case the efficient frontier becomes a crooked thread of piecewise linear segments wending its way through a space in which each security constitutes a different dimension. Different investors will be found on different straight-line segments. The point which is the wealth-weighted sum of each of them, that is, the market as a whole, will probably not be on the thread.

Thus the conclusion that the market index is efficient fails and so, too, fails the conclusion that expected return is a linear function of risk correlated with market return. While the empirical importance of this argument about the market as a whole does not appear to have been quantified, I have been unable to find a satisfactory rebuttal.

TRANSACTION COSTS

Suppose you already hold a portfolio of investments in closed-end emerging market funds, a Brazil Fund, a Mexico Fund, an Eastern Europe Fund, and so on. You have prepared your estimates of expected returns and their covariances. You carry out a Markowitz analysis. It tells you that you can improve your expected total return for the next year by 1% if you sell your Eastern European Fund and buy a new Russian Fund. Unfortunately, the bid-ask spread on the funds for the $20,000 you want to move is about 2%, suggesting a one-way trading cost of 1%. Counting both buying and selling, your total trading cost will be about 2%. Should you make the trade?

The answer depends on how long you expect to hold the new security and how long the return differential is expected to last. You could break even in two years, If you could depend on an extra 1% of return for, say, four years, the trade seems clearly attractive. But wait, shouldn't you go back to the Markowitz optimization and tell it about the high costs for this transaction? Perhaps it would then suggest some other portfolio rearrangement that offered better results after transaction costs.

Such problems are pervasive. The competitiveness of the market ensures that the potential for most investment managers to add returns will be on the same order of magnitude as transaction costs. Consequently, unless this part of the investment job is done well, transaction costs will eat up the potential benefit of the knowledge the active manager does bring to the situation. This wasted effort is the general result of most investors who attempt to add value to index returns through active trading.

So long as we are only dealing with one period we can always put transaction costs into equation (1) by creating two additional securities and slightly modifying the constraints. Thus, we have separate expected returns for the Eastern European Fund that we continue to hold, for the same fund that we contemplate buying, and for the same fund that we contemplate selling. The size of the potential sale is limited by what we already hold.[3] For investments we do not yet own, assuming no short sales we need put in only one security each. Thus, we can put transaction costs into the problem before we do the Markowitz optimization, using different transaction costs for each security if desirable.

That real investors must manage a sequence of investment periods, however, leaves a loose end. The analysis we spoke of assumes that the full transaction cost be amortized within a single period of analysis. What if we rebalance our portfolio every month, but our average portfolio turnover rate is only once every year? Then the transaction cost to be entered as input to the analysis should be substantially lowered, because it can be amortized over many months. Yet logically, how can we know our portfolio turnover rate and thus our amortization period if we have not yet done the Markowitz analysis that tells us how much we should trade?

This equilibrium answer to this circular question can be approached through iteration, either through multi-period simulation or through practical experience and rule of thumb. Clearly some policies are better than others. However, we may not always find the best combination of assumed transaction cost amortization and actual turnover rate. The guarantee that hill-climbing algorithms will do so that we are accustomed to in the basic quadratic programming problem with a positive definite covariance matrix does not apply to this more complex problem.

On the other hand, the *analytic* determination of optimal holding period is quite challenging. It depends on knowledge of the time-shape of the value-added curve, of active return statistical distribution properties, of the frequency of other opportunities, and, of course, of trading costs. It is really a problem in option theory whose exact solution requires solving stochastic differential equations. I am not familiar with anyone who is doing this in practice. I have provided an easier deterministic approximation as a reference.[4]

---

[3] Commercial optimizers calculate on the fly whether the net position of a single security is changing, and subtract trading costs where necessary. However, this is a matter of more efficient mechanics, not the intrinsic nature of the problem.

[4] Jarrod W. Wilcox, "The Effect of Transaction Costs and Delay on Performance Drag," *Financial Analysts Journal* (March/April 1993), pp. 45-54, p 77.

Now consider how much more complicated the trading cost problem really is if we are not willing to make this approximation of aggregate turnover rates. Suppose we wish to consider each stock on its individual merits. For an active investment manager, the size of the additional return to be earned after a trade is generally highest early and decays through time after the point of analysis. Referring to Chapter 4, it is obvious that the success of growth investors depends on being early. In contrast, the value investor dealing with market instability induced by momentum investors may face a longer period before the market turns. The added return pattern may be a very high additional rate of return that decays very rapidly for a specialist focused on earnings estimate revisions. Alternatively, for investment strategies focused on price-to-book ratios it may begin with a lower rate of benefit but one having a much slower rate of decay. In each case, the time integral of the value added must be large compared to the trading cost to justify the trade. However, the equilibrium turnover rates are very different. A successful trader focusing on rapid exploitation of earnings estimate information might turn his or her portfolio three times in a year. On the other hand, a value-oriented investor might turn over the portfolio only once in three years. Thus, their trading cost amortization schedules should be very different. Another implication is that the value-oriented investor is willing to hold much less liquid stocks.

What if the same stock is bought for two different reasons? The mind boggles at the complexity of an exact solution. This is a case where simulation of policy against a good database is probably the best available answer.

If we expect the optimizer to do more than simply provide guidance on the trades to be done, but to actually specify them, we may need additional features. For example, commercial optimizers may permit one to specify minimum transaction sizes. This is a good way of incorporating the administrative costs of conducting any transaction into the analysis. Thus, one might specify that any transactions be at least 0.25% of an institutional portfolio, or a bigger percentage of a smaller personal portfolio. The result, however, is a departure from Markowitz's easily solved quadratic programming problem.

An even greater sophistication is to incorporate variable transaction cost percentages. Percentage trading costs will generally be higher for very large transactions. For example, transaction costs may sharply accelerate as the purchase size exceeds a moderate fraction, say one-fourth, of the average daily trading volume. This is a serious problem for large institutional portfolios. One simple workaround within the framework of quadratic programming is to enter an additional constraint that purchases can be no larger than a cutoff fraction of the average market trading volume statistic. However, for some investment strategies it may be very desirable to have explicit tradeoffs between additional trading costs and value-added for larger trades. Consequently some commercial optimizers do incorporate this feature, although again at the expense of departing from the desirable single optimum region of quadratic programming.

LARGE NUMBERS OF SECURITIES

In Markowitz's original work he used three-stock examples. Ideal use of the framework would include all available stocks, which, if we include international stocks, are many thousands. Even if practical considerations limit you to the consideration of only a thousand, however, you will find that the quadratic programming problem as originally stated is too large. It will both take too long to run on a computer to be practical and suffer from too many statistical problems to provide accurate answers.[5]

Let us deal with the time problem first. The resources and time required to reach a solution to a quadratic programming problem at a given level of accuracy does not go up merely proportionally to the number of securities. You will not go far wrong if you imagine memory requirements to go up with n-squared and processing time to go up with n-cubed, where n is the number of securities in the covariance matrix. In modern computers the memory constraint is not too severe, but the processing time is. There have been advances in solution methods for quadratic programming problems that under some circumstances improve on the processing time relationship for large problems. Still, even if time went up only as n-squared, the full covariance approach described by Markowitz would require ten thousand times as long for a 1,000 stock problem as for a 10 stock problem. That is one reason why the original full covariance format is used for asset allocation studies involving only a few asset classes but drastic simplification is called for with a 1,000 stock universe. (Statistical error amplification is the other.)

In the early days, investment firms tried to reduce problem size by pre-screening the list of acceptable purchases before optimizing the portfolio return-risk tradeoff. Today a much more elegant approach shrinks the problem through factor analysis. That is, assume that:

$$r_{it} = \sum_j a_{ij} F_{jt} + \varepsilon_{it} \tag{2}$$

where

r_{it} = return for stock i at time t
a_{ij} = loading of stock i on factor j
F_{jt} = factor j realization at time t
ε_{it} = independent random disturbance for stock i at time t

The computationally expensive part of equation (1) is the term involving the covariance matrix, which for a 1,000 stock universe has over a half-million unique entries. Suppose we approximate each stock's return variation as com-

---

[5] Andre Perold provided an excellent early approach to dealing with these problems; see Andre Perold, "Large-Scale Portfolio Optimization," *Management Science* (1984), pp. 1143-1160.

posed of a linear function of even as many as a hundred common risk factors, plus one more for independent specific risk, as in equation (2). Even if we generously allow the number of factors to be 100, this will give a covariance matrix of the factors with only about 5,000 elements. If the factors are all independent of one another, there are more big savings possible, because the algorithm can rely on all but the diagonal elements being zero.

The factors can be returns on specific long-short portfolios selected to represent "growth," "momentum," "success," or the like. They can be industry average returns. They can be macro-economic factors like inflation changes. Alternatively, they can be pure statistical factors derived from a principal components analysis of the returns.[6] Principal components vary from period to period and may be difficult to interpret as coherent ideas. On the other hand, because they are independent of one another they can have important advantages in improving the ability to forecast the portfolio's risk. In any event, several commercial optimizer vendors supply estimates of such a factor structure, whether based on so-called fundamental factors, macroeconomic factors, or purely statistical groupings. They enable institutional managers to make, in most situations, reasonably accurate estimates of portfolio risk and arrive at efficient frontier estimates in minutes rather than hours or days.

Now let's open up the issue of statistical estimation. The inputs Markowitz suggests are in theory derivable from subjective probability estimates. But whether they are subjective or objective statistics from the past, the issue is whether they will forecast the future with sufficient accuracy to make the Markowitz analysis worthwhile. One of the characteristics of the quadratic programming problem is that its solutions tend toward unusual focus on outliers. For example, if two stocks have an unusually low correlation, they will both tend, other things equal, to be disproportionately weighted in the recommended portfolio. We can think of each input covariance as representing a random error plus a true value. The more different covariances we estimate, the greater the chance that we will observe an outlier that is based much more on chance rather than the true value. As the number of assets goes up, the number of separate covariances in the full covariance matrix goes up as the *square* of the number of assets. Consequently, the likelihood of the optimizer "diving" on erroneous low covariance inputs, or, conversely, taking long-short positions on a pair of apparently identical stocks, rises rapidly as the number of assets increases.

The true solution to this problem depends on better statistical estimation of risk and return, which we will expand on next, and cover more fully in a later chapter on risk estimation. However, as a simple heuristic, less is more. Factor analysis, by reducing the number of coefficients to be estimated, is one way to achieve this. Another approach is hierarchical investing. That is, first decide allo-

---

[6] Principal components are different weighted averages of the stock returns at hand. They are chosen so that the first component's correlation with the ensemble of stock returns has the largest possible value, the second the second largest, and so on. Each component must be uncorrelated with all those that have preceded it.

cation among a few large categories of assets, then decide by individual security. Each stage involves separate Markowitz optimization. Dividing this optimization problem clearly would be suboptimal given deterministic inputs. Still, what you are giving up in quadratic programming precision you may more than get back in greater robustness to errors in the estimates.

USING STATISTICAL ESTIMATES AS INPUTS

There is a strong analogy between (1) the problems of statistical analysis through multivariate least-squares regression and (2) quadratic programming to determine the best tradeoff between risk and return at the portfolio level. Both involve minimizing a sum of squares, and the success of both depends in part on the same characteristics of a covariance matrix. Consider two seemingly different but actually very similar problems. First, determine a weighted average of individual stocks that will best explain the variation in a benchmark return. In this problem we are subject to a linear equality constraint based on the weights and prevented from holding the benchmark portfolio. Second, find a single point on the efficient frontier that minimizes tracking error risk versus a benchmark return, with the weights subject to a constraint on portfolio expected return. These two problems are nearly identical, with the exception that the second has additional constraints for budget and non-negativity.

In multiple regression, the ability to forecast the dependent variable out of the sample from which you derived your estimates depends on your care in not over-fitting the model to coincidences by using too many variables. It also depends on your using only independent variables that are not too highly correlated among themselves. So, too, the principles of parsimony and independence to avoid multi-collinearity are at the root of better portfolio selection methods.

The basic idea of sensitivity to error depending on correlation among the independent variables can be grasped most simply in the case of the minimum variance point on the efficient frontier. Remember that the non-negativity constraint of Markowitz does not ban short sales, but simply means they use up capital at the same rate as long positions. Exhibit 1 represents two stocks, A and B, a high-flying technology stock and a stodgy regulated utility, respectively. Their risk in standard deviation terms is represented by the lengths of vectors from the origin O. A has more risk than B. The point −A represents a full short position in A.

Weights in each stock are represented by proportions of the vector lengths. These proportions must add to one (the budget constraint). The correlation between their returns is represented by the cosine of the angle AOB. That is, zero correlation implies a cosine of zero which in turn implies a 90 degree angle between two vectors. In this case, the angle indicates a strong correlation, characteristic of two stocks in the same market, but not necessarily in the same industry. Here the angle about 35 degrees implies a correlation of about 0.8.

Exhibit 1: Risk Minimization

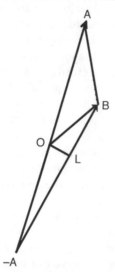

The risks of the portfolios attainable with positive combinations of A and B are the distances from O to various points on the AB line. (This is the line attainable by vector addition of fractions of the two component vectors.) Clearly the point of minimum risk is to hold 100% in B. Note that if A has a higher expected return, and no short sales are allowed, BA is the Markowitz efficient frontier. The expected return will "pull" the selected point along the frontier away from the point of minimum variance.

What happens if we allow short sales? Then we can reach any point along the line from −A to B as well. Still assuming A to have a higher expected return than B, the efficient frontier runs from L to B to A. The point L is at a minimum distance from O. It represents a minimum variance portfolio.[7]

Now consider what happens if we estimate correlation with an error. The true correlation is lower than we expect. In the case with no short sales, we will incorrectly assume a position along the line from B to A displaced toward A as far as our tolerance for risk will permit. An overestimation of the true correlation has caused a displacement in our position from the true position. However, the error is modest compared to the risk we have estimated that we were taking. In contrast, in the case with short sales, the same error in risk must be compared to a very much smaller assumed risk. It is not that the risk error is larger, but that it is larger relative to our expected risk. This is a good illustration of how much more sensitive long-short portfolios are to errors in our input estimates than are portfolios where the investments have positively correlated returns and no short positions

---

[7] There is a mirror low risk portfolio with negative B and positive A, but the total position would then be short. This solution is conventionally not considered, but could be.

are allowed. (Markowitz, by insisting that short-sales should be modeled as using capital, saves us from only the extreme worst cases of short-selling errors.)

In either case, consider what happens as the two securities become more similar, both in terms of risk and in terms of low correlation. The lines OA and OB become similar in length and the angle gets narrower. Suppose also that in fact they have identical expected returns, but that we estimate their expected return differences with random error. Suppose we estimate expected return with some error. It is very easy for us to decide to flip back and forth between holding A long and B short and holding B long and A short as the estimation error fluctuates. If we make an error in their correlation, the risk will be higher than we believe. Suppose our only error is in expected return. We will still both be running up transaction costs and perplexing our clients, if any. We may spoil the potential for a favorable ratio of return to risk that we might have enjoyed if we had invested in either A or B alone.

Even when short sales are forbidden, the existence of narrow angles (high correlations) among clusters of securities tends to push the solution to extremes. The more securities there are, the more such tight clusters there will be. Extreme solutions may amplify the impact of errors in the input estimates compared to such homespun portfolio allocation methods as equal weighting, and in any case they tend to be unstable. Instability can be offset in part by increasing the assumed trading cost, but errors in actual risk versus assumed risk cannot be so easily dealt with.[8]

There is now a professional literature on better estimates of the combination of expected return and the covariance matrix. Recommendations range from the complex (Bayes-Stein estimation)[9] to its commonsense approximation. I recommend the latter. Simply assume that the estimates that you have created are equal to the true value plus random error. Then try to eliminate some of the random error based on what you know about the error-generating process.

First, expected returns are likely to be inflated because of natural psychological over-optimism. You should use expected returns part way between a prior distribution based on skeptical theory and the result of your particular estimation process. Assuming all returns among a class of securities to be equal, for example, is usually a good starting point. That is, lower your estimates of returns for the "winners" and raise them for the "losers."

Second, you should weight your estimates of variances and covariances against a prior distribution. Simple risk priors are that all securities of the same general class have the same average variance, and that they all have the same average off-diagonal covariance. In each case, your task is then reduced to how

---

[8] If you are interested in reading more about this problem, a good introduction is given by Richard Michaud, "The Markowitz Optimization Enigma: Is 'Optimized' Optimal?" *Financial Analysts Journal* (January-February 1989), pp. 31-42.

[9] Philippe Jorion, "Bayes-Stein Estimation for Portfolio Analysis," *Journal of Financial and Quantitative Analysis* (September 1986), pp. 279-292.

much to weight these priors against your specific estimates. For example, you might find that giving the risk priors a 20% weight is adequate for stocks, but much more is needed for currencies. You might find that return priors deserve a much bigger weight than risk priors, perhaps 50% or more, and that off-diagonal covariance risk priors deserve more weight than diagonal variance priors.

We cannot leave single-period optimization without comment on the typical practice of imposing additional constraints on the portfolio selection problem. A variation is to add quadratic penalty functions for solutions that have extraneous "costs." Sometimes one of these is the simplest way to get additional information into the problem. For example, one could constrain overall average price/book of the portfolio if one wanted to assemble a fund that would be clearly recognizable as a "value" fund for marketing purposes. Often, though, the purpose is to be a further safeguard on risk. While such a practice can produce improved results, the alternative of modifying the problem will produce a more understandable result. These modifications include reducing the number of elements in the covariance matrix through a factor approach and for smaller problems shrinking the elements of the covariance towards cross-sectional priors. These steps will reduce the tendencies toward instability and underestimation of portfolio risk that the addition of constraints is meant to control. This is done to manage risk, because the investor doesn't trust the projection into the future of the covariance matrix.

SUMMARY

Summing up this chapter, Markowitz has been deservedly canonized. He has, as they say, forgotten more than most of us ever knew. But his method can be dangerous in inexperienced hands. In the next chapter, we go on to explore the less-familiar message of his 1959 book, that the single period mean-variance approach is merely a means to another end, approximating optimum long-term strategy. Before doing so, I quote from his closing remarks in his Nobel prize acceptance speech:[10]

> "…when I defended my dissertation as a student in the Economics Department of the University of Chicago, Professor Milton Friedman argued that portfolio theory was not Economics, and that they could not offer me a Ph.D. degree in Economics for a dissertation which was not in Economics. I assume he was only half serious, since they did offer me the degree without long debate. As to the merits of his arguments, at this point I am quite willing to concede: at the time I defended my dissertation, portfolio theory was not part of Economics. But now it is."

---

[10] Harry M. Markowitz, "Foundations of Portfolio Theory," *The Journal of Finance* (1991), pp. 469-477.

Chapter 6

Many-Period Investing

It frequently happens in the history of thought that when a powerful new method emerges the study of those problems which can be dealt with by the new method advances rapidly and attracts the limelight, while the rest tends to be ignored or even forgotten, its study despised.
Imre Lakatos, *"Proofs and Refutations," British Journal for the Philosophy of Science (1963)*

How do we know that an investment policy that will make us happy in the short run will not lead to problems in the long run? Conversely, are there successful long-run policies that we might miss if we confine our attention to the short run?

Harry Markowitz devoted a chapter of his 1959 book to long-run returns.[1] The single-period model on which the greater part of the book was focused was thereby given essential perspective. Through that chapter it finally becomes apparent that mean single-period return less a linear function of its variance can have very attractive properties as a utility surrogate in a longer-term context. He did so in that chapter not in the context of von Neumann-Morgenstern utility functions but by reaching out to another tradition. By showing that that mean fractional portfolio return less half its variance gives an approximation of the continuously compounded, or log, rate of return, Markowitz opened a door between the newer utility-based theories and competing ideas based on managing portfolios for long-term growth.

Despite this possible olive branch, the single-period analysis of the rest of his book quickly surpassed all rivals. It lent itself more easily to calculation and to use as a theoretical building block. It was built on the academically popular utility foundation and in turn served as a basis for constructing theories of aggregate market equilibrium such as the CAPM. Markowitz's approach soon overwhelmed its compound growth competitor. However, in 1971 Nils Hakansson published a remarkable paper that stimulated renewed interest in maximizing expected compound return.[2]

He showed explicitly how maximizing expected compound return could be mapped into the world of expected utility of terminal wealth. Some aversion to vari-

---

[1] Harry M. Markowitz, *Portfolio Selection: Efficient Diversification of Investments* (New Haven, Conn.: Yale University Press, 1959).
[2] Nils H. Hakansson, "Multi-Period Mean-Variance Analysis: Toward A General Theory of Portfolio Choice," *Journal of Finance* (1971), pp. 857-884.

ance could be readily explained as aversion to lower expected rates of growth. That is, to gain best expected compound return, one maximizes expected log return each period. For greater risk aversion he provided a two-parameter model that also considered variance of log returns. Like Markowitz, he could explain diversification and provide a single-period guide to policy that works well when repeated each period.

He used his model to argue omissions and defects in the single-period, quadratic nature of the Markowitz framework. For example, where there is a small risk of losing everything each period, variance will not be an adequate indicator of the risk of ruin in multiple periods. However, Hakansson's greatest point of difference with the conventional approach lay in his refusal to govern behavior by arbitrary utility functions on terminal wealth. Instead, he argued, the operation of maximizing a tradeoff between expected compound return and variability in compound return *induces* particular utility functions. As a simple example, a tolerance for variance risk greater than that required for maximum expected compound growth might be inconsistent with most investor's goals.

Hakansson also pointed out a plain, incontrovertible fact that is of interest to every professional investor and to most other investors. While increasing expected compound rate of return does not always increase *mean* long-term wealth, it definitely does increase *median* long-term wealth. This distinction is of great practical importance. It is most obvious for professional investors who are hired by others based on five-year records relative to a universe of competitors. However, many individual investors would also happily embrace better expected compound return as an investment criterion if they understood that it meant better median wealth.

Hakansson's work met with initial interest, misinterpretation, criticism, and finally neglect. Today only a small minority of financial economists work with expected compound returns, and many otherwise serious investors and students of finance are unaware of this approach to investing. I believe that there is a core of wisdom in the maximal expected growth rate approach that many investors are neglecting at their peril.

Today, maximizing expected growth is not very accessible for most of us for running day-to-day portfolios, because there appear to be no commercial optimizers based on the principle. However, it can be very helpful in setting policy, in adjusting the cost of risk with changing circumstances, and in those special cases where you really need it, as a basis for developing your own specialized techniques. Consequently we will review this tradition in some depth. I will also share my own ideas on how to place this theory on a firmer footing for conservative investors.

Along the way, I think you will find yourself slipping easily into some very advantageous ways of thinking about the investing process. We will proceed as follows:

- Winning coin flipping
- Extending Markowitz's multi-period return
- Hakansson, Merton, Samuelson and Roll

• Reconciling greater risk aversion
• Aftermath.

We will return to maximizing expected compound return in a later chapter on emerging markets. The idea of return superiority of an emerging market index *equal-weighted* by country over that of the CAPM-inspired market capitalization index can appear as black magic to those who do not understand these ideas. It is as though Markowitz came down from the mountain with the Ten Commandments and his followers promptly lost the second stone tablet.

WINNING COIN FLIPPING

When you toss a fair coin it will land with either "heads" or "tails" face up. Suppose you live in a world where your capital doubles if you receive "heads" and halves if you get "tails." Note that this is not "double or nothing," but "double or half." You begin with a dollar and must bet your entire fortune each toss of the coin. For example, suppose you toss the coin ten times. If you get all heads your terminal wealth will be $1,024. If you get all tails your terminal wealth will be $(1/1,024)$, or about a tenth of a penny.

Let us make the game a bit more competitive. You have an opponent who tosses coins of the same type. He has, however, two coins. At each toss, he bets half his capital on each coin. Therefore he as a 25% chance of doubling, a 50% chance of increasing by 25%, and a 25% chance of losing half of his capital at each turn.

Note that each period or turn your expected terminal wealth is the same as his, and your expected return for a single period is the same as his. If you begin with 1, then at the end of the turn, you have expected wealth of $0.5 \times 2 + 0.5 \times (1/2) = 1.25$. He has expected wealth of $0.25 \times 2 + 0.5 \times (5/4) + 0.25 \times (1/2) = 1.25$. After multiple periods, you will each have the same expected wealth. The successive coin tosses are independent, implying that the expected result of the sequence can be obtained by simply multiplying your identical expected wealth multiples at each step. However, as non-intuitive as it may at first seem, you will not have the same expected compounded return. We can demonstrate how practically important this distinction is by setting up a contest between you and your opponent.

Suppose that at the end of some fixed number of turns, the player with the greatest terminal wealth takes all the wealth of the other. What are your chances of winning? Since you are new to the game, we will allow you a handicap. If your wealth is equal to his, you win.

Rather than ponder the exponentially growing tree of compound probabilities here, we will resort to a simulation for the answer. Remember that you get the benefit of ties. Exhibit 1 shows the proportion of your winning cases as determined by simulation using 8,092 random two-player contests. The fit of the line to theory is imperfect only because of minor remaining sampling error.

Exhibit 1: Probability of Winning Against a Two-Coin Player

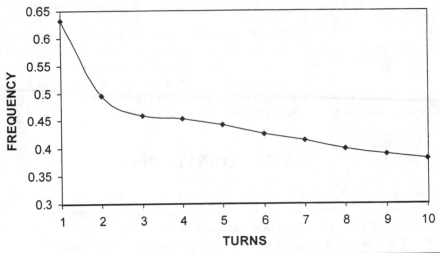

The horizontal scale shows the number of turns before we stop and determine the winner. The vertical scale shows the experimentally determined odds of your winning. With only one turn, the theoretical odds in your favor are 5:3, or 62.5%. With several more turns, the probability of a tie becomes quite small, and you might think you are playing a fair game. But are you? After ten tosses, your chance of winning is down to 38%. The more you toss, the worse you are likely to do. The moral is that it is better to be the player who can flip more coins if you want to have the highest return.

There are many interesting exercises possible with our coin flipping example. We could explore the effect of having more coins on the player's expected wealth: there is none. We could show the rate of deterioration of expected compound return from 25% in one turn to its asymptote after an infinite number of turns. We could show the dependence of the asymptote on increasing numbers of coins: one coin eventually gives 0%, two coins 12.5%, three coins 16.7%, and so on up to 25% for an infinite number of diversifying coins. We could show that diversification simultaneously reduces variance in terminal wealth while it increases median terminal wealth.

The coin-flipping game as given involves re-balancing wealth every period between the coins. We could show that not re-balancing but allowing each coin to retain its own winnings results in a lower expected compound return that deteriorates on average with increasing turns as more and more of the weight is shifted to fewer coins. (This should set one thinking about the desirability of index funds if there is any question about whether the market correctly prices long-run diversification benefits.) We could show that if the goal is to maximize the chance of achieving above median performance in a universe of single-coin investment managers you do best with the largest number of coins possible. However, there is an intermediate number of coins that is optimum for achieving first quartile.[3]

Some of these examples are given in more detail in an article I wrote titled "Investing at the Edge."[4] But the basic intuition should be clear already. Diversification can increase expected compound return and thereby your chances of winning multiple-period contests in which the investor with above-median results gets the prize. The benefit grows as the number of periods increases. If the prize goes only to those who achieve top quartile results, then you need less diversification of coins. Only if a tiny minority of performers get all the prizes, and if the prize is awarded after only a few turns, will you not benefit substantially from some diversification.

Now that we have shown why the determinants of compound return are both important and not entirely obvious, we have the proper motivation for the rest of the chapter.

EXTENDING MARKOWITZ'S MULTI-PERIOD RETURN

In the preceding discussion, you may have been mystified at my references to the difference between maximizing expected compound return and maximizing the expected terminal value. Why don't these give the same best policy for multi-period investments?

There are two different compound returns involved. Let T be the multiple of terminal wealth to initial wealth, and n be the number of periods. Equation (1) below (formally an inequality, not an equation) illustrates the two concepts.

$$\text{Expected}\left(T^{\frac{1}{n}} \right) \neq (\text{Expected}(T))^{\frac{1}{n}} \tag{1}$$

The expression on the left is one plus the expected geometric mean return, or continuously compounded return. The expression on the right is one plus the average return implied by the expected terminal value. There is nothing in probability theory that would ensure that the expected value of a number raised to a power be equal to the number's expected value raised to a power. They are equal only when n is 1. Consequently, these are two different concepts. In our coin-flipping example the term on the right was always 25%, whereas the term on the left varied between 0% and 25% depending on how many coins were flipped.

Rather, letting r_i be the return in the ith period, we have:

$$T^{\frac{1}{n}} = e^{\dfrac{\sum\limits_{i=1}^{n} \ln(1 + r_i)}{n}} \tag{2}$$

---

[3] Fractional numbers of coins can be approximated with a mixed strategy employing a different number of coins on some turns.

[4] Jarrod Wilcox, "Investing at the Edge," *Journal of Portfolio Management* (Winter 1998).

Note that the exponent on the right is the sample estimate of the expected value of $\ln(1+r_i)$. For any statistical distribution for which the expectation is finite, this exponent asymptotically approaches the true expectation for $\ln(1+r)$, a constant, as n increases. Since this is fixed, we have:

$$\text{Expected}\left(T^{\frac{1}{n}}\right) = e^{\text{Expected}(\ln(1+r))} \tag{3}$$

Note that we assume $1+r$ is non-negative. Markowitz expressed the function $\ln(1+r)$ in Taylor series form and then took its expectation in order to show that it depends not just on the expected r, which he labeled E, but also on its variance. We will do the same, but extend the formula through several more terms in order to show its dependence on higher-order moments of the return distribution.

One of the few articles in the professional investment literature of the last decade to treat expected compound return is the one by Booth and Fama.[5] They derive the same formula to be presented here, complete with higher-order terms.

The natural log function is continuously differentiable (smooth). It can be approximated to any degree of precision desired as a Taylor series. A Taylor series can be calculated centered on zero as a base, but in this case it will be more accurate for a given number of terms if it is centered around E, the expected value of r.[6]

We can express each period's log return as follows:

$$\ln(1+r) \cong \ln(1+E) + \frac{(r-E)}{(1+E)} - \frac{(r-E)^2}{2(1+E)^2} + \frac{(r-E)^3}{3(1+E)^3} - \frac{(r-E)^4}{4(1+E)^4}\ldots \tag{4}$$

Finally, we take the expectation of both sides of equation (4) to obtain equation (5), where $V(r)$ is the variance of r.

$$\text{Expected}(\ln(1+r)) = \left\{ \frac{\displaystyle\sum_{t=1}^{n}\ln(1+r_t)}{n} \right\} \cong \ln(1+E) - \frac{V(r)}{2(1+E)^2}$$

$$+ \text{Expected}\left\{\frac{(r-E)^3}{3(1+E)^3}\right\} - \text{Expected}\left\{\frac{(r-E)^4}{4(1+E)^4}\right\} \tag{5}$$

Note that the first-order term cancels out because the expected value of $(r-E)$ is zero. Markowitz, in his 1959 book, stopped at the squared term, but addi-

---

[5] David G. Booth and Eugene F. Fama, "Diversification Returns and Asset Contributions," *Financial Analysts Journal* (May/June 1992), pp. 26-32.
[6] If you would like to revisit calculus in order to see how this is done, see any reasonably comprehensive calculus text.

tional terms are useful for portfolios with high return skewness or kurtosis. If we substitute in equation (5) the conventional definitions for skewness $S(r)$ and kurtosis $K(r)$, then a convenient form is shown as equation (6).[7]

$$\text{Expected}(\ln(1+r)) \cong \ln(1+E) - \frac{V(r)}{2(1+E)^2} + \frac{S(r)V(r)^{3/2}}{3(1+E)^3} - \frac{K(r)V(r)^2}{4(1+E)^4} \quad (6)$$

Equation (6) provides intuition for understanding how variance of portfolio fractional return produces a drag on portfolio growth. In our coin-flipping example, the opponent with two coins got an advantage by reducing variance through diversification without affecting the expected single period return. Thus he increased his expected compound return. For Markowitz, equation (6) helped justify his choice of variance as the representation of risk that investors instinctively avoided through diversification.

Our extension to more terms helps explain why most investors also prefer positive skewness and less kurtosis. That is, they want downside protection and usually want protection against the catastrophic potential of the "fat tails" represented as kurtosis. In each case, they may be reacting to threats to their capital base that would unduly hinder compound growth. Diversification reduces these high order terms as well, both by reducing the variance represented in each term and also by reducing the skewness and kurtosis parameters.

Hakansson noted that maximizing expected compound return also maximizes the median terminal wealth. This is a long-term asymptotic result, but in most practical cases it is approximated closely after a handful of periods. Here is the reasoning, as I have reconstructed it.

If we assume that $\ln(1+r)$ has a statistical distribution with finite variance, then the statistical distribution of the sum of n such values becomes more and more similar to a normal distribution. This is a direct result of the Central Limit Theorem. The only inference we draw from this (although Hakansson drew more) is that the resulting distribution becomes more and more symmetric as n increases. This means that its mean is its median. Thus, maximizing expected compound return also maximizes median compound return. Rank order statistics are invariant under monotonic transformations such as obtaining terminal value by raising e to a power determined by return and time periods. Consequently, the terminal value implied by the median compound return is the median terminal value.

This shows that increasing expected compound return increases median terminal value. That is why our two-coin opponent beat us most of the time in the coin-flipping example.[8]

---

[7] Now we could convert this log result into fractional return by taking the antilog and subtracting one, if desired.

[8] If you want a more mathematical treatment of some of these properties, see Richard O. Michaud,"Risk Policy and Long-Term Investment," *Journal of Financial and Quantitative Analysis* (1981), pp. 147-167.

HAKANSSON, MERTON, SAMUELSON, AND ROLL

Compound growth maximization is neglected today as a direct result of the academic interchange that took place in the early 1970s. If you are to make use of it, you need enough context to defend yourself against the weight of opinion that resulted. And to be fair, you need to know where Hakansson stumbled. Here are the results of an afternoon spent in the rarely visited basement archives of M.I.T.'s business school library.

First, my editorial comment: Hakansson might have stopped with showing how one could use Markowitz's own thinking to improve on the fractional return mean-variance framework in certain rare cases, such as those with high skew or high kurtosis. Alternatively he might have tackled the edges of utility theory by merely pointing out the negative implications of risk-taking so high that it detracted from expected compound return. Again, he might have emphasized the practical implications of raising median results, allowing this to be received as a mere heuristic. If he had done any of these, his work might have been accepted as mainstream.

But he went further. He suggested *replacing* the Markowitz framework with a linear tradeoff between expected log return and the variance of log return. He suggested *drastically restricting* the acceptable types of von Neumann-Morgenstern utilities and giving them a secondary role. He suggested *abandoning* the quadratic programming algorithm. He advocated *destroying* the existing foundation beneath the CAPM. And for what? In most practical applications, at least for portfolios of NYSE-traded stocks, it was thought that there was little practical advantage for going to so much trouble.[9] It is remarkable that he was not tarred and feathered.

But it was not for these crimes his work was publicly criticized, but for more superficial mistakes in argumentation and logic. First, he stated that: "In the very long run, then, the investor...would experience a ... capital position almost surely greater than under any other policy." This applies very well to median results but seemed to be taken to apply to mean results. In that case, I believe he simply did not express himself clearly.

Second, he went beyond the simple maximization of the mean compound return to discuss tradeoffs between mean log return and variance of log returns. This he felt was needed to accommodate conservative investors. He then asserted that the mean-variance framework redone in log terms would result in optimum long-term expected utility for a broad class of utility functions expressed as wealth raised to a power. Hakansson went beyond the assertion that the Central Limit Theorem implies that multi-period compound returns are asymptotically normal. He further reasoned that their transformation into terminal values yielded a distribution sufficiently close to lognormal to assume they were exactly lognormal. This doesn't always work well when you are dealing at the tails with small

---

[9] Richard Roll, "Evidence On The 'Growth-Optimum' Model," *Journal of Finance* (1973), pp. 551-567.

probabilities multiplied by extreme returns. Based on this, he concluded that linear tradeoffs between mean and variance of log returns yielded optimal utilities for conservative investors using a broad class of utility functions based on powers of wealth. This proved a difficult position to defend.

The circulation of a 1972 working paper by Merton and Samuelson criticizing these two points seems to have effectively squelched much of the academic interest in Hakansson's ideas.[10] However, Merton and Samuelson conceded that Hakansson's model did imply optimal expected utility of terminal wealth if the utility function were logarithmic. They also agreed that even his broader assertions held if increasing the number of periods represented finer subdivisions of a fixed time interval rather than an increasing time interval.

To my way of thinking, Hakansson had the ammunition of original insight, but he was severely outgunned by brilliant conventional forces. Enough of my editorial! Listen to some highlights quoted from the key texts.

From Hakansson's 1971 paper:

> "Perhaps the single most important justification on behalf of the original single-period mean-variance model was that it generally implies diversification, while the maximization of returns does not. ... A mean-variance model, of course, is not necessary to obtain diversification. It is well known that [any] risk-averse von Neumann-Morgernstern rational investor will generally also diversify, for such an individual has a strictly concave utility function (of wealth)."

> "...diversification is a *must* for anyone interested in *maximizing expected return alone* over *more* than one period."

> "It is rather ironic, ex post, that the mean-variance model of single-period return and of total N-period return has received so much attention ... while mean and mean-variance formulations of average compound return over two or more periods have received no attention even though they
> 1) imply risk aversion without reference to the variance
> 2) are consistent with von Neumann-Morgenstern utility theory
> 3) are consistent with absolute preference
> 4) imply decreasing absolute risk aversion [risk aversion goes down with increasing wealth]
> 5) automatically insure solvency ...
> 6) imply that myopic investment behavior is optimal
> 7) provide a basis for the formation of mutual funds.

---

[10] Robert C. Merton and Paul A. Samuelson, "Fallacy of the Log-Normal Approximation To Optimal Portfolio Decision-Making Over Many Periods," Working Paper 623-72, M.I.T. Sloan School of Management (1972).

What structural properties of a portfolio model beyond these could one possibly hope for? The preceding irony is the more surprising in view of the presence of Chapter 8 in Markowitz's book, which touches on some aspects of the long run."

Now we read the reply from Merton and Samuelson:

"Thanks to the revival by von Neumann and Morgenstern, maximization of the expected value of a concave utility function of outcomes has for the last third of a century generally been accepted as the 'correct' criterion for optimal portfolio selection. .... it was appropriate that the seminal breakthroughs of the 1950's be largely preoccupied with the special case of the mean-variance analysis. Not only could the fruitful Sharpe-Lintner-Mossin capital asset pricing model be based on it, but in addition, it gave rise to simple linear rules of portfolio optimizing. In the mean-variance model, the well-known Separation or Mutual Fund Theorem [Tobin] holds; and with suitable additional assumptions, the model can be used to define a complete microeconomic framework for the capital market, and a number of empirically testable hypotheses can be derived."

"The desire for simplicity of analysis led naturally to a search for approximation theorems, particularly of the asymptotic type."

"...for others [Hakansson, point 1], an indefinitely large probability of doing better by Method A than Method B was taken as conclusive evidence for the superiority of A....Except to prepare the ground for a more subtle fallacy of the same asymptotic genus, the present paper need not more than review the simple max-expected log fallacy. It can concentrate instead on the asymptotic fallacy that involves... the Central Limit Theorem."

"...since the mean and variance of average-return-per period are asymptotic surrogates for the log normal's first two moments, Hakansson's average-expected-return seems to be given a new legitimacy by the Central-Limit Theorem [point 2]."

And after showing that Hakansson's mathematics showing the translation to power utility functions did not hold:

"Again the geometric mean strategy proves to be fallacious."

"This effectively dispenses with the false conjecture that for large T, the lognormal approximation provides a suitable surrogate for the true distribution of terminal wealth probabilities; and [therefore] with any hope that the mean and variance of expected-average-compound-return can serve as asymptotically sufficient decision parameters."

Now we read a paper by Roll, in which the Hakansson model is tested empirically, though jointly with aggregate market models and using conventional stocks rather than the kind of fringe investments that would show it to advantage. First, Roll's overall evaluation:

"Briefly, the growth-optimum model receives mixed support. In some tests it performs extremely well while the results of other tests are puzzling.

But contrast this with his specific conclusions based on predictions of similar expected returns across stocks:

"Thus, growth-optimum theory is strongly, even too strongly, supported by this test of its basic validity."

"In every case, the growth-optimum model was strongly supported."

Note his comments from the presumed joint test with the equivalent of CAPM as a superstructure and looking for dependence of expected return on the equivalent of "beta":

"On average across the six years, both the growth-optimum and the Sharpe-Lintner model seemed to have excessive intercepts and deficient slopes."

"Based on these results, one can only conclude that the two models are empirically identical. A qualification is in order, of course; assets whose returns are much more highly skewed (e.g., warrants), may permit a finer discriminatory test."

RECONCILING GREATER RISK AVERSION

An investment practitioner should not be constrained to models that happen to have already been used for the construction of the CAPM, a theory of the aggregate market. In this section I will share an idea I find useful for describing the portfolio selection problem for conservative investors in a compound return framework. I know of no software that implements these ideas; you may regard them as a gedanken, or thought, experiment.

Exhibit 2: Risk Aversion Induced by Different Reserves

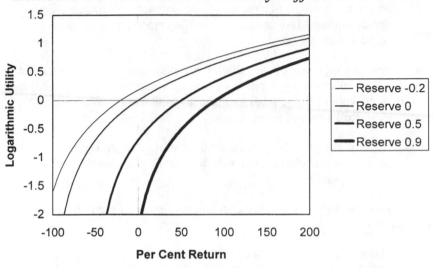

Hakansson successfully pointed out the defects in Markowitz for unusual cases, but his prescription for trading off expected log return against variance of log return to reflect different degrees of risk aversion did not win acceptance. There was, however, no problem in mapping into induced utility functions the result of simply maximizing expected compound return alone. The result is logarithmic utility.

Suppose we autocratically decide that this one utility function, the logarithmic curve, fits all, at least as an approximation to be applied each period. This is no worse than asserting the primacy of the quadratic curve. But what do we do to accommodate the full range of attitudes toward risk? Rather than use varying linear tradeoffs between expected return and variance as did Markowitz, I propose to use varying reserve levels of wealth. This notion has been used in another form as the foundation for constant proportion portfolio insurance, an idea we will explore in the next chapter. Imagine that each investor has a particular reserve level of wealth; to fall below it would represent disaster. As we would if we invested on margin, to get the true impact of a given profit or loss we must divide it not by our capital, but by the excess of our capital over this reserve. *To accommodate different propensities for risk-taking, variation in reserve levels takes the place of variations in Markowitz lambda.*

Exhibit 2 shows different implied utility curves for investors with reserve levels 0%, 50%, 90% and –20%. Absolute height is irrelevant to decisions. Remember from Exhibit 1 in Chapter 3 that risk aversion can be roughly imagined as indicated by the vertical difference between the utility curve for certainty results as shown and a straight chord between two points of equal probability. It is a product of the curvature, the starting slope of the line on which curvature operates, and the dispersion of potential outcomes along the horizontal axis that determines the loss of utility caused by risk.

Consider the reserve level 0%, which is represented in Exhibit 2 by the second line from the top. Only the line's slope and curvature determine the cost of risk. For this line, we see little potential for risk aversion among choices of very high returns, such as between a certain outcome of 190% or a 50/50 lottery between 180% and 200%. However, as we move leftward into negative territory, the combination of a steep slope and accelerated curvature implies that risk becomes costly. Thus, the same plus or minus 10% added on to a 50% loss means a great deal. Any probability of losing 100% would give infinitely less utility than a certain outcome that did not involve losing everything.

Suppose, as we can for portfolios of ordinary stocks, that we may ignore moments higher than the variance. Then we can use the Markowitz framework and the 0% reserve framework translates to a lambda of one. However, for extremely volatile or skewed or fat-tailed portfolios, additional terms of equation (6) will need to be considered.

Now consider a reserve level of half of initial capital. That is, to lose half of capital is considered equivalent to ruin. This case is represented by the third line from the top in Exhibit 2. It would typically apply if one has purchased stocks on 50% margin. It may also be relevant if one is an agent who may be fired for such a big loss, or if one has to face pension fund liabilities that can never be balanced with assets that have fallen so low. It is even the case if one is approaching retirement and cannot face living on such a reduced living standard.

In this 50% reserve level context, since the wealth denominator is only half as big, the expected returns are double (less interest if we are on margin). That is, the same profit or loss is divided by half the capital. But this doubles the standard deviation as well, which makes variance four times as big as it would be in the 0% reserve case. We can put the problem back into Markowitz terms in two ways. First, we could keep a lambda of one and recalculate our expected returns and covariance matrix with bigger returns. This would have the great merit of allowing us to expand our analysis to include the full equation (6) for maximizing expected return if variances, skew, and kurtosis are large enough to make it a noticeably better estimate of true expected compound return. However, I have not tried it in practice.

Alternatively, we can leave undisturbed the expected returns and covariance matrix and simply recast the linear tradeoff between expected return and variance so that it would yield the same portfolio selection. We do this by increasing the lambda from one to two. Of course, we have to remember to adjust peripheral elements as well. For example, trading costs must be doubled. We thereby abandon equation (6) as a tool for dealing with higher statistical moments of return. But such will generally be satisfactory in dealing with portfolios of common stocks.

Every lambda representing different degrees of risk aversion can thereby be mapped into our new framework using different reserve levels. If the reserve level is equal to current wealth plus the risk-free return, then investors will put all their funds into risk-free investments. If it is merely equal to current wealth, they can participate a little in equity investing. A 90% reserve is shown as the bottom line in Exhibit 2. This utility function implies a Markowitz lambda of 10.

Nothing in this decision framework forbids a negative reserve level. The impact of a reserve 20% below zero is shown as the top line in the exhibit. If the reserve level is negative, investors can take more risk than the naive (zero reserve) maximization of expected compound return would allow us to expect. The equivalent Markowitz lambda if returns are not adjusted is ⅚, or about 0.83.

What is the advantage of putting the portfolio selection problem into the structure of maximizing expected compound growth in the excess over a reserved level? There are many, and we have space to note only their main headings here.

First, we retain the expected compound return framework. With it, we can easily arrive at a typically adequate answer by optimizing the mean single-period return less half its variance through the Markowitz model. But our framework also would allow us to go to full expected log return maximization using equation (6) if we were to need to deal with the less usual cases noted earlier. If our reserves are non-zero, we should go to the trouble of adjusting returns by multiplying them by the ratio of wealth to excess reserves. This would be appropriate, for example, if we needed to live on our investment income and were tempted by the promise of income to create highly negatively skewed portfolio returns by owning stocks and writing calls on S&P 500 futures.

A second advantage of this system is that it allows us to suggest an appropriate lambda for investors who have known reserve levels. They may find specifying such "drop dead" requirements easier than specifying a return versus variance tradeoff. I have never had the privilege of working with an investment management client who knew or could comfortably specify his or her lambda.

Third, the framework explains and justifies what I have observed in practice, that risk-averse investors have a strong taste for avoiding downside risk (negative skew) and fat-tailed distributions (kurtosis). This is particularly true of agents, such as are most professional investors and pension fund directors. The framework also explains how investors should adjust their Markowitz lambdas if they lose money relative to their reserve level. This is a form of *portfolio insurance* or *dynamic hedging*, a subject to which we will return in the next chapter. The regular single-period Markowitzian framework has nothing to say about such practices.

Fourth, reserve levels clearly depend on outside income, consumption spending levels, and other circumstances. Their incorporation in the portfolio selection problem helps explain such phenomena as younger people holding stocks while older people often prefer bonds. The concept of time diversification that is often proposed to explain this problem is controversial for good reason. But the reserve concept is straightforward and unobjectionable. When investors are young their primary income is from employment, so that their reserve level can be very low, even negative. That is, they can afford to go into debt as a result of investment losses and still recover. Older investors on a retirement income have no other means of support and sensibly need a much higher reserve level.

Fifth, it helps explain the so-called "equity premium puzzle." Over long periods equity returns have been so high relative to risk-free returns that they could only be explained within the context of the CAPM by assuming investors were incredibly risk-averse. Yet we should not be surprised because the bulk of wealth is held by and for people for whom reserve levels are relatively high.

AFTERMATH

After the Merton-Samuelson critique, not much was heard about expected compound return investing. The greatest comparative advantage of the expected compound return framework over the Markowitz approach lies in the high-risk field of gambling. It is perhaps not surprising that the few economists and mathematicians who are its enthusiasts are also interested in the study of gambling problems.

For example, William Ziemba jointly edited in 1975 a book titled *Stochastic Optimization in Finance*. In it there is a chapter by Edward O. Thorp titled "Portfolio Choice and The Kelly Criterion."[11] Solid mathematical work by Kelly preceded Hakansson and it is in his language that the expected compound return criterion survives today among sophisticated gamblers. Kelly's framework keeps the size of bets in an ideal proportion to the size of the gambler's stake and the odds; it derives from the expected log return criterion.

Thorp agreed with the Samuelson-Merton critique of Hakansson's mathematics in extending the mean-variance framework to log returns. However he did not agree, as I do not, that this implies a problem with the simpler criterion of maximizing expected compound return alone, nor with the use of logarithmic utility. Thorp took his theories to the stock market, where he gained practical success, as he had a few years earlier at the blackjack tables.

In 1992 an article by MacLean, Ziemba, and Blazenko dealt with Hakansson's problem of providing for conservative investors by developing "fractional" Kelly strategies mixing the benefits of growth and security.[12] The authors' very practical operations research approach examines three gambling and one stock market trading application.

A CLOSING THOUGHT

Within the stock markets, increasing median terminal wealth through maximizing expected compound return is scarcely discussed. But it offers potential advantages for dealing with unusual investment problems and a convenient approach to

---

[11] Edward O. Thorp, "Portfolio Choice and the Kelly Criterion," in W. T. Ziemba and R. G. Vickson (eds.), *Stochastic Optimization Models in Finance* (New York: Academic Press, 1975).

[12] L.C. MacLean, W.T. Ziemba, and G. Blazenko, "Growth Versus Security in Dynamic Investment Analysis," *Management Science* (1992), pp. 1562-1585.

specifying different attitudes toward risk for everyone. If you are an active investor you may further benefit from its use because it is profoundly unfashionable and unlikely to be imitated widely in the near future.

Chapter 7

Options and
Their Dynamic Equivalents

*Results are what you expect, and consequences are what
you get.*
*Schoolgirl's definition, quoted in: Ladies' Home Journal
(New York, January 1942)*

The ideas that underlie the pricing of options, or contingent claims, are fundamental to investing. In this chapter we cannot hope to master the specialized tools
that are required to successfully trade in options *per se*. What we can do is better
understand options to better understand investing in stocks.

When I studied investments as taught by Paul Cootner at M.I.T. in the mid-
1960s, much was already known about the efficiency of the market, and the nearly
random walks that resulted. The problem of the proper pricing of options was a major
motivation for research characterizing the random nature of the securities markets.
Option concerns were a major part of the content of Cootner's classic compilation of
papers titled *The Random Character of Stock Markets*.[1] In it, a paper by Bachelier
from 1900 accurately portrayed options as founded on the diffusion of probability
from the starting point of today's prices. He noted even then the relevance of the "heat
transfer" partial differential equation from classical mathematics that would later
reappear in slightly more complicated form in the Black-Scholes option model.

However, the best modern translations of option theory still had not adequately captured the impact of arbitrage between the stock and the option. Even then,
Paul Samuelson, and later with his protege Bob Merton, still depended on investor
preferences in creating models of warrant pricing. Myron Scholes was a couple of
years ahead of me on the faculty at M.I.T.'s Sloan School. I remember him smiling
broadly and smoking a big cigar as he modestly narrated his exploits in consulting
with what I thought of as Wall Street. When I left the Sloan School for the "real
world," as we called it in 1973, I must admit that I had little idea that these familiar
people were busy creating a revolution that would still be growing 30 years later.

Their history is better told elsewhere and by others. For tightly reasoned
mathematical proofs, you will need to refer to a research-level treatise such as
Merton's *Continuous-Time Finance*.[2] For a clear exposition of principles of

---

[1] Paul H. Cootner (ed.), *The Random Character of Stock Market Prices* (Cambridge, Mass.: M.I.T.
Press,1964).
[2] Robert C. Merton, *Continuous-Time Finance* (Malden, Mass.: Blackwell Publishers, Inc. (revised) 1992).

option pricing at an intermediate level of mathematical sophistication, you might consult a good text, such as Hull.[3] What I will try to do here is to show option theory's broader application to active investing.

It now seems likely that all active investment strategies have their matching duals as portfolios of options. These portfolios have not only the mean return that active investors hope to add, but also variance, skewness, and kurtosis. That is, as active investors, we do not stand apart from investment return characteristics, merely selecting among those available from existing traded securities. Our varying intervention creates a wholly new pattern, a personal portfolio of hypothetical securities that must be added to the underlying assets to understand investment results.

EFFICIENT MARKETS AND BROWNIAN MOTION

In a well-developed market, speculators with information about future events quickly bid prices up or down until excess profits can no longer be earned by anticipating the forecasted event. If this bidding is practically instantaneous, what we observe as price changes will be dominated by unexpected returns, or surprises. Since surprises must occur with equal weight up or down, a *martingale*, the resulting price moves (plus dividends) appear to follow a random walk superimposed on an underlying upward drift based on equilibrium expected return. This phenomenon has been known since at least the beginning of this century. It was well documented by Cootner in 1964 using papers written earlier. Paul Samuelson upgraded the mathematical proofs as to why this randomness should be so in an article published in the M.I.T. Sloan School's *Industrial Management Review* in 1965.[4]

A key property of these random stock price changes is that surprises are practically continuous. Big surprises come less often, small surprises more frequently. There are surprises apparent when we examine price movements of liquid securities even on a time-scale of a minute or less. The pattern of jagged changes seen in broad strokes over a decade looks very similar to that seen under a magnifying glass over the course of a day. If one measures the absolute distance price movements traverse using yardsticks increasingly small, one gets an increasingly large total. These characteristics of self-similarity and fractional dimension place stock price histories squarely in the category of *fractals*, as defined by Benoit Mandelbrot.[5] The price trajectories are continuous (in reality only down to the level of eighths of a dollar per share). However, they are not differentiable in the sense of elementary calculus because their slopes do not approach a limit as time increments are decreased to zero.

---

[3] John C. Hull, *Options, Futures and Other Derivatives* (Upper Saddle River, NJ: Prentice Hall, 1997).
[4] Paul A. Samuelson, "Proof That Properly Anticipated Prices Fluctuate Randomly," *Industrial Management Review* (Spring 1965) , pp. 41-49.
[5] Benoit Mandelbrot, *Fractals and Scaling in Finance: Discontinuity, Concentration, Risk* (New York: Springer-Verlag, 1997).

Consider the great multiplicity of sources of surprising information, ranging from the daily "news" to individual decisions to save or consume that affect aggregate demand and supply for a particular security. This resulting statistical distribution of changes is characterized empirically by *variance roughly proportional to time interval*. In this, as well as in substantial independence between time-periods, stock price movements have the attribute of Brownian motion. This is the movement of microscopic colloidal particles suspended in solution that can be observed as the particles are randomly buffeted by colliding molecules traveling at different speeds and directions.

Mandelbrot argued in the 1960s that stock price changes are actually wilder than Brownian. Their distributions of returns have such fat tails they do not have finite variances. His paper arguing for this characterization, along with another by Eugene Fama explaining the awful consequences, is in Cootner.[6] Both are well worth reading. Mandelbrot also recently published a retrospective that may be more available to the reader without access to a research library.[7] This material is pertinent because it reminds us that real stock price series have substantially more large jumps over short periods than could be explained by Brownian noise. Nevertheless, his well-taken objections fall short, I believe, of obviating the latter's use as a starting point for analysis.

The independence of successive return surprises of bounded size leads through the Central Limit Theorem to the normal distribution of their sums across time. Since successive returns are compounded, in essence it is log returns that are summed. If this were not so, a large negative return could lead to a negative price! Assuming both independence and non-negative but bounded variance over every time interval implies that the limiting return distribution is lognormal.

Substantially higher than normal incidence of very large positive and negative log returns over very short periods exists for all securities markets, particularly at the level of individual stocks and for commodity and currency futures. Especially noteworthy was a day in October 1987 when the U.S. stock market fell about 20%. Second, in the real world there are also trading costs and trading is not exactly continuous. For both these reasons, we know that even under mild conditions option models based on arbitrage with a hedging position will be somewhat approximate. The existence of "jumps" in short-term prices and the similar imposition of discontinuous trading, whether through lack of liquidity or rational calculation based on trading costs, can make the Brownian model a rather poor approximation even for the limiting case of infinitesimal time increments. Nevertheless, the insights we obtain from option theory based on Brownian motion and free trading are fundamental.

Before going further in theory, let us work out a concrete spreadsheet example of the value of a call, the right to buy a security at a specified price at some future time.

---

[6] Cootner, *The Random Character of Stock Market Prices.*

[7] Mandelbrot, *Fractals and Scaling in Finance: Discontinuity, Concentration, Risk.*

OPTION VALUATION BY MONTE CARLO SIMULATION

Consider a stock currently selling at a price of 100 dollars. It will not pay a dividend. There are no transaction costs and no taxes. The short-term interest rate is 5%. How much would you pay for the right, but not the obligation, to buy the stock for a strike price of $100 in three month's time? (This right, exercisable only on the last day, is labeled a *European call*. The right to sell at a set price and time is termed a *European put*. If these two rights are liberalized to allow premature exercise, they are termed *American* call and put.)

Let us first tackle the question of the time value of money. Define current price S, exercise price E, time until exercise $T-t$, and interest rate r. There are many possible stock price values S_i at T. We have $S = 100$, $E = 100$, $t = 0.25$, and $r = 0.05$. Let the value of the option be H.

Suppose we were considering buying a right that *obligated* us to take delivery of the stock in three months, a "future." We would be indifferent as to whether we bought the stock itself now or bought the right plus a zero-coupon bond that matured for $100 in three months. Then we will sell the bond and use the proceeds to buy the stock at the agreed price. If other market participants follow the same logic, this arbitrage determines the price of our right. Its value is the stock's price today less the cost today of the bond. If the annualized interest on a 3-month bill is 5%, we would pay only $100/(1.05)^{0.25}$ for the bond, giving $1.21 as the value of our right.

Now let us return to the question of a call option that gives us the right, but *not* the obligation, of buying the stock three months from now.

For each possible outcome S_i

$$H_i = \max\left\{0, \left[S_i - \frac{E}{(1+r)^t}\right]\right\} \tag{1}$$

To determine the value of our option over all i, we must combine these values, accounting for the different possibilities. For now, suppose that the value of H is simply expected H_i.

Before constructing our simulation, we must decide on the form that we give to our model. Continuous option models beginning with Black and Scholes in the early 1970s have traditionally been written in terms of fractional return rather than log return. These two concepts approach the same limit as the time interval becomes infinitesimal. However, we should keep in mind for simulations using finite time differences that the underlying phenomenon is better modeled in terms of normally distributed log returns. Again, if this were not so, there would be a finite probability of a return that would lose more than starting capital.

For our Monte Carlo simulation, suppose that log returns have zero mean and 0.2 annual standard deviation. For now, we will leave open the question of what the mean should truly be, and merely examine the answers given this assumption.

Exhibit 1: Idealized Value of a Call

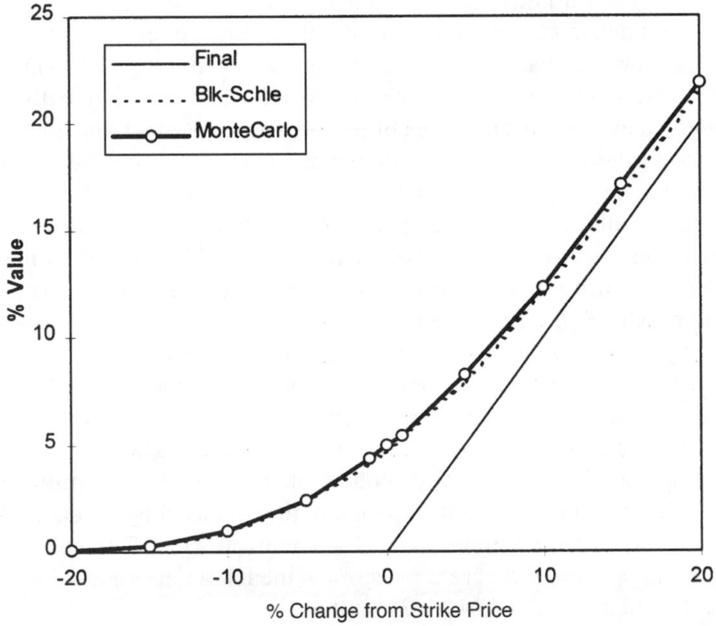

We can use the random number generator in a spreadsheet program such as Excel to create many log-normally distributed outcomes and simply observe where the mean value calculated for equation (1) lies.

In this case, I used as a normal distribution the sum of 12 uniform distributions between 0 and 1. I then subtracted 6 to get an approximately normal variate of mean 0 and standard deviation 1. I divided the 3-month interval into ten periods of 0.025 years, each of which had standard deviation of 0.2 times the square root of 0.025, or 0.0316 in log return. The realized log return in each period is our approximate normal deviate times this standard deviation. Taking the antilog of the sum of log returns over the ten periods and multiplying by starting price gives a terminal stock value S_i that is thoroughly log-normal. This exercise was repeated 10,000 times to get a mean value for the expression in equation (1). The entire procedure was then repeated for different starting prices.

Thus, Exhibit 1 shows results not only for a starting price of 100, but for a range of starting prices from 80 to 120. In each case the exercise price at expiration three months from now is 100. The horizontal axis is the difference between the initial stock price S and the exercise price E. The vertical axis is the value of the option. The dark solid line is the mean value of the H_i, our result from Monte Carlo simulation. The dotted line very near it is the theoretical value of the call as calculated by the Black-Scholes formula to be introduced later. The straight lines represent possible values of max(0, $S-E$), without taking time discounting into consideration. While our simulated result is only an approximation, grossly inadequate as a basis for trading options, it clearly has a similar shape.

The simulated result schedule of call option values for various starting stock prices shows the basic features of option values. Its slope is asymptotic to 0 for out-of-the-money calls and asymptotic to 1 for in-the-money calls. Its slope at-the-money between current prices of 99 and 101 ($S-E$ of -1 and $+1$) is approximately 0.5. In-the-money calls are valued at somewhat above the $S-E$ diagonal because E need not be paid until later.

How would the chart appear if we conducted trials with different parameters? If we were to reduce either the instantaneous risk level or the time to expiration $T-t$, the value of the option would move closer to the straight lines specifying max(0, $S-E$). The larger the risk, the less would be the curvature and consequently the higher the necessary valuation of the option. Also as we reduced the time to expiration, the in-the-money asymptote would approach the $S-E$ diagonal more closely. Finally, if interest rates were greater, the value of in-the-money calls would move above the $S-E$ diagonal by a greater margin.

Now we will examine two models of this process that provide greater insight. The first is the continuous approach, the one used by Fischer Black and Myron Scholes, and then generalized by Robert Merton. The second is built around binomial trees of discrete price movements, an approach developed by John Cox, Stephen Ross, and Mark Rubinstein.

THE STRANGE WORLD OF
FRACTAL (STOCHASTIC) CALCULUS

To understand the key insight of the Black-Scholes option pricing model you need to know about limits and partial derivatives.[8]

If variance is proportional to time interval, as it is with Brownian noise, standard deviation is proportional to the square root of the time interval. Recall that Δ symbolizes a small change. The equation below says that a small change in S, the stock price, divided by that price, is equal to a drift rate μ times the accompanying small change in time plus a normal random variable of standard deviation $\sigma(\Delta t)^{1/2}$. The square root of the change in time is implied when we say that variance is proportional to time interval.

$$\frac{\Delta S}{S} = \mu(\Delta t) + \sigma\varepsilon(\Delta t)^{1/2} \tag{2}$$

As the time interval approaches zero, the square root of the time interval grows larger and larger relative to the time interval. Thus, at sufficiently short intervals, return is dominated by the random component rather than by the drift component.

---

[8] For an introduction to calculus, see George B. Thomas, Jr. and Ross L. Finney, *Calculus and Analytic Geometry*, *9th ed.* (New York: Addison-Wesley, 1996). See Merton's *Continuous-Time Finance* if you want to dig into what is necessary to use these concepts in the world of random processes.

This dominance by the term proportional to the square root of the time interval at short intervals creates several striking statistical properties for the instantaneous properties of changes in S and in functions of S. Among these are the following, using the nomenclature of equation (2):

1. The variance of the fractional return $\Delta S/S$ is $\sigma^2 \Delta t$.
2. The correlation between a quantity H that is a function of S (with at least bounded third derivative) and S is either $+1$ or -1.
3. An *Ito process* is one in which a quantity S is determined as $\Delta S = a(\Delta t) + b\varepsilon(\Delta t)^{\frac{1}{2}}$ where ε is a standard normal variate, as it will be if the Central Limit Theorem applies, independent of past S, and where Δt goes to 0 at the limit, while a and b are functions of S and time t. For an Ito process, one can define

$$\Delta H = \left[\left(\frac{\partial.H}{\partial.S}\right)a + \left(\frac{\partial.H}{\partial.t}\right) + \left(\frac{\partial^2.H}{\partial.S^2}\right)\frac{b^2}{2}\right]\Delta t + \left(\frac{\partial.H}{\partial.S}\right)b\varepsilon(\Delta t)^{\frac{1}{2}} \tag{3}$$

and treat this as a partial differential equation. (Note that I have used a period after the symbol for partial differentiation merely as a typographical separator.) Equation (3) is *Ito's lemma*. It says that as time changes over small intervals, there will be two effects on H. The right-hand term gives a random effect on H dependent on the derivative of H with respect to S. There will also be a drift effect composed of three sub-parts. Its first two sub-parts are dependent on the derivatives (slopes) of H with respect to S (in turn dependent on t through a) and with respect to t. There will, finally, be a third sub-part, a rather surprising drift component proportional to the second derivative (curvature) of H versus S. The Taylor series expansion for ΔH as a function of changes in S and t includes a second-order term which squares $(\Delta t)^{\frac{1}{2}}$, bringing it to the same order of magnitude Δt as the other terms. In essence, if H is a function of S, and S includes a dominating stochastic term, then the curvature of H versus S generates a net drift as S bounces in either direction.
4. ΔH is also an Ito process.

We conclude, first, that if values of options can be expressed as differentiable functions of stock prices that behave as Brownian motion, they also will have Brownian motion, with perfect instantaneous correlation. This implies that some quantity of stock combined with a short position in the option can perfectly hedge the random fluctuation that dominates both of them at small time increments. Changes in value of such a hedged position will contain only drift elements and even higher-order terms. The latter can be ignored for instantaneous changes.

Second, Ito's lemma offers a description of changes in the value of an option (or other derivative security) that can be used along with boundary conditions to analyze its functional form. The boundary condition for a simple European call is that the value of the option at the time the option expires is equal to the greater of zero and the difference between the stock price and the exercise price.

Both these conclusions depend heavily on the time increment being very small. This need for small increments raises difficulties for discontinuities caused by adequate response to trading costs or by the somewhat similar impact of sudden jumps in price inconsistent with Brownian motion.

THE BLACK-SCHOLES MODEL

In 1973, Fischer Black and Myron Scholes won the race to obtain a solution to valuing options both adequate from a theoretical view and in a form suitable for empirical testing. They restricted their first effort to a European call with no dividends and constant variance. Robert Merton published a similar, but broader, result at almost the same time. Their solution has two parts: first, one sets up the correct partial differential equation; second, one solves it. The first part has significant economic content, and we can usefully outline their procedure. The second part draws on pre-existing mathematics, long used to solve problems like heat transfer in a physical body. Black and Scholes simply reported the solution as obtained in a textbook without further comment. Merton broke the solution down into components, but these depend on too much mathematical facility with partial differential equations to be useful here.

Let us set up the partial differential equation, first in stochastic form, and then simplified to ordinary variables. Equation (2) defines an Ito process for S, with the parameter $a = S\mu$ and $b = \sigma$. Ito's lemma defines another Ito process for H, which we will make into a European call option using our boundary conditions. Therefore we have the following two stochastic partial differential equations, equations (4) and (5).

$$\Delta S = S\mu(\Delta t) + S\sigma\varepsilon(\Delta t)^{\frac{1}{2}} \tag{4}$$

$$\Delta H = \left[\left(\frac{\partial.H}{\partial.S}\right)Su + \left(\frac{\partial.H}{\partial.t}\right) + \left(\frac{\partial^2.H}{\partial.S^2}\right)\frac{S^2\sigma^2}{2}\right]\Delta t + \left(\frac{\partial.H}{\partial.S}\right)S\sigma\varepsilon(\Delta t)^{\frac{1}{2}} \tag{5}$$

If we multiply equation (4) by the partial derivative of H with respect to S, and subtract the result from equation (5), two terms cancel out to form equation (6).

$$\Delta H - \left(\frac{\partial.H}{\partial.S}\right)\Delta S = \left[\left(\frac{\partial.H}{\partial.t}\right) + \left(\frac{\partial^2.H}{\partial.S^2}\right)\left(\frac{S^2\sigma^2}{2}\right)\right]\Delta t \tag{6}$$

This subtraction represents a portfolio of a long call and a short position of the stock, with the partial differential of H with respect to S as the number of shares sold short. For example, think back to our earlier Monte Carlo simulation of a call's value. The slope of the value of the call with respect to stock price was 0.5 at the money. At that point, a long call hedged by 0.5 shares of stock would have no risk, so long as our other assumptions held true.

Note that the dominant term at short intervals, the random term, has been eliminated. This was the purpose of the hedge. But the original contribution of Black and Scholes was to show that there is another benefit. The term depending on μ, the expected rate of return of the stock, has also been eliminated. It has exactly offsetting impact on the stock position and the call position. This means that the value of our hedged portfolio is not dependent on the expected return for the stock! It is therefore not dependent on general market equilibrium taking into account either varying investor expectations for average return or investor attitudes toward risk! This step puts option theory on much stronger ground than the CAPM, because it has many fewer assumptions.

What will such a hedged position earn? Because it will have no risk, it should in market equilibrium earn the risk-free rate r. Thus, we have equation (7), setting the change in the value of the hedged portfolio equal to the net capital invested or thrown off times r times the time interval.

$$\left[\left(\frac{\partial.H}{\partial.t}\right)+\left(\frac{\partial^2.H}{\partial.s^2}\right)\left(\frac{s^2\sigma^2}{2}\right)\right]\Delta t = \left[H-\left(\frac{\partial.H}{\partial.S}\right)S\right]r\Delta t \tag{7}$$

Looking at the left side of equation (7), the riskless earnings rate on the hedged portfolio is equal to the sum of two quantities. The first, of course, is the direct impact of the slope of the option value with respect to time. The second is the expected drift from the curvature of H with respect to S in the face of random variations in S. If we begin with the risk-free interest rate, we now know some specific requirements for the rate at which H depends on time, and for the curvature of H with respect to S given some particular level of stock return variance.

Finally, since the Δt can be divided through on both sides, rearranging we have the classic Black-Scholes partial differential equation,

$$\left(\frac{\partial.H}{\partial.t}\right)+rS\left(\frac{\partial.H}{\partial.S}\right)+\left(\frac{\sigma^2s^2}{2}\right)\left(\frac{\partial^2.H}{\partial.s^2}\right) = rH \tag{8}$$

subject to the boundary condition that $H = \max(0,S-E)$ when $t = 0$.

Assuming that you have no particular interest in learning how to solve such mathematical beasts, I will simply repeat the answer for the value of H in terms of S, t, and E that Black and Scholes presented in 1973.

$$H = SN(d_1) - EN(d_2)/e^{r(T-t)} \tag{9}$$

where $N(d_1)$ is the value of the cumulative normal distribution with argument d_1,

$$d_1 = \frac{\ln(S/E) + (r + \sigma^2/2)(T - t)}{\sigma\sqrt{T - t}}$$

$$d_1 = \frac{\ln(S/E) + (r - \sigma^2/2)(T - t)}{\sigma\sqrt{T - t}}$$

It is easy to confirm that in the limit as t approaches T the $N(d)$ terms go to either 0 or 1 depending on whether $S<E$ or $S>E$. Thus, the boundary condition is satisfied by equation (9). Confirming that equation (9) is in fact a solution to the partial differential equation (8) is more challenging, and I have not done so. However, we are assured by Merton and later by Cox, Ross, and Rubinstein that the Black-Scholes solution is correct.

OPTION VALUE OF BINOMIAL TREES

In case the continuous argument is unclear, we are going to come again to the same conclusions through discrete route. This is the binomial tree of discrete returns, introduced by Cox, Ross, and Rubinstein (CRR) in an extraordinary paper written in 1979. If you read only one paper on options from an original source, read this one, titled "Option Pricing: A Simplified Approach."

Their paper was written originally for pedagogical purposes. They credit William Sharpe with the suggestion of approaching the continuous case through the discrete route. In order to avoid the mathematically difficult Black-Scholes partial differential equation, they approach the normal distribution of log returns as the limit of the sum of binomial probability distributions. It turned out their approach was for most people easier and also far more flexible than the original.

Remember our coin flipping exercise in Chapter 6? Suppose we have one coin. It is priced at $1 per share. The number of shares is irrelevant. Each coin flip returns either 100% or −50%. Suppose we could buy a call on each share of the coin that may be exercised at $1 after a single flip. The risk-free interest rate is 25% per flipping period. What would be a fair price for the calls, each priced at H? Using the logic of CRR, we will set up a self-financing, perfectly hedged position as follows. It will be liquidated after the coin flip.

	Cash Flow Table (in $)		
	Now	After -50% Case	After +100% Case
Buy 3 Calls	−3H	0.0	3.0
Sell Short 2 Shares	2.0	−1.0	−4.0
Lend $0.80 at 25%	−0.8	1.0	1.0
Total	0.0	0.0	0.0

What does H have to be to avoid the possibility of a sure arbitrage profit by either the buyer or seller? Since the outcome is zero future net cash flow after the coin flip no matter what happens, H must be $0.4 per call.

Let's go through that again. Since there is no further gain or loss, we need only consider the instantaneous profit or loss in setting up the position. If H were cheaper than $0.40, one could make an excess return (no capital used and no time expired!) by buying the calls and offsetting their payoff under either outcome with a combination of a bond position and a short sale in the stock. If H were more expensive than $0.40, the same strategy would lose money. Thus arbitrage among coin speculators determines the price of a call. Such a mechanism may be used to determine the value of the call as long as the positive outcome is more, and the negative outcome is less, than the risk-free interest rate.

Note that that the fair price of the option does not depend on the probability of positive outcome versus the negative outcome! This is the same finding as with the Black-Scholes model. The only determinants are the risk-free rate, the price of the stock, and the upside and downside returns.

At this point in their argument, CCR note that when H is expressed as a function of its two payoffs, time discounted at the risk-free rate, the coefficients of each are non-negative numbers that sum to one. They note that one gets the same result as if these coefficients were probabilities and one lived in a risk-neutral world in which all returns were equal to the risk-free rate. To see this, examine equation (10), the value of a call for a single binomial set of outcomes.

$$H = [pH_u + (1 - p)H_d]/r \tag{10}$$

where

$$p = \frac{r - d}{u - d}$$

Here r is one plus the risk-free interest rate, u is one plus the stock's "up" return, and d is one plus the stock's "down" return. The letter p has been termed the risk-neutral probability. H_u is the value of the call after the "up" event, H_d the value of the call after the "down" event, and H the current value of the call. Since we are discussing a call for one period, H_u represents $\max(0, S_u - E)$, where S is the stock price and E the exercise price.

This formalism of calculating "risk-neutral probabilities" has wide application in option-theory as a mental shortcut. However, one should keep in mind that there is no such thing as a risk-neutral world other than as an algebraic device.

CCR then go on to show that this operation of equation (10) can be repeated for multiple time periods (multiple flips, in our example). Think of a tree lying on its side with the trunk at the left and more and more detailed branching to the right. The final branching is at the right edge. Imagine two parallel trees, one for the price of the stock and one for the value of the option. The value of the option for each of the possible choices before the last time period can be calculated based on the payoffs given the projected values of the stock. Then the process can be repeated, working its way back to the original first branching point. Options more complicated than European, or environments more complicated than constant variance, may require reference to the underlying stock price tree in keeping track of the values at the branches of the option value tree.

If the situation is very simple, the tree may be summarized by formula, as in the case of a European call. An example suitable for the latter is given as equation (11).

$$H = \frac{\left[\sum_{j=a}^{n} \left(\frac{n!}{j!(n-j)!} \right) p^j (1-p)^{n-j} (u^j d^{n-j} S - E) \right]}{r^n} \tag{11}$$

where n is the number of periods, E is the exercise price, S is the current stock price, n is the total number of periods, and a is the smallest non-negative integer such that $u^a d^{n-a} S > E$.

Otherwise, it is necessary to do more elaborate bookkeeping at each stage of backward recursion in the tree to keep track of changing conditions. For example, such an approach can be used to calculate numerical values for an option like an American put. This is the right to sell a stock at a specified price *prior* to a specific time, perhaps complicated by the payment of dividends at particular dates.

How do we choose u and d so as to be meaningful in a world of stocks rather than coins? Remember that the limit of the sum of binomial distributions is a normal distribution. Then we can choose u and d so as to recreate a normal distribution of log returns, an approximately Brownian motion process with mean $\mu(\Delta t)$ and standard deviation $\sigma(\Delta t)^{1/2}$.

Set:

$$u = e^{\sigma \sqrt{(T-t)/n}}$$

$$d = 1/u$$

where $T-t$ is the time to expiration and n is the number of time periods used for approximating Brownian motion. The higher is n the closer is the approximation. CRR show that, in the limit with increasing n, their formula converges to the Black-Scholes formula.

SOME IMPLICATIONS

What have we learned from the Black-Scholes-Merton continuous model? Suppose we can assume continuous trading and a stock process with bounded instantaneous variance. Suppose as well that we know what that variance is. Suppose we can freely borrow or lend. Then we know we can use a bond position to finance a perfectly hedged portfolio consisting of a call option less a short stock position. It is a significant advantage that we need not know the expected return for the stock nor for the option. The Cox-Ross-Rubinstein discrete model confirms this insight and broadens it to include many more situations.

Hayne Leland published a paper in 1985 titled "Option Pricing and Replication with Transactions Costs." In it he noted that, since Brownian motion requires infinite continuous trading, any trading cost makes pure option replication through dynamic trading self-defeating. If instead one trades at regular time intervals, Leland showed that the Black-Scholes formula should be modified. One does so by increasing the effective assumed variance linearly with the ratio of assumed transaction cost to the square root of the trading interval. This innovation made option replication practicable, although better policies make trades dependent on the size of price moves rather than time interval.

From both continuous and discrete models, we know that the proportion of the stock hedge required depends on the current stock price. This fact implies that we can replicate a call with a bond position plus a fractional short position in the stock only so long as we are willing to very frequently update the size of our positions. We will buy more stock as it goes up, and sell stock as it goes down in price. Conversely, if we find an investor with an active investment strategy of buying stocks after they go up, and selling them as they go down, we can say that investor's active policy approximates the action of either a put or call option. Both put and call replicators are momentum investors!

Recall from Chapter 4 what happens to a market as it has to cope with greater fractions of momentum investors. There is a limited "carrying capacity" for momentum investors beyond which the market becomes highly unstable. There is some reason to suspect that this limit might have been breached in 1987 in the U.S. stock market. Some suspect that that the "straw that broke the camel's back" was the existence of large amounts of funds engaged in the option replication strategies advocated by Leland and Rubinstein. In the event, the price "jumps" were bigger than expected and the transaction costs much higher than expected, so that the strategy was only partially effective in protecting against a downturn that it may have accelerated.

We may also note that the Black-Scholes model has not since 1987 been a very accurate model of the pricing of calls.[9] Out-of-the-money puts have become very expensive since 1987. Either investors are wrong or there needs to be significant adjustments to the model.

Nevertheless, having said all this, there is no escaping a very broad conclusion. There is a mapping between options and replicating active strategies. Combining portfolios of calls and puts of various long and short position sizes, strike prices and expiration dates, one can recreate an infinite variety of payoffs as a function of both stock price and time. Because of the theoretical problems posed by discontinuities, I do not claim that all possible active trading results can be duplicated by options. This strikes me as an unanswered question. But it is clear that many sterotypical patterns of active management can be replicated by portfo-

---

[9] See Mark Rubinstein, "Implied Binomial Trees," *Journal of Finance* (1994), pp 771-818, for a discussion of how to respond to the "smile," the variation of implied variance from options that differ only in their strike prices.

lios of options, and so better studied. Analyzing patterns of active management in terms of their replicating option portfolios has real potential for improving our understanding of the impact of our own behavior patterns as investors. In the remainder of this chapter we take up an obvious example.

CONSTANT PROPORTION PORTFOLIO INSURANCE

In the late 1980s, Andre Perold of the Harvard Business School wrote a working paper that described an active strategy much simpler than the Black-Scholes option replication strategy, but capable of producing comparable practical results. This idea reached publication only some years later as Black and Perold.[10] The idea was labeled Constant Proportion Portfolio Insurance (CPPI). It involves trading exposure between a safe asset and a risky asset. The exposure to the risky asset can involve leverage, perhaps typically through the use of stock index futures. There is no definite time to expiration. The floor is invested in the safe asset. The position in the risky asset is governed by equation (12).

$$\text{Risky Exposure} = k \times (\text{Wealth} - \text{Floor}) \tag{12}$$

The difference between wealth and the risky asset is an additional position in the safe asset, either long or short. The delta, or derivative of the portfolio with respect to changes in risky asset price, is, ignoring the effect of interest on the safe asset, the ratio of the risky exposure to wealth. If $k > 1$, delta steepens with increase in risky asset prices, as prices go up, and flattens to zero as prices go down.

This kind of policy is termed *portfolio insurance*. If $k = 1$, the policy simply allows initial positions to ride with returns, with no re-balancing. This still gives a mildly positively skewed return pattern. Constant asset allocation cannot be produced with a fixed k. Of course, if every price deviation is countered by a small compensating change in k, the initial proportions can be preserved and the average position of k will remain near 1. If $k < 1$, the policy will be a kind of value-orientation. The allocation of the risky asset will be reduced to below its initial position if its price rises.

Note that related policies may be followed implicitly by many investors in conjunction with momentum-based strategies without their being aware that they are approximating constant proportion portfolio insurance.

Often there is a further leverage cap limit placed on the extent of risky asset holdings. For example, no leverage may be allowed. Here we will first examine portfolio insurance without leverage caps, as this is the pure form.

---

[10] Fischer Black and Andre Perold, "Theory of Constant Proportion Portfolio Insurance," *Journal of Economic Dynamics and Control* (1992) pp. 403-426.

Exhibit 2: Value of CPPI with 80% Initial Floor and Multiplier of 5

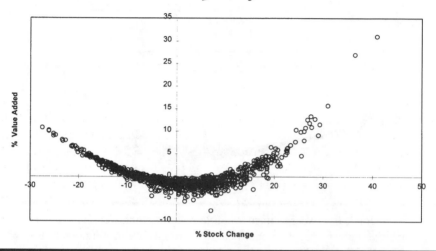

Exhibit 2 illustrates the value of such a policy for a thousand cases of different risky asset returns over a 3-month period. The broad intention of most users of such policies is to reproduce the action of a put, by protecting against downside risk. The example CPPI policy is based on a floor of 80% of initial assets to be invested in a risk-free investment yielding 5%. The risky investment is in stocks following lognormal returns with a mean of 0 and an annual standard deviation of 20%. To determine the stock position, the difference between wealth and the floor is multiplied by five. The total period of three months is divided into 10 sub-periods.

The Monte Carlo simulation is done with an Excel spreadsheet in the same way as before. However, in this case, we are simply looking at future values as a function of stock returns rather than trying to determine how best to calculate the present value as a function of initial price to exercise price.

The horizontal scale in Exhibit 2 represents the percentage change in stock price over the three months for each of the 1,000 sequences of random returns over 10 sub-periods. The vertical scale is the excess or deficit of the value of the portfolio over that of a hypothetical pure stock portfolio, expressed as a percentage of the initial wealth.

What we see looks very unlike a European put payoff function. Of course this exhibit differs from Exhibit 1 in that it concerns a put rather than a call, thus reversing the figure from left to right. But there are other more profound differences.

The first is that without a leverage cap such a policy produces a value added on the right-hand side of the exhibit as well as on the left-hand side. That is, the multiple of 5 times the cushion between wealth and floor causes high returns when stock prices enjoy a sustained rise. Thus, the payoff function is not like a put, but rather more like the combination of a put and a call.

Exhibit 3: Value of CPPI with 90% Initial Floor and Multiplier of 10

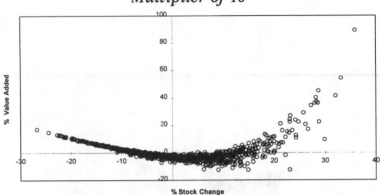

Second, the excess return when long-term stock trends have been either very positive or very negative entails a high probability of a moderate loss when prices finish close to where they started. This phenomenon of losses when movements see-saw back and forth is a characteristic property of portfolio insurance, and occurs even though we have put in no transaction cost.

Third, the resulting option payoffs are path dependent. (This would not be true if we had used infinitesimal time increments between rebalancing, but of course in that case real-world transaction costs would have been infinite.) This path-dependency means that the same final stock price can end up with substantially different value added (or subtracted) by a CPPI portfolio. The symptom of this path-dependency is a random vertical scatter around the curved central tendency of the payoff function.

Fourth, the variation in results for different paths is much greater in the case of positive stock returns than for negative stock returns. Substantial negative returns put the portfolio mostly into the safe asset from which there is by definition little variation in result. This characteristic is even more apparent as we lift the floor to 90% and the multiplier to 10, as in Exhibit 3.

Now for the real surprise. By suitable variations in the multiplier and the floor, one can obtain a very wide variety of payoff functions. Exhibit 4 goes back to a floor of 80% of initial capital, but increases the multiplier from 5 to 15. By allowing extreme leverage, the payoff function looks like that of an out-of-the-money call, plus a wild-card randomization.

Exhibit 5 goes even further by unconventionally reducing the multiplier to less than one, 0.5 in this case, and by allowing a floor of -100%, thus allowing one to lose double the initial capital. It is thus possible to achieve a payoff function that is the approximate reverse of that conventional CPPI with leverage. In this situation, one is paid for see-saw motions but loses heavily if there is a sustained price movement in either direction.

Exhibit 4: Value of CPPI with 80% Initial Floor and Multiplier of 15

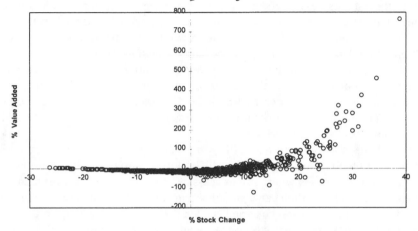

Exhibit 5: Value of CPPI with 80% Initial Floor and Multiplier of 15

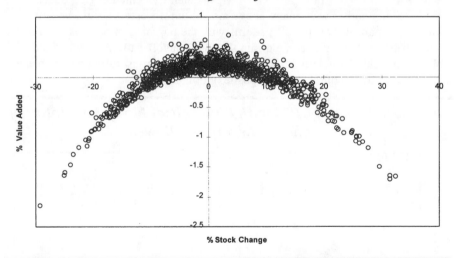

While these latter policies seem whimsical, they bear seeds of insight. The policy of Exhibit 4 comes closer to buying a lottery ticket on out-of-the-money calls. The policy of Exhibit 5 corresponds in exaggerated fashion to a value-oriented policy that sells stocks disproportionately as they go up, buys them as they go down, and is insensitive to any floor.

Anti-stability they may be, but momentum investors produce for themselves, absent transaction costs, positive skew, a desirable property for expected compound returns, as we saw in Chapter 6. On the other hand, deep value or contrarian investors may exaggerate downturns and fail to participate in upturns, thus giving themselves negative skew that will interfere with expected compound return. This ought to occasion some thought. Later we will see that value investors have generally enjoyed superior returns. Perhaps some of this results from a risk premium dependent not on variance but on negative skew.

Finally, Exhibit 6 shows CPPI as it is conventionally used, with a limit on the risky asset of 100% of wealth, so that no leverage is allowed. Now there is no call-like payoff for good stock performance. One trades likely losses if the price see-saws around its starting point against a well-defined put payoff if there is a substantial risky asset decline.

Perhaps a comment on CPPI is in order as a portfolio insurance tool. It can provide obvious substantial downside risk protection benefits. However, the balancing costs in cases where prices see-saw around a constant level tend to be hidden. Second, the method can also fail, as can any dynamic hedging trading pattern, if jumps in price are so large and sudden that the effective hedge ratio cannot keep up. For these reasons, which may lead to disappointment and misunderstandings, one should carefully consider whether the higher up-front costs of simply buying a put may be more practical. After all, traded option securities exist because they are a desirable alternative versus their dynamic hedging duals.

Said another way, many active momentum investors would be better off to duplicate part of their payoff patterns with the purchase of options. And active value investors, having become aware that their payoff patterns have an unfavorable component characteristic of writing options, might usefully counter-balance their policies by the purchase of opposite option positions.

Exhibit 6: Value of CPPI with 80% Initial Floor, Multiplier of 5 and No Leverage Allowed

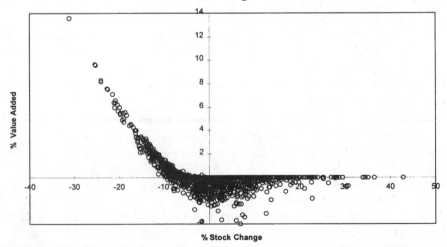

Chapter 8
The CAPM and Its Descendants

Myths which are believed in tend to become true.
George Orwell, *"The English People" (1944)*

You read about the Capital Asset Pricing Model (CAPM) in Chapter 3. It is diffi-cult to overestimate the impact it has had on the financial community. Despite its heroic and quite unrealistic assumptions, despite its abysmal success in empirical prediction, it remains central to financial thought. If a man from Mars were to examine carefully this set of beliefs that had so little possibility of being con-firmed empirically he would undoubtedly place it in the category of religion, not science. Yet it has accomplished a very great good. For millions of investors, it has prevented foolish investment policies through encouraging the development of index funds. The resulting index fund futures and their option derivatives have made markets more nearly perfect and better allocators of capital.

Bill Sharpe was first among equals as one of the CAPM's several inven-tors (Treynor, Tobin, Sharpe, Lintner, Mossin, refined by Fama and Black), and for decades its chief spokesman. I first met him in the mid 1980s. He utterly cap-tivated me by his generosity of spirit and down-to-earth manner. One of my prize memories is of him proudly showing off a new Markowitz optimizer he had pro-grammed for the personal computer. I promptly caused it to crash by entering a problem with equal expected returns for every asset. He kindly invited me to speak to his investment class, where I could expound my valuation theories. Yet for all that, and although I greatly respected the reductionist impulse that charac-terizes the CAPM, I found a great difference in outlook.

The CAPM is a descriptive theory predicting first-order effects. Its only success, and that is only approximate, is in predicting Markowitz efficiency for the market as a whole. It is wrong in predicting systematic risk as the only, or even an easily measurable, determinant of expected return. It is wrong in its pre-diction that everyone holds the same portfolio of risky assets. It entirely omits speculation, rational or otherwise, the subject of this book. It also eliminates the second-order effects that would be of most interest to the speculator. As I will argue later, even the form of Sharpe's recommendation that active managers be measured relative to the risk of underperforming a market-index benchmark is counter-productive for the skilled investor.

Testing and revising the CAPM became a new industry that has endured 30 years. It has produced so many academic and practitioner papers that I do not have space even to list many of the famous ones.

125

At the cosmic end of the scale we have the product of a few brave souls who have ventured to describe general equilibrium of both supply and demand for securities. I offer Cox, Ingersoll, and Ross,[1] but only as a reference for the mathematically intrepid. Next, there are more limited demand equilibrium theories that simply assume a fixed supply of securities, of which the CAPM was the parent. There are myriad variations on that theme: CCAPM, ICAPM, Int CAPM, Conditional CAPM and many others not popular enough to be labeled with their acronyms. Of this vast collection, we will discuss only two models offered by Merton. Narrower is the Arbitrage Pricing Theory proposed by Ross, and developed with Roll. Without seeking a more general equilibrium, it merely assumes a linear return generation process and that arbitrage profits across securities have been eliminated. Most specific of all and, so far as I can tell, of most practical benefit, is option theory. It examines the implication of the elimination of arbitrage profits between a single security and its derivatives. We introduced it in Chapter 7.

Of course as we know from Chapter 4 that even when we have both realistic and comprehensible equilibrium theories there is no necessity for the financial system to stay in, or even approach, equilibrium. The newspaper every day tells us that it does not do so, on many time scales.

For convenience I will repeat a small portion of Chapter 3 to remind you of the CAPM's features. Its first critical assumption is that the market is composed of many participants, each of whom is a von Neumann-Morgenstern utility maximizer considering a single-period investment choice in the Markowitz mean-variance framework. The investors are identical, except in their tolerances for risk. The second critical assumption is that there is an additional risk-free asset that may be freely borrowed or lent at a fixed rate of interest.

The CAPM assumes that information flow is instantaneous across investors. It assumes that investors all have the same investment horizon and all have equal access to all securities in the market. There are no taxes, transaction costs, preference changes nor changing availability of security returns contemplated. There are no restrictions on short sales.

Under these conditions, and assuming fixed supply of securities, equilibrium demand and arbitrage will together determine that every investor will hold the same portfolio of risky securities. They will differ only in the percentage of their wealth they lend or borrow of the risk-free asset. That risky portfolio, the market as a whole, will be on the Markowitz efficient frontier considering only risky securities. Every security will be priced so that its expected return is on the improved efficient frontier formed by the straight-line tangent (in mean-standard deviation space) passing through the risk-free rate and the market portfolio. This implies that specific risk uncorrelated with the market will not be rewarded by higher expected return. It also implies that expected return is a linear function of the expected regression coefficient of the security against the market portfolio, or beta.

[1] John Cox, Jonathan Ingersoll, and Stephen Ross, "An Intertemporal General Equilibrium Model of Asset Prices," *Econometrica* (1985), pp. 363-384.

Here are the topics we treat in the remainder of this chapter. The focus is on the needs of the active investor.

- Empirical tests of CAPM
- Inter-temporal Hedging
- Arbitrage Pricing Theory
- Market Segmentation
- Book/Price and Small Stock Returns
- Critique of Residual Risk Management

EMPIRICAL TESTS OF THE CAPM

In the first decade after its publication, the CAPM seemed to be supported by data. Clearly, stocks had higher long-term returns than bonds, and mutual funds with more risk had higher returns than those with lower risk. In my view, too little attention was paid to the fact that among stocks total return variance proved about as good as beta in predicting return. Neither was especially effective, but for a long while there was no alternative in the academic literature.

In private science, however, it was another matter. During the late 1970s, quantitative investment managers such as Dean LeBaron's Batterymarch Financial Management were busy exploiting the new-found power of the computer to find predictive relationships. Batterymarch and others were using price-earnings ratios, price to book ratios, and dividend yields as indicators of value. They got fabulous results, particularly with small capitalization stocks. It was great while it lasted! By the mid-1980s the cumulative impact of the news getting out to the competition, in part through the academic world, began to be felt generally.

The mills of the academic gods may grind slowly, but they grind exceedingly fine. Ultimately, the academic world rejected the CAPM as a factual descriptive model. The critical tests were those that found factors that were demonstrably more powerful than beta in three ways. They better forecasted average returns. They took away all beta's previously apparent statistical significance. And they could be used to construct portfolios superior to the market index in risk-return efficiency.

In 1977, it was price-earnings ratio that was used to rank portfolios. The low price-earnings portfolios dominated the market portfolio both in risk and return, and could not be explained by beta. Then in succession similar findings were made for small market capitalization (size), low price-to-book, and a variety of other value-oriented anomalies. Fama provided a comprehensive review of the many fine studies that forced the academic world to gradually doubt the descriptive powers of the CAPM.[2]

The major capitulation came only after 1992, when Fama and French published a definitive study, "The Cross-Section of Expected Stock Returns." (We

---

[2] Eugene F. Fama, "Efficient Capital Markets: II," *Journal of Finance* (1991), pp. 1575-1617.

will take a closer look at Fama and French in Chapter 14.) They showed that U.S. stock returns over a long period could be significantly predicted by two factors: *market capitalization* and *book-to-price ratio*. Furthermore, using these factors eliminated any evidence that systematic risk, measured by beta, separately affected expected return.

When Fama, one of the stalwarts of efficient market theory, finally accepted the anomalies, they became respectable for discussion. However, the academic world made minimal concessions to the need for intellectual change. Fama and French argued the possibility that the new factors simply reflected previously unmeasured risks. Others said the evidence was wrong because of survivor bias. Others defended the view that perhaps the theory was right, but we had been measuring beta against the wrong portfolio. But there was no returning to the old illusions. The CAPM must be exchanged for one of its children, or abandoned to the barbarians at the gate, the behavioralists who asserted market irrationality.

In the 1990s, the heat under microeconomics-based asset pricing theorists intensified from the discovery that additional expected returns were characteristic of autocorrelation structure rather than true random walks or Brownian motion. There seemed to be very short-term reversals of a month or so, intermediate term trending at annual intervals, and, finally, very long-term reversals on the order of five years.

Positive trending was particularly hard to rationalize as a risk premium. Again, the academic world lagged by at least five years private science as practiced by some quantitative investment managers and advisory services. At different times, both academics and practitioners found that positive analyst earnings estimate revisions and even 12-month past returns were predictive of future returns. These *momentum* strategies, essentially dynamic in nature, gave the behavioralists more ammunition. We will examine them in Chapter 9. But first we need to exploit fully the conclusions from equilibrium models more robust than the original CAPM.

INTER-TEMPORAL HEDGING

In 1973, Robert Merton, not satisfied with being a major contributor to the theory of options, published "An Intertemporal Capital Asset Pricing Model." In it he used the revolutionary continuous-time approach to fundamentally enlarge our conception of capital asset pricing equilibrium. I have seen many references in the investment literature to this work. However, some authors seem hardly to have read it, because they allege that it reproduced the conclusions of the CAPM in a continuous framework. So it did, but only under very special assumptions. More generally it went on to give us a new concept that allows an infinite number of additional risk premia beyond beta.

Merton leaves in place the CAPM's unrealistic assumption that all investors have the same forecasts of return and risk. However he relieves its other major restriction, that we are only interested in a single investment period. If we face multiple decision periods, we might want to consider whether in the next period we will be facing the same set of investment opportunities.

The same consideration also applies to changes in our future preferences, although Merton did not complicate his paper with this extension. For example, utility functions for investment might be altered by considering relations with future changes in wages. A variant known as the Conditional CAPM has emerged that considers the possibility that the risk tolerance for next period's beta will change.[3]

Using Merton's example of changes in investment opportunities, consider the role of long-term bonds. Their short-term return is dominated by changes in the interest rate. These changes are only partly correlated with the stock market and furthermore bear a fundamental relationship to investment opportunities more generally.

Long-term bond price increases hedge against the possibility of declines in the availability of interest from risk-free assets such as cash. Perhaps equally important, interest rates are influenced by the demand for capital for business expansion, a coincident indicator of prosperity.

If there should be a future economic depression, underlying business profit will decline and expected equity return conditional on that event would be lower than average. However, at such times, interest rates will also decline, raising long-term bond prices. Thus, if one buys a long-term bond today, one has hedged one's portfolio against a possible source of negative change in tomorrow's investment opportunities. As we know from Chapter 7, this hedge has a value that increases the bond's equilibrium price. Thus, unconditional expected returns for long-term bonds will be lower than could be justified by single-period thinking.

Let us leave Merton and do our own theorizing. Beyond the premium in return of stocks over bonds added as a group, consider differences in expected returns among stocks. A company with high long-term debt leverage will be the opposite of a recession hedge, and may carry extra expected return that cannot be fully explained by beta against the market portfolio.

Similarly, suppose a company tends to suffer disproportionately if there is economic depression because of its uncompetitive cost structure. If this sensitivity to reduced investment opportunities is not fully correlated with the risks of the market portfolio, its stock will require an additional risk premium beyond that indicated by beta. For example, the risk of bankruptcy could rise in a non-linear fashion relative to overall market conditions. We will show later the strong positive relationship between return on equity and price-to-book. Thus the return to low price-to-book may very well include a financial distress risk premium.

More, in times of lowered economic expectations, small companies will have disproportionately less access to bank loans than will have large companies.

---

[3] Ravi Jagannathan and Zhenyu Wang, "The Conditional CAPM and the Cross-Section of Expected Returns," *Journal of Finance* (1996), pp 3-54.

The market portfolio return may not be fully correlated with changes in the investment opportunity, perhaps in part because large-company stocks are propped up by arbitrage with lower interest-rate bonds. In that case, such small stocks should carry a financial risk premium.

Merton speculated that part of the observed flatness of the relationship between expected returns and beta might be the result of a long-bond factor. Note that this might happen, for example, if low price-to-book stocks had lower betas. Their higher financial risk premium could counteract their lower market beta in determining expected return.

It is not clear to me what is the practical difference between (1) a premium for shifts in general opportunities that do not perfectly correlate with market returns, and (2) priced risk that is not completely diversifiable because it is shared among a large minority of securities. These are the outcomes of Merton's ICAPM, on the one hand, and Ross's APT, to which we turn shortly, on the other. Neither can arise in the single-period CAPM and both have the same kind of symptom: additional risk premia.

Merton's paper opened the door for believing factors such as small capitalization and price-to-book receive separate risk premia that explain considerable degrees of long-term return. Beta ought not to be deprived of credit for some of this expected return. After all, the market as a whole also does respond to changing investment opportunities. And on the other side, expected return anomalies beyond beta's systematic risk may also derive from other sources, as we will later see. But Merton's argument is persuasive that there is a middle ground of risk premia beyond the market factor.

The consideration of inter-temporal risk premia offers a very practical way for active investors to approach investment problems. What was considered old-fashioned fundamental thinking now has the prestige of vanguard theory based on Ito processes. What kinds of general changes in investment opportunities and preferences does the investor have an unusual ability to withstand? For example, the investor with deep pockets may be able to ride out recessions with impunity, and so can effectively charge an insurance premium from other investors who cannot. Also, for every quantitative investor, inter-temporal risk premia should be a component of assessing fair value.

Attaching numbers to this process will be more difficult than estimating beta. Better, though, to have a rough idea of where you are headed than head in entirely the wrong direction with the wrong mental map.

For each kind of predictable variance in investment opportunity not fully reflected in the behavior of the market portfolio, there may be an additional risk premium. Since there could in principle be many such dimensions, the number of expected return factors based on risk premia unexplained by the CAPM that we may find is indeterminate. How many such factors are there? Can we determine how much influence each one has? Coming from a quite different angle, another school of thought has attempted to deal with this possibility.

ARBITRAGE PRICING THEORY

The Arbitrage Pricing Theory (APT) was originated by Ross in the late 1970s. It gained in significance with the appearance of some empirical support.[4]

Before proceeding to data, Roll and Ross noted that the residual popularity of the CAPM seemed to be based on confusion between its forecast of expected return based on beta and the observable empirical fact that most stock returns did seem to move together. That is, there was confusion between a linear model relating expected returns, which clearly did not hold, and a linear model relating observed returns to a single market factor, which did hold at least to a degree.

The CAPM proper makes no assumptions about the correlations of individual security returns. It asserts, however, that in a simple perfect market only the variability correlated with the market portfolio return will deserve a risk premium. Arbitrage between superior combinations of the market portfolio and the risk-free asset versus all other risky portfolios forces prices to line up with a linear function of the market portfolio risk. In a less simple or less perfect market this relationship does not appear to hold. For example, Merton had shown that it does not hold in multi-period models except under special conditions.

Roll and Ross supposed, instead, that observed returns for each security are linearly related to a risk-free rate plus a series of factors common to all stocks, plus an idiosyncratic specific risk term.

That is, for any short period:

$$r_i = r_f + b_{i1}F_1 + b_{i2}F_2 + \dots + b_{im}F_m + \varepsilon_i \tag{1}$$

where r is observed return for stock i, r_f is the risk-free interest rate, ε_i is the idiosyncratic risk, the various F_k are common factors that bear on every security, and the regression coefficients on these common factors are labeled factor loadings b_{ik}.

As a further simplification, suppose that the factors are uncorrelated among themselves, that is, they are orthogonal. Then very little needs to be assumed about utility functions to arrive at the conclusion that expected returns will follow the same pattern, with expected factor loadings replacing observed regression coefficients. That is, there will be a separate degree of risk aversion to each nondiversifiable independent risk.

The linearity of the return generation process plays the same role in the APT as does the linearity of risk that results from combinations of the risk-free asset and the market portfolio in the CAPM. Nothing can be said about the relative sizes of the various risk premia. If they arise through Merton's inter-temporal hedging mechanism, then the degree to which particular risks will interact with future investment opportunities or investor preferences will govern this.

The APT exercise then becomes one of, first, using statistical tools to identify factors, and, second, testing and estimating various factor premia. At this

---

[4] Richard Roll and Stephen Ross, "An Empirical Investigation of the Arbitrage Pricing Theory," *Journal of Finance* (1980), pp. 1073-1103.

point, economists meet *factor analysis*, a method developed in the "softer" academic disciplines concerned with such things as measuring intelligence and personality types from multiple test questions. Roll and Ross looked for independent factors that were priced in U.S. stocks during the 1962-1972 period. They concluded that there were from two to four, rather than the single factor predicted by the CAPM. The factors they found were purely statistical and could be described only by listing the stocks that had heavy positive or negative loadings on them.

In my 1970 dissertation at M.I.T., *Market Participant Cognitive Maps For Individual Common Stocks*, I had made heavy use of factor analyses of subjective attributes used in investment decision-making. These were extracted through psychological testing techniques from 40 investors, mostly institutional. My dissertation was written with encouragement from the Sloan School's accounting and social psychology departments with no participation by the finance department, which I then perceived as much too mathematical to be relevant. At my dissertation defense, the microeconomics and finance professors kindly let me through the gantlet. But they hardly knew what to make of factor analysis as a tool for finance. No one in either the micro-economics or the finance groups had any apparent experience with the technique, which they disdained because there was little developed statistical theory for hypothesis testing. Now ten years later the finance profession found that it needed factor analysis results for APT, but had little practical experience in working with it.

First, let me present some definitions. *Principal components* are weighted averages of individual attributes that collectively exhaust all variance in the sample. They are so constructed that each component is uncorrelated with all the others, and extracted in order of descending importance. There are the same number of principal components as there are attributes, unless some attributes are perfect linear functions of others. *Common factors* are nearly the same, but they exclude risk specific to only a single attribute (in this case, a single stock's returns). There may be only a few or no common factors. In the case of stock returns, we know empirically that there is at least one large common factor, the return of the market portfolio.

A very brief explanation of factor analysis as it applies to the APT is given in Campbell, Lo, and MacKinlay;[5] however this will not be sufficient if you are new to this technique. A better reference for the basic statistical insights would be Harman.[6]

The mechanics of factor analysis are best applied with a comprehensive statistical package such as STATA. However, here is the basic idea, together with a hint of the problems. Remember that these techniques in essence merely attempt to collapse a long list of descriptors to a more parsimonious list that can still adequately describe the original sample variation.

[5] John Y. Campbell, Andrew W. Lo, and A. Craig MacKinlay, *The Econometrics of Financial Markets* (Princeton, NJ: Princeton University Press, 1997).
[6] Harry Harman, *Modern Factor Analysis, Third Edition* (Chicago, IL: University of Chicago Press, 1976).

Consider height, weight, and age of company presidents. Suppose you measure these attributes for the companies comprising the Fortune 500. You find a strong positive correlation between height and weight, a moderate positive correlation between weight and age, and a small negative correlation between height and age. Standardize each variable by subtracting its mean and dividing through by its standard deviation. This makes the variances comparable across attributes. With these data, it is likely that a principal component analysis will find a strong component, call it "size," with positive loadings on height and weight and an indeterminate loading on age. A smaller second component may emerge, call it "lack of fitness," with a positive loading on age and a smaller positive loadings on weight and negative loading on height. The residual variance unexplained becomes the third component.

Each component has an *eigenvalue* that measures the percentage of total variance explained by the component (scaled by the number of original attributes). Principal components analysis always extracts components largest eigenvalue first. However, a subset of these components can be rotated and the total variance explained will remain the same. For example, in the case above, we may *rotate* the first two components to obtain two new ones, that together "explain" exactly the same variance. For example, we might rotate "size" so that height had a larger loading on it, and weight less. At the same time, we could alter "lack of fitness" so that weight had a larger loading on it. Together the two components could just as accurately map into their frame of reference each company president. When this is done, the first eigenvalue will be smaller than before, and the second larger than before, but their sum will be the same. Note that we also could rotate the three factors to produce a stronger eigenvalue for the third residual factor, which would be centered on age. The benefit of factor rotation may be that the factors are more concentrated on particular attributes, so we can understand them better. Or we can better get at the one component that is particularly important for some other use, such as forecasting length of tenure.

With that cryptic introduction to factor analysis, I have the following comments on the APT and the use of this technique to realize it in practice.

First comment:

It is important to remember whether one is trying to describe components of risk or trying to understand expected return. As we saw with the lack of correspondence between expected return and beta, these tasks are linked only very loosely. Although the APT makes many fewer assumptions than did the CAPM, it makes no pretense of being able to determine which risk components should be priced. Pure statistical principal component analysis of returns is remarkably effective at predicting the risk of a portfolio. It may be useless for forecasting expected return for individual securities.

One possible use for such statistically-based factor analysis is in deriving truly stock-specific residuals that may allow better forecasts of short term reversals.

Second comment:

The components or factors determined from stock returns are extremely unstable, for several reasons. Consider the problem of component or factor *rotation*. Suppose that two factors have similar eigenvalues. Very small differences in correlations from period to period can cause the particular statistical algorithm used to make very different choices in how the two factors are defined. However, together they explain almost the same variation in the new sample as the last.

Instability makes stock return factors more difficult to interpret. Two alternatives are often used.

In the first, one regresses individual stock returns against outside macro-economic disturbances, and call the regression betas loadings on these factors. This improves interpretation, but may lead to correlated factors that are neither very predictive of portfolio risk nor of individual stock expected return. Nevertheless, this approach should be investigated for active investment ideas. See, for example, Chen, Roll, and Ross,[7] which postulates economically significant factors such as responsiveness to changes in the long-short bond yield spread, in the corporate-government yield spread, inflation, and in industrial production. One can either investigate whether such factors carry long-term risk premia via the APT or use them mechanically to translate forecasts of macro-economic factors into return forecasts.

In the other, one can look to the stock characteristics that empirically are associated with differences in return from the market portfolio. These include both industry membership and such company characteristics as size, price-to-book, recent stock return momentum, and so on. This eclectic, atheoretic approach offers interpretable factors and intermediate ability to forecast portfolio return risk. It takes into account the undeniable correlations among stock returns from similar industries. It is widely used by practicing investors for both risk control and channeling particular "factor bets" into specific stock portfolios. Disadvantages include correlated factors and the strong possibility that some of the "factors" associated with long-term excess returns are coincidental attributes arrived at through widespread "data snooping." (Although I find it difficult to cite any single reference here, practicing professional investors will recognize the firm of BARRA, Inc. as a chief proponent.)

Both these alternatives offer more factor stability than does a purely statistical technique, although they may not be as useful for pure risk forecasting.

Third comment:

Because of its complexity, factor analysis still suffers from difficulties in hypothesis testing. Even very good economists instinctively reach for oversimplified statistical models to try to determine if factors are significant. Instead, I recommend using Monte Carlo simulations of random data generated in plausible ways to see how likely a "factor" results from chance. A factor analysis will always produce some apparent factors with eigenvalues greater than one.

---

[7] N. Chen, R. Roll, and S. Ross, "Economic Forces and the Stock Market," *Journal of Business* (1986), pp. 383-403.

Note that factor analysis by itself does not attempt to distinguish between random noise and true effects. In the earlier company president example, the residual third factor centered on age may be a true long-term relationship among attributes of company presidents, even though it will have a small eigenvalue. One *can* test whether an eigenvalue might have appeared by random chance given uncorrelated attributes, though not easily or with precision, but this procedure is not part of factor analysis proper.

Fourth comment:

Factor analysis will always produce a linear answer, even if the underlying relationships are non-linear. Any non-linear responses of returns to factors will be lost in the welter of apparent factors with eigenvalues too small to distinguish themselves from random ones. Similarly, factor analysis is not as effective as "cluster analysis" in discovering *hierarchical* relationships.

Consider another, primarily hierarchical, method of describing the variation in return among a long list of stocks. Extract the first market factor. Now extract a division of stocks that gives in some sense the maximum difference in return patterns between two groups of stocks. Suppose these turn out after the analysis to be interest-sensitive utilities and banks as opposed to expansion-loving stocks such oil drilling and timber. So far the procedure is not very different in result from factor analysis. Now maximally differentiate the first group, say into utilities versus banks. In parallel, maximally differentiate the second group into oil drilling and timber.

A new phenomenon now emerges. The underlying circumstances and risks that maximally differentiate members of the interest-sensitive group from one another are different from those that differentiate the members of the resource group.

Begin with the S&P500. We can construct a tree whose branches represent increasingly fragmented clusters of stocks, perhaps with General Motors and Ford, two large auto manufacturers, occupying adjacent twigs. When the tree is finished, all the variation in return will be described, just as when principal components uses as many components as there are stocks. But the nature of the description derived through hierarchical cluster analysis will be very different from that derived through factor analysis or principal components.

(In the late 1980s I once occupied 24 hours of processing time on what was then a large computer using my own special algorithm for cluster analysis on a thousand stocks' monthly returns over a ten year period. The results were fascinating and would have been very helpful to someone deciding how to organize a department of fundamental analysts.)

The point here is that both non-linear and hierarchical return structures will be largely ignored if you rely on factor analysis as your main way of understanding what is going on in the stock market.

Having said all that, the introduction of the APT opened new doors for thinking about capital asset pricing. So far as theory goes, however, the main change was a view of risk premiums enlarged to include multiple sources. The other major direction of needed progress, the removal of the CAPM's assumption that investors think the same way and have the same market access, began to gather momentum rather more slowly.

MARKET SEGMENTATION

From the beginning of the CAPM in the mid 1960s there have been those who were dissatisfied with the drastic assumption that all investors have the same expected return and risk for each security. Even a few minutes talking to real-world investors reveals that, for every well-known company, some investors think future returns will be much higher than do others. This discrepancy of the CAPM with observation creates a desire for a theory that is consistent with investor differences but still enables broad generalizations about market prices.

One of the founders of the CAPM, John Lintner, included a preliminary description of share prices when investor's judgments differ in his 1965 article in response to Sharpe.[8] This seems, however, not to have born much fruit in persuading his successors to take up the non-homogeneous judgment banner.

Bruno Solnik, writing in 1974 about the then less-central field of international investments, did better.[9] He noted that because of different exchange rate fluctuations with respect to different home currencies, investors in a world equity market living in different countries not only perceived risks as different; these risks *were* different. Clearly, at an international level the CAPM could not hold. However, for some time this seemed to be an isolated curiosity.

At this point, it will be useful to define *market segmentation*. I do so very broadly. Is not there a fundamental similarity in the effects of investor differences in home currency, in tax rates, in trading costs, in information available, and in interpretation of the same data? All of them cause two investors with the same risk preferences to have differential access to particular securities. Define market segmentation simply as any circumstance with this result, whether differences in access occur for reasons external or internal to the investor's thought process. That investors have different perceptions of expected risk and return may be considered as an example of market segmentation. Clearly all real-world markets are segmented in this sense.

In detail, it would be wise to model two investors identical in preference for return and risk as differing in their *probability* of buying the same security. That is, their individual access is a measure between zero and one. However, we are looking for first-order effects for the market as a whole. For this, it can be a useful simplification to think of large numbers of investors each having either zero or full

---

[8] John Lintner, "Security Prices, Risk, and Maximal Gains From Diversification," *Journal of Finance* (1965), pp. 587-615.

[9] Bruno H. Solnik, "An Equilibrium Model of the "International Capital Market," *Journal of Economic Theory* (1974), pp. 500-524.

access to any given security. The difference in these two views, between shades of gray for individuals versus varying fractions of on-off investors in a large population, may be ignored for our purpose in understanding aggregate equilibrium.

Let us go back to the CAPM. As Lintner pointed out, we cannot strictly ignore a stock's total risk.[10] Sharpe tended to do so, in two ways.[11] First, his formal result depends on assuming that an individual stock's weight in the market portfolio is so small that it can safely be regarded as zero. Second, he unnecessarily used examples in which returns are generated by a single underlying factor plus random noise specific to each security. I classify Fama as one of the founders of the CAPM because he makes the difference between Lintner and Sharpe clear, and in the context of a perfect market, immaterial.[12] As we will see, it becomes more significant in a real-world segmented market.

Even if we were to postulate a single factor model, which unrealistically minimizes the impact of return uncorrelated with the dominant market factor, we have more properly:

$$r_i = r_f + b_i(r_m - r_f) + \lambda(x_i)\sigma_i^2 \tag{2}$$

where

r_i = expected return on security i

r_f = risk-free interest rate

b_i = expected regression coefficient of i against the underlying market factor

r_m = expected return of the underlying market factor

λ = lambda, the cost of risk

σ_i^2 = variance of return for security i uncorrelated with the market factor

x_i = ratio of the value of security i to the value of the market.

As Sharpe pointed out, x_i would be vanishingly small in a perfect market with many securities.

Robert Merton in 1987, in his Presidential Address to the American Finance Association, illustrated the consequences for Equation 2 of assuming market segmentation.[13] His resulting paper is titled "A Simple Model of Capital Market Equilibrium with Incomplete Information." He created an elegant model of a market in which each firm's cash flows correspond to a single factor model plus specific risk. His security prices must adjust themselves so that this cash flow divided by price is an equilibrium return. The market is populated with on-off

---

[10] Lintner, "Security Prices, Risk, and Maximal Gains From Diversification."

[11] William F. Sharpe, "Capital Asset Prices: A Theory of Market Equilibrium Under Conditions of Risk," *Journal of Finance* (September 1964), pp. 425-442.

[12] Eugene F. Fama, "Risk, Return and Equilibrium: Some Clarifying Comments," *Journal of Finance* (1968), pp. 29-40.

[13] Robert C. Merton, "A Simple Model of Capital Market Equilibrium with Incomplete Information," *Journal of Finance* (1987), pp. 483-510.

investors, all with the same risk tolerance and the same wealth, each of which may have no access to some securities. His other assumptions are similar to those of the CAPM.

Under these conditions, he creates conditions under which the third term in Equation 2 can become significant. His result is equivalent to Equation 3.

$$r_i = r_f + b_i(r_m - r_f) + \lambda \left(\frac{x_i}{q_i} \right) \sigma_i^2 \tag{3}$$

where q_i is the fraction of investors who have access to security i.

Though x_i, the ratio of the firm's value to the market, may be tiny, suppose q_i, the fraction of the investor population wealth with access to it, is also small. Then the third term will be material.

Both x_i and σ_i^2 are functions of the value of the firm, which in turn is a function of q_i. Even the denominator of x_i, the aggregate value of the market, is a weak function of q_i. Consequently, the expected return is complex function of the model's parameters including q_i. However, the intuition is clear. The third term is proportional to the product of the security's specific risk and the ratio of the value of the firm to the total wealth of the investors with access to it. The fewer investors, the higher the expected return from it. It is also true that the fewer the number of investors, the lower the value of the firm.

In such a segmented market, specific risk is priced. But note that Equation 3 refers to stocks, not to their investors. The results for a Markowitz investor will depend on the degree to which investments in limited access securities are diversified. Also, Merton shows that in this model, and contrary to the CAPM, the market portfolio will not in general be efficient. Thus in a segmented market the investor with restricted access does worst, the market indexer better, and the Markowitz investor with full access best of all.

This market segmentation principle is fundamental to the success of investing through a value orientation. That in practice investors divide themselves into clienteles for different stocks provides additional benefits for those investors who participate in a wide range of stocks. The benefit is greatest for owning those stocks most neglected by others that also have high specific risks.

Merton's model is simplified to the case of a single underlying factor in firm cash flows. If the cash flows uncorrelated with the market are not independent of one another, that is, if there are multiple factors, the picture becomes yet more complicated. We can speculate on the general effect, however, by imagining that securities are subdivided into parts that pay off individually on each secondary common factor as well as on specific risk. Then the market segmentation model can be applied to each separately. For example, it may be that a large part of the investor population will not consider investing in tobacco stocks because of industry-wide problems that cut off consideration. Tobacco stocks as a class should therefore carry a premium. Within that group, there would then also be premia for each of the specific risks for particular tobacco companies.

The more segmented the market, and the higher its risks uncorrelated with the market as a whole, the greater will be the value added by over-weighting little-correlated and neglected investment opportunities. The additional risk premiums required by the system to compensate from market segmentation of otherwise diversifiable risks are exploited by the intelligent diversifier.

Note carefully how distant is this concept from the idea of additional return because of risk discomfort suffered by the investor. The burden is shifted to others in the system. In simple terms, the crowd gives up return by concentrating on popular stocks. Now come back to an example from everyday experience. If you refuse to even consider investing in companies near bankruptcy, I can exploit your distaste and obtain additional benefits for myself. If you as a US investor refuse to consider investing in Russia, I can do so and benefit. This is because Russian risks are high, mostly uncorrelated with the rest of the market, and you avoid them.

BOOK-TO-PRICE AND SMALL STOCK RETURNS

We previously surmised that the higher returns to small capitalization and low price to book confirmed by Fama and French could be partly explained by Merton's inter-temporal model of risk. But clearly they can also be partly explained by Merton's model of segmented markets. This realization pays deserved tribute to Merton, who gets credit not only for much of option theory but for two wholly separate explanations of the most obvious disconfirming evidence for the CAPM. It also links behavioral results to be presented in the next chapter directly with micro-economic models of asset pricing.

It does not require academic study to note that many people confuse good companies with good stock investments. Therefore they will not consider unsuccessful companies' stocks for their portfolios. Companies with low profitability tend to have low price to book, for good arbitrage reasons. The market segmentation model argues that such distasteful companies will receive excess returns. Note that this explanation of excess returns for low price-to-book is inherently more fragile than the inter-temporal one, which may go on so long as there is economic insecurity from business cycles. It can vanish when investors realize that they need not limit their access.

Similarly, consider the advantage to small-capitalization stocks first discovered about fifteen years ago. In Chapter 2, Exhibit 6, we saw that the power of "Factor X" to forecast stock returns in the US had declined sharply over the last fifteen years. It is now time to reveal that Factor X is actually small market capitalization, expressed in log form. One can make an argument that it would have declined somewhat because of the impact on inter-temporal risks because of a somewhat more stable business environment. However, the decline may have much more to do with increased access of small stocks to large institutional investors as trading costs have come down and more computer power has become available.

Declining market segmentation may also play a large role in explaining returns for emerging markets, a topic we will explore in a later chapter.

Note that there are two potential effects, an equilibrium return premium for high segmentation, and a transitory positive return as prices rise because of diminishing segmentation. Finally, returns subside to a level consistent with wider access.

The difference between the concept of equilibrium returns for limited access securities and the more transient world created by uneven information flow should be carefully noted. A widespread false impression of lower cash flow for a security may create limited access that enables the more diversified and thick-skinned investor to earn a premium through market segmentation effects. However, if the impression instead proves correct, the investor will suffer, because his portfolio was not on the true Markowitz efficient frontier. The key to segmentation return is limited access because of irrational or biased avoidance despite the "true" expected return and risk. Distinguishing between these two cases is typically quite challenging when no obvious barrier to investment such as taxation, trading cost or lack of data may be found. If it were not so, the natural competition in the market would likely soon discover the deception.

CRITIQUE OF RESIDUAL RISK MANAGEMENT

Seventeen years after his original CAPM contribution, Sharpe published "Decentralized Investment Management," an influential and fateful article suggesting practices for pension fund and similar organizations to use in managing their investment managers.[14] It was similar in spirit to the earlier work of Barr Rosenberg,[15] reinforced by Sharpe's faith in the efficiency of a readily identifiable efficient portfolio (the market portfolio). He argued for judging managers in terms of both the *excess return* they achieved beyond that of a benchmark, typically a market capitalization-weighted index, and *residual risk*. This risk was *not* to be the risk in excess of the benchmark risk in Markowitz terms. Instead it was the *standard deviation of the excess return*. While these risk ideas sound alike, they are totally different.

Consider the contradictory nature of the task Sharpe sets before the unfortunate active manager with true skill in forecasting. There is no reason to hire an active manager unless you believe his or her forecasts are better than the consensus expressed through the prices of the market portfolio. If so, then that manager will be able to find portfolios that have both higher return *and lower risk* than the benchmark. But Sharpe proposed not to reward the manager for lower risk, but to penalize such an effort insofar as the lower-risk active portfolio cre-

---

[14] William F. Sharpe, "Decentralized Investment Management," *Journal of Finance* (1981), pp. 217-234.

[15] Barr Rosenberg, "Institutional Investment with Multiple Portfolio Managers," *Proceedings of the Seminar on Analysis of Security Prices*, University of Chicago (1977).

ates returns that differ from the higher risk benchmark! The closest he comes to justifying this procedure is the following remark:

"In practice most clients explicitly or implicitly consider relative risk undesirable (over and above its contribution to absolute risk). In the case of a single active manager this is consistent with a belief that the manager's predictions are poorer than the manager considers them to be. This may well be a healthy attitude."

Of course, even though managers are undoubtedly overconfident, this logic does not support the relative risk practice unless one is willing to discount the manager's forecasts, not partially, but completely. Again, in that case, this is inconsistent with a need for decentralized management of active managers.

Meanwhile Barr Rosenberg founded a consulting firm that initially specialized in performance management based on his APT-like factor analysis of returns (BARRA). He recommended that "normal" portfolios be established as benchmarks centered on the manager's average style expressed in terms of return factors. This gave the manager no credit for reducing portfolio risk; it also gave no credit for the establishment of a wise normal portfolio that might take into account market segmentation effects. It prejudiced the evaluation of low-turnover value-oriented managers who were willing to invest in securities that clients would not have accessed on their own.

For a long time these practices held the high intellectual ground in discussions between large institutional clients and active investment managers. Their negative impact, however, became clearer with the increasing popularity of international investing. At one time, the EAFE capitalization-weighted index of international stocks carried over a sixty percent weight in Japanese stocks. The latter were selling at sky-high multiples as the world became convinced of the superiority of Japanese business practices. It became obvious both that the index benchmark was inefficient diversification and that managers whose normal portfolios maintained more reasonable price-to-book and price-earnings by strongly underweighting Japanese securities deserved credit.

Stung by such practices after they became prevalent in the consulting community, particularly as they applied to international investing, I wrote "EAFE is for Wimps." This article at least addressed the fallacy of overdependence on a poor benchmark.[16] I also discovered by trial and error that I could not create portfolios with lower absolute risk than the benchmark so long as I used residual risk rather than absolute risk in Markowitz mean-variance analysis. Fortunately, Richard Roll saw my work at a conference before I submitted it for publication. He politely pointed out that he had published an article that put the problem on firm theoretical ground.[17] He had established that it was impossible to generate such portfolios because the use of residual risk systematically excluded them.

---

[16] Jarrod W. Wilcox, "EAFE is for Wimps," *Journal of Portfolio Management* (Spring 1994).
[17] Richard Roll, "A Mean/Variance Analysis of Tracking Error," *Journal of Portfolio Management* (Summer 1992), pp. 13-22.

Exhibit 1: Suboptimality of Efficient Tracking Frontier (Return Based on Active Estimates)

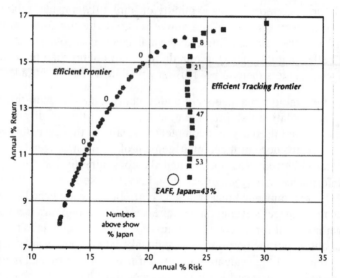

Consider a candidate portfolio of benchmark risk and highest possible return. It exists on the higher efficient frontier that results from superior active forecasts or at worst on the original passive efficient frontier. You cannot create a portfolio of equal return and lower risk without incurring residual risk penalties. Since you will not be rewarded for reducing absolute risk, this portfolio cannot dominate the first one if you are within the mean-residual variance framework. The efficient frontier that you trace between expected return and tracking error will be interior to the original efficient frontier when expressed in mean-absolute variance space. It will extend only rightward toward higher return and higher absolute risk from its starting point at the benchmark, which is the minimum residual risk position.

Exhibit 1 shows the general idea as I worked it out by trial and error under the constraints of no short sales and no leverage. Roll achieved quadratic curves based on theoretical parameters without these constraints.

In practice it is difficult to resist the continuing call by consultants for limits on residual risk versus a benchmark. Whenever a clear short-term benchmark is established, it provides an immense real-world pressure on agents to reduce residual risk. This pressure may stem from agent risk. It exists not only for investment managers but for the corporate employees and fiduciaries who administer pension funds. Underperforming a benchmark creates risk for the continued agency relationship even if it is within a pattern of reduced absolute risk for the pension fund beneficiary. In "EAFE is for Wimps" I made a modest proposal. If we want to recognize agent risk, we should put both kinds of risk in the objective function, with separate risk tolerances or lambdas for each.

That is, we should maximize a function like

$$\Phi = r - \frac{\lambda_a}{2}\sigma_a^2 - \frac{\lambda_r}{2}\sigma_r^2 \tag{4}$$

where the subscript a refers to absolute risk and r refers to relative risk or tracking error.

In practice this may be done with commercial single-risk Markowitz optimizers simply by optimizing with respect to residual risk around a benchmark that is a weighted average of cash and the true benchmark. The weight will be determined by the relative sizes of the two cost-of-risk lambdas. (This suggestion was made to me in conversation in the 1980s by Dan DiBartolomeo.) The selected portfolio may be further analyzed to determine its separate expected absolute and relative risks.

If you are an international investor, and having read this book changed only one aspect of your investing behavior, following this recommendation would be likely to have the greatest payoff for clients.

Chapter 9

Behavioral Finance

We are built to make mistakes, coded for error.
Lewis Thomas, *The Medusa and the Snail, "To Err is Human" (1979)*

The active investor may profit greatly from the investigation of human behavior. It provides a more accurate basis for understanding the market in which one operates. At least as important, it allows one to better diagnose flaws in one's own decision-making procedures.

THE MARKET AS THE SUM OF INDIVIDUAL BEHAVIOR

In 1986, The Journal of Business published a collection of papers presented at a conference titled "The Behavioral Foundations of Economic Theory."[1] Described as an opportunity for economist and psychologists to communicate, it was in essence a powerful attack on the descriptive adequacy of the von Neumann-Morgenstern utility theory. The axioms of their utility model underlie the theory of choice under uncertainty, the Markowitz model of portfolio selection, and in turn the Capital Asset Pricing Model (CAPM).

It had long been apparent that the von Neumann-Morgenstern formulation of the utility of lotteries was at best a model of how things ought to be, rather than the theory of how things are. However, economists had hoped that the deviations from it were random and the resulting aggregate useful.

This hope was at best a long-shot. It is hard to suppose that people optimize in detail even before probability enters the picture. During the 1950s, Herbert Simon modeled real world decision-making and found that people make decisions by *satisficing* rather than optimizing. That is, they search for problem solutions until they find only one or a small number of satisfactory solutions. They do not search exhaustively for the absolute best solution. However, economists could still imagine the errors made in this way to be small and offsetting, so that when aggregated across large numbers of market participants, the cumulative error might safely be ignored. Such a rationalization could explain with minimum theoretical concessions that few investors held anything like Markowitz optimum portfolios, while still clinging to the idealized picture of CAPM pricing at the market level.

---

[1] Amos Tversky and Daniel Kahneman, "Rational Choice and the Framing of Decisions," *Journal of Business* (October 1986), pp. 251-278.

What was achieved at the conference in the mid-1980s was to make it clear that financial economists could no longer ignore behavioral deviations from the optimization of *expected* utility. Strong, systematic biases arise when decision-makers confront the need for quantified judgments involving probabilities in uncertain environments. The biases generated are so universal that the law of large numbers can not be counted on for their minimization.

At the conference, the presentation likely most shocking to economists was that by Amos Tversky and Daniel Kahneman (K&T) titled "Rational Choice and the Framing of Decisions." It described experiments in which judgments reached in mathematically equivalent problems differed radically and systematically depending on how the task was presented, or *framed*. It was obvious that under normal circumstances humans do not estimate objective probabilities accurately. Worse for theory, we usually cannot even assemble a consistent personal subjective probability. The consequence is the unsettling reversal of preferences by the same person in various situations that to an economist would be equivalent.

Anyone who had been reading the psychological literature on decision-making under uncertainty would not have been surprised at this paper. It was a natural outgrowth of years of work led by K&T. Their research was originally published in the early 1970s; it was summarized in a 1982 book, *Judgment Under Uncertainty: Heuristics and Biases*, edited by Kahneman, Slovic and Tversky.[2]

In opposition, capital asset pricing models, beginning with the original CAPM, rely on a model of a market made up of participants who are perfect in their ability to calculate von Neumann-Morgenstern utilities. Some theorists had tentatively explored investor heterogeneity. But this effort did not go far. There was no logically imposed need to postulate differences in individual perception to arrive at a rational equilibrium at the aggregate market level once we assumed individual perceptions are perfect. For reasons of mathematical simplicity, the academic superstructure had thus been built on this thin reed of identical investor perceptions and perfectly rational and informed investors. Consequently, the behaviorist's attack on the ability of individuals to estimate probabilities in a way consistent with the statistical law of large numbers tends to undermine almost the whole edifice of theoretical finance.

INDIVIDUAL JUDGMENT UNDER UNCERTAINTY

K&T cite several threads of research from the 1950s that led to their work. At least one was readily available to students of business even in the 1960s when the CAPM was formulated. The 1978 Nobel Prize in economics went to Herbert Simon for his earlier work in bounded rationality. Simon emphasized empirical

---

[2] Amos Tversky and Daniel Kahneman, "Judgment Under Uncertainty: Heuristics and Biases," in Daniel Kahneman, Paul Slovic, and Amos Tversky (eds.), *Judgment Under Uncertainty: Heuristics and Biases* (Cambridge University Press, 1982).

research on human decision-making rather than mere observation of economic aggregates such as prices. He was not satisfied that he had understood a decision until he could model it by computer as an information-processing procedure. In doing so, he was forced to confront how far real decisions differ from the von Neumann-Morgenstern cum Savage model of rationality.

He found that real decisions are usually based on *heuristics* — rules of behavior or reasoning that only usually work, or that provide good approximations as opposed to exact or optimal solutions to problems. Heuristics solve simpler analogues of real problems. They are consequently easy to learn and apply by humans in complex situations. For example, classifying situations into stereotypes to which one always responds in the same way is a heuristic. "Always remain fully invested in stocks" is a heuristic. "Always diversify your portfolio so that no more than 25 percent is in one industry" is a heuristic.

In their research, K&T focused on the heuristics people use in making decisions involving numerical estimates in uncertain situations. It was already well known by the 1960s that we can not describe our behavior accurately, in part because our self-image is idealized. To discover what we actually do as decision-makers, it is necessary to set up controlled experiments and record behavioral responses. K&T and their students and colleagues devised a wide variety of experiments. They focused on three broad classes of heuristics that seem to bias numerical judgments of facts and probabilities made under conditions of uncertainty, creating substantial errors. K&T named them *representativeness*, *availability*, and *anchoring*.

Representativeness

Representativeness is essentially reasoning by stereotype. It is also revealed by the desire for a familiar story to explain events and by the expectation that a small sample should contain all the recognizable characteristics of a large sample. It causes us to ignore some of the factors that should objectively affect our assessment of probability, such as sample size and elementary logic. Here is a classic example where logic is ignored from K&T's "On the Study of Statistical Intuitions."

Subjects are given descriptions such as a following:

"Linda is 31 years old, single, outspoken, in very bright. She majored in philosophy. As a student, she was deeply concerned with issues of discrimination and social justice, and also participated in anti-nuclear demonstrations."

Then the subject is given two possible true statements:

A) "Linda is a bank teller."
B) "Linda is a bank teller who is active in the feminist movement."

Most subjects with no formal training in statistics tend to think that B) is more probable, even when cues are given that suggest that this is logically impossible.

Other experiments showed the frequent irrelevance for subjects of sample size. This is true even for experts in the field of study, if they have not been formally trained in statistics and cued to use the trained responses. For example, here is a question asked of squash players:

> "As you know, a game of squash can be played either to 9 or to 15 points. Holding all other rules of the game constant, if A is a better player than B, which scoring system will give A a better chance of winning"?

K&T reported that "Although all our informants had some knowledge of statistics, most of them said that the scoring system should not make any difference." Clearly, however, the longer game gives more opportunity to the player with the greater skill to overcome random effects that might dominate a smaller sample. Representativeness bias also tends to make subjects conclude that a preponderance of evidence within a very small sample is worth more than a slight edge within a very large sample. It makes us over-generalize profitable rules we have found in small samples of experience. With only a slight stretch in the original meaning, it can be used to account for the prevalence of conclusions drawn from trying many different rules on the experience of a small sample. This is the dreaded *data mining* (over-fitting) error.

Availability

As decision-makers, we often estimate frequency not from the total available sample but from the cases most easily remembered or most easily constructed. This bias K&T term *availability*. Here is one of their examples:

> Consider the letter *r*. Is *r* more likely to appear in
> — the first position in English word
> — the third position?

Most subjects judge the first position more frequent; the true answer is the third position. Words *beginning* with *r* are easier to retrieve from memory.

In the same way, as investors we tend to give more weight to extreme or recent events as typical, because they are most easily remembered.

Anchoring and Adjustment

Anchoring happens when we answer questions starting from an initial value, but then must make an adjustment. Usually the adjustment is inadequate. This causes logically equivalent judgments to be strongly dependent on situational framing. Here is an example given by K&T of how one can demonstrate the resulting bias.

For a group of test subjects, ask for an estimate of the number of countries in Africa. For one half the group, begin by asking whether the number is higher or lower than 75. Then ask for the actual best guess. For the other half of the subjects, ask whether the number is higher or lower than 25. Then ask for the best guess. The average response for the first group will be substantially higher than for the second group.

The anchoring effect clearly may be used in manipulative sales and negotiation tactics. It can also be seen in a surprising context in which estimates of dispersion are anchored around a central best guess. For example, suppose subjects are first asked for their estimate of the Dow Jones Industrial index of stock prices a year from now. Then they are asked to estimate a range within which they have 98% confidence the actual value will fall. The resulting range will be substantially compressed relative to the true range of experience. For example, 30 percent of the true outcomes, rather than 2 percent, may lie outside this range. This phenomenon makes subjects act as though they were overconfident of their initial forecasts.

K&T find it striking that the heuristics causing the three biases are so ingrained that they are very difficult to overcome purely based on practical experience within a particular decision arena. More rational estimation typically occurs only after formal training, and then only when there are strong cues that the problem solution should draw on the specific techniques used in that training. Even professionally trained experts often fall prey to these ingrained heuristic biases of representativeness, availability and anchoring.

Leaving Kahneman and Tversky, there are several other obvious sources of bias that are familiar to every student of psychology. We have already referred to satisficing, the tendency to stop searching after an apparently adequate perception, answer or explanation has been found. I offer two others that are extremely pervasive.

COGNITIVE DISSONANCE AND GROUP INFLUENCE

Suppose you meet and like both Joe and Dan, but then you discover that Joe and Dan dislike one another intensely and articulately. The chances are great that eventually your attitude will change to favor one and cast off the other. In the same way, it is difficult for our minds to hold any two views that cannot easily be reconciled. That is, faced with conflict, our minds unconsciously seek better balance and tend to forget or discard the least well-integrated perception or attitude. This phenomenon was labeled *cognitive dissonance reduction* by Leon Festinger.[3]

Festinger postulated that when the mind holds two contradictory views, a discomfort is produced that will tend to be relieved in one of several ways. The less important or less central view may be rejected. It may be distorted to become more consistent, even if this involves some fairly complicated invention. Finally, additional supporting facts may be gathered for the more important view. Festinger's theory has been supported in many contexts.

---

[3] Leon A. Festinger, *A Theory of Cognitive Dissonance* (Stanford, CA: Stanford University Press, 1957).

Like K&T's notion of representativeness, which I label stereotyping, cognitive dissonance reduction can operate at such low levels that we may never give the odd fact any attention, or even perceive it. Unlike stereotyping, however, cognitive dissonance reduction refers to our ability to gradually erode and re-fit well-established ideas until they mesh with our total outlook. This integration may be an essential part of mental health, but it can severely restrict our ability to learn new ways looking at things. For an investor it is especially dangerous, because it may cause us to hold onto a position long after disconfirming facts are available. It also causes us to expose ourselves too much to sources of information that confirm our pre-existing ideas. And it causes us to believe that good companies have good stocks, whereas the reverse is at least as often true.

John Donne wrote "No man is an island." It is certainly true that most of us belong to groups — a family, workgroup, friends. These groups have attitudes, norms, language and opinions that have a powerful impact on our thoughts. In 1936, M. Sherif described a series of classic experiments on the formation of influential group norms that had no basis in fact.[4]

Sherif took advantage of a perceptual illusion called the autokinetic effect. One perceives a stationary dot of light in an otherwise dark room to be moving. Sherif asked subjects to orally estimate the distance the light moved when they were alone and when in groups. Individuals making judgments by themselves established their own average estimates, varying from 1 to 10 inches. When later judgments were made in groups of three subjects, personal estimates converged until a consensus was reached. After several sessions, subjects accepted a standard estimate in place of their own judgments. In subsequent individual sessions, subjects still were influenced by that group norm.

Group opinion is extremely persuasive, not only in the everyday world, but in the world of investing. One of the highlights of my experience as an investor has been in watching a group of senior investment people trying to reach consensus on new investment ideas. Irony occurs when a firm priding itself on its contrarian investment strategies attempts such an exercise. Even though achieving an unusual and contrary viewpoint is a near logical impossibility in such a committee context, the group can not resist trying for agreement. When finally a candidate idea is adapted to make agreement possible, the group may recognize its lack of originality and resolve to try harder the next time.

In a way, group influence is like cognitive dissonance reduction, but on a larger scale. Individuals feel the need to agree with the group — and if they do not, they are often rejected or diminished in status. This may be a useful mechanism in a group deciding the best way to build a bridge. But it may squeeze out any profitable ideas in a competitive market. Being precisely right in one's estimate of fundamentals is usually not as important as being only approximately right about something the market is not expecting.

---

[4] M. Sherif, *The Psychology of Social Norms* (New York: Harper and Row, 1936).

APPLYING THE PRINCIPLES OF BEHAVIORAL FINANCE

I take the principles of behavioral finance to be the exploitation and avoidance of representativeness, availability, anchoring, satisficing, cognitive dissonance reduction and group influence. If we do not learn them, we are at the mercy of the unconscious heuristics our species has evolved over hundreds of thousands of years before stock markets became part of our environment. If we do not learn them, we are at the mercy of the unconscious heuristics our species has evolved over hundreds of thousands of years before stock markets became part of our environment. If we do not learn them, we are at the mercy of the unconscious heuristics our species has evolved over hundreds of thousands of years before stock markets became part of our environment.

K&T noted the extreme slowness with which decision-makers learn on their own to overcome biases in making numerical judgments under uncertainty. When it comes to investing, it is not so surprising that people are even slower to learn. First, the stock market is even more different than are K&T's test situations from the environment in which our heuristic behaviors have evolved. Cause and effect are hidden in a world so competitive that most of what one believes is already in the price of the stock and so is useless for prediction. Second, since the market is relatively efficient, any investment rule that does not rapidly cause bankruptcy is likely to achieve results indistinguishable to the naked eye from any other. Thus, buying stocks that have recently split two for one gives results similar to buying stocks whose presidents have graduated from the Harvard Business School. For that matter, results are similar when buying stocks whose names begin with the letter "*S.*"

It is true that some learning occurs, and in the very long run, those with better investment strategies tend to survive and to prosper at a greater rate. However, this is rather offset by turnover within the investor pool and by the fact that most investors' income from owning stocks is secondary to their employment or business income.

This does not mean that one cannot benefit from training in this regard. Here are some suggestions:

Representativeness – Each investment opportunity has some elements that are different from precedent. This is why we need risk control.

Availability – Quantify as rigorously as the data will allow. For example, assemble similar instances and use statistical techniques. Do not assume recent events will continue.

Anchoring — Again, quantify. Remember that major change is likely to be underestimated, and the range of possibilities is larger than you think.

Satisficing — Search longer and harder for better explanations, better econometrics in model building, faster execution of ideas and so on. Most investors give up before pushing themselves to the limit of their capability.

Dissonance reduction — Sometimes it is more important to hang onto a discordant fact than to construct a coherent theory. Learn to live with ambiguity. Do not discard data that does not fit your hypothesis.

Group influence — Anchoring merely sets up the potential for trends; group influence greatly amplifies it. If most of what *you* know is already in the market price, the same is true in greater measure for the group consensus.

You can also use a knowledge of behavioral finance to exploit the mistakes of others. Some biases are so endemic that the only way they can be kept in check is through the development of opposing professional cynics. These are investors who make their living by exploiting the inadequate heuristics of others. The difficulty which the average actively-managed mutual fund has in beating index funds suggests one of two things. Either there is a plentiful supply of such cynics or most such experts are insufficiently skilled in spotting biases, both their own and those of others. As an active investor, I tend to subscribe to the latter thesis.

In any event, it would appear that assessing particular types of market opportunities for the biases they exploit and for the likely competition among non-consensual thinkers and implementers is a critical skill for active investing. While many so-called market anomalies may be traced to risk premia, it is likely that many more are simply mistakes in information processing. They reappear whenever the core of skilled active investors flags in its efforts, or when the market is confronted with novel situations.

One area where risk premia cannot be offered as an explanation is that of autocorrelation of returns. In many time periods and across many foreign markets, we see a pattern of short-term reversals, intermediate-term momentum or trend, and very long-term reversals. Academics have tended to focus least on the short-term reversals, ascribing them rather casually to bid-ask spreads. My hypothesis, stemming from behavioral finance, is as follows. Short-term reversals occur because anchoring in terms of value brings in supply or demand in reaction to price movement from a small group of very attentive players. This anchoring also sets up the conditions for a trend when there is substantial new information. Group influences (or their imitative equivalent) amplify the attraction of new players that results in exaggerated trends. Finally, longer-term reversals take place when price action departs far enough from underlying economic reality or when the supply of momentum players is exhausted.

Good empirical studies on momentum and reversal are reported by DeBondt and Thaler[5] and by Chan, Jegadeesh and Lakonishok.[6] The DeBondt and Thaler study also explores the so-called January effect, the excess returns of prior losers and small stocks in January, within this context. The Chan *et al.* study shows that stock analyst earnings estimate revisions also have had predictive value based on momentum.

Event studies of the rapidity with which certain very concrete announcements are incorporated in stock prices are briefly described in Fama[7] and in the

---

[5] Werner DeBondt and Richard Thaler, "Further Evidence on Investor Overreaction and Stock Market Seasonality," *Journal of Finance* (1987), pp. 557-581.
[6] Louis Chan, Narasimhan Jegadeesh, and Josef Lakonishok, "Momentum Strategies," *Journal of Finance* (1996), pp. 1681-1713.
[7] Eugene F. Fama, "Efficient Capital Markets: II," *Journal of Finance* (1991), pp. 1575-1617.

econometrics book by Campbell, Lo and MacKinlay.[8] Some of these show a high degree of market efficiency. In other cases there is evidence of momentum that could be interpreted simply as lack of availability of information but equally well as anchoring-induced slowness in changing minds based on readily available information.

What about our other bias-causing heuristics? One of the most striking features of the stock market is the wide disparity of opinions held by investors. Rather than integrate knowledge into a consensus worldview, each investor specializes in a particular nexus of ideas and facts. It seems likely that the phenomena of availability and cognitive dissonance reduction initiate this specialization, which may be further reinforced by group interaction with like-minded individuals. However, the degree of heterogeneity even within small groups can be surprising. My personal experience within the Boston investment community is that of the coexistence of very different viewpoints and methods of information-processing. These exist among people who frequently eat lunch together and even among those at the same investment firm. Of course, I may have been sensitized to such differences by my own research, performed decades earlier at a time when there was almost no audience for behavioral modeling of investors.

A METHOD OF MEASURING DECISION ASSUMPTIONS

My Ph.D. dissertation (Massachusetts Institute of Technology, 1970) was titled "Market Participant Cognitive Maps for Individual Common Stocks." In 1972, the MIT Press was kind enough to publish a reworked version as a monograph, *A Method for Measuring Decision Assumptions*.[9] I think it was kindness, because the book only sold about 1200 copies. What I had done in that book was very far from the CAPM. It was very far from anything in finance, except for work by Geoffrey Clarkson,[10] who had used the Simon approach of computer modeling of heuristic rules, and by Paul Slovic.[11]

Clarkson had spent a great deal of time modeling a single decision-maker. My objective was to capture a substantial part of an investor's decision-making process, and, like Clarkson, to do so in a way that would reflect how decisions were actually made. However, I wanted a method that depended even less on the ideas used by the measurer, and that would be more useful in the rough and tumble of real organizations. I worked with forty investors, mostly institutional, and achieved an average R-squared of about 30% in forecasting their stock ratings by a procedure that took about four hours of each investor's time. Most of the attention was spent on getting the investor's subjective stock attributes right.

---

[8] John Y. Campbell, Andrew W. Lo, and A. Craig MacKinlay, *The Econometrics of Financial Markets* (Princeton, NJ: Princeton University Press, 1997).

[9] Jarrod Wilcox, *A Method for Measuring Decision Assumptions* (Cambridge, MA: MIT Press, 1972).

[10] Geoffrey Clarkson, *Portfolio Selection: A Simulation of Trust Investment* (Englewood Cliffs, NJ: Prentice-Hall (1962).

[11] Paul Slovic, "Analyzing the Expert Judge: A Descriptive Study of a Stockbroker's Decision Process," *Journal of Applied Psychology* (1969), pp. 255-263.

From today's perspective, I would improve the design of the experiment and the subsequent analysis in many ways. I will describe the part of my approach that still seems fresh, and that could be most helpful to you if you wish to model your decision-making. My other purpose is to give credibility to my main finding, that of great variety in approach by different investors.

The general attack begins with a technique used by some cognitive psychologists called the Role Repertory Test to elicit relevant stock attributes. It then goes on through factor analysis to produce simple multiple regression models that could be validated with fresh samples.

The Role Repertory Test works as follows. First you prepare a list of varied roles; I used 20 roles. Here are some examples:

1. The stock in which you first made a substantial profit
2. The stock in which you first took a substantial loss
3. Your present favorite stock
4. The stock you most dislike

...

10. A stock you like which a friend doesn't like
11. A stock you know little about

...

20. A stock which you should have waited longer to buy.

These role labels are written ahead of time on 20 index cards, each given a number. The subject is first asked to write on each card the name of a stock that fits the role. Then the cards are presented in triads, chosen ahead of time to provide a good mix of comparisons. I used 20 triads. A voice recorder is then turned on and the interview begun. The triads are presented one at a time. For each, the subject is first asked to group the stocks into the two that are most similar and the one that is most different, using attributes that would be relevant in the subject's decision-making.

The researcher then retires and listens to the tape-recording, and prepares for the subject a form that listed the labels the subject used for attributes. Here is an example:

Subject No. 37, May 20, 1969, a security analyst, sorting Falstaff Brewing, Needham Packing, and Digital Equipment:

Subject: "In a vague way you can organize these according to their business, again, Falstaff Brewing and Needham Packing both being in segments of the food industry, Digital Equipment involved in computer applications. The — I would look next at management, and because Digital is one I'm not close to, I can't evaluate their management. Falstaff, again, is weak here, and Needham is new and untested, operating — it's a company that has a concept and is trying to develop it. I don't think these fall together very neatly in any respect...."

Exhibit 1: Sample Post Interviewing Notes:

food industry	computer applications
weak management	not so
new untested management	not so
has a concept, trying to develop it	not so
slow market growth	rapid market growth

Exhibit 2: A Sample Response To Questionnaire

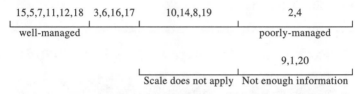

Researcher: "How would that affect your attitude toward a stock to know it was, let's say, computer versus food?"

Subject: "Again, to answer that I would try to quantify the growth rate, the growth potential of their industries, and I know that the computer — that the segment of the computer business that Digital is in — has a very rapid growing potential, as opposed to the brewing industry, which is perhaps 12 percent to 15 percent a year, and the meat packing business, which *could be* in the 15 percent range also, which Needham's concepts proved realistic. So the answer is — you would think that if, all things being equal, that Digital would have a greater potential, but on the other side if they don't — if they're not a quality management and so on, there could be much greater risk as well."

Exhibit 1 summarizes this material into five potentially useful attributes. This is done for each triad for which new attributes emerged. Perhaps days later, the subject fills out a questionnaire in which each of these attributes can be turned into a scale. The subject listed the role numbers of the original stocks in as many categories within the attribute as he or she cares to. The vertical lines between categories shown in Exhibit 2 were drawn by a subject, allowing him to specify a number of gradations comfortable to him. (The example is for a different subject than the one reported in the tape transcription.)

Each stock's position on the ordinal scale is coded as though it were a cardinal number. Then the scales are factor analyzed. This accomplishes two things. First, although the individual scales possess a mix more of ranking than distance information, the linear combination of several such scales in a factor score produces a rating that has more cardinal (distance) information. This is similar in principle to MDS, Multimensional Scaling, a multivariate statistical technique that uses ordinal distance rankings to produce a numeric metric. Second, factor analysis greatly reduces the number of potential explanatory variables. A Monte Carlo simulation may be used to produce empirical eigenvalue cutoffs for significant factors. Thus, ratings on 20 stocks on perhaps 30 attributes can often be condensed to three or four factors. (See Exhibit 3 for examples.) The transformation matrix to produce the factor scores can be used to convert attribute descriptions of fresh stock observations on new stocks to measures on the same scales. These can be regressed against a dependent variable. I used a rating of twenty possible gradations obtained from the subject as to whether the stock is suitable or unsuitable for one's portfolio.

Exhibit 3: Examples of Attribute Factors Used To Judge Stocks

Investor Type	Factor Loading	Antithesis	Thesis
7. Professional	0.72	large capitalization	small capitalization
Trader (likes Thesis)	0.81	high volume	low volume
	0.72	not likely to ever be in or out of vogue	subject to sharp changes depending on whether in or out of vogue
15. Mutual Fund			
Investor First Factor	0.89	variable growth	steady growth
(likes Antithesis)	0.71	speculative	not speculative
	0.91	unpredictable	predictable
Second Factor	0.71	unfavorable stock performers over last 5 years	favorable stock performers over last 5 years
(likes Thesis)	0.85	not well managed for its industry	very well managed for its industry
	0.74	poor historical growth record	good historical growth record
19. Individual			
Investor First Factor	0.74	serves declining market	serves rapidly growing market
(likes Thesis)			
	0.73	not sophisticated in the use of financial instruments	sophisticated
	0.87	growth record is poor	growth record is good
	0.84	management not very capable	has very capable management
	0.88	far behind competitors	moves into innovations ahead of competitors
Second Factor	0.97	stock has recently been falling more in down markets and rising less in up markets than others in its group	stock has recently been falling less in down markets and rising more in up markets
(likes Thesis)	0.93	stock has fallen rapidly in last six months	stock has risen rapidly in last six months
22. Individual Investor			
First Factor	0.78	not so	considerable institutional participation
(likes Thesis)	0.84	thin market	has broad ownership

Exhibit 3 (Continued)

Investor Type	Factor Loading	Antithesis	Thesis
Second Factor (likes Thesis)	0.76	long-term technical demand is worsening	long-term technical demand is improving
	0.76	short-term technical demand is worsening	short-term technical demand is improving
	0.82	stock price has recently moved down by a large percentage	stock price has recently moved up by a large percentage
26. Trust Officer First Factor (likes Thesis)	0.80	not so	glamour growth stock
	0.85	has been an unexceptional stock performer	has been an exceptional stock performer
	0.80	a former market favorite which has fallen out of grace	not so
	0.74	low P/E	high P/E
	0.78	not so	a management play, management has demonstrated ability to grow
	0.80	way down from all-time highs	near all-time highs
Second Factor (likes Thesis)	0.93	little potential for very high growth rate	high potential for very high growth rate
	0.76	earnings stalled	earnings growing rapidly
28. Trust Officer First Factor (likes Thesis)	0.76	stock extremely volatile	stock not volatile
	0.77	management incapable	capable management
	0.86	questionable management	honest management
	0.79	short history	long history

In my study I gathered two additional samples in this way, a modeling sample and a validation sample. Today I would have attempted to collect data on many more stocks to get models that were based on larger samples than my groups of twenty. On the other hand, many fundamental investors do not know larger numbers of stocks well.

As time went on after 1972, there was no call for my diligence in measuring decision attributes, but I have never forgotten the most important and incontrovertible lesson. Investors are not homogeneous. Again, Exhibit 3 gives a limited sample of significant factors for investors whose models were strongly validated, with r-squared's on the order of 0.5 to 0.7. Each factor is represented by its loadings on the attributes used to define it.

This is a small sample of the types of attributes used. Overall, there are elements of each of the factors present in the investment literature, but their distribution across investors is a mosaic. What I found in 1969 was highly tilted in favor of growth and momentum, reflecting the biases described in this chapter. These information processing styles created great opportunity for value investors then. This opportunity may exist in different quantities today.

WHITHER INVESTMENT THEORY?

If individual decision-makers are imperfect, it is still possible to cause them to interact in such a way that their aggregate comprises an efficient market. After all, this is the essence of Adam Smith's theory that sufficient competition can produce a perfect market.

To draw an analogy from elementary physics: the relationships among pressure, density and temperature of gases in containers can be understood (Boyle's Law) without modeling the course of action of each individual gas molecule. Attempting to model a financial market by extrapolating the properties of individual investors is similar to attempting to model a hot air balloon the hard way, molecule by molecule.

I am not familiar with any good arguments why equilibrium finance cannot be reconstructed to deal with heterogeneity and bounded rationality of individual investors. What is needed is a model of restoring forces that permit the development of investor sub-populations. The growth in activity by sub-populations will exploit any imperfections until market efficiency is restored up to a limit imposed by well-defined measurement and transaction costs. This seems to me a task well within modern mathematical and conceptual capabilities, once the bottleneck is truly identified within the finance profession.

It may turn out that still more useful models may be obtained by characterizing specific archetypes of investor policies interacting with one another in the presence of real economic disturbances. We took first steps toward such a model in Chapter 4. The Santa Fe experiments described in Chapter 3 represent a more comprehensive approach. The non-linear complexity of such market models requires computer simulation to analyze thoroughly. In a formal sense, such models can only produce what we put into them, as in any logical deduction. However, in practice the unpredictability assured by the complex interaction of quasi-random elements constitutes opportunities for inductive reasoning. This may be done in artificial worlds of staged degrees of complexity. It will be, then, an open *empirical* question whether investors employing von Neumann-Morgenstern estimated utilities or even Markowitz optimal portfolio selection will survive in and dominate such environments. Equilibria and relatively efficient markets will likely emerge with or without this utility construct.

Chapter 10

Trading Costs and Taxes

*Many have dreamed up republics and principalities that
have never in truth been known to exist; the gulf between
how one should live and how one does live is so wide that
a man who neglects what is actually done for what should
be done learns the way to self-destruction rather than self-
preservation.*
Niccolò Machiavelli, *The Prince (1514)*

Trading costs and taxes are frictions. In a world of competitive investors they are
traps for idealists and opportunities for realists.

Average active returns appear to be near zero. That is to be expected if
active investors are in equilibrium. As a first-order approximation, then, trading
costs must be on the same order of magnitude as average return forecasting ability. At the margin, understanding how to manage trading costs may be of equal
importance to understanding how to add value through better return forecasts.

Taxes are another source of friction, another wedge between idealized
market positions and the real value of holdings. Like trading costs, capital gains
taxes are levied only at the point of sale, the timing of which is up to the owner.
Unlike trading costs, capital gains tax effects can be either positive or negative. If
prices go down, it will be to the advantage of the investor to sell and realize the
loss in order to gain a tax benefit. If prices go up, the owner has an incentive to
hold the stock in order to defer the tax. Attention to managing after-tax returns
can have a material impact on long-term results.

TRADING COST ENVIRONMENT

Trading costs come in layers, like onions, with each additional layer providing further damage to performance. Institutionalized trading helps buyers and sellers to
connect with one another more efficiently. If one trades through brokers at the New
York Stock Exchange, the first layer of cost is *brokerage commission*, which covers most of the mechanics of order processing, and any *transaction taxes*. The next
layer is half the *bid-ask spread*, the difference between the highest price bid for a
purchase and the lowest price asked for a sale. The bid-ask spread reflects both the
cost of inventory for specialists who tie up capital in providing liquidity and the
adverse selection effect. The latter arises because the reactive side of the trade
must charge against the possibility that the buyer or seller initiating the trade truly
has information about which way the price is going to go in the future.

For larger trades, prices will likely be executed outside the original bid-ask spread. That is, the spread will be pushed up or down until new buyers or sellers are drawn into play. This creates a layer of *market impact* transaction costs. An extension of this layer, less visible, comes when one includes the *opportunity costs* from not executing trades because transaction pressure has driven prices to the point where the trade no longer makes sense. Andre Perold coined the term *implementation shortfall* to include all the layers of the trading cost to this point.[1] Implementation shortfall can be measured by summing (1) commissions and taxes, (2) the difference between the price actually paid and the price when the initial decision to trade took place, adjusted for total market movement, and (3) opportunity cost for trades not completed. The latter is measured as the difference between the price after some pre-determined interval, perhaps several weeks, adjusted for overall market movement and the price at the point of the original decision to trade. This kind of trading cost is subject to a great deal of random variation, and is reasonably accurate only when conducted over a fairly large sample, say 100 or more similar trades.

There is even a further layer of trading costs that can be assessed by running a paper portfolio with very frequent (for example, daily) trading in contrast to a real portfolio. This more inclusive difference in return I label *performance drag*.[2] This concept includes not only implementation shortfall on the trades intended but the additional loss of return that occurs because trades are self-censored. That is, there are profits to be gained from potential transactions, but since they do not exceed trading costs the transactions are never initiated. In moving from real trading to a paper portfolio, trading costs are reduced, more trades become profitable, turnover increases, and the potential for active return goes up.

Implementation shortfall trading costs are influenced by many factors; they show strong differences by type of security and by the size and technology of the market within which trades take place. Costs range from several basis points (hundredths of a percent) for very liquid futures to perhaps 25-75 basis points for typical institutional trades to 2%, 4%, or higher for less liquid stocks, particularly very small stocks or those in emerging markets.

TRADING COST AND MARKET STRUCTURE

Trading costs affect market structure. For example, they encourage market segmentation, with the consequences we noted in Chapter 6. Most obvious among these are domestic versus foreign barriers. There is also some segmentation by size. For example, large institutions with active investment strategies find it challenging to invest in the smallest companies because of illiquidity with respect to large purchases.

---

[1] Andre F. Perold, "The Implementation Shortfall: Paper versus Reality," *Journal of Portfolio Management* (April 1988).

[2] Jarrod Wilcox, "The Effect of Transaction Costs and Delay on Performance Drag," *Financial Analysts Journal* (March/April 1993), pp 45-54, p.77.

Trading costs help encourage the formation of intermediary mutual funds, and especially index funds. Trading costs provide economies of scale to specialist firms who can afford to carefully manage the process.

Trading costs create illiquidity risk, and thus increase required return. This is likely part of the reason for the higher expected returns observed in the past for small-capitalization stocks, and still observable for *very* small capitalization stocks.

High trading costs prevent the exercise of certain high-turnover strategies and thus impede the flow of information to the marketplace. Reduced trading costs accelerate the flow of information into portfolios. We see this effect, for example, as more efficient trading technology and more liquid markets have helped make attractive strategies based on short-term inefficiencies created by momentum in changes in analyst earnings estimates.

REDUCING IMPLEMENTATION SHORTFALL

There have been a number of professional journal articles intended to help institutional investors organize the effort to reduce trading costs.[3] The emphasis is on the trade once it has been initiated, and on measurement as a first step to control.

In practice, effective trading is a craft-oriented rather than theoretical topic. There are decisions as to whether it is better to be a patient trader, with tight price limits, or to trade promptly at market prices. Should one use public advertising and competitive bids, or conceal the trade activity as much as possible? Should one trade through open outcry, through a specialist, or through an electronic mechanism that allows more complex price limit rules? Such questions have no single right answer for every type of trade.

There are basic normative rules of thumb, though I would not elevate them to theory:

1. Take into account average daily volume before you trade. Once small fixed costs are covered, trading costs are a rising function of the size of the trade relative to recent average daily volume.
2. Trade in the most efficient markets at the times they are most liquid. Experiment with electronic trading exchanges. The old-style mechanisms still do not take account of the possibilities offered by the computer for coordinating orders across different securities, and may possibly afford conventional specialists too easy profit.
3. Use patient, public methods if you are a passive investor. Use faster, more secret methods if you are a momentum investor.
4. Use low-trading-cost futures covering many securities where they can be substituted for individual "physical" securities.

---

[3] For an example, see B.M. Collins and F.J. Fabozzi, "A Method for Measuring Trading Costs," *Financial Analysts Journal* (March/April 1991).

5. Do not leave a large limit order in the marketplace over a long period; you provide a safety net (a free option) for traders who wish to front-run you by taking the same side at a slightly more generous price, and who will push the price just out of your reach.
6. Use order substitution if it fits your investment style — that is, order several similar stocks with tight price limits, and cancel the unfilled orders as soon as you succeed on a substitute security. (This idea of order substitution is from Evan Schulman, founder of Lattice Trading.)[4]
7. Do not cultivate a reputation as a clever trader; you will pay for it as counterparties charge you extra for presumed adverse selection effects.
8. Finally, feed back detailed information about trading costs to your portfolio construction process.

MINIMIZING PERFORMANCE DRAG

There is one part of trading cost reduction that cannot be left to traders — the prevention of trading costs by proper matching of intended portfolio turnover to the problem. This can be regarded as minimizing performance drag. When trading is for rebalancing to maintain desired portfolio proportions, there are theoretical studies based on Ito calculus as to the proper kind of least-cost policy. These take the form of threshold asset proportion ranges within which trades are not worth doing, together with a rule that causes rebalancing back to the outer limit of the range. Such rules are slightly impractical because they do not take into account the fixed costs of trading, treating trading costs as proportional to trade size. (When more realism is added, one would reduce the number of very small trades by trading back to well within the asset proportion range.)[5]

The problem of substituting one actively-selected security for another is both more interesting and harder than mere passive rebalancing of asset proportions for risk control purposes. To make it clearer without complication, and without stochastic calculus, I will both disregard the total portfolio and use a simplified, deterministic model of active return.

The following mathematics, although unpretentious, may require some study. In return, you will receive a clear understanding of the nature of the answer to the circular question posed in an earlier chapter. That is, the solution to Markowitz optimization depends on the holding period over which trading costs may be amortized. That holding period depends on the solution to the Markowitz optimization. How do we break the loop? We do it, to a first approximation, as follows.

Active return R_t is assumed to start at some initial value A_o for each holding, and to decline exponentially with time as e^{-kt} since initiating a holding, where

---

[4] I learned this from Evan Schulman while we were both at Batterymarch Financial Management.
[5] See Michael Magill and George M. Constantinides, "Portfolio Selection with Transaction Costs," *Journal of Economic Theory* (1976), pp. 245-263.

k is the exponential rate of decay and t is time since purchase. We assume that there is a steady supply of equivalent replacements. What is the optimum holding period H and what is the minimum performance drag D? How do these depend on round-trip transaction cost (C), initial rate of active return (A_o), and its time rate of decay (k)? We will determine these by maximizing average rate of return (R_a).

We have by definition

$$R_t = A_o e^{-kt} \tag{1}$$

Exhibit 1 shows an example of such a process, punctuated by repeated transactions.

In this exhibit, the initial alpha A_o is set at 0.1, k at 4, and C at 0.01. In a year, the value added is about 2.2%. This picture might be appropriate for a very high turnover strategy focused on earnings estimate revisions. In this case, the holding period has been set at 0.2 year, but as we will see, for these parameters the optimum holding period is about 0.35 year. Exhibit 1 thus shows positive active value added that could be somewhat improved by lengthening the holding period.

By elementary calculus,[6] and remembering to subtract the trading cost, the relative value of the holding after one holding period H will be:

$$e^{R_a H} = (1 - C)e^{\frac{A_o}{k}(1 - e^{-kH})} \tag{2}$$

Exhibit 1: Five Successive Trades

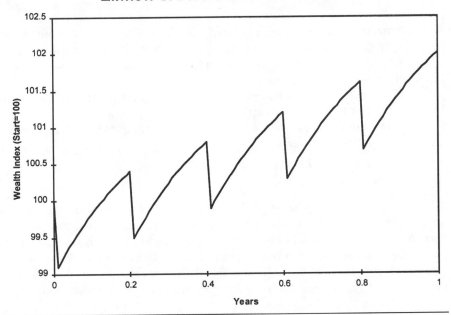

---

[6] The kind found in George B. Thomas Jr. and Ross L. Finney, *Calculus and Analytic Geometry,* 9th ed. (New York: Addison-Wesley, 1996).

Therefore, the average return is found by taking the natural log of both sides and dividing by the holding period.

$$R_a = \frac{\ln(1 - C)}{H} + \left(\frac{A_o}{kH}\right)(1 - e^{-kH})$$ (3)

To determine the H which gives the maximum average return, take the derivative of the right-hand side with respect to H, and set it to zero. This gives the following equation, after some rearrangement of expressions.

$$\frac{1 + kH}{e^{kH}} = \frac{\ln(1 - C)}{(A_o/k)}$$ (4)

While the value of kH, the allowable decay in active return, and therefore of H, is not immediately calculated from this formula, it can be readily derived by iteration. First, though, let us simplify the right-hand side by defining Q, the *implementation difficulty* of the trade.

Define:

$$Q = -\frac{\ln(1 - C)}{(A_o/k)}$$ (5)

This simplifies the notation to:

$$\frac{1 + kH}{e^{kH}} = 1 - Q$$ (6)

As implementation difficulty approaches 1 from below, the value of optimum H goes to infinity. That is, the trade should never take place if Q is 1 or greater. This will be found to be the case when equation (3) indicates a zero or lower average active return after transaction costs.

The value of kH can be determined by using the hill-climbing facility in Excel, or through the following iterative procedure.

Set an initial guess for kH at $\sqrt{2Q}$. Then iterate provisional guesses for kH using the following scheme:

$$kH_n = \ln\left[\frac{(1 + kH_{n-1})}{(1 - Q)}\right]$$ (7)

When there is no further change, divide the answer by k to determine the optimal holding period H. The answer for typical institutional equity investing strategies may vary from a month or two for some rapid-decay earnings estimate momentum strategies to five years or more for a slow decay value strategy with high trading costs.

Once optimal holding period is calculated you can calculate the minimum performance drag, the loss relative to a paper portfolio with no trading costs.

Define:

$$D = A_o - R_a$$ (8)

Exhibit 2: Calculating Optimal Holding Period and Average Return

		Momentum			Value		
Trading Cost C		0.010	0.020	0.024	0.010	0.020	0.030
Initial Alpha A_O		0.100	0.100	0.100	0.045	0.045	0.045
Time Decay k		4.0	4.0	4.0	0.5	0.5	0.5
Implementation Difficulty Q		0.40	0.81	0.97	0.11	0.22	0.34
Initial Seed for kH		0.90	1.27	1.39	0.47	0.67	0.82
Iterations for kH	1	1.15	2.47	4.44	0.51	0.77	1.01
	2	1.28	2.90	5.26	0.53	0.82	1.11
	3	1.34	3.01	5.40	0.54	0.85	1.16
	4	1.36	3.04	5.42	0.55	0.87	1.18
	5	1.37	3.05	5.42	0.56	0.88	1.19
	6	1.38	3.05	5.43	0.56	0.89	1.20
	7	1.38	3.05	5.43	0.56	0.89	1.20
	8	1.38	3.05	5.43	0.57	0.89	1.20
	9	1.38	3.05	5.43	0.57	0.89	1.20
	10	1.38	3.05	5.43	0.57	0.89	1.20
Estimated Optimal Holding Period H		0.35	0.76	1.36	1.13	1.78	2.41
Optimal Avg. Return R_a		0.025	0.005	0.000	0.025	0.018	0.014
Performance Drag D		0.075	0.095	0.100	0.020	0.027	0.031

Minimum performance drag can be calculated using equations (8) and (3) once optimum holding period is determined. It has been shown that the minimum performance drag is always greater than twice the optimum average trading cost per time period, usually far greater.[7] Thus, reductions in trading cost per trade, the implementation shortfall, can have a striking impact on reducing performance drag and increasing realized return. The greatest benefits in terms of reduced ratio of D to A_O will be for strategies with rapid rates of active return decay after trade initiation, or high k, such as those based on revisions in analysts' earning estimates.

Exhibit 2 carries out all these calculations for the example in Exhibit 1, as well as for several other combinations of trading cost, initial value added, and rate of time decay.

In Exhibit 2 the three left-most examples might be for a "momentum" process exploiting estimate revisions, with an initially high, but rapidly decaying, value added. If the trading cost is higher than about 2.4%, the optimal holding period explodes and the average return goes to zero. In the 1% trading cost case (0.5% one-way), turnover is (1/0.35) or 286%. There is a very large remaining performance drag that might be exploited if cheaper trading methods could be found. On the other hand, the "value" process shown in the three right-hand columns has much lower initial returns, but its value-added decays relatively slowly over time. It is much less sensitive to increases in trading costs. Note that it pro-

---

[7] Wilcox, "The Effect of Transaction Costs and Delay on Performance Drag."

vides material value-added even when round-trip trading costs are as high as 3%. It is much slower in terms of annual turnover, about (1/1.13) or 88% in the 1% trading cost case, and only 41% in the 3% round-trip trading cost case.

As a further step within this framework, you can also easily estimate the impact of time delay on the trading process.[8] The resulting loss of active return from delay causes obvious injury, in part through the further lengthening of the optimum holding period *subsequent* to the initial delay because of lower initial alpha. Momentum-type strategies (with fast decay rates) suffer far more from delay than value-type strategies.

Once you work out for yourself how sensitive average value-added return is to trading costs and time delay, your attitude toward the importance of managing trading will be forever altered. Many investment organizations appear to devote far less management attention to this function than it deserves based on its potential for improving performance. Remember, the benefit to reducing trading costs cannot simply be estimated on current turnover. As trading costs decline, optimal holding periods shorten, turnover increases, and more value added can be captured.

THE TAX ENVIRONMENT

Taxes are much like trading costs — they get in the way of active strategies. Unlike trading costs, comprehensive treatment of taxes is an immense task. Multiple government bodies may levy taxes on the same transaction. These taxes may be at different rates for different entities: individuals, personal holding companies, and insurance companies, for example. Taxes differ by types of income such as dividends, capital gains, and inheritance. Taxes differ by type of security. Domestic versus foreign stocks, foreign exchange and municipal bonds, for example, may all be treated differently. Then there is the complication that gains from short periods are treated differently from those for longer periods. Also, losses may be used as offsets for gains, but subject to complicated rules.

A reasonably full treatment of taxable investing would therefore require an entire book. Here we must simplify the tax picture dramatically.[9]

IMPACT OF TAXES ON THE MARKET

An equilibrium model for the capital markets including taxes must make even more assumptions than did the CAPM proper. George Constantinides derives such

---

[8] See Wilcox, "The Effect of Transaction Costs and Delay on Performance Drag."

[9] If you want to take the next step toward understanding the underlying theoretical ideas, I recommend the several papers: George M. Constantinides, "Capital Market Equilibrium with Personal Tax," University of Chicago Graduate School of Business, Working Paper (February 1980) and George M. Constantinides,"Capital Market Equilibrium with Personal Tax," *Econometrica* (1983), pp. 611-636.

a model, and draws some modest conclusions.[10] For example, the market portfolio is no longer efficient, and the substitute is complex and essentially unmeasurable because it depends on the original cost positions for the embedded unrealized capital gains. It will not surprise you to learn that expected pre-tax return no longer depends simply on beta versus the market portfolio but also on tax premiums. Assets with tax advantages have lower pre-tax returns. His model does not explore what happens when there are borrowing or lending constraints and so does not lead to the complicated tax clientele effects observed in the real world.

I offer my own qualitative hypotheses regarding the effect of taxes on the market. They are neither rigorous nor quantitative, but may serve as a reminder of effects to watch for.

1. Taxes create market segmentation and clienteles. The effective tax on dividends is higher than that on realized long-term capital gains, and much higher than on unrealized capital gains. Consequently, other things equal, taxable owners should prefer securities with no dividends. (Of course, income needs may preclude this.) Non-taxable investors such as pension funds should prefer securities with higher dividend yields. (Pension funds should also not be very interested in low-yield but tax-exempt municipal bonds.) Note, however, that very broad diversification is available to both taxable and non-taxable shareholders. Therefore, there will typically be little undiversifiable specific risk in the aggregate segment, and thus little segmentation return of the sort described in Chapter 8.

2. Taxes do affect pricing and expected return, though not primarily through the segmentation effect. For example, we should expect higher pre-tax returns from stocks with higher dividend yields. The reason is that capital gains taxes are generally lower and, what is more important, they can be deferred. This effect has been reported in the past for U.S. stocks; however it is not so obvious today.

3. Capital gains taxes, because they are applied to gains only when they are realized through sale, cause taxable investors to hold portfolios that tend to become less diversified through time.

4. Because capital gains taxes tend to reduce willingness to sell in the presence of pervasive long-term increases in market prices, they reduce the efficiency of the market in incorporating new information.

5. Finally, if the motivation to take losses and let gains ride were prevalent, it would destabilize the overall market by inducing a kind of momentum investing. That is, the supply of sellers would fall when a stock goes up and increase when it goes down. However, in practice this effect seems

---

[10] Constantinides, "Capital Market Equilibrium with Personal Tax."

more than counterbalanced by behavioral biases that cause many investors to be irrationally reluctant to sell at a loss.

MAXIMIZING AFTER-TAX RETURN

Because of the mathematical complexity of finding best policies for maximizing after-tax return, the best approach may be to create a Monte Carlo simulation for each different investment problem. Constantinides provides analytics for a simple case based on Ito calculus on his way to establishing the individual investor conditions needed for an equilibrium market model.[11] He also provides crucial additional detail on dealing with taxes in the presence of transaction costs in an earlier working paper.[12]

Here we merely note the broad ideas for improving after-tax return. This is an area where reasonable guesses based on general principles will be a great deal better than nothing.

First, if you have a higher tax rate than other security-holders, bias holdings in favor of tax-advantaged securities. This includes not only municipal bonds, but also stocks that receive favorable tax treatment, such as those with no dividends.

Second, defer taxes by giving some thought to the tax calendar. Realize losses this year and gains next year. Do not pay high short-term capital gains taxes when by deferring a sale for eighteen months you can pay a substantially lower long-term capital gains tax. Try not to sell stocks with large unrealized capital gains if you are in poor health and likely not to live much longer, or you will deprive your heirs of an opportunity to avoid the tax.

However, the most important idea of all is to realize losses and defer realizing gains. This idea can be reinforced by initial purchases that make this situation more likely to develop to your advantage. That is, act so that you will remain well-diversified and get more opportunities to realize losses early while deferring gains. Let us explore these latter ideas in more detail.

LONG-TERM AFTER-TAX RETURNS

We begin with a simple deterministic model. Most long-term portfolios rather early develop market value in excess of cost. They would incur a tax liability were the portfolio to be sold. That potential tax liability has some of the characteristics of an interest-free loan from the government, except that it is always just proportionate to the difference between price and original cost. In accounting balance sheet terms, the portfolio assets are original cost plus market appreciation. Owner's equity at liquidation is the sum of these, less potential tax liability.

---

[11] Constantinides,"Capital Market Equilibrium with Personal Tax" (1983).
[12] Constantinides, "Capital Market Equilibrium with Personal Tax" (February 1980).

Suppose we initially define after-tax return as the annual percentage change in the owner's liquidation value. (This ignores the complication of *tax option value*, to which we return in the next section.)

Then we define:

$$L = P - T(P - B) \tag{9}$$

where

L = liquidation value, or owner's equity
P = market value
T = tax rate
B = cost basis

If we define after-tax return (r_a) as the percentage change in that liquidation value per unit of time, we can derive the following:

$$r_a = \frac{r_p}{1 + \dfrac{T(B/P)}{(1-T)}} \tag{10}$$

where

r_a = after-tax return
r_p = pre-tax return

Equation (10) applies to the very, very long term. It gives insight into the long-term equilibrium conditions of various policies. However, it should not be used to make realistic quantitative choices even in a deterministic case. This is because it does not take into account the transients that result if initial B/P is very different from long-term equilibrium B/P. Actual tradeoffs should be worked out using a spreadsheet with year-by-year calculation of the quantities of interest. These include sales, capital gains, and taxes. You will need to supply assumptions of passive price growth, value added through active management, capital gains tax rate, turnover, initial B/P ratio, dividend rate, and dividend tax rate. This simulation can be done deterministically as a first pass, and then stochastically by assuming randomized stock returns of a given risk level.

However, equation (10) does help us grasp the basic principles. When a stock is bought, P equals B, so that after-tax return is simply pre-tax return times one minus the tax rate. Thus an active policy that adds pre-tax return will be initially more attractive than a passive policy. With a passive buy and hold strategy, as P grows through time, however, B/P declines to very low levels. This causes after-tax return to asymptotically approach pre-tax return. Over longer periods, it may or may not put the after-tax return of a buy and hold strategy above that of active management that continues to provide added pre-tax return but requires turnover and so cannot achieve very low B/P ratios.

This is just another way of saying that the interest-free loan from the government can provide leverage that scales up after-tax return on the liquidation value to pre-tax levels. Consequently, as prices drift up relative to cost-basis, after-tax return of the holding increases and positions tend to become locked in. That is, greater and greater benefits from better alternative uses of the money have to be contemplated to make a sale worthwhile.

THE TAX OPTION

A more sophisticated approach to understanding the impact of realizing gains and letting profits run takes into account the probabilistic nature of returns. It then becomes apparent that the value of a taxable holding with the option to establish a tax benefit is higher than if there is no choice. The size of this tax option value will, of course, depend on whether the stock price is close to its original cost basis (high option value), or far above it (little value). It also, not surprisingly after you have read Chapter 7, depends positively on the return variance of the stock.

The tax-timing option value goes down with increasing transaction costs. Without transaction costs, the proper rule would be to immediately sell any security priced below cost. With transaction costs, one must establish an action price threshold substantially below the original cost basis so that the tax benefit is not eaten up by repeated trading costs. This causes smaller opportunities to be missed.

Let us explore the case of no transaction costs, no dividends, and no forced liquidations. The investment horizon is indefinitely long. Consider a recently purchased stock. We are going to establish three conditions for its value to us as a taxable owner.

First, we know the flatter slope of value versus price at all price points less than cost and also the steeper slope at a point where price is infinite. If the price goes up, we can choose to hold on, and, as we saw in equation (10), the eventual rate of return will approach that of a tax-free asset. Thus, for prices far above cost, value goes up at the same rate as price. On the other hand, suppose the price were to go down below cost. Then we can sell the stock and realize immediately a tax benefit of the tax rate times the loss. The proceeds are used to buy a substitute stock. The value therefore goes down from original cost exactly as liquidation value, at a rate equal to price change times the difference between unity and the tax rate. This will be true for every point on the curve where price is less than cost.

Second, because of arbitrage between fresh purchase and holding an established position, the holding value when price equals cost is cost.

Third, because of arbitrage between shares of the same stock bought at different prices, the slope of value versus price can not have any discontinuities.

Taking these three facts into account, the value of the stock to us must be a smooth curve looking something like line A in Exhibit 3.

Exhibit 3: After-Tax Value With and Without Option

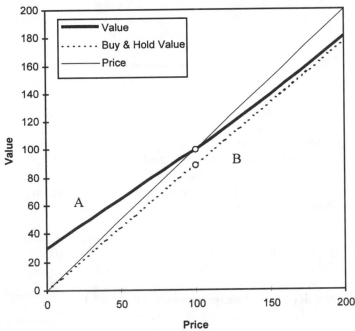

The sharpness of the curve as it changes slope will depend on the variance of returns. That is, for a high variance stock, a modest price rise will not steepen the slope very much. This is because there will remain a large chance of a future loss sufficient to put value to the left of cost and therefore on a flatter slope. The result is analogous to the impact of high variance on the value of a call option. In both cases, high return variance causes the value to vary more smoothly with price.

The characterization above depends on our willingness to sell to realize a loss. In contrast, consider what happens if we buy a stock and resolve never to sell it. Since the holding period is infinitely long, this cannot change our ultimate slope to the right of cost. However, on the left, since we will not liquidate the stock to realize a tax benefit, the value goes down at the same rate. Adding arbitrage conditions, the result must be the straight line B in Exhibit 3.

The difference between lines A and B is the value of the tax timing option. In the exhibit, the cost-basis is 100, the tax rate 30%, the risk-free rate 5%, and the annual standard deviation of return 25%. The vertical distance between the small white circles on lines A and B is the value of the tax timing option at the point where price equals the cost basis. In this example with no transaction costs, dividends, and no forced liquidations, the tax timing option is worth about 11% of the purchase price. If we choose never to consider the option of selling early to realize a loss, we never gain a tax benefit, and we lose this part of what we paid for the security.

Constantinides provides both a formula for this option value, and a formula that includes the impact of transaction costs,[13] but I shall not reproduce them here. However, it is very worthwhile to state the general dependence of the option value on various parameters based on Constantinides' analysis:

1. The tax timing option value at the time of purchase can range from almost nothing to on the order of 20% or more of the value of the stock, depending on plausible ranges of parameters.
2. Its value is higher for cases where the difference in results from holding and liquidation are most extreme: both when variance is high and the time horizon long.
3. The higher the transaction cost, the lower the value of the timing option. This is both because of direct costs and because you must wait for bigger, less frequent losses to make the tax reduction benefit per trade large relative to the transaction cost.

As an example of the formula result, assume a personal holding company capital gains tax rate of 28%, no dividends, and an after-tax riskless rate of interest of 5%. The formula indicates thresholds between about 10% and 40% below cost-basis for stocks with one-way trading costs of between 1% and 2% and annual standard deviation of return of between 10% and 40%.

Stocks with low variance should be harvested earlier because the chance may not come again. Stocks with low transaction costs should also be harvested earlier because net profit per trade will be greater.

ARRANGING FOR AFTER TAX OPTION VALUE

The ideas behind tax option value tell us that we can improve after-tax returns not only by correctly harvesting tax benefits through loss realization, but by prearranging that the value be high.

We can buy stocks with high variance. Note that this need have little impact on the total risk of the portfolio if we make sure the variance comes as diversifiable, or specific, risk. Typically, for example, small volatile stocks, which may have low betas, will provide better tax benefits with lower risk than the most popular growth stocks, which are often highly correlated with the market.

We can also enhance the value of tax options by reducing the need for forced liquidations. The skewed nature of long-term returns assures that eventually a very few stockholdings will have multiplied themselves in value many times, while the large majority of stocks in the portfolio will provide mediocre returns. The portfolio as a whole may therefore become so concentrated in a few stocks that

---

[13] See Constantinides,"Capital Market Equilibrium with Personal Tax" and "Capital Market Equilibrium with Personal Tax."

overall portfolio risk will escalate. However, by starting with many more different holdings than ordinarily required, one reduces the need for future rebalancing. This will lengthen the effective horizon and further increase the value of the tax option.

As a sophisticated taxable investor, you start with a portfolio of many different securities, each high in diversifiable risk. You harvest tax benefits as losses become available. As the years pass, it may become more difficult to justify fresh purchases, although cash flow from dividends and the availability of high-alpha strategies offer that potential. If one has chosen wisely, however, it will probably never be necessary to rebalance merely for the sake of risk control. After the first decade, after-tax returns will likely compound at a rate similar to those of the non-taxable investor. That is, the long-term bite of taxes will only be at liquidation, and will no longer affect compound rates of return except through foregone active value added. You may even be able to engage in further active investing through gradual increases in debt leverage offset by protective futures positions.

The essence of competitive investment strategy in the real world may turn on using frictions like trading costs and taxes to your advantage.

Chapter 11

The Dynamic Market of Individuals

*It is not from the benevolence of the butcher, the brewer,
or the baker, that we expect our dinner, but from their
regard to their own interest. We address ourselves, not to
their humanity but to their self-love, and never talk to them
of our necessities but of their advantages.*
Adam Smith. *The Wealth of Nations (1776)*

After observing real individuals operating in real markets, economists have postulated idealized individuals interacting together to create idealized markets.
Although they have aided our understanding, they have discarded much that could
be useful to us as active investors. As investors, you and I have no obligation to
simplify the world for science.

This brief chapter is a speculative essay formed around an analogy
between a *market* and an *ecology*. Let us view the stock market as an ecology of
competing and complementary species. We may find it as rich and colorful as the
teeming tropical forests. This qualitative perspective may help us apply our reductionist quantitative models more successfully.

Frequently one finds investment practitioners happy that their methods
are becoming more popular. If you believe that as others share your beliefs they
will become more profitable, this chapter may be particularly helpful.

COMPLEXITY THEORY

The literature of "complexity theory" is now vast and goes far beyond the simple
feedback models in which it originated and on which we have space to tarry. I
note here for your reference two thinkers I believe have been most influential:
Benoit Mandelbrot and John Holland.

Mandelbrot showed how very simple local rules could lead to many of
the fantastically complicated structures found in nature. We briefly noted in an
earlier chapter his work on the statistical structure of securities returns. However,
his indirect influence through the idea of fractal dimension, and in turn through
better understanding the nature of chaotic processes, is broader.[1]

---

[1] Benoit Mandelbrot, *The Fractal Geometry of Nature* (W H Freeman & Co., 1988).

Holland showed new ways to model the process of evolution of problem-solving structures. He first brought us the idea of genetic algorithms and then went on to outline higher-order learning mechanisms both at the individual and ecological levels.[2] We will return to genetic algorithms in Chapter 21.

In Chapter 3 we discussed in a favorable light a stock market simulation developed under the auspices of the Sante Fe Institute. This is an organization that can reasonably lay claim to being at the heart of new work in this fast-growing field. I find myself wanting to express caution here. As in the California gold strike of 1849, there is froth of unsound enthusiasm. Yet real gold nuggets lie at the root of the hyperbole. One unifying generalization is that of *emergent phenomena*, unexpected behaviors that arise in ensembles of components.

Consider hydrogen and oxygen, two gases at normal temperatures. Could we predict drinkable water from their combination? After we had seen the conversion from gases to liquid, or the reverse, we could begin to construct a model in which this is possible, but probably not before. Similarly, if we began by observing the real world of individuals who possess potentially tradable goods, but had never seen a market in operation, we would find it difficult to imagine its properties. We would imagine neither its efficient resource allocation in a static sense nor its encouragement of specialization and further gains in productivity.

Emergent phenomena are those that are hard to predict from a naive look at the components. One of the root causes of difficulty of prediction is feedback. I defined it and gave some simple illustrations of negative and positive feedback in Chapter 4. Negative feedback regulates behavior around some equilibrium point, as in a thermostat that turns on the air-conditioner when a room gets too hot. Positive feedback promotes continuation of change. It promotes processes of growth, but also of decay. For example, a winning college basketball team makes it easier to recruit talented new team members. Alternatively, a losing team makes it harder to recruit good players.

Linear feedback systems, negative or positive, are easiest to understand and to learn. They exist where variables are at most added or subtracted from one another in determining rates of change. In such cases, we can simply add together the effects of multiple disturbances to determine the combined behavior. There may be a simple tendency to oscillate at a defined frequency, to amplify certain disturbances by a defined ratio, or to grow at a well-defined rate. If there are only a few and easily observable interacting feedback loops, discovering these properties is a relatively straightforward quantitative task.

Several factors can make feedback systems hard to discover and predict. They are non-linearity of the relationships within causal loops, the inter-reaction of multiple loops, and the dispersion of causal links outside the perspective of any one person.

If the impact of one variable on another is a non-linear function, or if two variables are multiplied or divided, the resulting feedback system is non-linear.

---

[2] John H. Holland, *Adaptation in Natural and Artificial Systems: An Introductory Analysis With Applications to Biology, Control, and Artificial Intelligence (Complex A)* Reprint Edition, Bradford Books (1992).

Non-linearities make such systems very much harder to exhaustively predict. There are no existing quantitative tools for exhaustively analyzing more than the simplest of them. Non-linear systems may have multiple modes of behavior, and even simulation may not reveal all of these. We saw the results of a very simple non-linearity in the market simulation of Chapter 4. It resulted in a system that could be stable in the face of small disturbances, but flip into violent oscillations when hit by a single large disturbance.

Feedback systems may involve the interrelationship of many feedback loops operating at similar time-scales; just a few may make the behavior of the total system seem to have a "mind of its own." For example, my Master's thesis at M.I.T. was based on a simple model of the economy in which there were two main negative feedback loops. One was for adjusting inventory and the other for adjusting production capacity. There were also two main groups of positive feedback loops. The first of these linked income from both production and capacity investment to consumer spending. This generated sales, and thus affected both production and capacity utilization. The latter further influenced investment in new capacity. (Did you note the four distinct loops?) The second was a single loop that subtracted capacity available for production whenever it was needed to build more capacity. Thus, a shortage of capacity for a time engendered further decreases in capacity. A key non-linearity was in the link between capacity utilization and new investment in production capacity. There was no reaction until usage began to be a high percentage of capacity.

This system at times generated short-term inventory-based business cycles. At other times, tight capacity locked in a long-lasting boom followed by an even longer-lasting depression. The system could also exhibit relatively smooth growth without much instability, depending on modest changes in parameters and types of disturbances. Despite having re-simulated this system several times over the intervening decades, I still am not entirely confident of my understanding of all its potential behaviors. Most real systems of interest are far more complicated.

Finally, suppose the causal links that make up a feedback loop are distributed through the interaction of more than one person. Then the individuals involved may have no sense that they are involved in a feedback system. Thus the feedback system is never defined and so cannot be the basis for prediction. Each participant perceives the resulting system behavior as out of his or her control. The same thing can happen when feedback behavior is so slow relative to the experience of a single observer that characteristic impact on oscillations, growth, or decay is not perceived as endogenous. A good example of a feedback system that is not readily visible to its participants is a speculative bubble. Favorable news stimulates new investments and recruits new investors, which stimulates further good news and further new investments and recruits.

One of the insights of complexity theory is that positive feedback is all around us, although under-analyzed by equilibrium-seeking economists. Brian Arthur, a leader in the Santa Fe Institute's economics efforts, has long argued the importance of positive feedback in economics.[3] He noted that early experience in an industry could produce a lock-in effect leading to dominance, not only because of economies of scale, but because of learning curves. Of course, clients of the Boston Consulting Group knew decades earlier of the "experience curve," in which costs tend to fall by a given percentage every time accumulated experience doubles. The existence of experience curves leads to great competitive value for market share. The case of the Microsoft Corporation may also make this phenomenon obvious to the reader. It came to dominate the personal computer software market in the late 1990s after a small early lead in operating systems two decades earlier.

While negative feedback is important to maintain organizations, positive feedback is essential in their formation and growth, indeed in the formation of any social institution. Positive feedback converts the random to the organized. As one very important example, markets are created by positive feedback from liquidity of available supply and demand to trading volume and back.

Because of positive feedback, small differences in environment show up as large differences in types of dominant organism, organization, or behavioral strategy. We should not be surprised, for example, to find substantial differences in winning stock market strategies for markets in countries with different reporting and insider-trading regulations, different trading costs, and so on. Similarly, a fundamental analyst whose techniques work well in a high-technology growth industry may be unable to function well in a mature or regulated industry. We should also not be surprised to find that successful speculators and traders have a very different set of heuristics from those we use in daily life.

Can you force yourself to act as though most of what you know is already reflected in prices and is therefore useless? To sell on good news and buy on bad? To gracefully accept failures rather than trying to turn them around by hanging on? To make a practice of disagreeing with your peers? If you can, you have probably become a specialist by dint of exposure to a speculative market environment.

When one finds a complex organization, it is much easier to conceive of a central directing force than it is to understand it as the result of interacting decentralized units. Can you find a watch and not imagine a watchmaker? It is easier to model a single "representative investor," assigning to him or her superhuman cognitive complexity, than to conceive of a relatively efficient market of different types of individuals interacting according to simple rules. A real market cannot be understood by looking at a single real investor, nor should it be modeled that way, just as an ant colony cannot be understood by looking at a single ant. Complexity theorists counterbalance this tendency toward postulating a central or representative decision-maker by showing through computer simulation how complicated organizations and behaviors arise from simple elements.

Complexity theorists are particularly critical of conventional economics and, by extension, financial economists. The economist's usual focus on equilib-

---

[3] W.B. Arthur, S.N. Durlauf, and D. Lane, *The Economy as an Evolving Complex System II*, Santa Fe Institute Studies in the Sciences of Complexity, Addison Wesley Longman (1997).

rium does not describe mechanisms for achieving equilibrium nor when the mechanisms are ineffective. Sometimes economists have been forced to deal with dynamic behavior, as in forecasting business cycles or economic growth. But even then they have tended to focus on the easier mathematics of aggregate national accounting entities rather than the disaggregate differences in knowledge and income that often propel the system. The great economist Joseph Schumpeter showed in the 1940s the enormous impact on business cycles and financial markets of detailed innovations and their diffusion through the industrial structure. But he was the exception that proves the rule — his approach fell immediately out of fashion.[4]

In the real economy, there is a complex of hierarchical structures, institutions, and networks of communication and influence not dealt with easily by mathematics even in a static sense. The dynamics are even worse — not only within the existing structure, but of the structure itself. As economic agents accumulate experience, they adapt. This changes the environment for other agents, changing global properties of the economy. Continuous adaptation is forever creating novel niches for specialists. Recruitment of new players causes the system to forget earlier mistakes. This constant process of change helps insure that the system stays well away from equilibrium. Obviously the same is true in the stock market, which because of the high speed in which adaptation can take place is even more unstable.

Feedback need not be of the conventional engineering type which one models with a fixed structure of differential equations. It can produce changes in more complex structural representations such as genes or corporate 5-year plans. (We will return to these kinds of structural feedback when we discuss genetic algorithms in Chapter 21.) Feedback can even produce structures that survive by producing randomness.

Consider the children's game of "rock, paper, and scissors." Two players simultaneously show one of these symbols. Rock crushes scissors, scissors cut paper, paper covers rock. The game is played repeatedly, with a penalty paid by the loser at each trial. Each player's strategy consists of trying to forecast the other's next move while making one's own move unpredictable. Inherent uncertainty and chaos is created as the players become more skillful. The same is true in many complex systems where there are adversarial or even competitive relationships. The stock market can be thought of as producing randomness through competition in forecasting.

In nature, the revision of species' strategies occurs on the time-scale of genetic evolution, as predators grow longer fangs and prey become fleeter or better armored. In the economy the adaptation takes the length of a product development cycle or an advertising campaign. In the stock market, one deals with a time-scale of reaction that may be on the order of months, days, or even, in some trading situations, minutes.

Complexity theorists argue that traditional mathematical tools do not promote deep understanding of adaptive nonlinear networks. I do not entirely

---

[4] Joseph Schumpeter, *Business Cycles, A Theoretical, Historical and Statistical Analysis of the Capitalist Process* (New York: McGraw-Hill, 1964).

agree — sometimes traditional mathematical tools do produce deep understanding — that is how they got to be traditional. But the Santa Fe group does have a point. The inherent non-linear complexity, instability, and uncertainty of speculative securities markets lend themselves to simple models to only a very limited degree.

ECOLOGY

The literature of biology is probably two orders of magnitude larger even than the theory of complexity that attempts to encompass and jump-start it. Here, condensed, are the basic ideas that lead directly to ecologies, our analogy for the markets.

Living things must overcome the Second Law of Thermodynamics: that in a closed system, entropy (lack of structure, random disorder) tends to increase. This implies that living things, which must create order to grow, must have access to resources. The latter, being limited, ensure competition for resources and the tendency for survival of the fittest.

Evolution has produced a strategy of reproduction that allows adaptation to various environments. Our reproductive blueprint, as is true for everything in our experience higher than a virus, is carried in strings of DNA, the genes. A dominant plan for flexible exploitation of different environments and rapid adaptation to changes within it has been the creation of sexual reproduction, which creates constant shuffling of different genes within a range. The range is limited, however, by barriers to successful mating between individuals that are too different. This preserves a degree of successful specialization. The pool of individuals who can mate with one another form a species. The species, not the individual, is the basic unit of the study of ecology.

An ecology is an interdependent system of species living together in a particular kind of environment. Surviving natural ecologies are highly efficient in their use of the environmental resources, and as a system, typically highly resilient in the face of periodic disruptions such as floods, fires, and droughts. However, they undergo periodic revision, sometimes from natural causes, such as long-term changes in temperature and moisture, or when invaded by new species.

I propose an analogy. Let us seek to understand the stock market as an ecology of different types of investor behavior. The external resources are corporate earnings, information for forecasting changes in earnings, and the arrival of new participants with assets derived from other sources such as employment. The roles and governing ideas are more fluid than in genetic systems, but there are sufficient barriers to exchange so that we can observe high degrees of specialization in the way participants behave. The role of the genes is assumed by particular ideas of how one may earn returns. One can describe a dynamic market of individuals buying and selling securities as though they were organisms competing for information predicting prices. In this analogy, the cultural ideas that govern their decisions are genes competing to reproduce themselves. They do this by attracting new individuals. The role of the environment is taken by the available technology of communication and institutional arrangements for information gathering and trading.

An individual's progeny can benefit from the process of sexual shuffling of genes to enable rapid adaptation to changing environments. Similarly, an investor benefits from sharing a mix of ideas with a relatively small group of investors of similar but slightly differing persuasions. But the common belief that an investment approach becomes more valuable as it is more widely shared is short-term indeed. The sharing of one's ideas might enhance the pricing of existing investments, but it will also make it more expensive to take new similar positions in the future. The analogy between investment approaches and species makes it clear that one does not want the analogies to famines and parasitic diseases caused by overpopulation within a particular investment approach.

Species can be characterized in terms of general strategies for survival. Large ecosystems such as tropical jungles develop tremendous variety and specialization. The species that survive may be slow to reproduce because they must maintain a high degree of efficiency to meet the intense competition. Smaller and more transitory environments, such as small islands or patches of forest destroyed by fire or volcanic action, attract risk-taking species that depend on lack of competition. Such species reproduce heavily to compensate for losses, and they are far-ranging in search of new environments.

The securities markets have become huge and varied. There are different types of securities — stocks, bonds, money market, and a host of derivatives, not to speak of commodity futures and real estate interests. There are differences by country that allow specialists to flourish. Subtle differences like magnitude of trading costs, depth of market and changes in government regulation play the roles of temperature, rainfall, and natural catastrophes. We see extreme repetitive specialization and trading efficiency in traders working with earnings estimates revisions. They are in sharp contrast to the frontier types who scatter their seed to the various emerging markets in the hope of hitting a few good ones without much global competition.

Ecologies with many alternate pathways in the food chain are generally quite stable. When they are simplified, however, they may show striking boom and bust cycles of population and prosperity. These are generated by the combination of inherent explosive birthrates of some populations, the long lags in building up limiting predator populations or in destroying the carrying capacity of the environment, and the non-linearities of species interaction.

An important topic in ecology is the dynamics of predator-prey relationships. In an ecology there are many connections between the populations of many different species, not only predator-prey, but competitors and symbionts. The whole forms a vast and intricate set of non-linear feedback systems.

There is a famous set of differential equations, the Lotka-Volterra predator-prey equations, that describe the interaction of two species, one of which preys on the other. If there are not enough predators, prey population grows to exceed environmental carrying capacity. Population overshoot will lead to an eventual decline, which may be to very low levels if the overshoot is great. This oscillation can be markedly amplified by predator population cyclicality in response to prey availability. The system will also be highly non-linear because the rate at which predators find and eat prey is a function of the *product* of the two populations.

Consider the investor types modeled in Chapter 4. Rephrasing the dynamic behavior in ecological terms, momentum investors feed off opportunities initially created by laggard fundamental analysts who do not quickly exploit all the available information. They also flourish where growth investors who are sensitive to changes in earnings prospects are insensitive to price. In turn, value investors exploit the extremes of pricing created by the environment created by the combination of growth and momentum investors.

Indexers are insensitive to the price relationship between stocks and cash. In small quantities they are harmless free-riders. In large quantities, however, they tend to destabilize the system by being willing to hold stocks no matter how high their prices go. They avoid being exploited in a variety of ways, but they are grist for the value player's mill at market tops.

This analogy suggests that the best rewards for a particular type of investment strategy will depend on the relative participating populations of investor species. For example, some value strategies nibble away at small arbitrage differences created by growth investors insensitive to price. But when the market has become dominated by momentum thinking, and new momentum investors are being continuously recruited, there are no tops and bottoms to exploit. In that case, value investing can be cruder in measurement of fair value, but must be more sophisticated in waiting for the momentum players to destroy the carrying capacity of the environment for momentum thinking.

The analogy with predator-prey population dynamics also helps us understand when the market will be most stable. For example, if there are two kinds of prey, multi-prey predators can differentially focus on the more available type of prey, preventing its growth to such high unsustainable peaks as in the simpler context of only one type of prey. The analogy suggests we should beware of growing homogeneity of investor thinking — it helps engender booms and busts. On the other hand, the *contrarian* investor with patience may sense a rare opportunity in existing homogeneity of opinion carried to extremes of valuation. The market as ecology analogy gives support not only to what is conventionally called technical analysis, but also to the quantitative measurements of investor participation provided by mutual fund reporting of holdings and cash flow.

When choosing an investor species to join, it is probably unwise to attempt the active investing style that has been most popular over the past decade, because it may be highly over-populated.

THE INSTITUTIONAL ENVIRONMENT

Market environments are set by institutions — not only organized exchanges but also by the technology available to the investor. The invention of the stock exchange led to greater liquidity and lower trading costs. It also led to niche roles: specialists, floor traders, brokers and fundamental analysts for hire. The invention of electronic trading aids and the Internet is breaking up some of these institutions and creating new ones for on-line trading and securities research.

The history of the market is expressed both in books and in electronic databases that allow simulation of various investment strategies; these can change the environment. Certainly it has become much harder to earn extra returns on those market inefficiencies that have been described in academic journals such as the *Journal of Finance*. This process is a special hazard for quantitative investors. We test our return forecasts on history, at the same time as other quantitative investors are doing the same. Having observed the process, we disturb it so that history tends to repeat itself less often. The better our collective memory, the more varied future history is likely to become.

As liquidity improves, additional short-term trading strategies become profitable. As electronic databases became available, both fundamental comparisons and ability to exploit imperfections in analyst earnings updates become enhanced. It would appear that the Internet allows much greater access to the market by the retail public. One could hypothesize, for example, that not only will life get harder for conventional brokers, but, if the new retail participants are unsophisticated, life might conceivably get easier for skilled fundamental analysts.

In a broader sense, the availability of computers and computerized databases is constantly changing the nature of successful strategies. Fortunately, not all markets are changing at the same rate, or starting from the same position. It is still possible to use techniques that used to work well in the United States in less developed markets. Even in the United States, the continued recruitment of new unsophisticated investors who pay little attention to what has worked over long periods of history tends to prolong the life of old active investing techniques.

One of the biggest changes in the environment has been the invention of new forms of securities that package risk in different ways. First among these is the index fund. But second come the many more complex types of derivative instruments. These include futures, options, options on futures, and swaps. They change the environment so that it is easier to bet on negative information, easier to hedge particular risks, and cheaper to trade, allowing higher frequency asset allocation. While they are poorly understood, they provide niches for pioneers and specialists.

Finally, stability of business and social institutions is another factor affecting the investing environment. When institutions, which provide stability in our lives, break down, our investment time horizon is shortened. This creates longer-term opportunities for specialists with long horizons. This kind of reasoning is particularly applicable in emerging markets with periodic upheavals.

In today's markets, domestically-focused investors need to adapt to global and emerging markets, currency, and various useful derivatives. International investors must adapt to the European currency union. All investors need to learn to get maximum leverage from computerization and better communications. Even a qualitative fundamental analyst can greatly improve information gathering on a global scale by using the Internet regularly. Every investor must continually adapt to the changing effectiveness of his or her tools.

Ecologies are never in complete equilibrium — but there are varying degrees of stability. Current markets appear to me to have little tendency to come to equilibrium. The causes include not only a changing environment but also an ample supply of new uninformed investors and the growing popularity of index funds insensitive to market price levels. On the other hand, there is a strong possibility that over longer horizons gradual increase in depth of world global markets may eventually create enough integrated investor variety to make them more stable.

Chapter 12

Valuation Models

Nowadays people know the price of everything and the value of nothing.
Oscar Wilde, *The Picture of Dorian Gray (1891)*

Is the common stock of the General Electric Corporation expensive, or is it cheap? It all depends. There is no one best valuation model for stocks. The valuation model most appropriate for corporations to use in making acquisition decisions may not be most useful to the outside investor who has less available information and many more alternatives to consider. The best model for stock picking may not be the best model for comparing stocks as an asset class to bonds or to cash. Think of valuation models as structured frameworks for arbitrage decisions. The best model takes into account our available information and the comparison we want to make.

We always have the alternative available of simply using a regression model linking expected return to various indicators, leaving fair value implicit. However, a valuation model does make us consider fundamental determinants of equilibrium prices that may give us clues as to where to look for useful indicators.

In this chapter we will first examine the choice between stocks and cash. Then we will deal with decisions just among stocks. Limiting ourselves to these two choices de-emphasizes the direct comparison of a specific stock to its financing costs. This latter perspective, while vital to the management of corporations, and valuable to some fundamental analysts, is largely outside my experience as a quantitative investor. There are a multitude of ways in which one can parse the ingredients of stock value. I have selected only two, but they are fundamental.

A valuation model sufficiently detailed and accurate for perfectly explaining today's price would be of no use except as a list of ingredients we must predict. What we hope to do with a valuation model is to provide an approximation with errors. We want the approximation to be close enough so that there is a noticeable and not too prolonged tendency for errors to correct themselves.

Fundamental analysts frequently complicate their valuation models in an effort to make them more accurate. For example, they may make a judgment in each case how long above-average profit growth will continue. Alternatively, they may ask what is the value of the firm if we separately value each of its major product divisions. However, the resulting frameworks can require so many judgmental inputs that they are of little use to the quantitative investor seeking statistical significance. In the end, quantitative investors are usually driven toward simple, focused valuation models that can be tied to objective data or current consensus forecasts of the near-term future.

185

STOCK MARKET FAIR VALUE

As I write, the price to book ratio (*P/B*) of the U.S. stock market is over 4. The current market value of the companies traded is four times the difference between the cost of their assets and the debt used to help finance them. If we take into account modest inflation since the purchase of those assets, we might suppose that this still represents roughly three times replacement cost. This high ratio is unusual not only in the history of the United States but also of many other countries. Does it imply anything about future returns? That is, can we take the *P/B* ratio and use it as a simple valuation model?

Before pursuing that question further, let us come at the problem from a different direction. Are there arbitrages that bound the prices within which U.S. stock prices will fluctuate? What variables would be the focus of such arbitrages?

We can imagine and observe very different types of arbitrage for a company's stock, depending on who is the decision-maker:

1. *The company.* When stock prices are high, companies can issue more stock without paying as much for it in terms of dilution of claims on the existing assets. At a price of three times replacement cost, they can create two dollars of profit for every equity dollar they invest in their business. In contrast, when prices are low, companies can increase return on equity by repurchasing their own shares. This arbitrage involves price to book ratios.

2. *Other companies.* When stock prices are high, companies will pay cash to expand through their own original investment. When prices are low, it will be more efficient to buy up another company with a depressed stock price. While there are exceptions when one must get into a business more quickly than it can be grown internally, the purchase of lower price-to-book companies is the overall tendency. Very high transaction costs may cause this arbitrage to be operative mostly when stock prices are at extremes. If the buying company believes it can radically change profitability of the assets, the relevant arbitrage involves price/book. If not, the relevant comparison is most likely in terms of price/cash flow, or for some stock-conscious managements, price-earnings ratios.

3. *Investors.* They can select among stocks, cash or bonds (as well as other alternatives such as real estate or a bigger personal home). There is a comparison between stocks and cash, between stocks and bonds, and between bonds and cash. Stocks provide participation in economic growth. Bonds insure against future hard times in the economy. Cash, including short-term treasury bills and government-backed bank interest, provides greatest current safety. The relevant equity arbitrage comparisons will be in terms of interest rates versus dividend yields, or versus earnings yields, or perhaps earnings yields plus expected growth in earnings, depending on how conservative the investor.

4. *Foreign investors*. They compare using additional factors representing currency risk and tax and regulatory differences.

Each of these arbitrages works differently, emphasizing different measures and comparisons. Altogether, the relevant bound changes depending on the situation.

In 1998, the U.S. stock market seems reasonably competitive with bonds and cash; to those who focus on arbitrage by investors it seems supported by low interest rates. However, to those who focus on arbitrage by corporate decision-makers between direct investment and secondary investment, things look different. The new capacity under construction and the boom in new stock issues make it seem as though the market is over-priced and due for a correction.

What arbitrage offers the greatest remaining opportunity? Let us construct a valuation model for the U.S. stock market based on arbitrage by companies, simply using *P/B*. This means that we are focusing on the effects caused by those who are in a position to influence corporate profitability of assets deployed. We ignore the impact of earnings, dividends and competing interest rates. We do so in part because the market we trade in is inherently more efficient than the one corporations trade in. This is because of the absence of high transaction costs needed for control and for new financing and for physical expansion. We want to take advantage of the most imperfect arbitrage first. It is also helpful that general opinion seems to be that the relationship between *P/B* and future returns for the market as a whole is too weak to be useful.

The following analysis is based on quarterly data from the Morgan Stanley Capital International Perspective. The database includes 22 countries, of which the United States is number 22. It extends from the beginning of 1970 through June 1996. The STATA statistics program is used to produce the analytical results.[1]

Exhibit 1 examines the range of the *P/B* ratio for the United States. (Of course in 1998, we are well above the top of the *P/B* range shown here.) For the United States, *P/B* has ranged from 1 to 3.23 during this period, with a median of about 1.6.

We next look both at the United States and at the sample of 22 countries as a whole. We will refer to the global pool of observations to gain greater confidence in any U.S. relationship between *P/B* and future returns. In the absence of evidence for U.S. uniqueness, we want to consider the more secure conclusions that can be arrived at by looking at many times as many data.

Note in Exhibit 2 the quartile boundaries. We will use them later. The first distribution is for the United States, the second for 22 countries. The range of values for the second sample is considerably broader. The variable *pbln* refers to the natural logarithm of the *P/B* ratio. This transformed variable is somewhat more symmetrical in distribution, always a useful property in statistical estimation. It is also associated with the PB-ROE valuation model to which we will turn in the second section of this chapter.

---

[1] *Stata 5 Users Guide*, Stata Corporation, College Station, Texas, 1997.

Exhibit 1: U.S. Range for Price/Book

. sum PB if ZINDIV==22,de

PB

	Percentiles	Smallest		
1%	1	1		
5%	1.1	1.04		
10%	1.17	1.07	Obs	87
25%	1.33	1.1	Sum of Wgt.	87
50%	1.6		Mean	1.78
		Largest	Std. Dev.	0.5714486
75%	2.15	3.08		
90%	2.61	3.21	Variance	0.3265535
95%	2.91	3.23	Skewness	0.81238
99%	3.23	3.23	Kurtosis	2.809228

Exhibit 2: U.S. and Global Log Price/Book

United States

. sum pbln if ZINDIV==22,de

pbln

	Percentiles	Smallest		
1%	0	0		
5%	0.0953102	0.0392207		
10%	0.1570037	0.0676586	Obs	87
25%	0.2851789	0.0953102	Sum of Wgt.	87
50%	0.4700036		Mean	0.5290607
		Largest	Std. Dev.	0.3059909
75%	0.7654678	1.12493		
90%	0.9593502	1.166271	Variance	0.0936304
95%	1.068153	1.172482	Skewness	0.3478653
99%	1.172482	1.172482	Kurtosis	2.092214

Global

. sum pbln,de

pbln

	Percentiles	Smallest		
1%	−0.8209805	−1.237874		
5%	−0.4780358	−1.07881		
10%	−0.2744368	−1.049822	Obs	1677
25%	0.0392207	−1.049822	Sum of Wgt.	1677
50%	0.3920421		Mean	0.3333014
		Largest	Std. Dev.	0.4417248
75%	0.6312718	1.589235		
90%	0.8329091	1.589235	Variance	0.1951208
95%	0.9593502	1.593309	Skewness	−0.366984
99%	1.368639	1.61343	Kurtosis	3.330689

Exhibit 3: Regression of Quarterly Returns versus Log P/B

. regress flrtnusd pbln if ZINDIV==22 (US)

Source	SS	df	MS			
Model	0.004198707	1	0.004198707			
Residual	0.465283165	84	0.005539085			
Total	0.469481872	85	0.005523316			

Number of obs	=	86
F(1, 84)	=	0.76
Prob > F	=	0.3864
R-squared	=	0.0089
Adj R-squared	=	−0.0029
Root MSE	=	0.07443

flrtnusd	Coef.	Std. Err.	t	P>|t|	[95% Conf. Interval]	
pbln	-0.023453	0.0269376	−0.871	0.386	−0.0770215	0.0301155
_cons	0.0449041	0.0161807	2.775	0.007	0.0127271	0.0770811

. xtreg flrtnloc pbln,fe

Fixed-effects (within) regression

sd(u_ZINDIV)	=	0.020787	Number of obs = 1655
sd(e_ZINDIV_t)	=	0.1122856	n = 22
sd(e_ZINDIV_t + u_ZINDIV)	=	0.1141935	T-bar = 75.2273
corr(u_ZINDIV, Xb)	=	−0.4730	R-sq within = 0.0286
			between = 0.0329
			overall = 0.0182
			F(1,1632) = 48.08
			Prob > F = 0.0000

flrtnloc	Coef.	Std. Err.	t	P>|t|	[95% Conf. Interval]	
pbln	−0.0531692	0.0076678	−6.934	0.000	−0.068209	−0.0381295
_cons	0.0495417	0.0037339	13.268	0.000	0.042218	0.0568654
ZINDIV F(21,1632) =			1.431	0.093	(22 categories)	

. xtreg flrtnloc pbln uspbln,fe

Fixed-effects (within) regression

sd(u_ZINDIV)	=	0.0209636	Number of obs = 1655
sd(e_ZINDIV_t)	=	0.1123009	n = 22
sd(e_ZINDIV_t + u_ZINDIV)	=	0.1142409	T-bar = 75.2273
corr(u_ZINDIV, Xb)	=	−0.4745	R-sq within = 0.0289
			between = 0.0307
			overall = 0.0185
			F(2,1631) = 24.31
			Prob > F = 0.0000

flrtnloc	Coef.	Std. Err.	t	P>|t|	[95% Conf. Interval]	
pbln	−0.0542661	0.0078091	−6.949	0.000	−0.069583	−0.0389492
uspbln	0.0308131	0.0413899	0.744	0.457	−0.0503699	0.1119961
_cons	0.0490663	0.0037886	12.951	0.000	0.0416352	0.0564973
ZINDIV F(21,1631) =			1.435	0.091	(22 categories)	

We regress the next quarter's return (in log return format) against today's log price/book. Exhibit 3 shows three regressions. The first is for the United States alone. The second is for the larger sample. The third is for the larger sample but also tests whether the United States is significantly different in its response from the larger sample. The second and third regressions are specialized forms of regression, "fixed effects regression," used for isolating time-series effects within each country. In this case, we do not want to contaminate the time-series effects with cross-sectional effects. In the next section, we will use the same technique in reverse to avoid contaminating cross-sectional effects with time-series effects. See the STATA manuals or Johnston(1997) for an explanation of fixed effects regression.[2]

We will assume that the assumptions of the statistical significance tests used in ordinary least squares regression are met only closely enough so that the resulting t-statistics are a plausible guide to useful relationships.

The first regression in Exhibit 3 shows that we get the postulated sign for the United States, but the relationship considering this sample by itself is not statistically significant, with a t-statistic of −0.87. However, the second regression indicates a t-statistic of −6.93 when we pool data from 22 countries. This statistic is inflated, because in reality our observations are now correlated rather than independent. The proper correction is arduous. I will content myself here with asserting that for stock problems you will be safe in dividing the resulting t-statistics by 2 or 3, which in this case would still give a useful result. Thus, the global sample encourages us to construct a valuation model based on P/B for the United States.

The third regression adds a new independent variable, the product of $pbln$ and a dummy variable that is 1 for the United States and 0 everywhere else. It shows that the difference in response for the United States and the rest of the world is not significantly different, with a t-statistic of only 0.74. This confirms our use of the larger sample to help us determine an appropriate relationship for the United States.

Note that returns in each country are in local currency, because we are only trying to understand local effects through time. We are not interested here in which country is the better buy.

There are good reasons to believe that the arbitrage that causes reversions in prices is more effective at the extremes of P/B, because of threshold effects based on transaction costs. However, we may be observing mostly the extremes at the high end, since there has not been a major U.S. depression since the 1930s. That is, we may see stronger effects in this sample at the high end of the range, because the low end really is not very low, at least for the United States. We can investigate this by looking at the difference in average return across quartile boundaries in Exhibit 4, again possibly reinforcing our findings on the United States by looking at the larger global sample in Exhibit 5. (For the sake of brevity, we are not try to correct the global quartile ranges for cross-sectional effects.) Note that return averages within $pbln$ quartiles are the same as those within P/B quartiles, since the pool of observations is identical.

We see that in the United States, the average quarterly return in log terms has been 0.0445 for the cheapest P/B quartile. This drops to 0.0343 for the middle two quartiles. It drops faster, to 0.0174, or 1.76%, within the most expensive P/B quartile. Thus there appears to be a greater response at the high end, although we do not have enough U.S. observations to be very sure of this.

---

[2] Jack Johnston and John Dinardo, *Econometric Methods* (4th Ed.) (McGraw-Hill 1997).

Exhibit 4: US Returns By P/B Quartile

Low P/B Quartile
. sum flrtnusd if pbln<=.285 & ZINDIV==22 & pbln~=.

Variable	Obs	Mean	Std. Dev.	Min	Max
flrtnusd	21	0.0445061	0.0810587	−0.103809	0.204814

Middle P/B Quartiles
. sum flrtnusd if pbln>.285 & pbln<=0.765 & ZINDIV==22 & pbln~=.

Variable	Obs	Mean	Std. Dev.	Min	Max
flrtnusd	44	0.0343084	0.0713958	−0.1475056	0.184237

High P/B Quartile
. sum flrtnusd if pbln>.765 & ZINDIV==22 & pbln~=.

Variable	Obs	Mean	Std. Dev.	Min	Max
flrtnusd	21	0.0174071	0.0744759	−0.2616813	0.0922813

Exhibit 5: Global Returns By P/B Quartile

Low P/B Quartile for Global
. sum flrtnloc if pbln<=.0392 & pbln~=.

Variable	Obs	Mean	Std. Dev.	Min	Max
flrtnloc	398	0.0468139	0.1106458	−0.3154025	0.5684622

Middle P/B Quartiles for Global
. sum flrtnloc if pbln>.0392 & pbln<=.631 & pbln~=.

Variable	Obs	Mean	Std. Dev.	Min	Max
flrtnloc	843	0.0370303	0.102517	−0.4147649	0.6441225

High P/B Quartile for Global
. sum flrtnloc if pbln>.631 & pbln~=.

Variable	Obs	Mean	Std. Dev.	Min	Max
flrtnloc	414	0.0079333	0.132829	−0.5704275	0.4365792

The same kind of phenomenon is also apparent within the much larger global sample. Average quarterly log returns in the cheapest quartile are 0.0468. This drops to 0.0370 for the middle two quartiles and then plummets to 0.0079 for the most expensive *P/B* quartile. Our analysis indicates that we should expect greater impact on returns from reducing stock holdings at the high end of the *P/B* range than from increasing them at the low end.

We have established sufficiently for practical purposes that fair price-to-book value is worth our attention. Having discovered a useful attribute, however, does not in itself provide a fair value point on that attribute. The latter will depend on the type of arbitrage we are contemplating and on whether we want to make any adjustments from the historical sample period.

Here is a rather simple approach based on company arbitrage and assuming that the past historical return and *pbln* distributions were typical. Suppose we consider that investment in new plant and equipment will earn a return on equity of ROE, for example 13%, or in quarterly log return terms, 0.0305. Then substituting into the first regression in Exhibit 3, we can estimate, assuming that our historical period was long enough so that it's ROE was typical, that fair value *pbln* occurs when

$$0.0305 = 0.0449 - 0.0235 \, pbln$$

or, *pbln* = 0.613, implying *P/B* = 1.85.

We might want to estimate expected return around this point from reversion to fair value using the regression coefficient of −0.0235. Alternatively, we might want to estimate a piecewise linear regression with a flatter slope for lower values and a steeper slope for higher values of current *pbln* versus fair value *pbln*.

If we wanted to determine fair value with respect to arbitrage by investors operating strictly within the secondary markets, our job would be much more complicated. Suppose we do wish to compare the expected stock return to cash returns. Then we must estimate an additional risk premium for stock investments before substituting the sum of cash returns and risk premium into the left side of our regression equation. Unfortunately, what is a fair value for risk premiums seems to vary widely from one period to another. We may decide to use a very long-term historical average risk premium of about 0.015 per quarter. If current short-term t-bill rates are 0.013 per quarter, then we might say that our regression requires that

$$(0.013 + 0.015) = 0.0449 - 0.0235 \, pbln$$

or *P/B* = 2.05.

Is fair value a *P/B* of 1.85 or 2.05? There may be two or more different arbitrages at work, and we cannot say much about the central tendency without knowing more about the relative activity of two different types of decision criteria or decision-makers. Suppose we had stuck to a regression format without bothering to detour through valuation models and an estimate of fair value. Then the analogous question would be whether the underlying stochastic process were stable, and if not, what its current state was versus the estimation history.

A still more complicated arbitrage is that between the stock market and the long-term bond market. It poses at least three additional problems. First, stocks and bonds may *both* be priced far from their respective fair values. Second, there is information content in bond prices that we need to exploit. For example, it would do no good to figure that high price-earnings-multiple stocks are fairly priced versus bonds if bonds have low interest rates because they are being used as disaster insurance. Third, bond pricing also includes a risk premium, in part because of the risk of inflation, but the risk of bonds is not along the same dimension as the risk of stocks. Ultimately the comparison of risk premia requires an assessment of the relative likelihood of two types of risk, for which we may have no quantitative model.

THE PB-ROE MODEL

Many stock valuation models are based, directly or indirectly, on dividend discount models. That is, a stock is worth the present cash value of future dividends, making the implicit arbitrage a specific stock versus cash. We have already noted that such models require a more explicit estimation of risk premia than is comfortable. This should make us prefer models in which we can assume risk premium differences are small, such as those for arbitrage between stocks of similar companies. Another equally problematic issue is that of time horizon. The dividend discount model does not use much in the way of near-term information, leaving much of the value of a company to be determined by events that happen too far in the future to be forecast directly. Partly for that reason, the second generation of valuation models converted dividend projections to earnings or cash flow, which measure dividend-paying capability at an earlier stage. Such models are also more useful to corporate managers, who care less about dividends.

During the last few years, third-generation models have become popular that translate the present value of the future dividend stream into present book value plus future differences between return on equity and costs of equity capital.[3] Incorporating present book value puts a large component of stock price into the present, where it easy to forecast. For each period in the future, one takes the present value of the product of future book value and the difference between ROE and the cost of capital. At some point in the future one fixes the assumption and calculates a terminal value.

Not only is the forecasting time horizon thus shortened, but book value and ROE are better suited for forecasting purposes than the earlier-emphasized dividends, earnings, cash flow and their growth rates. The underlying reason is that the latter are largely first differences, or derivatives with respect to time, of the former. Given relatively clean accounting, the difference between earnings and dividends is the time derivative of book value. Going to the more difficult level of forecasting changes in these quantities, earnings growth is ROE times book value growth, usually small but easy to forecast, plus book value times change in ROE, often large and very difficult to forecast. Empirically, past ROE is a reasonably good predictor of future ROE. In contrast, past earnings growth has almost no correlation with future earnings growth.

There is another reason for the newfound popularity of price models based on book value and surplus ROE. Fama and French made respectable for academics the investigation of P/B.[4] In contrast, this increase in desire to use P/B is illogical for the investor because published results make a model weaker in

---

[3] James A. Ohlson, "Earnings, Book Values, and Dividends in Security Valuation," *Contemporary Accounting Research* (1995), pp. 661-687.

[4] Eugene F. Fama and Kenneth R. French, "The Cross Section of Expected Stock Returns," *Journal of Finance* (June 1992), pp. 427-465.

terms of forecasting returns, not stronger. Nevertheless, there are so many different possibilities for exploiting such models that they remain worthwhile.

We will arrive at a similar model, the PB-ROE model, but begin by taking stock price changes, rather than future changes in fundamental variables, as our starting point. The PB-ROE model and the book value plus surplus earnings model are relatives. The difference is that we begin here with an explicit consideration of two different sources of arbitrage and work toward a structure that lends itself to objective econometric estimation.

Though I do not claim that I was the first to notice a useful relationship between price-to-book and return on equity, my explorations of it came well before a focus on book value returned to respectable finance circles. Because of inflation and differences in accounting, it was in fact very common at that time to hear from anyone with a pretense to an MBA that "book value is meaningless."

In 1975 I was working as a management consultant with The Boston Consulting Group. Toward the end of my time there, I happened to plot the price/book of Polaroid against its return on equity, year by year, working from Value Line data. The company had had marvelous profits. As return on equity increased, so did their stock price, with *P/B* going up to over 10, in a straight line when plotted on a log scale versus return on equity, and then falling in a straight line back down as profits began an inexorable decline. This was a lucky observation, because very few such histories exist with a wide-enough return on equity range to see the relationship clearly through time rather than cross-sectionally. I filed the empirical relationship away but had no idea whether it had any theoretical basis.

The next year I embarked on my own as a management consultant with a contract from a Midwestern industrial company. One of my assignments was to determine the causal factors governing their stock price. With nothing to do in the evenings for a week at a time in the local library of a small town, I worked out a rationale for the log-linear relationship I had seen between *P/B* and ROE. For proprietary reasons, I did not publish the result for eight years, though it gradually disseminated through my business contacts, first in management consulting, and then in several investment firms.[5] Here is how I reasoned then and now.

Stock returns are composed of both dividend yield and price appreciation. We can partition price as the product of the price-to-book ratio and book value. Thus, in any small time increment, the percentage change in price is the percentage change in book value plus the percentage change in the price-to-book ratio plus a vanishingly small third term which is their product. Then shareholder's return over a short interval is dividend yield plus percentage price change plus the percentage change in *P/B*. If stock price is at fair value, then the expected value of this expression is the required shareholder return, more usually called the cost of equity capital. This relationship is summarized in equation (1).

---

[5] Jarrod Wilcox, "The P/B-ROE Valuation Model," *Financial Analysts Journal* (January/February 1984), pp. 58-66.

$$k = \frac{D}{P} + g_B + \frac{\Delta\left(\frac{P}{B}\right)}{\left(\frac{P}{B}\right)} \tag{1}$$

where:

k = shareholder return
D = dividend per share
P = price per share
g_B = growth rate in book value per share
B = book value per share
Δ = the difference operator.

Equation (1) holds for both actual and expected returns. Looking into the future, the variables on the right are expectations, and on the left, the return is that required by shareholders, the equity cost of capital.

Starting from equation (1), we will derive a differential equation in P/B. If we know the values of the other parameters, and if we can postulate an end result toward which P/B is tending, then we can solve the differential equation and discover the appropriate current P/B that constitutes fair value. The intuition is that if the current dividend yield plus growth in book value exceed the required shareholder return or cost of capital, initial P/B must be expected to decline in order to achieve market clearing. The only way that can happen is if current fair value is higher than its final value. Similarly, if there is currently no profit, no growth and no dividends, the required shareholder return must come from an expected increase in P/B. This can only happen if its current fair value is lower than the terminal equilibrium value.

Note that two different types of arbitrage are involved. In the primary investment market, companies will push book value and market value toward an equilibrium relationship, but this will happen over a relatively long time period because of various types of transaction costs. Over rather shorter periods of time, investors in the secondary market work toward an equilibrium in which stocks of similar risks have similar expected returns. Note also that we structure the model within a continuous framework rather than in annual increments over an infinite period.

In common with the academic literature, we will here assume for simplicity that long-term equilibrium P/B is 1. This has several implications that are not strictly true. As the simplest example of why not, consider inflation. Typically, B is measured as historical accounting book value rather than replacement value; thus it will be understated, and equilibrium P/B will be measured as greater than 1. Another possibility is that there exist barriers to entry that may create a wedge between costs of capital generally and the profitability of particular high-profit companies, industries or countries.

We saw in the previous section evidence that equilibrium P/B in the United States in the last several decades appears to be on the order of 1.8. If we take a conservative view that our sample did not include as much of the low tail as would be appropriate — that is, that we were not adequately discounting an economic depression — we might reduce this to, say, 1.6. The remaining gap between 1.6 and 1 will result in our model biasing the implied cost of capital. This is not important for our purpose here, because we do not compare stocks with cash. (We could, however, if we measure expected ROE, get an estimate of changes in the cost of capital over time.) That is, the cost of capital will be neither an input nor a required output of the model as we will use it. If this were not true, however, we could simply substitute a number like 1.6 as a terminal value for *P/B* and re-derive the model along the lines shown next.

The time differential equation in *P/B* is expressed as equation (2), with the *terminal value* boundary condition that *P/B* = 1 at time *T* in the future.

$$\frac{d(P/B)}{dt} = (P/B)(k - g_B) - \delta \qquad (2)$$

subject to

$$(P/B)_{t = T} = 1$$

where

d = the derivative operator
t = time
T = the time when *P/B* equals its final equilibrium value, assuming the initial time is zero.
δ = the ratio of dividends to book value, *D/B*, taken to be a constant.

Here we take each parameter as a constant, although it is possible to derive solutions for more complicated assumptions. This amounts to assuming that the cost of capital, the dividend yield on book value (not price) and the growth rate in book value are constant until time *T*. Empirically, dividend yield on book is considerably more stable than dividend payout ratio, the ratio of dividends to earnings. Assuming so-called clean surplus accounting, ROE is the sum of dividend yield on book and growth in book, so we assume constant ROE until *T*.

At *T*, there is an implicit assumption that thereafter ROE = *k*, so that the derived *P/B* = 1. This rectangular assumption for surplus ROE as a function of time may seem unnatural, but again, because we make the same sort of assumption for all stocks, and because we are comparing only among stocks, it will have small effect on stock-to-stock comparisons.

Equation (2) is not a difficult differential equation to solve as compared with, say, the version of the heat equation used by Black and Scholes to get a closed-form option value. In outline, I approached it by a change of variable to negative time, making *P/B*=1 the *initial value*, rather than the terminal boundary condition. This allowed the straightforward use of a LaPlace transform to obtain equation (3) as the solution.

$$P/B = \frac{\delta}{(k - g_B)} + \left(\frac{k - r}{k - g_B}\right) \times e^{(g_B - k)T} \qquad (3)$$

where:

r = expected return on equity, ROE, in turn equal to $\delta + g_B$

The left-hand term in equation (3) may be familiar to you as an infinite horizon valuation model of P, except it divides through by B to get P/B, and except that it uses growth rate of book value where convention uses growth rate in dividends. The right-hand term summarizes the required transient to equilibrium conditions that the infinite horizon model lacks. In that right-hand term we have substituted r for $\delta + g_B$.

P/B does depend somewhat on dividend policy. Dividends reduce value if expected ROE is greater than k. Dividends increase value if the expected ROE is less than k. The modern finance assertion of the irrelevance of dividends does not apply here, because we assume ROE fixed and no other sources or uses of company financing. However, the impact of dividend policy on P/B is typically small compared to the total variation of P/B as a function of ROE. We can take advantage of this fact to derive a much simpler approximation for P/B.

Suppose one expresses the exponential function at the far right of equation (3) using a Taylor series in g_B around k, then multiplies by $(r - k)/(g_B - k)$ as in the equation, and adds the left-hand term from the equation. Then one is left with a series in increasing powers of $(g_B - k)$ whose first two terms are identical with the analogous Taylor series for e raised to the $(r - k)T$ power. This is shown as equation (4). The remaining higher-order terms differ in equations (3) and (4) but slightly, and are identical if dividends are zero. Even with dividends, the approximation of equation (3) by equation (4) will be tolerable so long as second-order effects are modest, that is, so long as the differences between expected ROE and the cost of equity capital are moderate.

$$P/B \cong e^{(r - k)T} \qquad (4)$$

Finally, taking the natural log of both sides, we derive equation (5), which is suitable for use in regression, to which we turn next.

$$\ln(P/B) = -Tk + Tr \qquad (5)$$

We can estimate this relationship by substituting our own expected ROE for r and regressing log P/B against it. If we have been careful to use reasonably comparable stocks in terms of risk (which relates to k) and uncertainty of future ROE (which also relates to T), the resulting best fit line estimates fair value within the group. We may choose to buy stocks below the line and sell those above the line. In effect, we have adjusted the P/B fair values of the previous section for differences in profitability.

If we assume that expected ROE is measured accurately, then the slope of the best fit line, the regression coefficient, estimates T. (If we wish, we can correct for errors in variables to get a better estimate, which will tend to give a longer time horizon estimate.)

Note, though, that if we measure expected ROE with error, for example if we approximate it with historical ROE, we cannot separate $k + (ROE - r)$ into separate components to estimate k without bias. This becomes practically important because the market often appears to expect future profitability to be better than the past. Thus we cannot use this approach by itself to separate optimism from a low cost of capital.

There are many degrees of sophistication we can apply to such an analysis. We can use either historic ROE or analyst estimates of future ROE. We can go into greater detail by examining market and book values after potential dilution from stock options. We can try to account for differences in dividend policy holding uncertainty in ROE constant or differences in uncertainty of ROE based on the standard deviation of past ROE holding dividend policy constant. However, in the examples which follow we will stick to simple techniques.

EXAMPLE OF PB-ROE ANALYSIS

This section is based on data provided by Value Line for U.S. stocks. The sample begins with about 600 stocks in 1982, a number that increases to somewhat over a thousand by 1996. To make the example somewhat more manageable, I have used only one month of data in each year, June valuation and July returns. The data are influenced by survivor bias, since companies from the early years that no longer are traded are excluded. Since we expect more survivor bias for earlier years, we can evaluate it by examining differences in the power of PB-ROE residuals to forecast returns year by year. We have also excluded from the sample on an *ex ante* basis those companies where current ROE is unlikely to measure expected ROE for the future. This is done by excluding outlier companies where current ROE is less than −20% or greater than 60% or where current book value is negative. We also throw out companies where five-year standard deviation of ROE is greater than 15%.

A good use of the PB-ROE model is as a framework for industry analysis, equally valuable for quantitative and qualitative analysts. The best first assumption is that current ROE is a good approximation for future ROE. Then we plot P/B on a log scale against historic ROE. By limiting our sample to companies within the same industry, we make the gap between historic ROE and expected ROE more consistent. Exhibit 6 shows such a chart as of June 1996 for the U.S. ethical drug industry. The best fit line gives a slope of 3.55 years for the investment horizon, and an implied $k + (ROE - r)$ of minus 17.5%. If we assume the true cost of equity capital were on the order of 12%, this implies truly amazing optimism.

Exhibit 6: Ethical Drugs, SIC 2834
Value Line, June 1996

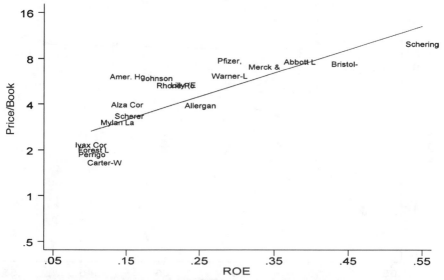

Such displays can be useful for qualitative fundamental analysts as a way to get a quick sense of relative profitability and of what the market thinks of the quality and persistence of current company earnings. In Exhibit 6, the most profitable company is Schering-Plough, the least profitable Ivax.

Relative *P/B* valuation in the exhibit is well explained by relative current ROE, with an R-squared of 67%. In this case, R-squared is not a definitive measure for judging the tracking ability of fair value for price. The reason is that we have divided both the dependent and independent variables by the same variable, book value, thus introducing some additional correlation. However, it is a useful indicator for comparing PB-ROE models for different industries or time periods.

Two companies in Exhibit 6 are valued much higher than their current profitability would suggest — American Home products and Pfizer. On the other hand, Carter Wallace is valued well-below the best fit line. Often such discrepancies reflect concrete and justifiable reasons for expecting future relative ROE to be different from current ROE. Sometimes they reflect true differences in cost of capital, dividend policy or investment horizon. However, they may instead reflect market inefficiencies we can arbitrage by buying companies below the diagonal best-fit line and selling those above the line.

The slope of the best-fit line, assuming dividends are moderate, reflects the investment horizon before one assumes that ROE reverts to the mean. In the case of the highly profitable drug industry, the slope is somewhat flatter than usual. This is sensible since such high profits are an irresistible incentive for competitors to expand within the industry, which would have the effect of reducing future profits.

Exhibit 7: Drugs Compared with Electric Utilities
Value Line, June 1996

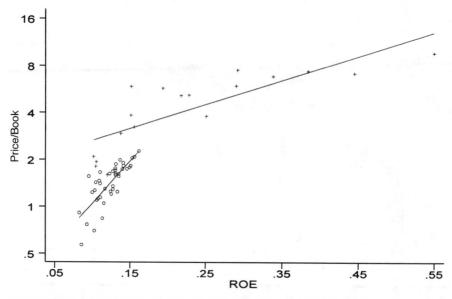

On the other hand, in more mature industries such as electric utilities, returns may be rather stable, allowing much longer investment horizons. This is accentuated by the regulated nature of the industry. Exhibit 7 shows a lower, shorter and steeper best-fit line for electric utilities in PB-ROE space. Its slope gives an estimated time horizon of 12.44 years. (A broader investigation across industries would show a moderate inverse relationship between past standard deviation of ROE and measured T.) The electric utility best-fit intercept combined with the slope gives and estimate for k + (ROE − r) of 9.6%. If we assume a typical cost of equity capital at 12% (6% risk-free plus 6% risk premium), then the expected deterioration in ROE from current values is 2.4%. Unlike the case for the drug industry, this implied change is easy to imagine based on increasing competition for the electric utility industry. The R-squared of the fit is 62%.

If we add all industries in the Value Line sample as of June 1996, we get the cloud of points shown in Exhibit 8. The slope is 4.11 years, the implied k + (ROE − r) is −6.4%, implying very substantial optimism of about 18%, and the R-squared is only 33%, far less than the fit within a single industry.

The eye can also pick out an S-shaped relationship, with a central slope substantially steeper than 4 years, but flatter slopes at ROE's less than 5% or greater than 25%. This is consistent with a world in which threshold effects are important, so that ROE differentials are less likely to persist once they reach extreme levels. If desired, this fit could be estimated using a non-linear regression.

Exhibit 8: All Industries
Value Line, June 1996

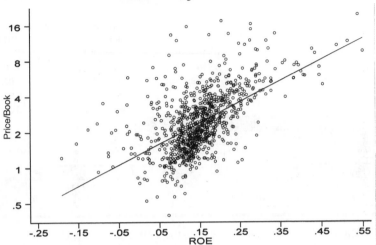

Exhibit 9: Log P/B versus ROE, Pooled By Year
June, 1982-1996

. xtreg pbln roe if year>=82,fe

		Fixed-effects (within) regression
sd(u_year)	=	0.2342962
sd(e_year_t)	=	0.4683727
sd(e_year_t + u_year)	=	0.5237058
corr(u_year, Xb)	=	-0.0104

Number of obs	=	11088
n	=	15
T-bar	=	739.2
R-sq within	=	0.3340
between	=	0.0002
overall	=	0.2947
F(1, 11072)	=	5552.61
Prob > F	=	0.0000

pbln	Coef.	Std. Err.	t	P>|t|	[95% Conf. Interval]	
roe	3.971157	.0532928	74.516	0.000	3.866694	4.07562
_cons	0.1284342	.0086974	14.767	0.000	0.1113857	0.1454827
year	F(14,11072) =		157.399	0.000	(15 categories)	

A history of intercept and slope year by year would indicate steadily rising optimism. Implied future ROE's are far higher than current ROE's necessary to justify current prices by 1996. This trend has continued through mid 1998 as I write.

Exhibit 9 pools the data from each of 15 years to get a typical slope. This time a fixed-effects regression is used to separate these cross-sectional effects from any possible contamination by time-series effects. The average investment horizon is 3.97 years. This gives greater weight to more recent years since there are more company observations in more recent years.

Exhibit 10: Return Based on Relative P/B
(July, 1982-1996)

. xtreg frtn resid

			Random-effects GLS regression		
sd(u_year)	=	0.072131	Number of obs	=	10783
sd(e_year_t)	=	0.1194899	n	=	16
sd(e_year_t + u_year)	=	0.1395733	T-bar	=	438.091
corr(u_year, X)	=	0 (assumed)	R-sq within	=	0.0254
			between	=	0.0013
			overall	=	0.0203

theta							
min	5%	median	95%	max	chi2(1)	=	280.69
0.8016	0.8016	0.9368	0.9449	0.9449	Prob > chi2 =	=	0.0000

frtn	Coef.	Std. Err.	z	P>|z|	[95% Conf. Interval]	
resid	−0.0344635	0.002057	−16.754	0.000	−0.0384953	−0.0304318
_cons	0.0509262	0.0180876	2.816	0.005	0.0154752	0.0863772

Having briefly gotten a feel for the behavior of the PB-ROE model, we now assess whether it could help us forecast returns. We will forecast only July's returns for each year, and use fixed effects regression to isolate cross-sectional comparisons from time-series contamination. (Remember, we do not want to compare stocks with cash, but only with each other.)

We will first establish a base line based simply on log P/B. For each year, we measure deviations from average log P/B in June of that year. Then we pool these residuals across all 15 years to forecast July returns. The final regression is fixed effect, to avoid any possible contamination by time-series effects. (Alternatively, we could have transformed the dependent variable by subtracting the mean July return in each year.)

Exhibit 10 shows the result. We do not need the addition of ROE to a P/B model to forecast returns. The t-statistic is −16.75 and the R-squared created by cross-sectional effects is 2.5%. Keep in mind, that this effect might be exaggerated or even created by survivor bias. That is, low P/B companies are more likely to fail or to be acquired and thus drop out of the sample. They thus never reveal likely inferior stock returns. The remaining low P/B stocks are those which by surviving are more likely to have provided favorable stock returns.

Now we will examine whether there is any improvement from using the PB-ROE model.

Exhibit 11 shows the result of using as our forecast the residuals of a separate log P/B - ROE regression each June. R-squared has been increased to 3.8% while the t-statistic has been strengthened to −20.60. This result is even more powerful when we consider that survivor bias is less for this model. This is because fewer low P/B stocks will have positive return forecasts and more high P/B companies will have positive return forecasts. The PB-ROE criterion has the correct sign in 13 of 15 years, while the P/B criterion has the correct sign in 12 of 15 years. However, the PB-ROE criterion was more effective based on t-statistic than the plain *P/B* criterion in 11 out of the 15 years.

In each case, there is some combination of survivor bias and instability of process leading to less effectiveness with time. When year-by-year t-statistics are calculated for each model there is a fairly strong trend for each to become less negative through time. Still, both worked well during the last two years of the sample, 1995-1996.

MORE THOUGHTS

In the next chapter, we briefly treat technical models. There is a natural opposition between valuation models and technical models in that when prices increase the former tend to sell and the latter tend to buy. This opposition gives rise to a deeper relationship. As we saw in Chapter 7, a policy of active buying into trends underlies the constant proportion portfolio insurance (CPPI) policy. This replicates the consequences of buying both a put and a call option. Then it must be that valuation models, which take the opposite side of each trade, can give rise to an active trading pattern that replicates selling a combination of a put and a call. CPPI involves paying an implicit option premium when the total price excursion does not get far because of see-saw movements. Concurrently, following a strong value model such as *P/B* involves collecting an implied option premium when there have not been lengthy price trends. Thus, one should be careful that any sample in which a valuation model is evaluated has a fair representation of extremely positive and extremely negative price trends. Otherwise, one may confuse an option premium for alpha, the ability to earn active returns.

Exhibit 11: Return Based on Relative PB-ROE
(July, 1982-1996)

. xtreg frtn resid

			Random-effects GLS regression		
sd(u_year)	=	0.0721342	Number of obs	=	10783
sd(e_year_t)	=	0.1187199	n	=	16
sd(e_year_t + u_year)	=	0.1389164	T-bar	=	438.091
corr(u_year, X)	=	0 (assumed)	R-sq within	=	0.0379
			between	=	0.0013
			overall	=	0.0304

theta							
min	5%	median	95%	max	chi2(1)	=	424.46
0.8029	0.8029	0.9372	0.9453	0.9453	Prob > chi2	=	0.0000

frtn	Coef.	Std. Err.	z	P>|z|	[95% Conf. Interval]	
resid	−0.0526365	0.0025549	−20.602	0.000	−0.057644	−0.0476291
_cons	0.050842	0.0180877	2.811	0.005	0.0153908	0.0862932

Chapter 13

Technical Heuristics

It's the height of folly to want to be the only wise one.
François, Duc de La Rochefoucauld, *Sentences et Maximes Morales (1678)*

The body of investment lore known as "technical analysis" stands in the same relation to finance as "alternative medicine" to scientific medicine. Technical analysis as practiced by many investors has much in common with cult and superstition. Yet just as certain folk herbs really do reduce fevers or produce a sense of well-being, there are elements of technical analysis that produce useful investment results. In this chapter, we point out both some quackery and some valuable heuristics in the body of trading and technical analysis lore.

In discussing technical analysis, various topics from earlier in this book are worth recall. In Chapter 4 we portrayed decision policies as filters on price signals. Remember also the overconfidence revealed by behavioral finance in Chapter 9. Pertinent, too, is the need for capital growth theory to manage expected compound return in high-risk situations that we examined in Chapter 6. Another important concept for understanding the results of technical analysis is the equivalence introduced in Chapter 7 between active trading patterns and option positions. Finally, we should recall the existence of fat-tailed return distributions when using econometric techniques introduced in Chapter 2 to investigate the likelihood that our results could have been achieved randomly. All these concepts are helpful in understanding and evaluating technical analysis.

Most technical analysis has to do with high-frequency investing, or what we know as trading. We respect that convention here and take traders as our subject population. Many amateur traders seem to burn out after a season or two. Those who remain have accumulated wisdom we should respect because of its survival value. On the other hand, without the use of rigorous statistical analysis, it is entirely too easy to generalize based on limited experience. For every thousand traders flipping two-sided coins, there will likely be one who has won ten times in a row, 2^{10} being 1024. This person naturally thinks he or she has developed a very high skill in coin flipping. Thus we cannot trust self-appointed trading experts. We should give most credit to ideas that have been used successfully by many traders over very long periods, or where we have valid econometric tests.

Many quantitative investors divide to conquer. They separate as much as possible the process of forecasting returns from that of building ideal portfolios, and again from implementation in trading. In contrast, most traders seem to intertwine all parts of the process. Consequently, trading techniques encompass not only spotting good trades but also risk control and control of one's emotions. Successful traders have a well-rounded view of what it takes to survive and flourish in competitive markets, one that quantitative investors should emulate.

The technical analyst's general assumption is that most fundamental information is already incorporated in prices. Consequently one can profit more from a close study of the market's internal price dynamics, along with volume and open interest, than from a study of the external economic stimuli. Some representative views on how best to trade, and on the technical analysis that underlies much of it, are found in Eng(1988),[1] Schwager (1989),[2] and Elder (1993).[3] The methods used have been around for a long time in slightly different forms. In Drew(1941)[4] the historian can find detailed description of two broad classes of technical methods: those that identify trends one should ride, and those that identify turning points or trading range boundaries. The former included in 1941 the Dow theory, the 10% filter rule, and various calculations based on moving averages. The latter included spreads in price action between speculative and investment grade stocks, or between volatile and stable industries. It also included the use of the product of volume and price change to determine both the trend (when Buying Power and Selling Pressure were moderate) and reversal points (when there was a severe imbalance). Both groups of methods relied in part on subjective interpretation of charts.

The more modern descendants of these market technician methods are covered in the book by Eng. This is not the most popular of such how-to manuals, but it is comprehensive. Nearly 50 years after Drew, enough experience had been gained for Eng to hypothesize as to the market contexts in which particular technical methods would work better or worse. For example, he makes a sharp distinction between the methods most useful in trading (mean-reverting) markets versus trending markets, between bull trending versus bear trending markets, and among the transition situations. Critical of course is one's ability to tell which market context is governing in time to take his advice!

Here are examples of the methods Eng describes: Moving Averages, Relative Strength, Percentage R, Oscillators, Stochastics, Point and Figure, Tic Volume, On-Balance Volume, Bar Charts, Astronomical Cycles, Elliot Wave Theory and Gann Analysis. I am particularly struck by the unembarrassed way he treats trading based on astrological charts, including phases of the moon and positions of the planets Mars and Saturn.

As noted in Chapter 1, Schwager's book is a fascinating account of interviews with traders who have made, and sometimes lost, enormous sums of money.

My favorite in this list is that by Elder, *Trading for a Living*. A psychiatrist by training, he describes only a modest set of technical tools. He more than

---

[1] William F. Eng, *The Technical Analysis of Stocks, Options & Futures*, Richard D. Irwin, 1988.
[2] Jack D. Schwager, *Market Wizards: Interviews with Top Traders* (New York, N.Y.: New York Institute of Finance, 1989).
[3] Alexander Elder, *Trading For A Living*, John Wiley & Son (1993).
[4] Garfield Albee Drew, *New Methods for Profit in the Stock Market* (Boston: The Metcalf Press, 1941).

compensates by emphasizing more than most sources the importance of control both of risk and of one's emotional behavior.

TECHNICAL HEURISTICS AND INVESTMENT PRINCIPLES

Technical methods vary from vague to extremely precise. Some well-known, successful traders concentrate on their policy or system, leaving little scope for judgments that might be ruled by emotions. Once a trading model is tuned to a particular market, its implementation is systematic. This provides a benefit parallel to one of the central benefits of quantitative investing, control over emotions that may interfere with judgment.

An important control over emotions is the pre-specification of stop-loss rules. For example, a chartist following a trend will normally place a buy order accompanied by a stop-loss sale order at a price just below the bottom edge of recent trading ranges. He or she willingly exchanges the prevention of large losses for the consequent many small losses. It is this selling discipline, not diversification, to which many traders refer when they use the term "risk control."

A few years ago I wrote an essay in which I contended that it was generally much harder to sell than to buy.[5] One of the key causes is conflict between different criteria that cause indecision. The number of criteria to be considered increase after purchase, while the perceived alternatives decrease, making disabling conflict more likely. Quantitative investors usually overcome this by establishing a single quantitative rule that governs both buying and selling. Traders using technical approaches overcome it in their own fashion — by religiously applying stop-loss orders that are automatically triggered if prices move against them.

The speedy realization of small losses combined with reluctance to take small gains that characterize good traders has another benefit, however. It is one often not appreciated in mainstream finance. As we saw in Chapter 7, such an activity pattern affords a rough approximation to constant proportion portfolio insurance, or the combination of simultaneously buying a put and a call on the underlying security. Why would this kind of behavior be found among the survivors of the trading game?

An underlying rationale for this is found in Hakansson's capital growth theory, which we reviewed in Chapter 6. Such a trading pattern applied to an undiversified portfolio will produce positive skewness in returns, which from equation (6) in that chapter contributes to expected compound return. An obvious part of this contribution is the reduction of the chance of ruin in a single period. Without positive skewness, the enormous capital volatility many traders assume would otherwise seriously damage expected compound return through the variance drag effect.

---

[5] Jarrod Wilcox, "Selling Bottlenecks: Causes and Treatments," *Financial Analysts Journal* (March-April 1994), pp. 49-54.

The other part of trader's risk control is a policy of not risking more than a certain percentage of trading capital on a single trade. For example, the amount may be limited to no more than 1% of current capital. This directly reduces total return variance to permit positive expected compound growth. Many traders operate on margin, so that the percentage of their remaining capital at risk grows explosively as their losses mount if they maintain their trading position. Continually monitoring the amount at risk relative to remaining capital can enable the trader to adjust trading position more intelligently. The result intended is to maintain a positive expected compound return during the midst of volatile markets and possibly volatile emotions.

How can quantitative investors take advantage of these heuristics? Maintaining positive skew and optimally managing portfolio return variance would be helpful in the exploitation of market inefficiencies most institutional investors avoid as too risky. When adequate returns require the use of margin, or where the limited number of securities available for a class of arbitrage does not permit effective diversification, trader's heuristics will help. Example applications could include hedging of foreign currencies back to a single home currency, leveraging short-term bonds, and tactical asset allocation between US stocks and cash.

Some technical methods are used to identify trends and some to identify turning points. The thesis from the nineteen twenties and thirties was that groups of investors (as described in Chapter 4) produce interpretable patterns as news spreads with varying speeds, providing trends. Less informed retail investors jump on trends to produce overbought and oversold conditions readily discovered by market technicians. Perhaps the key insight to be gained in this chapter is that the resulting traditional technical analysis methods simply assume this kind of inefficiency in the market. They do not detect whether it is still there for the exploiting.

Momentum trading, agreeing with the crowd, seems inherently easier to learn than its contrarian opposite. This may be because of its similarity to conformist, consensus heuristics used in other occupations. It is also true that over any given investment horizon, playing the reversal game up and down requires twice as many trades as playing for a trend. It is therefore more suitable for specialist traders with access to specially low trading costs. Possibly for these reasons, there seems to be an excess of trend-following traders over those who specialize in picking turning points.

The underlying mechanism of technical methods for capturing trends may be quantitatively understood as smoothing or sampling a stream of prices to eliminate "random" high-frequency elements so that the low-frequency elements stand out.

Let me explain this engineering approach. A time-series of prices of finite length and amplitude may be approximated as the sum of sinusoidal waves of different periodicity. Such a sum is known as a Fourier series. We can visualize what happens when we apply a linear operator such as a moving average to such a time series. We do this by thinking of the effect it will have on each of these component sinusoidal curves separately, and then summing the result. For example, suppose the moving average is calculated from the average of the last 26 days of prices. Then the sinusoidal series component with a period of two years will not be much affected, except to delay it by a small fraction of its period. On the other hand, the component sinusoid with a period of four days will be almost completely obliterated. In total, the initial price signal will be transformed in two ways. First, it will be delayed by about 13 days. Second, its high-frequency components will be filtered out. What remains will look like a series of trends.

Sampling, rather than smoothing, will produce similar effects. If one measures prices at monthly intervals, one eliminates high-frequency daily information. If one measures only every quarter, still more will go.

For an example of moving averages, see Exhibit 1. It shows a sequence of stock prices, together with a 13 day exponentially weighted moving average and a 26 day exponentially weighted moving average. An exponentially weighted average works exactly as the "smooth" function used in Chapter 4. It is created as in equation (1), where S is a smoothed function of X, and D is a smoothing time-delay parameter.

$$S_t = S_{t-1} + \frac{X_t - S_{t-1}}{D} \tag{1}$$

According to standard technical analysis, the slope of such a moving average measures the price trend. In Exhibit 1, the trend is clearly very favorable. Furthermore, a purchase rule that suggested buying when prices approach the 13-day moving average would have been even more profitable than holding the stock throughout. Unfortunately, Exhibit 1 is simply a sequence of randomly-generated stock prices assuming a lognormal return distribution with an annual mean of 0.1 and standard deviation of 0.4.

Exhibit 1: Trending Stock Prices, 13-Day and 26-Day Moving Averages

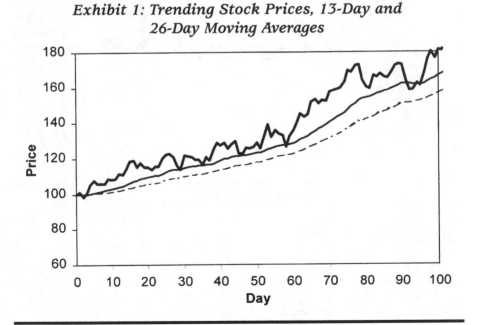

Exhibit 2: Changing Trend Stock Prices, 13-Day and 26-Day Moving Averages

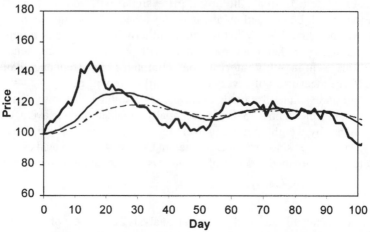

Exhibit 3: Trading Range Stock Prices, 13-Day and 26-Day Moving Averages

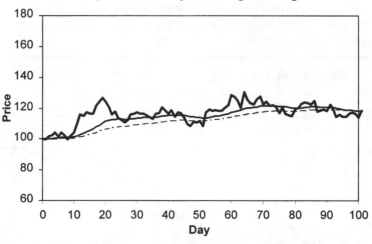

Exhibits 2 and 3, which look quite different, were generated using different random numbers drawn from a random population with exactly the same mean and standard deviation!

The measurement of a trend through using a moving average cannot detect what most investors mean by a trend: that is, a sequence that predicts future above-average returns. If one assumes ahead of time that there will be a predictive trend because one believes that the market is inefficient, then the moving average can tell you its likely direction. But without that prior belief, it is rather useless.

Detection of non-random trends, that is, predictive ones, is much more difficult than many novice market technicians or traders imagine.

Old-fashioned technical methods detected turning points by looking for signs of over-reaction by the least informed investors. For example, one used the ratio of odd-lot trades to total trades, or the ratio of an index of speculative stocks to investment grade stocks. This may have worked reasonably well. However, as the market has matured, these methods have become less useful and less popular. But alternatives are still often used based simply on prices, or better, on prices combined with volume, or for futures, with open interest.

If a moving average spots the trend, then the difference between a price-series and its moving average might be supposed to pick up the shorter-term information useful for spotting a turning point. But what if the price series is very noisy? The solution proposed by many is to use the difference between a short-term moving average and a longer-term moving average as a signal. This is the foundation of the technical device known as an "oscillator." There are a variety of ways to interpret such differences, but all suffer from the same basic problem. That is, they assume market inefficiency rather than detect it. The inadequacy of their basic structure for predicting returns, at least when used by themselves, is somewhat disguised. This is because the scope for different behavior of the tool depending on the length of the two averaging delays is quite large. Usually one can adjust the parameters so that a system would have "worked" to some degree for a given security over a given period.

Having made these criticisms, I do not mean to imply that such methods can never work. They can work if the market is sufficiently inefficient or if one has ancillary information. The artificial stock market simulation studies done at the Santa Fe Institute, cited in Chapter 3, indicate that trend-following approaches are likely survivors in any market where instability of agent rules is likely. The investor population can produce this instability either by changing its policies in response to changing environments or by recruiting new, inexperienced investors. Another way of saying this is that when fashion predominates, trend-following will be associated with survival. (Paradoxically, so will its opposite, fundamental value investing.)

It would take yet another book to thoroughly explore the various technical approaches that might have some value. Instead, I will pick and choose among interesting ideas. Here are some I believe to be worthy of further research:

1. Market technicians frequently use price information in conjunction with volume information. There is a close positive connection between volume and price volatility. This suggests that an analogue behavior for quantitative investors is to explore the connection, positive or negative, between predictive trends and the market's typical bursts of activity that result in temporary high return variance.

2. Quantitative investors often use fundamental analyst earnings estimate revisions as a momentum indicator. In a sense, this is a kind of technical analysis, if we regard analysts as part of the market's internal mecha-

nism. Might estimate revision signals also be more fruitful in conjunction with volume or volatility information?

3. The old-fashioned indicators of turning points were based on differentiating between the signals given off by amateurs versus professionals. Unfortunately, the odd-lot indicator of fifty years ago does not work so well today. But we now have available government-required reports on holdings of mutual funds of different types.

4. Looking at price charts has the salutary effect of forcing the investor to recognize the extremely "fat-tailed" nature of returns, as outlined by Mandelbrot.[6] It may not be strictly true, as he used to assert, that the tails are so fat that return distributions have no finite variance. But it is true that our measure of that variance often materially increases as we collect more history. In the crash in October 1987, the daily fall exceeded by twenty times the standard deviation of returns measured previously. If we were dealing with true log-normal returns, this would have been essentially impossible.

THE APPLICABILITY OF OPTION THEORY

At the close of Chapter 12 I noted that just as momentum investing produced results equivalent to simultaneously buying a put and a call, value investing could do the opposite. The nature of value investing is to make more money when volatile securities oscillate within valuation ranges. The nature of momentum investors is to make more money (relative to their peers) when volatile stocks pursue very extended trends, either up or down. If one were to measure the overall success of value investing in a fat-tailed return world, one would want to think about the possibility that the result included an option premium that is not recognized as such. We do not recognize it because we do not observe in a bounded period the potential extreme range of returns postulated by Mandlebrot.

There is a strict analogy within the technical analysis world. Momentum investing (I use this term as synonymous with trend-following) will produce an option-buying payoff. Attempting to profit from counter-trading at the boundaries of trading ranges will produce an option-selling payoff pattern. Exhibit 4 illustrates with Monte Carlo simulation.

This simulation does not have fat tails. It is based on twenty days of a randomly generated daily return based on a log normal return distribution with annual mean 0.1 and annual standard deviation of 0.4. Five hundred random sequences are plotted. The horizontal axis shows the cumulative log return of the simulated

---

[6] Benoit Mandelbrot, *Fractals and Scaling in Finance: Discontinuity, Concentration, Risk* (New York: Springer-Verlag, 1997).

underlying stock after twenty days. The vertical axis shows the log return value added over a cash benchmark for one of two trading rules. The black diamonds show the results of a momentum or trend-following strategy. The hollow circles show results for the opposite strategy, one that acts as though there were a flexible trading range, with bets for reversals as the range boundary is approached.

The trend-following strategy is as follows. At the end of each day with sufficient history, the cumulative five-day log return is calculated. A fraction of assets equal to five times that number is invested in the stock for the next day. If the five-day return has been negative, then the investment is in a short position. Any remaining assets are left in cash, which for simplicity earns no interest. In other words, the bet is proportionate to a five-day trend. The opposite trading range strategy is exactly the same except that the fraction of assets used is of the opposite sign, or minus five times the cumulative 5-day log return.

In Exhibit 4 the black diamond outcomes of the momentum or trend-following strategy form a pattern shaped like the letter U. The empty circles are the mirror image, and form a hump. The momentum strategy pays an option premium. At the far left and right, the premium is more than offset by value added from trend-following. The opposite trading range strategy receives a premium when reversals are common — that is, in the center of the range. However, when extended trends occur, as at the far left and right, the trading range strategy loses significant capital.

Exhibit 4: Option Properties of Trading Rules

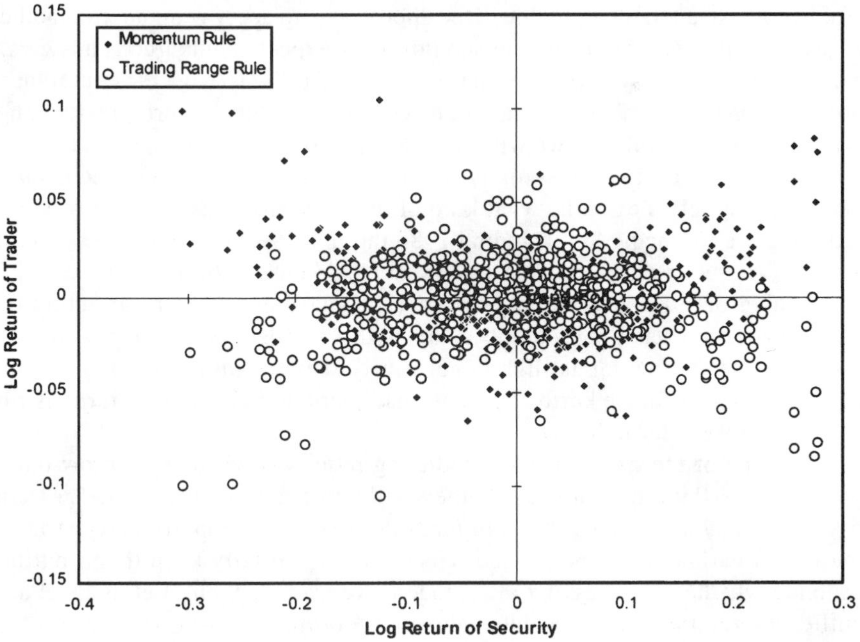

Exhibit 5: S&P500 Daily % Return Characteristics, 1983-1997

	Percentiles	Smallest		
1%	-2.255484	-20.46693		
5%	-1.296524	-8.278941		
10%	-0.8672445	-6.865681	Obs	3913
25%	-0.360112	-6.768304	Sum of Wgt.	3913
50%	0.0304093		Mean	0.0538248
		Largest	Std. Dev.	0.9337595
75%	0.4837679	4.925407		
90%	1.029203	5.115224	Variance	0.8719069
95%	1.434614	5.332677	Skewness	-2.919973
99%	2.329069	9.099362	Kurtosis	69.52025

There is much more vertical scatter than shown in the option payoff patterns for CPPI in Chapter 7. That is, the same final security return can have very different payoffs to the trading strategies. Unlike perfect (continuous, zero trading cost) CPPI, there is substantial path dependence in the strategy payoff.

STUDY OF A SIMPLE TECHNICAL RULE

What should a quantitative investor do when confronted with a technical analysis tool hypothesized to be profitable? One approach is to apply econometric methods to test its efficacy. Of course, one should rarely expect unambiguous answers. If certainty were readily available, the market would likely have closed down the profit opportunity before one had a chance to exploit it. Nevertheless, such an exercise can be useful, and we will give a simple example here.

We will try to forecast daily returns of the S&P500 Index of the US stock market. First, let us examine what kind of distribution we have. The statistics in Exhibit 5 are for the period including 1983 through 1997.

We see in Exhibit 5 that the lowest return during the 15 years was −20% (in October of 1987) and the highest 9% a few days later. The mean return over the whole period was 5 basis points a day, with a standard deviation of a little less than 1%. The distribution is slightly negatively skewed, with a very high kurtosis of 69. For reference, the kurtosis of a normal distribution is 3; this return distribution certainly has fat-tails.

One of the first issues in predicting returns is whether to throw out the outliers if we think they are so few they will be very difficult to model. Alternatively, we may keep them, thinking that otherwise a disproportionate amount of the return variance will be missed. Here we will initially keep them, but later examine whether it makes any difference if we exclude them. Let us label as an outlier any return with an absolute value of 5% or more.

We are going to test for the predictive power of a "reversal." To keep things simple, we will define the pattern in terms of quartile return boundaries as found in Exhibit 5. That is, we will look for "up" movements of at least 0.48% or "down" movements of at least −0.36%. We will define a reversal as either an up movement preceded by two daily down movements, or a down movement preceded by two up movements. If any of the three preceding days had movements in between the threshold definitions for up and down movements, we will count the whole pattern as a non-reversal. We define a variable "reversal" to be 1 for an up day preceded by two down days, −1 for a down day preceded by two up days, and 0 otherwise.

If the distribution were normal and successive days "nearly" independent, the probability of any one day being a reversal by this definition would be about 2/(4x4x4), or 3.1%. The actual number observed is quite close, 3.4%. The most reversals are observed in 1987 (26) and the fewest in 1995 (2). Nineteen ninety-seven was a more active year, with 15 reversals.

We will divide our sample into two, using odd days of the month (1, 3, ...31) for our estimation sample, and even days (2,4,...30) as our validation sample. If we decide to keep our model, we can combine the two samples to get its best estimate. We can also test the model throwing out the instances of outlier returns. Finally, we can look just at rebounds off the bottom (defined as an up day preceded by two down days).

Exhibit 6 shows three regressions. The first is of daily S&P500 returns (SRETDAY) against "reversal" for the odd days. The second is a test of the fit from that model as a predictor for the return on even days. The third predicts SRETDAY from reversals just within the even days.

Exhibit 6 shows that the reversal pattern did quite well on the odd days, with an average pickup in return of 28 basis points (0.28%) on up days and -0.28% on down days, for a t-statistic of 2.45. This has a significance level of 1.4% on a two-tailed test, but since we predicted the direction, it appears significant at a 0.7% level (one-tailed).

Sadly, we cannot take this relationship very much for granted in the future. The t-statistic can be thrown off by extreme outliers that happen to correlate with the reversal signal. We earlier saw that the underlying distribution is far from normal in the extreme tails. This disquiet becomes tangible when we look at the validation sample. The third regression in Exhibit 6 indicates that in this sample the reversal signal only picks up 14 basis points, and the t-statistic is reduced to 1.26, not quite significant at the 10% level one-tailed. Unless we think there is a true structural difference between odd and even days of the month, we have to admit that our estimate is less certain than our initial regression would suggest.

We might suspect that the stronger effect in the odd-day sample depends on outliers, and indeed it includes some large movements from the crash periods in 1987 and again in 1990. Exhibit 7 excludes outlier days, those with returns with absolute values of greater than 5%. This exclusion greatly reduces the effectiveness shown in the odd-day sample while slightly increasing it in the even-day sample. Now, on a one-tailed basis, the significance level in each is consistent at about 10%. The odd-day estimated impact is 15 basis points and the even-day impact is 14 basis points.

Exhibit 6: Estimate of Reversal Predictive Power

. regress SRETDAY reversal if odd

Source	SS	df	MS
Model	5.61590606	1	5.61590606
Residual	1859.91063	1994	0.932753578
Total	1865.52654	1995	0.935101023

Number of obs = 1996
F(1, 1994) = 6.02
Prob > F = 0.0142
R-squared = 0.0030
Adj R-squared = 0.0025
Root MSE = 0.96579

SRETDAY	Coef.	Std. Err.	t	P>|t|	[95% Conf. Interval]	
reversal	0.2814102	.1146868	2.454	0.014	0.0564917	0.5063287
_cons	0.029419	.0216303	1.360	0.174	-0.0130014	0.0718393

. more
. predict fitodd
. regress SRETDAY fitodd if even

Source	SS	df	MS
Model	1.28084768	1	1.28084768
Residual	1542.0163	1915	0.805230446
Total	1543.29715	1916	0.805478681

Number of obs = 1917
F(1, 1915) = 1.59
Prob > F = 0.2074
R-squared = 0.0008
Adj R-squared = 0.0003
Root MSE = 0.89735

SRETDAY	Coef.	Std. Err.	t	P>|t|	[95% Conf. Interval]	
fitodd	0.5107641	0.4049783	1.261	0.207	-0.2834807	1.305009
_cons	0.0624518	0.0236468	2.641	0.008	0.0160755	0.108828

. more
. regress SRETDAY reversal if even

Source	SS	df	MS
Model	1.28084765	1	1.28084765
Residual	1542.0163	1915	0.805230446
Total	1543.29715	1916	0.805478681

Number of obs = 1917
F(1, 1915) = 1.59
Prob > F = 0.2074
R-squared = 0.0008
Adj R-squared = 0.0003
Root MSE = 0.89735

SRETDAY I	Coef.	Std. Err.	t	P>|t|	[95% Conf. Interval]	
reversal	0.1437342	0.113965	1.261	0.207	-0.0797744	0.3672428
_cons	0.0774779	0.0204954	3.780	0.000	0.0372823	0.1176736

These effects are small, but potentially economically significant, since trading in S&P500 futures is very liquid. For one-way trading costs of 3 basis points, we might conservatively project a profit of about 8 basis points per reversal. There is also the possibility of much larger returns when the market is disrupted by outlier days, as in the aftermath of the October 1987 crash.

Exhibit 7: Reversal Effectiveness Omitting Outliers

Reversal Effectiveness Omitting Outliers
. regress SRETDAY reversal if odd & abs(SRETDAY)<5

Source	SS	df	MS
Model	1.64975524	1	1.64975524
Residual	1275.79851	1990	0.641104779
Total	1277.44827	1991	0.641611384

Number of obs = 1992
F(1, 1990) = 2.57
Prob > F = 0.1088
R-squared = 0.0013
Adj R-squared = 0.0008
Root MSE = 0.80069

SRETDAY	Coef.	Std. Err.	t	P>|t|	[95% Conf. Interval]	
reversal	0.1535978	0.0957502	1.604	0.109	-0.0341834	0.3413791
_cons	0.0426134	0.0179492	2.374	0.018	0.0074123	0.0778145

. predict fitodd3
. regress SRETDAY fitodd3 if even & abs(SRETDAY)<5

Source	SS	df	MS
Model	1.28390035	1	1.28390035
Residual	1344.84405	1910	0.704106833
Total	1346.12795	1911	0.704410231

Number of obs = 1912
F(1, 1910) = 1.82
Prob > F = 0.1771
R-squared = 0.0010
Adj R-squared = 0.0004
Root MSE = 0.83911

SRETDAY	Coef.	Std. Err.	t	P>|t|	[95% Conf. Interval]	
fitodd3	0.9368974	0.6938182	1.350	0.177	-0.4238234	2.297618
_cons	0.0428604	0.0351543	1.219	0.223	-0.0260844	0.1118052

. regress SRETDAY reversal if even & abs(SRETDAY)<5

Source	SS	df	MS
Model	1.28390038	1	1.28390038
Residual	1344.84405	1910	0.704106833
Total	1346.12795	1911	0.704410231

Number of obs = 1912
F(1, 1910) = 1.82
Prob > F = 0.1771
R-squared = 0.0010
Adj R-squared = 0.0004
Root MSE = .83911

SRETDAY	Coef.	Std. Err.	t	P>|t|	[95% Conf. Interval]	
reversal	0.1439054	0.106569	1.350	0.177	-0.0650984	0.3529092
_cons	0.0827848	0.0191903	4.314	0.000	0.0451486	0.120421

Exhibit 8 shows the combined sample estimate for reversals. With more degrees of freedom, the t-statistic on the top regression is notably better, even without including outlier days. The final t-statistic is about 2.0, with a significance level of 4%, or 2% one-tailed. The bottom regression shows the same estimate for "rebounds," which are the subset of reversals in an upward direction. Upward rebounds appear to be more pronounced than downward reversals, with an estimated return of 19 basis points, but the difference is not statistically significant.

Exhibit 8: Best Estimate of Reversal and Rebound Effects

. regress SRETDAY reversal if abs(SRETDAY)<5

Source	SS	df	MS
Model	2.84968339	1	2.84968339
Residual	2622.21769	3902	0.672018885
Total	2625.06737	3903	0.672576832

Number of obs	= 3904
F(1, 3902)	= 4.24
Prob > F	= 0.0395
R-squared	= 0.0011
Adj R-squared	= 0.0008
Root MSE	= 0.81977

SRETDAY	Coef.	Std. Err.	t	P>ltl	[95% Conf. Interval]	
reversal	0.1469445	0.0713585	2.059	0.040	0.007041	0.2868481
_cons	0.0623095	0.0131213	4.749	0.000	0.0365842	0.0880348

. regress SRETDAY rebound if abs(SRETDAY)<5

Source	SS	df	MS
Model	2.60996818	1	2.60996818
Residual	2622.45741	3902	0.672080319
Total	2625.06737	3903	0.672576832

Number of obs	= 3904
F(1, 3902)	= 3.88
Prob > F	= 0.0488
R-squared	= 0.0010
Adj R-squared	= 0.0007
Root MSE	= 0.81981

SRETDAY	Coef.	Std. Err.	t	P>ltl	[95% Conf. Interval]	
rebound	0.1934969	0.0981899	1.971	0.049	0.0009885	0.3860053
_cons	0.0591669	0.0132416	4.468	0.000	0.0332057	0.085128

Overall, this particular technical tool looks profitable, but it is a small profit earned infrequently. It would not be sufficient to justify practical action in isolation. However, a practical quantitative daily trading model is likely to consist of a collection of such individually low-powered tools.

In short, technical analysis does have something to offer the skeptical quantitative investor. But you will need patience in sorting out the useful bits. And you need to resist the siren call of your own evolution that tries to see patterns in random data.

Chapter 14

Econometric Modeling of Market Imperfections

Now here, you see, it takes all the running you can do, to keep in the same place. If you want to get somewhere else, you must run at least twice as fast as that!
Lewis Carroll, The Red Queen in Through the Looking-Glass (1872)

There is a hierarchy of problem solving in investment work. On a day-to-day basis, one is busy with implementation details regarding assessment of individual securities and trading. With a bit more perspective, it is possible to discern overall patterns of activity that can be defined as return forecasting and portfolio construction. This insight is a profound contribution by the pioneers of academic finance to investment practitioners. Insofar as constructing a good return forecast is a relatively independent activity, the conventional tools of statistical estimation and hypothesis testing can be brought to bear. These "econometric" tools offer an efficient way to discover predictive indicators. Thus it is important that as a quantitative investor you have a mastery of basic econometrics.

Yet for their true mastery in an investment context, it is vital to note that neither the framework of academic finance nor of classical econometrics is more than a useful approximation. Consider the following step-by-step deepening of the investor's problems.

First, financial data often do not conform to the conventional assumptions of the more elementary body of statistical techniques. Elementary courses do not much deal with real everyday investment problems of extremely fat-tailed distributions, complicated correlation structures, mixing of time-series and cross-sectional data, unstable processes and so on.

Next, the problem of constructing the best return forecast is not truly independent of the problem of constructing a best portfolio. That is, minimizing mean-squared error within a regression, even a fancy one, is too narrow an objective function in the context of finding the best portfolio. As the simplest example, the best forecast across a large sample of stocks may be inferior in portfolio construction to a differently based forecast that gives greater predictability for larger stocks. The lack of the same forecast usefulness for small versus large stocks reflects constraints against short-sales, differences in trading costs and even the requirements of reducing residual risk versus capitalization-weighted benchmarks.

Third, the problem of managing a portfolio is a dynamic one that takes into account features such as trading costs that couple successive portfolio problems. The best forecast of one-month returns, if it implies high turnover, will be inferior to another forecast of lower statistical significance in forecasting one-month returns but greater persistence over a longer period.

Going to a higher level of problem definition in another direction, the forecast problem is embedded in a stochastic learning problem. For example, according to conventional statistics, a model with a higher R-squared, adjusted for degrees of freedom, will be preferred. But if it is selected from hundreds of possibilities (the data-mining problem), it reflects an inefficient learning procedure that is unlikely to generalize to the future.[1]

Finally, investors do not operate in a vacuum against nature. They are involved in a game-theoretic, dynamic system in which their investment success reflects the trends in investment policies of competitors. Assume that the underlying stochastic return generating process is unstable because competitors are continually learning better, or at least more fashionable, methods. Then an emphasis on new or unconventional methods will gain higher rewards. In contrast, perfectly conducted econometric research that reproduces the same findings likely to be already fashionable may even have a perverse impact on investment results. In today's competitive world, one might be better off with a low t-statistic on a hypothetical obscure signal such as the length of tenure of the company's president.

Thus this chapter begins with a famous quotation from the Red Queen used to describe competitive races where all that counts is maintaining a lead. Quantitative investment research is not science proceeding at a leisurely pace. It is a race, with no end in sight, and it must be tempered with a practical awareness of larger issues. Econometrics is an imperfect tool for this problem, but to the extent it can be used to speed our learning process and produce useful innovations, it is the best tool we have.

In this chapter, we further display the practice of econometrics in investment work. First, we will conduct a simple econometric study of our own, pointing out useful heuristics that are important for the quantitative investor. We will look for the "January effect," the tendency for small stocks to do especially well in January. I will use this opportunity to share my research tastes and prejudices. Second, we will review three important examples of econometric research from the investment literature. They include Fama and French,[2] Chan, Jegadeesh, and Lakonishok,[3] and Campbell and Shiller.[4] Besides useful review of particular findings, these examples will give us an introduction to some additional techniques.

---

[1] This topic of data-mining or data-snooping is covered very well in John Y. Campbell, Andrew W. Lo, and A. Craig MacKinlay, *The Econometrics of Financial Markets* (Princeton University Press, 1997).

[2] Eugene Fama and Kenneth R. French, "The Cross-section of Expected Stock Returns," *Journal of Finance* (1992), pp. 427-465.

[3] Louis K. C. Chan, Narasimhan Jegadeesh, and Josef Lakonishok, "Momentum Strategies," *Journal of Finance* (1996), pp. 1681-1713.

[4] John Y. Campbell and Robert J. Shiller, "Valuation Ratios and the Long-Run Stock Market Outlook," *Journal of Portfolio Management* (Winter 1998), pp. 11-26.

OUR OWN EXAMPLE — SMALL STOCKS RETURN PREMIUMS AND THE JANUARY EFFECT

The following example presents most of the econometric problems and their treatments found in investment work. It is organized to provide a kind of checklist of issues for the reader's studies.

In the late 1970s and early 1980s, it became fashionable to note that small stocks had higher average returns than did big stocks. Academics then discovered that most of this effect seemed to occur in the first few days of January. The reasons were mysterious, although various hypotheses were made rooted in tax effects and behavioral quirks. Mid-1983 was possibly the peak of the small stock experience. Less has been heard in recent years of small stock superiority, and especially of the January effect. In this chapter we explore the validity of the idea from a longer perspective.

Sample Selection

To begin, we need data. We will use the electronic database provided by Value Line. Since it preferentially includes those companies of current interest, rather than dead companies that were alive in earlier years, it has the relatively common problem of survivorship bias. However, this will be irrelevant for our purpose of investigating the superiority of January versus other months for relative small stock performance. It is relevant, however, to the overall finding of a small-stock return premium. The reason is that stocks low in market capitalization are differentially more likely to be dropped from the database if they have poor subsequent returns. Survivor bias should be worst in the earliest years of whatever sample we select.

I have most readily available the 19 years and one month beginning December 1977 and ending December 1996. Within that sample, we must restrict our attention to those companies and dates with price, dividend yield, and number of shares available. The remaining sample includes only 428 companies at the beginning, rising gradually to 1,080 at the end. The apparent growth in numbers reflects more the birth and death of companies within Value Line's universe, together with their not carrying forward data on dead companies, than it does growth in their coverage.

Since these data are monthly we have a very large dataset to work with — about 175,000 observations. What is the most efficient way to learn from these data? There is so much evidence available that it is clumsy to work with it all at one time; consequently, I will follow the idyllic procedure of splitting the observations equally into a model estimation sample and a separate validation sample. Then we can test whatever we discover against the fresh evidence in the other half of the sample.

Although a suitable way to test a hypothesis, this classic procedure is not necessarily the most efficient use of the data for estimation purposes. Suppose I split the sample in two and give two different researchers different halves as their model estimation samples. They must each select a favorite prediction model without seeing the other half of the data. They then test this model on a swapped validation sample. Each concludes that their model should be accepted in whole or in part or not at all. This use of the second sample serves well enough for hypothesis testing after model estimation. But is it the best estimation model? Suppose at this point I construct my model predicting return as the average of the return predicted by the two previously separate researchers. Will not my model be superior to each of theirs?

If we wish to learn anything beyond our prior hypothesis, what is the best procedure? Any revision of our hypothesis other than outright rejection of the original structure might conceivably be labeled data-mining. But the term data-mining should be reserved for hypothesis revisions that worsen future predictions. Otherwise, when we revise our hypothesis we are simply learning. How can we improve the odds that what we learn from the sample will generalize out of sample and thus not constitute data-mining?

We can structure our data exploration so that it maximizes the chance of carrying over out-of-sample by requiring consistency across subsamples of the sample available. This tends to reduce the impact of outliers and to focus attention on the variables least sensitive to structural change. One can usefully iterate this procedure. For example, if the final model were developed by requiring consistency among several subsamples of companies, it might be additionally validated by requiring consistency between odd and even years.

Sometimes it *will* be fruitful to articulate a differentiated model by sub-sample, for example a model of bank stock returns as compared to manufacturing stock returns. This process sharply increases the temptation and opportunity for data-mining, overfitting the model to the sample. In such cases, a separate valida-tion sample or sub-sample is particularly useful. For example, one might first split the sample using every other company ranked alphabetically by name, and then require consistency across these two samples in the differences between banks and manufacturers.

This cycle of limited data exploration followed by pruning based on requiring consistency across sub-samples is my personal heuristic. I believe it is a logical extension of the notion that model validation is essentially the requiring of consistency across a model estimation sample and a validation sample. It is a search for robustness across samples. It will be confused with data-mining. But it is essentially different if, as I argue, it *increases* rather than decreases the chance that the resulting model will work out of sample. Usually such a model will be more parsimonious than would otherwise be developed.

Another issue very much worth noting is the care needed in splitting the sample if one is dealing with a process that is changing through time. In this case, we should not segregate large blocks of time between estimation and validation samples, but instead efficiently mix different time periods in both. Otherwise, we will unnecessarily tend toward a model not robust across time, or perhaps, seeing failure in the validation sample, we will end with no model at all.

It is relatively common to select earlier data as the model estimation period and later data as the test period. There is an advantage here if the later data is unavailable to the investigator who may data-mine the earlier sample. However, this advantage is often more than offset by structural changes. In an unstable process such as that found in the shifting fashions of investment behavior, this procedure maximizes rather than minimizes the difference between the two samples. It also confounds two very different problems. On the one hand, we have the typical statistical issue of data-mining that results from a high number of potential hypotheses relative to a small number of independent data. On the other, we have the much more difficult problem of adaptive learning in the face of a changing environment. Selecting samples that span different time periods focuses attention away from variables whose structural changes would otherwise have to be explicitly modeled to get good results.

For our present study of the January effect, we will select two samples based on their initial ordering within the Value Line database. We select the evenly-numbered companies as our model estimation sample and the odd-numbered companies as our model validation sample. This assures a random sampling.

We have not yet discussed the proper time interval the sample should span. There is a tradeoff between the greater statistical degrees of freedom, and therefore the greater confidence, gained by using more observations, versus the possibility of less relevance because of subsequent structural changes in the data. The correct choice must depend on the statistical power needed to find a weak effect versus the speed of environmental change.

This decision is complicated because to some extent the environment changes cyclically rather than unidirectionally. It is said that clothing styles worn on social occasions tend not to look like the styles of one's parents, but may well bear a resemblance to those of one's grandparents. So, too, do fashions in investing tend to be cyclic. It may sometimes pay to weight the observations of the last few months very heavily to pick up a style still emerging. At the same time, there is a competitive argument for including 15-year old observations with as much weight, or even more, as for observations three years old. The purpose is to take advantage of the possibility that very old ideas may come back into fashion. Most market participants will expect the future to be like the past several years, not the very recent past and not like the poorly remembered "ancient history."

For our study of the January effect, we will use all 19 years available to us. We will weight these years equally to keep the example simple.

Data Conditioning and Model Structure

We will use STATA statement format to make the details of our example as explicit as possible. We first calculate next month's total return *frtn* as follows:

. quietly by ZINDIV: gen frtn = 100*((PRICE[_n+1]+DPS[_n+1]/12)/PRICE-1)

The monthly data are sorted first by company (*ZINDIV*) and then by month (*ZDATE*), here indexed as _*n*. The foregoing simply says that within each company, return is calculated as a percentage based on next month's price and estimated dividend per share (*DPS*) compared to this month's price. Note that this database has no record of actual dividends declared during the month. That fact forces us to estimate the dividend based on the annual dividend Value Line estimates, and prorate the effect to a single month. A different choice would have been to forecast price returns excluding dividends, but this would have introduced still more difficult problems of bias. Keep in mind that it would be wise to check our example study using the actual monthly profile of dividend payments before investing based on our findings here.

Note that we have chosen not to express returns in log form. The log form would be useful for time-series forecasts of a single asset's returns. However, our problem is portfolio construction period by period. In this case, it is more important to forecast the portfolio result, and that will be a weighted sum of the stock's arithmetic returns each period.

Should we forecast returns, including the ups and downs of the market as a whole, or would it be better to forecast each month only the cross-sectional differences among returns? If the underlying relationship truly applies to total return rather than to excess return, the latter will imply a modest econometric inaccuracy, but this is material only if there are relatively few assets.

The bigger issue lies elsewhere. If we had a truly complete forecast of each stock's total return, then we would also have a good forecast of monthly differences from the mean. However, the market is so efficient that, however useful our forecast model for earning returns in a portfolio sense, it will explain only a small fraction of the individual stock's total return. In choosing between econometric approaches, we are choosing between small slivers of that total variability, and these slivers have different practical relevance.

A concrete example is in order. I once did a study of asset allocation between stocks and bonds on a global basis. World average price-to-book was a useful predictor of world average stock returns. Unfortunately world stock price-to-book also was a predictor of world bond returns in the same direction with a somewhat comparable magnitude. Thus, it was useless as a predictor of the difference between stock and bond returns.

We will not be considering allocations between stocks and cash, and we note that the differences among stocks in expected return based on market beta seem from other studies to be quite modest. Consequently, we choose to forecast *excess* returns over cross-sectional means.

The following STATA code accomplishes the subtraction of the unique mean return for each next month, and then calculates descriptive statistics on the resulting excess return.

```
. egen frtnmn = mean(frtn),by(ZDATE)
. gen frtnx = frtn - frtnmn
. sum frtnx,de
```

frtnx				
Percentiles	Smallest			
1%	−20.9586	−82.36		
5%	−12.60005	−78.03786		
10%	−9.408678	−77.23414	Obs	87846
25%	−4.940997	−74.82349	Sum of Wgt.	87846
50%	−.4702471		Mean	−6.43e−09
		Largest	Std. Dev.	11.71061
75%	4.160643	494.5071		
90%	9.474096	800.1474	Variance	137.1384
95%	13.67557	906.4333	Skewness	30.64531
99%	25.31902	1322.33	Kurtosis	2668.466

The resulting excess return's mean is now essentially zero. The standard deviation is 11.7% per month, or just over 40% annualized. The peculiarities of the return distribution are the large positive skew of 30 and the enormous kurtosis of 2,668. These suggest high positive outliers. Indeed, we see that although the 99th percentile of the excess return distribution is only 25%, the four largest observations range from about 500% to over 1,300%!

Of course, we should expect arithmetic returns to have positive skewness and high kurtosis if they are generated by something like a log-normal distribution. Let us examine the distribution of excess log returns, which should make skewness vanish, and kurtosis much smaller.

```
. gen lfrtn = log(1+frtn/100)
. egen lfrtnmn = mean(lfrtn),by(ZDATE)
. gen lfrtnx = lfrtn - lfrtnmn
. sum lfrtnx, de
```

lfrtnx				
Percentiles	Smallest			
1%	−0.2285644	−1.883817		
5%	−0.1271221	−1.759434		
10%	−0.091979	−1.387244	Obs	87846
25%	−0.0451942	−1.385378	Sum of Wgt.	87846
50%	−0.0006987		Mean	−1.33e−10
		Largest	Std. Dev.	0.0901243
75%	0.0444675	1.764736		
90%	0.0934027	2.209974	Variance	0.0081224
95%	0.1304574	2.284595	Skewness	0.9073399
99%	0.2268546	2.707331	Kurtosis	46.7281

We see from this vantage point very modest skewness, but still quite high kurtosis — or fat tails, since a normal distribution has a kurtosis of 3, not 46.7. Of course we know from Mandelbrot, Fama, and others that stock return distributions are not truly log-normal, having greater dispersion, or "fat" tails, but here we see it for ourselves. We might also suspect that several very high returns that account for the still high kurtosis might conceivably be data errors. If so, we should either correct them or remove them from the sample.

Let us assume, however, that in this case all the observations are valid. We still have a decision to make. Should we *winsorize* the data — that is, bring in the outliers toward the mean? The advantage of winsorization is that we will reduce the impact of a very few outlier return observations on the relationship we find. The disadvantage is that we will not gain any information on relationships that do govern the extreme values. We may experience a loss in information because such outlier returns will be a part of the total portfolio return we are trying to construct.

I approach this quandary in the case of our study of the January effect as follows. If sacrificing a handful of data points in 88,000 will appreciably reduce kurtosis, I will winsorize. The outlier observations would have been too few to model separately, and by reducing kurtosis from 2,668 we will likely reduce the forecasting variance in any OLS regression. Thus, I arbitrarily set a 200% maximum return for our observations, reducing 19 higher excess return observations to that figure.

```
. gen frtnxw = frtnx
. replace frtnxw = 200 if frtnx>200
. sum frtnxw,de
```

			frtnxw		
	Percentiles	Smallest			
1%	−20.9113	−82.36			
5%	−12.56947	−78.03786			
10%	−9.379884	−77.23414	Obs		88402
25%	−4.908188	−74.82349	Sum of Wgt.		88402
50%	−0.4175602		Mean		1.208306
		Largest	Std. Dev.		18.40186
75%	4.275156	200			
90%	9.816416	200	Variance		338.6283
95%	14.52182	200	Skewness		8.346649
99%	35.48227	200	Kurtosis		90.1606

This winsorization has reduced kurtosis for the transformed variable from over 2,600 to 90, still large, but more tolerable.

For the independent variables, where preserving outliers is less critical, I prefer to reduce kurtosis to 10 or below before attempting OLS (ordinary least-squares) regression.

Our key independent variable is market capitalization, which we will convert to log form. We do this both to provide a more statistically manageable distribution and because a log form gives a more plausible causal relationship. Then we reset the sample to include only the observations for which both forward excess return and log market capitalization exist. These will be labeled *OK*.

Another critical issue is whether the model will be usable for forecast purposes because all the data needed are available in a timely fashion. Prices meet this criterion, but market capitalization may not. For our example, we will lag data on the number of shares by six months to make sure it would have been available for the forecast.

We have slightly improved our method by making sure that the mean of all variables within this sample is zero. This requires subtracting the mean for log market capitalization and re-subtracting the new mean of our return variable. This nicety makes sure that we will end with a regression whose intercept is zero and requires no interpretation. We note that the conditioned size variable is very nearly normal, with a near-zero skew and a kurtosis of 3.

```
. quietly by ZINDIV: gen mktcap = SHARES[_n-1]*PRICE
. gen lmktcap = log(mktcap)
. gen OK=1
. replace OK=0 if lmktcap==. | frtnxw==.
. egen frtnxwm = mean(frtnxw) if OK,by(ZDATE)
. replace frtnxw = frtnxw - frtnxwm
. egen lmktcapm=mean(lmktcap) if OK, by(ZDATE)
. gen lmktx=lmktcap-lmktcapm
. sum lmktx,de
```

		lmktx		
	Percentiles	Smallest		
1%	−3.064978	−6.471973		
5%	−2.095595	−6.447474		
10%	−1.603871	−5.562202	Obs	87721
25%	−0.849741	−5.542977	Sum of Wgt.	87721
50%	−0.080687		Mean	−7.45e−10
		Largest	Std. Dev.	1.323953
75%	0.8111315	4.704186		
90%	1.745313	4.706092	Variance	1.752851
95%	2.312665	4.706391	Skewness	0.1440559
99%	3.155127	4.760564	Kurtosis	3.325943

We also create a dummy variable whose value is one if next month's return occurs in January, zero otherwise. This dummy variable is multiplied by log market capitalization. The resulting product will allow us to represent any extra effect of market capitalization on return during January.

```
. gen january =0
. replace january=1 if month ==12
. gen janlmkt = january*lmktx if OK
```

Estimating Predictive Relationships

We first estimate correlation coefficients. Then we estimate separate linear relationships between next month's return and each of our two predictive indicators.

. corr frtnxw lmktx janlmkt if OK
(obs=87721)

	frtnxw	lmktx	janlmkt
frtnxw	1.0000		
lmktx	-0.0670	1.0000	
janlmkt	-0.0348	0.2914	1.0000

. regress frtnxw janlmkt if OK

Source	SS	df	MS
Model	10124.5786	1	10124.5786
Residual	8334990.06	87719	95.0192098
Total	8345114.64	87720	95.1335459

Number of obs	=	87721
F(1, 87719)	=	106.55
Prob > F	=	0.0000
R-squared	=	0.0012
Adj R-squared	=	0.0012
Root MSE	=	9.7478

frtnxw	Coef.	Std. Err.	t	P>|t|	[95% Conf. Interval]	
janlmkt	-0.8806035	0.0853095	-10.322	0.000	-1.047809	-0.7133976
_cons	-8.60e-09	0.032912	0.000	1.000	-0.0645072	0.0645072

. regress frtnxw lmktx if OK

Source	SS	df	MS
Model	37455.6329	1	37455.6329
Residual	8307659.01	87719	94.7076347
Total	8345114.64	87720	95.1335459

Number of obs	=	87721
F(1, 87719)	=	395.49
Prob > F	=	0.0000
R-squared	=	0.0045
Adj R-squared	=	0.0045
Root MSE	=	9.7318

frtnxw	Coef.	Std. Err.	t	P>|t|	[95% Conf. Interval]	
lmktx	-0.4935563	0.0248182	-19.887	0.000	-0.5421998	-0.4449128
_cons	-7.44e-09	0.032858	0.000	1.000	-0.0644013	0.0644013

We see from the correlation coefficients a negative relation between excess log market capitalization and next month's excess return. This is also true in January. The first regression shows that the effect was notable in January measured in isolation. We note a regression coefficient of −0.88% for every increase of 1 in log market capitalization, or of a multiple of 2.7 in market capitalization. Since there is a large range available, this could be a very useful relationship in a portfolio sense. On an individual stock, however, it is a very small proportion of total variance, only 0.12 of 1%, or 0.12%.

The second regression shows that by keeping track of small stocks in all 12 months we account for much more of the total variation, 0.45%. However, the impact per month is only about half as big as in January alone.

Now we will regress next month's returns against both explanatory variables at once to estimate their separate effects.

. regress frtnxw lmktx janlmkt if OK

Source	SS	df	MS
Model	39593.0114	2	19796.5057
Residual	8305521.63	87718	94.6843479
Total	8345114.64	87720	95.1335459

Number of obs =	87721
F(2, 87718) =	209.08
Prob > F =	0.0000
R-squared =	0.0047
Adj R-squared =	0.0047
Root MSE =	9.7306

frtnxw	Coef.	Std. Err.	t	P>|t|	[95% Conf. Interval]	
lmktx	−0.4576415	0.025941	−17.642	0.000	−0.5084855	−0.4067975
janlmkt	−0.422962	0.0890225	−4.751	0.000	−0.5974453	−0.2484787
_cons	−8.15e-09	0.0328539	0.000	1.000	−0.0643934	0.0643934

This third regression puts the January effect into much better perspective, because adding a special incremental return for that month increases R-squared only to 0.47%. The marginal impact of small size for January (−0.46−0.42, or −0.88) appears materially greater than for other months (−0.46). However, because the January effect can be applied for only one month a year, pursuing the increment is of little importance overall.

Of course, in practical terms the January effect is even less important as a source of profit, because taking an additional small stock position just for January would cause extra trading costs. For example, suppose the small stock alternative reduced log market cap by 3, and we took advantage of it only for January. Then the regression estimate gives an estimate of 2.6% gross profit, but we must pay four times the one-way trading cost to have achieved this result. If the one-way trading cost were 0.5%, there would be a profit of 0.6%. This is much inferior to holding the same small stocks all year, earning 3 times 0.46% per month, or 1.38%. Even if we trade among such small stocks once a year, at a cost of 1%, amounting to 0.08% per month, we receive a net monthly value added of 1.3%. Thus, even if the January effect is real, it appears practically insignificant unless we need to trade at the right times for other reasons.

How likely is it that the observed relationship is an effect of chance rather than an enduring relationship? At face value with so many observations, we have very good t-statistics for both the common effect ($t = -18$) and the January effect ($t = -5$). For each, there appears to be less than 0.0005 probability of the true coefficient being zero and appearing this different from zero simply by chance. However, as we shall see, the true significance level is much different.

OLS Assumptions About Residual Errors

We have already gone a long way toward a proper model by keeping the number of variables low, by having many observations, and by not searching among many different formulations to estimate our effect. These practices minimize the overconfidence that comes from too much data-mining. We now consider problems arising from complexity in the structure of the regression residuals.

We first consider heteroscedasticity, that different observations may come with different degrees of random dispersion. There is no point in testing for it here, because it is always present in work with stocks. Different industries, different time periods, different stock characteristics have different variance in excess return. These risk differences flow through as variance in the residuals of whatever return forecast model we are trying to construct.

Heteroscedasticity does not bias our estimates; it only means that they have greater variance than we think. We could, if we wished, model the variance of different types of return observations, and arrive at a weighting scheme for observations that could improve the accuracy of our estimate. For example, it is typical that small stocks and stocks with higher recent squared excess returns are more likely to have higher unexplained variation. Thus small stocks and stocks with high recent squared returns would get less weight in our regression, with the weights proportional to the reciprocal of the estimated variance. However, unless we develop an excellent model of variance differences, this procedure can lead to more trouble than it is worth. The reason is that errors in our variance estimates may disturb the final regression estimates as much as did the original heteroscedasticity.

In this case, we content ourselves with a robust estimate of the t-statistic that takes account of apparent heteroscedasticity without changing the estimate. For example, in STATA we can use something called the Huber-White sandwich estimator of variance to correct our t-statistics.

```
. regress frtnxw lmktx janlmkt if OK, robust
```

Regression with robust standard errors

Number of obs	=	87721
F(2, 87718)	=	133.09
Prob > F	=	0.0000
R-squared	=	0.0047
Root MSE	=	9.7306

frtnxw	Coef.	Robust Std. Err.	t	P>|t|	[95% Conf. Interval]	
lmktx	−0.4576415	0.0332066	−13.782	0.000	−0.5227261	−0.3925569
janlmkt	−0.422962	0.1061759	−3.984	0.000	−0.6310659	−0.2148581
_cons	−8.15e-09	0.0328539	0.000	1.000	−0.0643934	0.0643934

We see, as promised, no change in regression coefficient. We also see only a modest reduction in t-statistic.

Still another problem that might arise is one of autocorrelation of error through time. This can be investigated by looking at the correlation of successive residual errors of the regression. We begin with a set of fits to the regression model, labeled *pfrtnxw*.

```
. predict pfrtnxw
. gen rfrtnxw = frtnxw - pfrtnxw
. sort ZINDIV ZDATE
. quietly by ZINDIV: gen rfrtnxw1 = rfrtnxw[_n-1]
. corr rfrtnxw rfrtnxw1
(obs=87165)
```

	rfrtnxw	rfrtnxw1
rfrtnxw	1.0000	
rfrtnxw1	−0.0091	1.0000

As is usual in stock market work, the residuals are sufficiently uncorrelated to make the assumption of error independence through time an excellent one.

A much more serious lack of independence exists among residuals for different stocks observed at the same time. For example, if the market is going up during the month, high-beta stocks will all tend to have positive excess returns and low-beta stocks all tend to have negative excess returns. Even more difficult to sort out, clusters of stocks in the same industry will tend to have similar excess returns in a particular month. The net effect of this is to reduce the implicit degrees of freedom to some lesser number. There is no precise equivalent number of degrees of freedom for a factor structure. However, in very rough terms, the equivalent number of degrees of freedom might be 10 instead of the roughly 500 we thought we had each month when we counted the number of stocks. We can get a lower bound t-statistic if we assume that there is *complete* correlation, either positive or negative, among the excess returns of all stocks for a given month. In the present study, we have 229 time periods, so even in this worst of all cases we would have a chance to find significant results provided our hypothesis is simple. The true equivalent t-statistic is undoubtedly better, but we cannot be more precise in measuring it without more detailed modeling of the clustering relationships across stocks of their residual errors.

```
. regress frtnxw lmktx janlmkt if OK, robust cluster(ZDATE)
```

Regression with robust standard errors				Number of obs	=	87721
				F(2, 227)	=	27.60
				Prob > F	=	0.0000
				R-squared	=	0.0047
Number of clusters (ZDATE) = 228				Root MSE	=	9.7306

frtnxw	Coef.	Robust Std. Err.	t	P>|t|	[95% Conf. Interval]	
lmktx	−0.4576415	0.0687016	−6.661	0.000	−0.5930159	−0.3222671
janlmkt	−0.422962	0.2762688	−1.531	0.127	−0.9673412	0.1214171
_cons	−8.15e-09	6.17e-09	−1.322	0.188	−2.03e-08	4.00e-09

The small stock effect seems intact. However, we now see that there is a possibility that, given sufficient clustering of excess returns, the January effect, with a worst-case t-statistic of only −1.5, might be rather inflated by coincidence. The overconfidence that comes from mistakenly assuming independent observations is a subtle trap for quantitative investors relying on OLS assumptions.

Structural Issues

Multicollinearity, that is, intercorrelation among the explanatory variables, will not necessarily lead to forecast error. But in such cases small variations in the sample can cause large and deceptive variations in the individual regression coefficients. Our two explanatory variables have a correlation among themselves of 0.29, which is a little high, but not serious. The form we used earlier allowed us to easily test whether January's incremental small cap effect was significantly higher than the base relationship; we rely on the t-statistic of -5 for the incremental January term.

We can, if we wish, transform the two variables to a different form in which they have less correlation with each other. We do so very simply in this case by replacing the general effect with one that applies every month except January. In the following, each t-statistic merely tests whether the coefficient for the pertinent months is different from zero, not whether they are different from each other. Now the incremental January effect must be inferred from the difference in the two regression coefficients, and there is no test for whether the difference is significant. In this case, we gained nothing and gave up a valuable test. However, the general approach of transforming variables to reduce multicollinearity is a good idea in many other cases.

```
. gen nojan=1-january
. gen nolmktx = nojan*lmktx
. regress frtnxw nolmktx janlmkt if OK
```

Source	SS	df	MS
Model	39593.0114	2	19796.5057
Residual	8305521.63	87718	94.6843479
Total	8345114.64	87720	95.1335459

Number of obs =	87721
F(2, 87718) =	209.08
Prob > F =	0.0000
R-squared =	0.0047
Adj R-squared =	0.0047
Root MSE =	9.7306

frtnxw	Coef.	Std. Err.	t	P>ltl	[95% Conf. Interval]	
nolmktx	-0.4576415	0.025941	-17.642	0.000	-0.5084855	-0.4067975
janlmkt	-0.8806035	0.0851591	-10.341	0.000	-1.047515	-0.7136925
_cons	-8.15e-09	0.0328539	0.000	1.000	-0.0643934	0.0643934

```
. corr frtnxw nolmktx janlmkt
(obs=87721)
```

	frtnxw	nolmktx	janlmkt
frtnxw	1.0000		
nolmktx	-0.0594	1.0000	
janlmkt	-0.0348	0.0000	1.0000

We assume in OLS that the residuals are uncorrelated with the values of the independent variables. One implication is that the postulated linear relationships exhaust the predictive content of the explanatory variables. But what if the small stock effect is a non-linear effect of market capitalization that we did not capture by transforming that variable before running our OLS regression?

We approach this issue by rank ordering stocks by market capitalization each month and then pooling the data within a market cap decile across time periods. That is, stocks in the largest 10% in January 1984 are pooled with the likely somewhat different list of the largest 10% of stocks ranked in March of 1992, and so on. Exhibit 1 shows the mean excess return for the stock-month combinations that occur within each decile, or tenth of the sample, plotted against the median market capitalization for that decile. The mean return is very high for the smallest decile, and then slopes downward rapidly through the third decile, decelerating to a nearly flat slope in the largest half of the sample.

(Note that for ease of interpretation the horizontal axis shows the median decile value for 1996, the last year of our sample. The true median market capitalization for each decile within our sample would have been considerably smaller, because capitalization has grown enormously for all deciles, especially before accounting for inflation, since the earlier years.)

The average impact of size on returns in any one month has been very clearly non-linear! We could test this assertion by incorporating non-linear features within our list of explanatory variables and re-running the OLS. For example, a reasonable model would add a dummy variable if the stock were in the smallest three deciles, and another term that was the same dummy multiplied by excess log market cap.

In practical terms, there was very little benefit to investing in the seventh decile as an alternative to the tenth decile. This covered a range of between about $3 billion for the seventh decile median to about $20 billion for the tenth decile median in 1996. This non-linearity is exactly what we would expect if small stock investing incurred threshold effects such as illiquid trading and lack of information that served as barriers to many investors. But it means our basic linear model is flawed.

Exhibit 1: Monthly Excess Return versus Market Capitalization by Decile

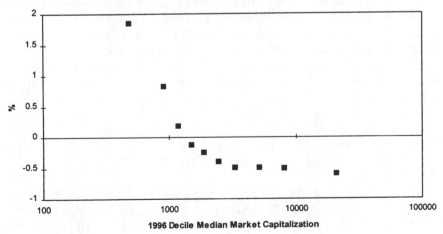

Exhibit 2: Regression Coefficients by Year

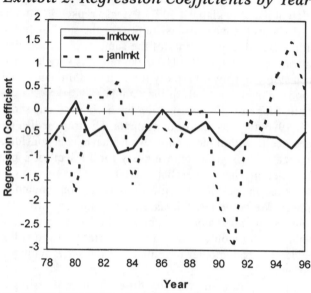

If time and space permitted, we could go on to develop and test an OLS model incorporating terms that were non-linear functions of log market capitalization. We might well find that most of the January effect occurs within the smallest stocks. However, we have other topics to cover in our example.

Unstable Process

In a changing environment, most return forecasting models will fail to a degree if asked to work in a successive period, independent of any model overconfidence caused by data-mining. When estimated with a fixed OLS regression structure, such models will exhibit a correlation between residuals and time. Just as we investigated the dependence of our model's relationships on the level of market capitalization, or at least its decile ranking, we can investigate its dependence on time.

One excellent approach is simply to divide one's sample into subsamples during different periods. Then test whether these subsamples have different regression coefficients from the total sample using the dummy variable approach shown in the preceding paragraphs. This would tell us how stable the relationships might be. Very often in investment work they can be shown to be unstable. This frequent occurrence forces us as practitioners to decide whether the instability is for cyclical reasons or, in contrast, the result of a long-run trend caused by increasing market efficiency.

We show in Exhibit 2 the regression coefficients for the common small cap effect and the incremental January effect within annual subsamples. In each case, the desired effect is a negative coefficient. The general small capitalization benefit has stayed relatively constant, with some random variation. The January effect, however, shows much greater year-to-year variation and has been perverse during the last three years of the sample. Even if we believe it is real, its inconsistency should give us pause. Not only as agents are we subject to risk of unhappy clients, but as principals, as we saw in an earlier chapter, returns with high variance have reduced expected compound return.

We would like a more formal test of whether there has been a secular trend, either in overall small stock effects or in the incremental January enhancement of small stock expected returns. We therefore introduce a time interaction term, with time being measured from the approximate midpoint of our sample.

```
. gen year = int(ZDATE)
. gen month = int(100*(ZDATE-year)+.001)
. gen sdate = year-1+month/12.0
. gen time = (sdate-1977) - 9.5
. gen tlmktx = time*lmktx
. gen tjanlmkt = time*janlmkt
. regress frtnxw lmktx tlmktx janlmkt tjanlmkt if OK, robust cluster(ZDATE)
```

Regression with robust standard errors

			Number of obs	=	87721
			F(4, 227)	=	16.33
			Prob > F	=	0.0000
			R-squared	=	0.0048
Number of clusters (ZDATE) = 228			Root MSE	=	9.7302

frtnxw	Coef.	Robust Std. Err.	t	P>|t|	[95% Conf. Interval]	
lmktx	−0.4487103	0.069056	−6.498	0.000	−0.584783	−0.3126375
tlmktx	−0.0120492	0.0121462	−0.992	0.322	−0.0359828	0.0118845
janlmkt	−0.467153	0.2526572	−1.849	0.066	−0.9650063	0.0307002
tjanlmkt	0.0420137	0.0434327	0.967	0.334	−0.0435691	0.1275965
_cons	−7.70e-09	6.22e-09	−1.237	0.217	−2.00e-08	4.56e-09

Remember that these regressions have very conservative t-statistics that assume complete clustering within stock returns of a given month. Taking a more generous view, even a t-statistic of about 1 tells a story. The regression indicates a probable improvement in the overall small stock effect with time, but a probable decline in the January increment with time. Alternatively, if we believe that the returns are extremely clustered, there is little or no evidence of change. On balance, however, this analysis indicates further ground for caution in trying to exploit an incremental effect for January.

Recall also the survivor bias issue. The sign of the regression coefficient for our time-interacted small capitalization effect, *tlmktx*, is negative. Our evidence supports the notion that the small market capitalization effect is real. However, as we saw in the section on non-linearity, it is largely confined to small stocks that are likely not to be heavily represented in most institutional portfolios.

We could also investigate differences among industries in the small capitalization effect and in its January enhancement. It is likely that we would find some to be statistically significant. However, one needs to be unusually cautious about data-mining in such an exercise, and I will not pursue it here.

Validation Sample

We will use our simple two-variable model based on the even-company sample to construct a forecast within the odd-company validation sample, and then regress next month's actual excess returns in the odd-company sample against it.
The model is:

forecast excess return = −0.457*lmktx −0.423*janlmkt.

The predicted next month's return using this formula on the odd company sample will be labeled *peven*. We have the following successful validation, robust against our super-conservative clustering t-statistic.

```
. gen peven = -.463*lmktx -.447*janlmkt
. regress frtnxw peven if OK, robust cluster(ZDATE)
```

Regression with robust standard errors

Number of obs	=	91876
F(1, 227)	=	71.15
Prob > F	=	0.0000
R-squared	=	0.0049
Root MSE	=	9.824

Number of clusters (ZDATE) = 228

frtnxw	Coef.	Robust Std. Err.	t	P>|t|	[95% Conf. Interval]	
peven	1.04697	0.1241182	8.435	0.000	0.8023985	1.291541
_cons	-8.56e-09	6.65e-09	-1.287	0.199	-2.17e-08	4.54e-09

The regression coefficient is close to one, while the forecast fit is as good as in the sample from which it was estimated. In practice, at this point, one would now use the combined sample to modestly refine the regression coefficients of the predictive model. However, our validation sample was useful in forcefully supporting the contention that we did not over-fit the model to our first sample through extensive data-mining.

Overall, we have shown that the small-cap effect appeared alive and well, at least among the smallest U.S. stocks. However, the incremental January effect has been less reliable and of marginal practical importance taken in isolation. The issue of survivor bias does not affect these conclusions. The issue of better data that incorporates precise dividend payment dates might conceivably strengthen the case for the January effect, as could the details of a non-linear model with a focus on the smallest stocks. The weight of the evidence is in the other direction, however. For our purpose here, however, it is sufficient that we have shown practical ways of dealing with a number of critical issues in applying econometrics to investing.

EXAMPLES OF ECONOMETRIC RESEARCH FROM THE INVESTMENT LITERATURE

In this section we will briefly review three important pieces of econometric research on potential market inefficiencies. For each, we will describe decisions on database, data conditioning, findings, and methods of dealing with complexities associated with statistical distributions of residuals, model structure, time instability, and data-mining.

Fama and French

"The Cross Section of Expected Stock Returns," by Fama and French, published in 1992, is a landmark in the field of finance. It put the nail in the coffin of the Sharpe-Lintner-Black CAPM model as a simple descriptive theory for use in the teaching of finance. That is, it confirmed the low power of measured beta to predict cross-sectional differences in return absent a knowledge of the future market return. It also showed that book-to-price ratio and size of market capitalization had generally subsumed other indicators such as leverage and the earnings-to-price ratio in successfully forecasting average return differences.

The authors' objective was in part focused on testing the CAPM rather than on the best forecast for investment purposes. This biased their procedure toward elaboration of different methods of measuring beta and on separating its effects from those of size, while somewhat neglecting other issues of importance to the investor. Nevertheless, such a study, if performed before the resulting knowledge became generally available to practitioners, could be immensely helpful to the quantitative investor.

The variables studied were total return as predicted by:

> beta (systematic risk),
> market capitalization (size),
> the ratio of assets to equity (leverage),
> the ratio of book value to market value (B/M, the inverse of P/B), and
> earnings to price (E/P).

Their choice of sample was appropriate. The period was long enough to capture a variety of market conditions (1963-1990). They used the Compustat database, which has fewer survivor bias problems than Value Line. They used the CRSP return database, which gives precise data on returns rather than relying on average dividend yields in its calculation. The stocks covered by these databases formed the initial universe, restricted further to the companies listed by the NYSE and the AMEX exchanges or included in NASDAQ's list. They further restricted their sample to exclude financial sector companies. This solved compatibility problems regarding leverage.

On the other hand, they did not save a validation sample, and reported only a single split of their sample into two time periods in which they simply compared regression coefficients with no formal tests. That is, they made little attempt to control for data-mining or model inconsistency across sub-samples. In view of their academic purpose and relatively parsimonious model, this is understandable.

Similarly, they did no data conditioning on returns. This likely did not affect their broad conclusions. They did condition the independent variables. They replaced negative earnings E/P with a separate dummy variable to partially deal with its U-shaped functionality. They also excluded the few cases of negative book value. They took the log form of both B/M and size, substantially reducing their skewness and kurtosis.

Fama and French paid considerable attention to data availability of balance sheet and income statement variables, lagging them by at least six months, or more if fiscal years did not fall in December. They did not do so for beta, however, as noted below.

Their model structure reflected a tradition in finance — the Fama-Mac-Beth procedure. This is a two-pass procedure for dealing with beta. It then combines cross-sections and time-series.

In the first pass, a relationship between the return of each stock and the market or average return is developed. Fama and French tried several different beta estimation procedures here. These were intended to get accurate rather than investor-usable estimates of beta — that is, they involved examining information from later time periods to help determine an accurate beta for the current month. I have some qualms about this procedure for quantitative investors, though it seems acceptable for a test of the CAPM.

In the second pass, beta is combined with other explanatory variables in a cross-sectional regression each month across the total returns of each stock. Then the mean regression coefficients for each variable are taken as the regression estimate, with a t-test available to take into account the variance in the coefficient among the different time periods. Again, this procedure was adequate in this case to produce a reasonably powerful overall test of their hypotheses.

The Fama-MacBeth procedure attempts to gain some of the advantages of pooling data across the different time-periods. However, in its focus on dealing with beta it leaves something to be desired in efficient handling of other information. The t-test of the mean cross-sectional regression coefficients against its variance across time periods leaves out all information as to how large is the cross-sectional sample. This is somewhat analogous to assuming clustering of residuals across stocks. In contrast, consider directly pooling the data in a single regression, as we did in studying the January effect. Then one has both an upper bound t-statistic based on an assumption of fully independent observations in a single period as well as a lower-bound t-statistic based on fully clustered observations.

A second Fama-Macbeth disadvantage is that it does not take advantage of the greater range of independent variables across the pooled sample and so has less resolution in discovering a weak relationship. A third disadvantage is that it gives equal weight to all sub-periods. In doing so, it disregards that the dependent variable has much greater variation in some periods. It has no offsetting advantages that I can see versus using pooled samples with both the dependent and independent variables in excess over cross-sectional mean form.

Fama and French pay considerable attention to the strong negative correlation, or multicollinearity, between beta and size. They disentangle them with a separate analysis of 100 portfolios formed by separately ranking beta deciles within each size decile. They find that the internal beta deciles do not produce further differentiation of average return and conclude that previous findings of beta influence on expected return simply reflected the size effect. This is excellent technique. However, similar results might have been obtained by regressing beta on size each period, calculating the residual beta unexplained by size, and using the result as a substitute for beta in testing its ability to forecast return.

They also find a negative correlation between size and B/M, not surprising since size is proportional to price and B/M proportional to the reciprocal of price. They note the impact on the regression when one or the other is omitted, which is good. However, they could have gone further and perhaps saved their readers much confusion if they had made the following transformation.

$$\text{Log size} = \log \text{book value} - \log(\text{B/M}) \tag{1}$$

Thus a negative regression coefficient on Fama and French's size factor represents an incremental positive regression coefficient on the B/M factor.

Rather than regress returns against both size measured as log market capitalization and log (book value/market capitalization), which have a fairly strong correlation (-0.26) built in because of log book value's lesser range, they could have used log book value and log (book/market). In my experience, this leads to reduced multicollinearity. In this case it will also lead to enhancing the coefficient for the ratio of book value to market value.

Fama and French deal effectively with autocorrelation (it is not material) and probably wisely do not get into the issue of heteroscedasticity. However, the Fama-Macbeth procedure is susceptible to heteroscedasticity of variance across time, which they do not test, nor do they adjust their t-statistics for it. They do look at decile portfolio results, a procedure that might pick up important non-linearities. Their size deciles do not show the same non-linear pattern we saw in our January effect study, except for an unusually big jump in the average return of the smallest decile. The difference in findings might reflect their generally earlier period. At any rate, their procedure is excellent in this regard.

They do not provide a table or plot of regression coefficients across time, except to provide us with a single split between an early and late period. However, the split does seem to support their contention that the effects measured are not subject to rapid secular change. When they do this comparison, they do not put it in a form that would permit an easy test. If they had used the pooled regression method, they could have secured a formal t-test of the incremental effect of being in the second sample. This could have been done by adding new variables premultiplied by a dummy variable signifying inclusion in the second half. The inclusion of time-interacted variables would also have been useful.

On balance, however, the 1992 Fama and French study establishing size and B/M as return predictors stands as an excellent example of effective econometrics for investment work.

Chan, Jegadeesh, and Lakonishok

The authors of "Momentum Strategies," Chan, Jegadeesh, and Lakonishok, did for momentum indicators some of what Fama and French had done for size and book-to-market. They were not concerned with measuring beta's value as a predictor of average returns — CAPM as descriptive theory was already moot. What they did was to show that positive changes in price and earnings information were associated with later positive returns. This needed to be done particularly carefully because nothing in modern finance, which regarded any predictable extra return as mere risk premium, could justify it.

Chan *et al.* began with the now-familiar database of Compustat fundamentals and CRSP returns. To this was added the IBES information on analyst consensus earnings estimates. They included financials like banks, there being no reason to exclude them. The period they used was somewhat shorter and more recent than that of Fama and French; they used the period 1977-1993.

The basic structure of the analysis was similar, with two parallel parts. One examined buy and hold performance of equal-weighted portfolios formed from deciles or other percentile splits of observations sorted by the independent variables singly or in combination. The other looked at Fama-Macbeth mean cross-sectional regression coefficients. The latter offers an unbiased but not fully efficient means of estimation relative to a directly pooled sample of variables transformed by subtracting cross-sectional means, as discussed in the critique of Fama and French. The authors gave an unusual twist to Fama-Macbeth by transforming each independent variable into its percentile rank at the time. This gives an undisclosed but presumably helpful effect in making the regression more robust. Such a procedure can be helpful or harmful in different situations. In this case, we are uninformed as to the comparison.

Their basic dependent variables were total return, not excess return, measured over 6-month and 12-month intervals. They did not winsorize these. Their independent variables were *price momentum*, measured as prior 6-months return, and three measures of earnings information improvement. The first was *earnings surprise*, measured as the change in quarterly earnings from those of the year-ago quarter. The second was *abnormal return around earnings announcements*, measured as the excess return over an equal-weighted market average from two days before through one day after the earnings announcement. The third was *earnings estimate revision*, measured by calculating monthly change in earnings estimates for the current fiscal year, divided by prior month's price, and then taking a 6-month average of that.

They appear to have carefully recorded dates when information first became public. This is superior to Fama and French's 6-month lagging of fundamental information, although it implies vigilance and expense for practitioners seeking to duplicate their results.

They found that each of these variables had a somewhat independent predictive effect. Price momentum tended to be relatively more important in predicting longer-term returns. These findings held up even in the presence of a size variable in their Fama-MacBeth regressions. Inexplicably, the authors did not include B/M ratios in these regressions.

Chan *et al.* made no obvious attempt to control data-mining through testing on randomly-selected or hold-out subsamples. In my experience the IBES database typically contains extreme outliers that might be considered data errors. Although they do not report attempts to condition their data, by basing their analysis on ranking they effectively accomplish the same reduction of the impact of outliers as would have winsorization. However, by relying on a ranking procedure, they simultaneously disregard much potentially valuable distance information through the rest of the distribution.

Their regression analysis does correct for the inflation of t-statistic caused by monthly observations of the overlapping 6-month or 12-month time-periods for the dependent variable.

The authors, by including the portfolio decile study, convincingly show non-linear effects. There seems to be, for these variables, more return slope information in the tails than in the center of the independent variable ranges. However, it would have been good to see a formal statistical test of significance of the non-linearity.

Chan *et al.* do pay considerable attention to multicollinearity among their selected independent variables, as well as bringing in the size effect as well. However, their omission of book-to-market ratios in the Fama-Macbeth regressions is troubling and unnecessary given their sample and database; B/M was a known powerful return predictor then.

They attempted to compensate for this omission by time-series analysis. This was modeled after a later Fama and French work that postulates a three-factor risk structure based on market risk, size, and B/M.[5] To measure the factors associated with these last two, they constructed long-short portfolios based on extremes in size and book-to-market. They then did separate time-series regressions of returns for a high momentum and a low momentum portfolio incorporating the market return, the size factor return, and the book-to-market factor return. The results gave a positive intercept for the high momentum portfolio and a negative intercept for the low momentum portfolio. They interpreted this as demonstrating that the momentum anomaly was little dependent on the size and B/M effects.

This procedure seems doubtful. Their interpretation that one can measure a relationship equally well whether cross-sectionally or through time, with the

---

[5] Eugene Fama and Kenneth R. French, "Multifactor Explanations of Asset Pricing Anomalies," *Journal of Finance* (1996), pp. 55-84.

same coefficient, is a good one only if the true relationship is indifferent in that way. In many cases, time series slopes are markedly different from cross-sectional slopes. Second, they seem to mix forecasting risk with forecasting a bias in the mean. That they have controlled for the impact of B/M on monthly return variations does not imply that this controls for differences in the long-term mean.

Chan *et al.* do no exploration of relationships by time-subsamples. They do, however, study the subsample defined by largest-half market capitalization. This categorization is correctly carried out each period rather than once for the whole sample. They find that the momentum effect is slightly weaker for larger stocks, but still very strong. This is an important finding, because portfolios restricted from short-sales and managed to keep tracking error low are better able to take advantage of the scope for underweighting offered by larger stocks. It is also true that larger stocks generally have lower trading costs.

The complication of the model to handle different sized stocks can take several forms. It can be done with sub-samples and separate OLS regressions, as is done here. Better, the two relationships could have been combined in one regression with premultiplier dummy variables like the one we used for our study of the January effect. This nesting of an incremental variable list makes easier the formal test of the significance of incremental regression coefficients. It could also have been done with interactive variables that allow one to make smooth-curve transitions between different size categories.

Finally, Chan *et al.* look for, and find, interaction effects. Using two-way sorts, they find that price momentum confirmed by earnings momentum has an unusually powerful positive predictive power. This discovery could also have been made by including an interactive product of the two variables within a regression.

Campbell and Shiller

Market timing is a controversial topic: you could earn enormous additional returns if you knew when to get out of the stock market, but the record of most investors on this score is unimpressive. A 1998 study by Campbell and Shiller titled "Valuation Ratios and the Long-Run Stock Market Outlook" restates the old arguments in econometric form.[6] They seek to forecast long-term returns, as well as to provide information about the efficiency of the stock market. They conclude that the stock market was so high in 1996 (not to speak of early 1998) that it forecasted below-average stock returns for many years to follow. Their conclusion brings to bear evidence in a new way.

They examine annual stock return, dividend, and earnings data for the Standard & Poor's 500 Index of the U.S. stock market for 1926-1996, combined with a predecessor series beginning in 1872. Note the effort to get the longest possible sample — this is appropriate not only because they are interested in long-term returns but also because, as we will see, they face challenging econometric problems. They also examine some shorter term data on foreign countries based on Morgan Stanley (MSCI) index data.

---

[6] Campbell and Shiller, "Valuation Ratios and the Long-Run Stock Market Outlook."

Campbell and Shiller illustrate the predictive power of dividend yields and a price to smoothed earnings ratio (10-year average earnings) in forecasting returns. They study three intervals: return over 1 year, 10 years, and most unusually, the time until the valuation ratio next crosses its full-sample average.

They condition their data by dividing through prices, dividends, and earnings by a producer price index. This is an attempt to make returns, growth in dividends, and growth in 10-year average earnings all as comparable as possible even though they traverse periods with very different inflation rates.

The first evidence they present is based on scatterplots of cumulative growth in dividends and cumulative stock returns as functions of prior year dividend yield. Each point's time horizon is variable — it is the time until the dividend yield next crossed its full sample average of 4.73%. There are no points plotted for the years since 1983, as dividend yields have remained below this average through 1996. Since the dividend yield crosses its average only 29 times during the sample period, there are only 29 non-overlapping observations, but there are as many points on the plot as years between 1872 and 1983. The time intervals range from one to 20 years. The authors point out that there is almost no correlation between dividend yield and subsequent cumulative dividend growth over this flexible horizon. However, there is a quite high positive correlation between dividend yield and subsequent cumulative return over these periods. They conclude that this means that the dividend yield does not forecast much about future dividends, but a great deal about future (at least long-term future) cumulative returns. And indeed, the scatterplots are visually very impressive, with an R-squared of 64%.

They provide no separation of data into a model estimation sample and validation sample, nor division of the data into subsamples that could be examined for consistency. At first glance, the simplicity of their model and the large number of observations would rule out much data-mining. However, they point out that they have for the flexible horizon case a rather small number of non-overlapping observations — 29, or if they analyze 10-year returns, only 12. Consequently, data-mining is an issue to be considered even in such a spare and elegant study.

Campbell and Shiller condition variables by correcting for inflation. They also properly lag dividend yield for availability. With index data, there is less need to be concerned with winsorization, and they do not winsorize.

The authors refer to small-sample bias. However, they do not explicitly describe for the investment practitioner the nature of the problem. Therefore I will digress here to present my own simple simulation. We examine the common problem that occurs when one regresses a time-series of returns against ratios such as dividend yield, price-to-earnings or price-to-book.

Exhibit 3 shows a single simulated time series of prices over 10 years. Consider that there are no dividends, that we want to forecast return based on price-to-book ratios, and that book value stays constant through the entire period. The data are drawn from a Monte Carlo simulation with log normal returns, a 0.15 annual risk, and to put the problem in its purest form, a zero-mean annual return. We are to do a study of return predictability in possession of the entire 10-year's worth of sample history.

Exhibit 3: Simulated Price Series

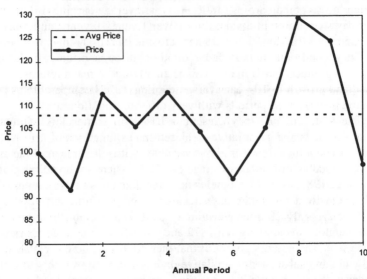

Suppose first that we use just current price to predict next period's return. Since we know the sample average price, we can use it as a weak estimator of next period's price. If today's price is below average, then we should predict that the next period's return will be positive. Thus, in the in-sample fit, there will be a negative correlation between today's price and tomorrow's return. But by construction prices are generated randomly; thus, despite our finding of a correlation, there will be absolutely no power to forecast outside the sample!

The same negative correlation will tend to show up when we forecast based on price-to-book value or price to smoothed earnings, where price is in the numerator. A corresponding positive correlation will tend to be found for dividend yield, with price in the denominator. These all occur because book value, smoothed earnings and dividends fluctuate much less than do prices, together with the fact that price is contained in both independent and dependent variables.

From whence do these correlation biases come? Note again that price appears both in the dependent and independent variables. We also know the sample average for the independent variable. Thus, then, we have information helpful in predicting within the sample the next price. Finally, we therefore can predict the return from comparing the current price to that estimated next price. This is a subtle form of look-ahead bias.

The degree of bias in the estimated correlation coefficient relative to the out-of-sample correlation coefficient is greater the smaller the sample and the larger the return variance. Exhibit 4 shows both the mean estimation bias and the standard deviation of the bias in the extreme case where the price-relative measuring stick — in this case book value — is absolutely flat. It is based on 500 trials with a mean log return of 0.10. In realistic cases, of course, the measuring stick — dividends, book value, or smoothed earnings, would also tend to increase, reducing the bias more rapidly, but the basic principle remains the same.

Campbell and Shiller's study at first sight seems to have plenty of observations, so that this bias would seem quite small, and one for which they may have applied a correction. However, the actual bias extent, and therefore the necessary full correction, is not clear because of the much smaller number of non-overlapping observations.

Think of the heteroscedasticity involved in comparing cumulative log return for one year versus 20 years. Recognizing the difficulty in interpreting observations taken from variable time horizons, the authors also present results for fixed 1-year and 10-year horizons. They find that dividend yields after all do predict dividend growth over a 1-year horizon, with low dividend yields (high prices) predicting growth in dividends, just as the efficient market would suggest. However, this goes away and is even reversed at the 10-year horizon. They find that dividend yield has only a very slight ability to forecast 1-year returns, but a considerable slope in predicting 10-year returns. These results are all in accord with their earlier presentation with one exception. The degree of scatter is much higher, and the corresponding R-squared much lower, for the 10-year constant time horizon as opposed to the variable horizon. They conclude that they need a better forecast variable and subsequently turn to an analysis of price to smoothed earnings. I find this difference rather mysterious and worthy of further investigation.

Exhibit 4: Deceptive Time Series Correlations
Simulated Log Returns versus Prior P/B

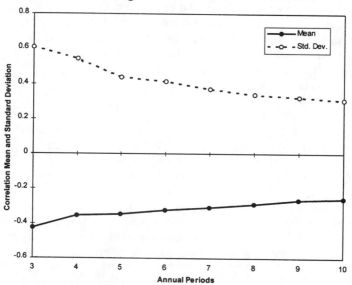

At this point, the authors' emphasis on R-squared requires critical comment. Their use of a flexible time horizon is based on the time to crossing a mean determined by knowledge of the entire sample. Campbell, in a personal communication, notes that this is not necessary; the same approach could have used, for example, a mean based only on observations available prior to the current date. However, as implemented by Campbell and Shiller the variable horizon brings in a new kind of look-ahead bias, one that goes beyond that described in Exhibit 3, and which would be generally less familiar in its statistical properties. In general, look-ahead bias inflates R-squared. Beyond this, any use of overlapping observations, present even in the 10-year fixed horizon case, greatly inflates R-squared. The authors undoubtedly are familiar with methods for adjusting t-statistics and thus statistical significance for overlapping observations. However, R-squared, which also corresponds to the visual fit of the scatter plot, is not so adjusted.

Campbell and Shiller report a serious Monte Carlo analysis (serious, as opposed to my own trivial example in which I did not model changes in the valuation yardstick). The analysis provides a distribution of results in the form they had earlier reported, but based on data that by construction has no return predictability. This baseline and its distribution largely resolve the issues I have indicated in terms of statistical testing. One modest shortcoming in their approach, however, is the common use of a log-normal return distribution rather than one with fat-tails. This undoubtedly inflated statistical significance.

When one's model structure deviates far from classic OLS assumptions, Monte Carlo analysis is the best, and possibly the only, way to get a clear read on the significance of results.

Campbell and Shiller go on to show that the price to smoothed earnings ratio is an even better explainer of future (in-sample) returns than is dividend yield. They also show generally similar results for foreign countries, with some exceptions, based on the much shorter sample since 1970. These additions raise no new methodological issues and add some additional weight to their conclusions.

Proper econometric treatment of financial time series is more challenging than cross-sectional analysis. However, in many cases, time-series regression according to the OLS model can be made less problematic by dealing with innovations in explanatory variables as opposed to using their absolute levels. Where this is not possible or sufficient, there is a large armory of time-series-oriented statistical weapons extending OLS that you may wish to pursue from other sources. Remember, however, that the instability of the market structure may limit the effectiveness of approaches dependent on precise knowledge of problem structure.

One of the most interesting of these time-series approaches is the Kalman filter. It is a kind of generalized adaptive regression that can deal with complex time-series problems in a reasonably understandable way. For example, suppose we think that the "normal" dividend yield toward which future dividend yields must trend over time is itself subject to random shocks that each have a permanent effect. The Kalman filter can take into account such structural changes.[7]

---

[7] Andrew C. Harvey, *Forecasting, Structural Time-Series Models and the Kalman Filter* (Cambridge University Press, 1989).

SUMMING UP ECONOMETRICS

Investment practitioners should view formal statistical tools as an accelerant to the learning process in a race against competitors. Properly used, they are a great improvement over unaided intuition. But their benefit requires considerable investment of time, exposure to best practice, and access to the appropriate data. It also requires retaining a perspective that keeps investment objectives, not technique, foremost. The market structure is always changing and the greatest rewards will likely go to simple, robust methods applied promptly and creatively.

Chapter 15
Risk Assessment and Portfolio Construction

*Blind fear, that seeing reason leads, finds safer footing than
blind reason, stumbling without fear.*
William Shakespeare, *Troilus and Cressida (circa 1600)*

Markowitz optimization of expected return and risk is the foundation of modern portfolio theory and a great step forward in our understanding of how to manage investments. However, without a proper appreciation for its limits, it is probably the single most dangerous weapon in the armory of quantitative investing. Quantitative investors need to know how to properly manage portfolios using it. They need to know a good deal more, as well, to provide a broader perspective on what can be a narrow, mechanical exercise. In this chapter we will discuss a philosophy of risk management, risk forecasting, portfolio construction, and detailed "optimizer" problems, choices, and solutions.

RISK MANAGEMENT PHILOSOPHY

In 1980, I joined one of the leading investment firms of the day. The firm not only employed Markowitz optimizer techniques, but used them to organize its investment strategies into electronic trade lists. This work was revolutionary in that it was largely made explicit through computer programs rather than implicitly carried out by portfolio managers.

I noted then a homely fact about covariances that no one seemed to be discussing in the practical application of optimizers at that time. I first came upon it in 1983 when looking at the correlations between returns among country stock indices. The correlations were generally lower on a monthly basis than on a quarterly basis! And the resulting optimal portfolios were very different! (It is even possible that two assets will have negative correlation in returns when measured on one time scale and positive correlations when measured on another.) Optimal Markowitz portfolios cannot be defined without reference to the length of the period over which the investment is to take place. But many practitioners and academics of the day were applying optimizers without thinking very hard about such issues, issues that were quite material to practical success in risk control.

Despite such problems of inattention to details, the practice of controlling risk by balancing of expected return against statistical measures of return volatility has become steadily more widespread. It represents a transition from management of risk by trial and error to management of risk by systematic approach. On the other hand, such systems are inherently complicated and subject to unexpected and sometimes detrimental behaviors. My overall conclusion from experience has been that overconfident quantitative risk control can easily get one into more trouble than old-fashioned diversification by asset type and industry stratification.

Markowitz optimization has also led to trouble of a different sort through its transmutation into a tool for managing decentralized investment managers and index funds. In this process, Markowitz's concept of managing against total risk has declined and the idea of managing residual risk against a narrow benchmark has replaced it. In essence, this means that cash is no longer part of the effective benchmark. There is no doubt that the average portfolio manager is not very good at market timing in the ordinary trading ranges. But who will speak up for caution when the U.S. stock market is as high as it was in early 1998, with prices reaching four times purchase cost equity? It will certainly not be the manager whose charter is a 3% annual expected tracking error versus the S&P 500. In consequence, the entire stock market becomes more susceptible to speculative booms and busts.

At the same time, optimization with respect to covariance risk has been made less adequate as the main tool for risk control by the spread of derivative security usage. Even simple derivatives such as puts and calls are highly non-linear and time-dependent in their risk characteristics. More complicated options, the kinds with special names invented on Wall Street, are still more non-linear and conditional on special events. Even the most seasoned investment professionals have great difficulty in appreciating their investment risk characteristics.

Derivatives often provide low transaction cost ways of taking long-short positions that seek to hedge away some risk while exploiting others. This desirable result may be amplified through the use of leverage. However, a fact of life in the real world is that no two securities are perfect offsets all the time. As Markowitz pointed out, and as we have noted in an earlier chapter, small errors in estimated correlation coefficients between securities can imply huge relative increases in risk for long-short positions.

Out of unhappy experiences with unexpected events has come the "value at risk," or VAR, movement for evaluating the extreme downside tail of the return distribution for portfolios. The advent of non-linear derivatives, and the growing recognition that Mandlebrot was largely right in regarding conventional statistics as subject to gross errors in dealing with extremely fat-tailed distributions, have both been contributors to the impetus for VAR.

VAR takes many forms, but a best-practice example might be to ask the following. What is the 99th percentile of losses the portfolio should be expected to incur within a two-week period? Answer with a Monte Carlo simulation of your portfolio return given its sensitivity to factor risks, and the likely fat-tailed distributions of their returns. This strikes me as a very healthy response to the inadequacy of the historical covariance matrix for indicating the severe risks of most concern to institutional investors. Conceptually, the techniques required for properly conducting VAR are those discussed earlier in this book. Use Monte Carlo analysis rather than historical distributions, adequately reflect the non-linearities in your instruments, and be sure to consider fat-tailed return distributions as inputs rather than relying on the log-normal distribution.

I look forward to the day when risk control is seen in a still larger context — that of capital growth theory. Evaluating risk in terms of expected compound growth against a capital base furnishes a much more complete picture than does the single-period covariance matrix. It gives a more adequate treatment of return skew and fat-tails and it tells us when variance is so high that it cannot be optimal. And it also gives more meaning to risk aversion. Suppose we extend Hakansson's ideas to deal with expected growth rate of *net capital* after a given reserve percentage particular to the investor. Then we can encompass any degree of risk aversion within the goal of maximizing expected compound growth rate of net capital given that reserve percentage. (Refer back to Chapter 6 if you have missed this critical concept.)

Real investors are concerned with several types of risk. For the principal investor, these include both conventional portfolio risk that is measured as the variance of portfolio arithmetic return and the additional characteristics of return distributions, captured by skew and kurtosis, necessary for optimizing expected capital growth. Intermediary or agent investors are concerned with a different array of risks. These include both the risk of not tracking a benchmark closely enough and the risk of failing in some other client expectation that might cause a business setback. There is no end to the possible institutional conventions whose threatened breach constitutes agent risk. Both types of investors react in ways that depend on their risk aversion.

What is the probability of worldwide economic depression or banking crisis, or of an outbreak of small-scale nuclear war? In a larger sense, this concern with event risk is a reflection of Mandlebrot's observation that the measured annualized variance of financial returns typically rises with longer lengths of time. The infrequent catastrophe cannot readily be extrapolated from limited windows of experience. Because risk estimation will always be subject to this error, no matter how scientific we become, there will always be at least some role for what seem to be arbitrary conservative constraints on investment positions.

RISK FORECASTING

Our discussion of risk forecasting must be compact to fit within the scope of this book. In the remainder of this chapter we will confine ourselves to discussing risk in the context of Markowitz optimization. The reader is assumed to have access to an "optimizer," in this case a computer program for solving the quadratic programming problem. We will divide our topics as follows:

- sensitivity of portfolio optimization to input error
- averaging Monte Carlo simulation results

- use of factor analysis
- forecasting individual risk elements
- forecasting multiple inputs.

Averaging Monte Carlo simulation results is a corrective action that takes into account the special sensitivity of optimization to error in the inputs. In parallel, factor analysis, conventional among commercial optimizer vendors, organizes the input data in a way that decreases this sensitivity by simplifying the problem. After discussing these general topics, we go on to consider more specific techniques for improving the input estimates.

Sensitivity to Input Error

Classic Markowitz optimization selects asset weights such that they maximize an objective function composed of the expected portfolio return less the product of a risk sensitivity parameter times expected portfolio return variance. The weights must sum to 100% and will typically also be required to be non-negative. Portfolio expected return is just the sum of the products of the weights and the expected returns for each asset. A more elegant formulation is to regard it as a vector product of the weight vector and the expected return vector. In the same language, the portfolio return's variance is the matrix product of: (1) the row vector of the weights, (2) the square matrix of covariances among the assets, and (3) the column vector of the weights.

Risk estimation as part of this process consists of estimating the covariance matrix of returns. Recall that each element of the covariance matrix is composed of the product of three ingredients: the correlation coefficient between two security returns and each of their standard deviations. That is, the covariance matrix is itself the product of a column vector of standard deviations, a square matrix of correlation coefficients, and a horizontal vector of standard deviations. The diagonal elements of the covariance matrix running from upper left to lower right are the variances of each asset's return.

In the Markowitz framework, the covariances refer to absolute returns. However, often in practice the covariances used are of residual, or excess, returns above and below a benchmark.

The conventional optimization finds the maximum of the objective function by treating each expected return and expected covariance as if it were known, but of course it is not. Therefore, the optimization that results will incorporate any errors in both the expected return vector and the covariance matrix. It will do so in a way that is very sensitive to outliers.

To see this, suppose that we consider a portfolio of ten assets. In reality, the returns of each asset are randomly generated with identical means, standard deviations, and zero intercorrelation with the others. However, we must estimate the risks and mean returns based on only ten observations.

Even if we accurately estimate the expected returns as all equal, and use the ten observations only for estimating the covariance matrix, the result will be that the

optimization puts disproportionate weights on pairs of assets with least sample correlation and least standard deviation. This resulting portfolio will have increased risk
over an equal-weighted portfolio. It will also tend to be unstable. Since the heavily
weighted securities are those with unusually high error (differences in estimated
parameters from the group as a whole), we can say that optimization maximizes the
weight given to error. This bias toward error will be greater the fewer the observations
or the more unstable the underlying process. It will also be proportionately greater
the greater the number of assets. This happens because the number of elements in the
covariance matrix in which separate errors (two standard deviations and a correlation
coefficient) may be combined goes up as the square of the number of assets.

When we add errors in expected returns to the process, the tendency to
heavily weight assets estimated with error is increased still further. Again, the larger
the number of assets, the surer is the chance that a few of them will appear to have
combined properties of high expected return, low individual risk, and low correlation.

Finally, just as Markowitz forewarned, the whole process becomes even
more hazardous if short sales are allowed, because the sensitivity of apparent
portfolio risk to small errors in estimated correlation coefficients will be greatly
increased. In more concrete terms, investors will be faced with catastrophes as
asset pairs that appeared to hedge one another turn out to be imperfect hedges
with more observations.

Averaging Monte Carlo Simulation Results

If optimization is sensitive to error, why not carry out many optimizations with
slight variations in input, each of which will result in an "optimal" portfolio, and
then in some way average these to obtain a more robust solution? That is what is
proposed by Richard Michaud.[1] I believe it to be an excellent suggestion. With
apologies to Michaud, I will simplify it to what I regard as its essence.

Let us take the example of the 10 identical stocks with independent returns
cited earlier. From each we have 10 sample returns. Assume for simplicity that we
will estimate the future mean returns in some other way and estimate only the covariances from this sample. We do so with high sample error since there are only 10
observations. From this, we have sample standard deviations and correlation coefficients. Then we generate 100 simulated repetitions of this dataset from a multivariate
normal distribution with these parameters. From each of these simulated datasets,
derive new sample covariances, and then a new efficient frontier of optimal portfolios.
(Remember that the efficient frontier is the set of portfolios with the highest returns
for each level of risk, with risk running from that of the minimum variance portfolio
to that of the portfolio consisting of the single asset with the highest returns.)

The first thing you will note is large variation in efficient frontier content
and its risk and return locus relative to the efficient frontier derived from the initial dataset. This ought to give us pause in trying too hard to achieve optimality,
when so many different portfolios are so close together in a statistical sense. For

---

[1] Richard O. Michaud, *Efficient Asset Management* (Cambridge, MA: Harvard Business School Press, 1998).

example, an equal-weighted portfolio may be found to be well within any reasonable confidence interval within which the efficient frontier is estimated to lie.

Returning to our example, there will be 100 minimum variance portfolios and therefore 100 weights for the first asset for the robust minimum variance portfolio. Take the average of these as the robust weight of asset number one. Repeat for each asset and then check the combined portfolio against any problem constraints. Now move on to construct a robust portfolio for other points along the efficient frontier.

Michaud advises rank ordering portfolios by risk along each efficient frontier, and then taking the average within the same percentile. For example, one has 100 portfolios each of which had median (50th percentile) risk in its efficient frontier. Average the weights of these median risk portfolios to get a more robust median risk portfolio. This exercise can be repeated for as many different risk percentiles as desired to fill in the portions of the efficient frontier of interest.

There is no reason for a portfolio to chase differences in apparent optimality that are not statistically significant. Michaud's is a heroic procedure, the only one that treats the efficient frontier as a statistic, with all that that implies, rather than as a result derived from precise inputs. For quadratic programming problems such as this, an average solution will generally be a good solution. It's special merit is that it will be relatively insensitive to changes in estimated risk from a few added observations. The robustness of the result will often lead to a better implied risk forecast and typically lead to reduced turnover.

We now turn to alternative approaches for solving this problem through conditioning the input covariance matrix in some way and then doing a single optimization.

Use of Factor Analysis

Full covariance analysis is today used mainly for problems with less than about 50 assets. Instead, one uses an abbreviated approach based on factoring the covariance matrix into a relatively small number of common factors on which each stock has loadings. One then need deal mainly with the covariance matrix of factor returns, which will be much smaller than the full covariance matrix, and correspondingly less susceptible to magnifying error. Commercial risk structure vendors provide loadings of hundreds and sometimes thousands of stocks on each risk factor, plus estimates of their specific risks and any necessary covariances among factors. Their factor structures for return risk are usually designed for monthly or weekly return intervals.

The factors may be constructed in several ways, each with advantages. Purely statistical principal components analysis of the past several years of weekly returns will show a great deal of structure that may be predictive for a few months. If one desires risk control without frills, one will be happy with the result. The disadvantage is that the apparent principal components or factors will in general be neither very meaningful nor stable through time.

Probably the most popular approach is to cluster stocks by industry, with a factor for each industry, and to combine this with about a dozen special long-short portfolios that each characterize some particular dimension such as high book/price versus low book/price, large versus small capitalization, and so on. With the advent of international investing, such risk models can get much more complicated, involving country and currency effects.

Two other approaches also have a following. One uses sensitivity to movements of asset class index returns as factor returns. Thus there is a stock market factor, a bond factor, a small stock factor, a growth stock factor, a value stock factor, and so on. The other approach is a remnant of the early days of the APT return model. It reflects factors based on sensitivity to changes in external economic stimuli such as changes in interest rates, inflation, or industrial production.

Since each approach has a commercial market, we can assume each has advantages for particular quantitative investors. My experience is that purely statistical methods such as principal components analysis are adequate and may be superior because they involve no preconceptions. However, the argument has been raised by others that any factors used for risk estimation should be understandable and congruent with those used in the formation of expected returns. For example, if one bets on low price-to-book, would it not be useful to know directly how much risk that would imply? Of course being able to isolate the P/B factor risk is a convenience, and, alternatively, having a factor structure that did not at least indirectly reflect that implied risk would be a problem.

Estimating Single Elements of Risk

The confidence intervals around estimated standard deviations and correlations are surprisingly wide. That is, it takes surprisingly large samples to estimate these parameters accurately. In general statistics, one notes that the central tendency, usually the mean, is easier to estimate than the standard deviation. Even so, for distributions with very fat tails, such as the Cauchy, which arises from taking the ratio of two normal distributions where the denominator can be zero, the best estimate of the central tendency will involve throwing out considerable information from the tails. This need to discard or at least winsorize (pull in to an outer bound) information in the tails in the presence of fat-tailed distributions is at least as true for covariances as for measures of central tendency.

For example, if deleting one observation from a hundred will change a sample correlation from 0.2 to 0.8, then it is likely that this point is an outlier that should be discarded. When we do so, we are acknowledging that the observations come from something other than the normal, or even log normal, distribution. Unfortunately, without a prespecification of the exact return distribution we are facing, determining where to apply such cutoffs will remain a skill rather than a definite algorithm.

Another way to improve estimates of single elements of risk is to take into account variation through time. It is an empirical fact that high volatility returns tend to cluster by period. An autoregressive scheme that estimates variance as a function of recent observed variance may be constructed by regressing squared returns against past squared returns, assuming mean returns near zero.

Another empirical observation is that return correlations are higher for very large excursions. That is, assets are traded in slightly segmented markets. If there is little overall volatility, the separated motions of each can be rather independent. On the other hand, on really big trading days like those of the stock panic in October 1987, correlations increase sharply. This changing correlation process could also be modeled

However, as we move beyond the variance diagonal of the covariance matrix, the problems of modeling time dependency become ones of estimating multiple parameters and correspondingly more challenging. If we model covariances, they imply a product of two standard deviations and a correlation coefficient. How do we insure that the results are consistent both with the variances on the covariance matrix diagonal and with an implied correlation coefficient lying between plus and minus one? A typical resolution is to micro-estimate variances, and therefore standard deviations, based on recent events, while estimating correlation coefficients over a full sample.

Simultaneous Estimation of Multiple Elements

When we try to forecast more than one quantity it is frequent that the implied residual error terms of the multiple equations will not be independent, but will be correlated. There are methods for directly addressing such problems as systems of equations, but they do not scale well to more than a handful of regressions. An alternative for medium to large covariance matrices is factor analysis, which attempts to restructure the covariance matrix so that it is produced by a relatively few possibly correlated factor risks, and a larger number of uncorrelated specific risks.

Another way to reduce error and use information across sample inputs to the Markowitz optimization is through the use of Stein estimators, also called shrinkage estimators because they shrink outlying estimates towards an implicit Bayesian prior. The simplest example of a Stein estimator is that for estimating mean return.

Suppose that one has a prior assumption that cross-sectional differences in expected return are zero, and one will deviate from this Bayesian prior only with reluctance. (This is a useful assumption if we believe that our return forecasts are based to a degree on data-mining or are subject to process instability.) Then one might divide the original estimates of difference from the zero mean by a parameter that is positively related to the time-series variance in forecast estimate for that particular asset. That is, we assume extreme forecasts are more likely to be in error. We will also reduce dispersion in our forecasts overall.

Stein estimators also exist for the covariance matrix. They may take as their prior equal covariances across stocks, equal correlations, or any of a variety of other forms. Michaud, and especially Ledoit, are useful references on Stein estimators for portfolio optimization.[2]

Finally, there are ad hoc methods that have some of the properties of Stein estimators and some implied properties of factor analysis. For example, a heuristic I have invented is to assemble a Bayesian prior covariance matrix that is equal in its variance diagonal and equal in all its implied correlations. Then I shrink the actual differences in the sample covariance matrix part-way toward this prior. Another approach is to categorize stocks in groups. Then calculate the average return within the group. Finally, calculate the inter-group correlations. These can be combined with the average standard deviation within each group to create Bayesian prior covariances that can be applied to every element in the original stock covariance matrix, either as a shrinkage target or as the final estimate.

All these methods tend to produce better out-of sample correlation between *ex ante* and *ex post* portfolio risk, as well as more stable weight allocations. You will also observe solutions that tend to allocate more similar weights to similar securities rather than going long one and short the other.

OPTIMIZER ISSUES AND PRACTICAL SOLUTIONS

This section catalogues a variety of issues that quantitative investors who use optimizers for portfolio construction must resolve on a day-to-day basis. It is purely pragmatic, reflecting largely my own experience.

Non-Intuitive Solution Changes

Many people find that optimizers produce what appear to be radically different solutions from month to month. This is non-intuitive, and causes them to lose faith in the output. Approaches to making the solution more robust in the face of statistical error in the inputs, such as averaging Monte Carlo simulations, factor analysis and Stein estimators, will cure many of these fluctuations. Another help is making sure that realistic trading costs are added to the objective function. This will filter out many portfolio changes that otherwise would be proposed. If these steps don't fully resolve the problem, one must reform intuitions. That is, portfolios that to you or I look very different, perhaps because of different concentrations by industry, may look very similar to the optimizer because they have very similar levels of expected return and risk.

Constraints

Besides typical non-negativity constraints, it is also possible to add a variety of other departures from the basic Markowitz optimization and still retain the char-

---

[2] Oliver Ledoit, "Portfolio Selection: Improved Covariance Matrix Estimation," Sloan School of Management at MIT (Working Paper, November 1994).

acteristics of the original quadratic programming framework. There will be no deceptive local maxima and the global maximum of the objective function will be reachable by following successive trial solutions up the gradient as closely as possible. The permissible additions include any linear constraint on the weights. Examples might be that the maximum position in asset number two be less than 10%, or that the dividend yield of the portfolio be at least 3%. (It is also possible to add to the risk term additional penalties quadratic in the weights, but this is not the focus here.)

Position constraints are fail-safe mechanisms for risk control and may also be used by investment managers to satisfy client requirements. For example, depart no more than 2% from the benchmark weight in any one stock, or no more than 5% active weight in any one industry. Or, no more than 10% of the portfolio may be invested in emerging markets, and so on. Such constraints are often a crutch for preventing poor and unstable diversification, and may often be slackened once more robust estimation procedures are instituted. One wants enough constraints to protect against disaster, but should keep in mind that each constraint will tend to worsen the opportunities for value added.

At any one time, one is confronted with a single efficient frontier. Therefore a constraint against taking more than a given amount of risk merely puts part of the efficient frontier out of bounds, and does not interfere with the core of the optimization. However, if one views optimizations as one of a sequence in which expected returns and covariances are changing, and the constraint on expected risk is constant, there is a significant loss in information passing through. At the times when we have more information, that is, a higher ratio of expected return to expected risk, we will not take full advantage of it. And when we have little differences in return, if we have a lower bound on risk we will overplay our hand. It is much better to control risk through a bigger lambda, or risk aversion parameter, than to put in a fixed risk limit that takes frequent effect.

It is possible to think of constraints on turnover as a linear constraint on the total of assets bought, as distinguished from assets simply held. Thus, depending on how it is implemented, a turnover constraint may not interfere with the optimization potential of the problem. It will, however, further restrict the flow of information from return forecasts to portfolio holdings.

Finally, there are constraints that do not truly fit within the quadratic programming paradigm. For example, one may add to the optimizer a facility for producing recommended trades only in round lot sizes. This kind of constraint is practically very useful but likely to cause the optimization algorithm difficulty in finding the best solution.

Individually, each constraint has a purpose that seems to justify it. Collectively, however, the system of constraints will generally be paid for in a reduced ratio of active returns to realized risk. The need for constraints is often a confession that the input data are faulty, and when these have been corrected it is wise to keep constraints loose enough so that they are not normally binding.

Managing the Trading Process

The first choice one has for managing the trading process as stimulated by the optimizer is the choice of the risk aversion parameter. For, the more closely one holds to a conventional capitalization-weighted benchmark, generally the lower the turnover. One also indirectly affects trading by choosing the frequency with which the optimizer will be updated. In my experience I have used daily, weekly, monthly, and quarterly optimizations. The best interval will depend on the size of active return forecasts, the rate at which they decay, as well as on trading costs.

I have already commented on turnover constraints, voicing the conclusion that one should not use them without strong reasons. It seems to me that it is better to install trading costs, which may be specific to each security, and a trading cost amortization period, which may apply to every security. Determination of amortization period is a circular process, since until we have observed typical turnover rates, we cannot judge how many periods a newly bought security is likely to be held. However, the circular logic can be readily solved through iteration. I usually amortize trading costs over a shorter period than implied by the turnover rate. This is a practical way, admittedly imperfect, to compensate for possible data mining in either the return forecast or the risk forecast. However, it would be better to condition these forecasts directly.

One of the most effective ways to control trading is simply to forecast returns in a way that emphasizes persistent forecast elements. This can be done by constructing the forecasts from longer-period returns, or even weighted averages of returns from multiple periods. The econometric problems in this procedure are challenging: either sharply reduced degrees of freedom or overlapping observations that require more advanced statistical knowledge to implement. Alternatively, and this is my preference, one can exponentially smooth all forecast input variables before entering them into a forecast regression. This has the great advantage of allowing one to stay with non-overlapping return observations in a conventional framework for hypothesis testing and confidence intervals. Either way, one increases the persistence of the forecast. That is, one can sometimes improve the portfolio result by giving up some high-frequency forecasting capability in return for forecasts of greater persistence.

Multiple Levels

It is not always a good idea to include the full detail of the asset allocation problem within one optimization. For example, consider allocating among stocks and bonds in a global portfolio. The dispersion for expected stock returns will typically be much greater than for bond expected returns. Suppose we do not condition these dispersions. If holdings are selected from the positive tail of expected returns, disproportionately more stocks will be put in the portfolio. For example, suppose there is a benchmark of 60% stocks and 40% bonds; the resulting allocation may be 70% stocks without reflecting any forecast that the average stock will outperform the average bond.

Of course if one fully trusts all the detailed level estimates, one should implement this plan. But if outlier estimates are less reliable than more conservative estimates, it would be a poor plan. A safer procedure, even though by definition sub-optimal, would be to first allocate between stocks and bonds based on average characteristics for each asset class. Then one can use the result as a constraint on the total proportions of stocks and bonds in a second optimal allocation at the detailed security level.

The detailed allocation can be done as follows. Pool the detailed stock and bond allocation problems but retain the constraint on overall proportions. This does run the risk that changes in stock allocations will be transmitted through the optimization to less-warranted changes in bond security allocations. However, the offsetting advantage is that it potentially improves the return to risk ratio of the entire portfolio through taking advantage of specific stock-bond combinations. For example, in an international balanced portfolio, it might make less sense to overweight Japanese bonds if it were likely that Japanese stocks were also to be overweighted.

Simulation Capability

Without historical simulation, one has little reason to trust the accuracy of an optimizer or its implicit risk estimation. It is useful to compare forecast risk with actual risk in two ways. First, what is the bias, or difference in average predicted risk and realized risk, usually measured as the ratio of standard deviation in return? Second, what is the risk tracking? This can be tested by running a time-series regression between portfolio forecast squared return and realized squared return. (An idea of success can be gotten even without adjustments for the mean being different from zero.)

Second, one wants an overall measure of effectiveness in coupling return forecasts to active positions to actual returns. For example, one might simulate the entire process dynamically over a period of, say 15 years. In this simulation, to the extent practical both return and risk forecasts should be based on rolling windows without taking advantage of later data except by choosing forecast input variables.

The simulation can provide overall statistics on value added and its ratio to annualized risk as standard deviation, the so-called information ratio. It will also provide evidence on such risk-related ideas as drawdown, the maximum cumulative loss from a previous peak. The distribution of returns may provide the basis for a Value at Risk Monte Carlo simulation.

The existence of such a historical simulation capability that allows linking your forecasts to portfolio construction is today a rarity, even for commercial vendors. But as a quantitative investor you should pursue such a toolset until you attain it, for it is very nearly indispensable in maintaining an effective quantitative investment process.

Chapter 16

Performance Analysis

Know thyself.
Inscription on the Oracle of Apollo at Delphi, Greece (circa 600 BC)

It is a truism that what is measured is what is managed and, ultimately, what is improved. Best current measurement practice among many investment managers is largely an adaptation of standard cost accounting. We begin by introducing this approach, which analyzes differences between benchmark and actual returns at various levels of detail. Then we will return to a deeper level of performance analysis in which we divide the process of portfolio management into three functional parts. These are *return forecasting, portfolio construction*, and *trading*. We initially describe techniques for measuring performance within each of these parts as if they were fully independent. Then we go on to measure how well the parts are coupled together. The ideal is practical statistical quality control and improvement. Though the inherently high residual noise in investing makes the kind of quality control system inspired by Deming seem far-fetched at first glance, striving for that ideal appears on examination to be quite practical.[1]

STANDARD COST ACCOUNTING

In 1970 I joined the faculty at M.I.T. I taught in the accounting department, which we somewhat grandly called "management information for planning and control." My mentor in this assignment was Zenon Zannetos, an original thinker who stressed the importance of standards as "substabilities" around which organizations could be managed. Actual performance along many dimensions could best be managed in comparison with these standards. The difference between actual and standard performance could be managed as though it were a statistical control process. Zenon's contribution was his appreciation for the fact that standard cost accounting systems then in use within many large corporations provided grist for that statistical mill. That is, sequences of *accounting variances* could be analyzed using operations research techniques. (Note that "accounting variance" is not defined as statistical variance but simply as the single-observation difference between actual and standard.)

---

[1] Mary Walton, *The Deming Management Method* (New York: Dodd, Mead, 1986). W. Edwards Deming is credited with helping to revive the Japanese economy during the 1950s through spreading the gospel of statistical quality control.

261

For a brief idea of what standard cost accounting is about, consider the following. In the records of an automobile manufacturer, there will be defined a standard cost to manufacture an automobile. That standard cost is made up of the standard cost of various parts. Short-run costs are often thought of as having a fixed and marginal component. Thus, the standard cost of manufacturing a part will depend on a planned, or standard, volume over which one allocates the fixed period cost. It will also depend upon a standard number of labor hours to carry out various operations and on a standard wage per hour. The whole assembly of standards comprises a plan. Standard cost accounting consists of an analysis of the difference between total planned and actual costs into constituent parts.

As the accounting variance is analyzed at each level of the organization, it will be broken down according to the arithmetic logic involved in the plan. Suppose the cost of a car consisted of the *sum* of an engine and a body. Then one would want the car cost variance to be analyzed further as the sum of an engine variance and a body variance.

Suppose also that the cost of a car body can be analyzed as the arithmetic *product* of pounds per car body times the cost per pound. Then there will logically be three components to the total body variance. These are: (1) the standard cost per pound times the variance in pounds, (2) the standard weight per car body times the variance in cost per pound, and (3) an interaction term that is the product of the variance in weight times the variance in cost per pound. Convention will assign the typically much smaller interaction term to one of the other two. Thus, we might have only two variance components recorded by the cost accounting system. For example, we might have the weight variance multiplied by the standard cost per pound as one part, and the actual (not standard) weight multiplied by the variance in cost per pound as the second part.

Standard cost accounting is potentially a very flexible tool because there is no one best way to break down the plan into its component parts. For some purposes, for example, an automobile manufacturer would do better not to break down the car's cost by part and subassembly but rather by the type of resource that goes into it. Suppose management structure is by function rather than by automobile part. Then we might want standards and variances aggregated by research costs, engineering costs, advertising and sales costs, dealership support, and manufacturing. The latter could be further analyzed into fixed capital depreciation, inventory carrying costs, raw materials, and assembly.

The ideas of standard cost accounting apply equally well to the revenue generation side of business, and to the analysis of value added and profit. Particularly when enhanced by statistical techniques, it can also be useful for us as investors interested in analyzing and improving our performance.

A sequence of variances in value added by a particular operation constitutes a time-series that can be analyzed for its statistical characteristics. We will want to measure the level and rates of change of its mean and variance, and seek to relate these to particular conditions. We can also use measured standard deviation to judge how unusual individual events are. This might help us to decide which individual events are worth further investigation or special handling.

When I became a portfolio manager in the early 1980s, this standard cost accounting discipline was already familiar to me. The only difference was that standards were replaced by benchmarks.

To illustrate, in international equity investing, value-added could be broken down into two parts: country selection and stock selection. (The third interaction part was usually lumped with stock selection.) That is, in investing versus an EAFE benchmark with given country weights and given index performance within each country, one goes on as follows. Country selection value-added is defined as the sum across countries of the country selection value-added for each. The latter is defined for one country as the product of (1) the difference between individual country benchmark return and a common portfolio benchmark return, and (2) the difference in the country's weight in the portfolio and its weight in the benchmark. Stock selection value-added is defined as the sum across countries of the stock selection value-added within each. The latter is defined for each country as the product of actual portfolio country weight times the difference between the actual and benchmark returns within that country. Note we use actual country weights in the calculation of the stock selection variance so as not to omit the interaction effect between country selection and stock selection.

For an investor specializing in U.S. stocks, the same method may be applied, but with industry sectors substituted for countries. Of course the same method can also be applied to the asset allocation decision between cash, bonds, and stocks. It can also be applied to dividing between local stock value-added and currency value-added, or any other breakdown that portrays the structure of the decision.

Exhibit 1 shows a simplified hypothetical performance report for a single month. This is constructed for a hypothetical global equity fund in which stock selection plays a minimal role. (Any stock selection variance is here lumped with trading costs and any mid-month transactions that cannot capture full-month returns.) The analysis is therefore focused on variances divided by country and by implementation results versus idealized beginning-of-period returns.

Note in Exhibit 1 the positive variance for overweighting Italy. This is calculated by multiplying two differences: that between 6.15 and 1.29, the overweight, and that between 9.58 and 2.07, the excess return.

Even though simplified, Exhibit 1 still is comprehensive enough to avoid three traps for the unwary. First, the country selection variances are analyzed using the difference between each country's index return and the overall benchmark return. If, alternatively, one had simply multiplied active weights by country index returns without subtracting the overall benchmark return, the variances would not be so useful for diagnosis of good and bad decisions. Second, cash, which is present to some degree in every portfolio, is included in the analysis. It is given an index return equal to the going cash return, even though it is not included in the MSCI indices. Third, all the unexplained variances with actual returns are highlighted as an implementation variance. This forces consideration of trading costs, even when they are not otherwise captured.

Exhibit 1: XYZ Fund Performance Analysis for December 19XX

Benchmark: MSCI World Equity Index
Benchmark Return: 2.07%

	Beg. Fund Weight%	Beg. Bench Weight %	Index $ Return %	Country Selection Variance
North America				
Canada	6.52	2.29	0.94	-0.05
United States	30.11	39.34	1.47	0.06
Total Weight	36.64	41.63		
Pacific Rim				
Australia	4.02	1.57	2.04	0.00
Hong Kong	0.00	1.86	3.27	-0.02
Japan	18.70	23.61	5.11	-0.15
Malaysia	0.00	1.29	5.81	-0.05
New Zealand	0.13	0.29	1.23	0.00
Singapore	0.63	0.72	7.35	0.00
Total Weight	223.46	29.33		
Europe				
Austria	1.13	0.14	2.54	0.00
Belgium	5.40	0.72	5.6	0.17
Germany	0.13	4.01	3.06	-0.04
Denmark	0.00	0.43	2.47	0.00
Spain	5.90	1.00	4.66	0.13
Finland	0.00	0.43	-15.62	0.08
France	8.16	3.72	4.22	0.10
Ireland	0.50	0.14	2.33	0.00
Italy	6.15	1.29	9.58	0.37
Netherlands	6.78	2.29	4.33	0.10
Norway	0.00	0.29	2.55	0.00
Sweden	1.13	1.29	-2.25	0.01
Switzerland	0.38	3.43	3.91	-0.06
United Kingdom	3.64	9.87	2.65	-0.04
Total Weight	39.27	29.04		
Cash	0.63	0.00	0.47	-0.01
Totals	100.00	100.00	Country Selection Variance	0.58
			Implementation Variance	-0.12
			Plus: Benchmark Return	2.07
			Equals: Actual Fund Return	2.53

Exhibit 2: Summary of Monthly Variances for XYZ Fund 19XX

Benchmark: 70% MSCI World Equity Index, 30% Salomon World Government Bond Index

	Return %	Annual Risk	Reward/Risk
Bond-Stock-Cash Allocation	0.32	0.35	0.91
Equity			
North America	−0.35	0.29	−1.21
Pacific	−0.51	0.43	−1.19
Europe	−0.63	0.71	−0.89
Bonds	−0.42	0.34	−1.24
Currency	0.33	0.69	0.48
Implementation	−1.22	0.68	−1.79
Sum of Monthly Variances	−2.48	1.50	−1.65
Due to Compounding	−0.45		
Account Return	17.11		
Benchmark Return	20.04		
Annual Variance*	−2.93		

* Variance is defined for this entry as: Account Return − Benchmark Return

Such records are more useful if they are accumulated for multiple periods. Then averages and standard deviations may be produced. Note that when this is done the sum of the monthly variances does not equal the variance for the total period. That is, the total period variance is instead the difference between compounded actual return and compounded standard return. However, the difference is generally modest and can be included in a longer term report such as Exhibit 2 as a variance "due to compounding." Again, the example is altered to be hypothetical, although loosely based on a real case.

The left-hand column in Exhibit 2 represents the sum of 12 more detailed monthly variances in each row. The sample standard deviation of each row is multiplied by the square root of 12 to get an annualized risk (standard deviation) for that variance. In this case, results are quite poor in country selection, both for equities and bonds, particularly given low risks taken. Furthermore, there is a large negative variance for the year assigned to implementation, which in this case could include some combination of security selection, monthly timing, and trading costs. One could also add management and custodial fees to get a complete picture. There were modest bright spots in broad asset class selection and in currencies.

The calculation of a reward to risk ratio is not very meaningful for such a short sample, but I have included it for completeness.

Real reports of this type are considerably more complicated because they separate stock selection from country or industry sector selection. For example, each country would be represented by both a country selection variance relative to a higher-level equity benchmark and a stock selection variance relative to each local equity benchmark, using the method described earlier.

What I call the standard cost accounting framework has achieved considerable acceptance within the institutional investment community. However, there are deficiencies to this approach that make it only a first step in performance assessment.

First, the subdivision of variances by asset class, country or industry may or may not reflect the way the investment process is actually managed. For example, it may not distinguish between the effectiveness of different decision functions, such as forecasting as opposed to portfolio construction. It therefore may not reveal the critical bottlenecks whose relief could most improve the process.

Second, seldom is the analysis of return variances carried out with the statistical rigor necessary given the essentially random character of the largest part of the process. Too often, no tests of statistical significance are made before drawing conclusions.

Third, there are often conflicting objectives between those measured and those who want the measurements for evaluation purposes. In this context, the foregoing lack of focus on actual organization of the investment process and on its statistical nature tend to produce "gaming" of the system. When performance measurement is not relevant to true process improvement by those measured, human nature will often find a way to subvert it.

MEASURING RETURN FORECASTING PERFORMANCE

In what follows, we assume throughout that the quantitative investor actually constructs an explicit forecast of excess return. This is in itself a marked innovation that allows for improved measurement and control of the value-added process. An explicit forecast is a substability, a place of separation between relatively independent disturbances. How can we measure its quality?

We can use the same framework that we used to derive our forecast first, with two important differences. First, since the data are unfolding in real time, there is no possibility of look-ahead bias or data-mining. Second, we may well refine our forecast model during the sequence of observations. What we are measuring is the totality of our forecasting process, not just the most recent method employed.

Suppose, for example, that we are interested only in whether to be in cash or in an index of the stock market. We forecast the difference in return between stocks and cash. We keep a record of both our forecast difference and the actual difference in returns. The difference between actual and forecast is the forecast error. To make a concrete example, suppose we are interested in daily forecasts and we have already accumulated 50 days of data.

Our first step is to examine the statistical distribution of our forecast errors. One of the tenets of statistical quality control I find interesting in its application here is that one should initially focus on the outliers. That is, inspect the forecast errors for strong outliers, and attempt to account for these first. Only outlier observations deserve individual close inspection, and the ability to forecast or prevent outliers is often the first step to process improvement.

Exhibit 3: Cross-Sectional Forecast-Actual Return Correlation

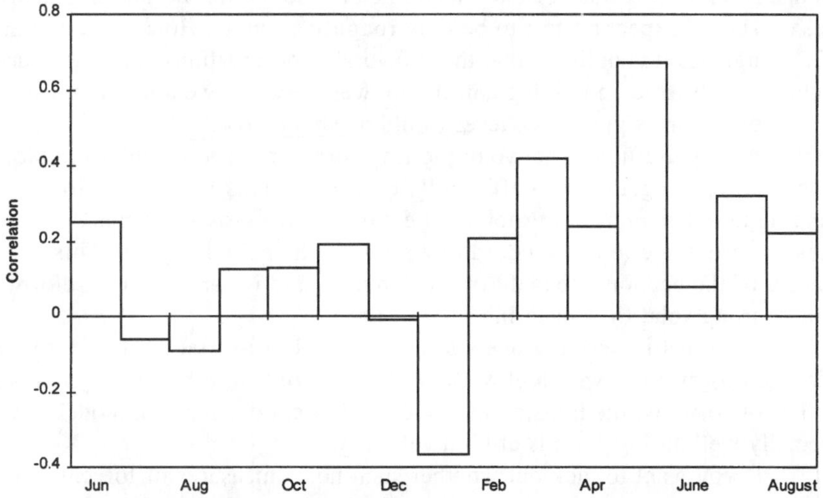

Second, we examine forecast errors for evidence of autocorrelation, or runs. These may be behavioral in nature or they may be related to some slow-moving outside disturbance. For example, suppose we use a value model such as the difference between dividend yield and interest rates to forecast the level of stocks. Then we might find that it works much better in periods coming out of economic recession than when the economy is going into recession.

Third, we can use linear regression (OLS) of the relationship between the actual stock-cash return difference and its forecast to get an idea of the power of our forecast. This will generally be a robust measuring tool if we have sufficient observations, say 50. (That is not to say that we will have enough observations to show our result is non-random, but only that the assumptions of OLS t-tests based on normality will be useful.) We can estimate the reliability of our conclusion using the t-statistic for the null hypothesis that the regression coefficient is zero.

There are other supplementary measures possible. We may decide to reduce the impact of remaining outliers by tracking the correlation of ranks of actual return differences against ranks of forecasts. If we have enough observations, we may even divide forecasts into sorted deciles and look for non-linear relationships between forecast and actual. Is there valid information just in the tails of the forecast, or is it spread throughout its range?

In more complicated situations we will want to forecast the returns of a large number of assets. We can track the time-series sequence of cross sectional correlation coefficients, calculating averages and standard deviations as well. A real example from forecasting currency hedging returns is shown as Exhibit 3. In this case, each bar represents a monthly average of weekly correlations between forecast and actual hedging returns for nine currencies. The mean correlation during this period is 0.15, and the monthly standard deviation is 0.24. With only 15 months, and knowing that correlation coefficients do not follow a normal distribution, we should expect a t-test to be only roughly accurate. However, a t-statistic of 2.48 suggests it is unlikely that these favorable observations could have arisen by chance if the true underlying correlation were zero. (If we took the t-test literally, the two-tailed significance level would be about 2.6%.)

A very useful alternative to plotting correlation coefficients is to plot the cross-sectional regression coefficient's t-statistic. This will take into account changing numbers of assets. Another alternative is the cross-sectional correlation times the cross-sectional standard deviation of the actual returns. This gives a measure of the economic benefit of the forecast, and is particularly useful when there is strong volatility clustering.

Note that in deriving one's forecast model, it is often useful to give less weight to observations with high variance because of heteroscedasticity in residuals. The opposite is true in using the model. We want our forecast model to work especially well during periods of high volatility.

If you want to pick out whether such noisy measures of forecast quality are getting better or worse over time, it will often be necessary to smooth them. A smoothed version may reveal patterns to the eye such as calendar effects or a relationship with the business cycle.

Of course, all the usual tools of econometric analysis are applicable to analyzing forecast errors further. The comments made earlier regarding examination of the forecast error series for outliers and autocorrelation also apply here.

MEASURING PORTFOLIO CONSTRUCTION PERFORMANCE

The next elements in the investment process are risk forecasts and the subsequent construction of the portfolio.

In principle, the techniques of the preceding section are also available for analyzing each element of the forecast covariance matrix. In practice, this is unusual, both because of the extra complexity and because most investors harbor the reasonable belief that forecasting returns is much more important than forecasting risks. I must confess that I, too, have often sinned in this regard.

A frequently cited rule of thumb is that an error in expected return is 10 times as important as an error in standard deviation in determining optimal portfolio position. And the latter is twice as important as getting the correlation right. This is clearly an oversimplification that is highly context-dependent. But similar beliefs cause the more sophisticated approaches to assessing risk noted in Chapter 15 to be underutilized. Risk forecasts often go unrecorded and are unavailable for performance assessment.

This is regrettable, not only because the rule of thumb may not apply everywhere, but also because it usually is easier to forecast risk than to forecast return. It may even be 10 times easier!

If risk forecasts are recorded, it is most cheaply done at the aggregate portfolio level. It is not difficult to compare the average of the portfolio risk forecasts to the actual standard deviation of return over the period to see if we have a biased forecast.

However, a better comparison may be done using the methods described in the preceding section, but transforming return deviations by squaring them. First, calculate the actual excess return each period by subtracting the sample mean. Square each of these actual excess returns to form the *actual*. Second, each period square the forecast portfolio standard deviation of return to obtain your *forecast*. Then continue as described in the prior section, examining the forecast errors for outliers and runs, and regressing actual against forecast with the consequent OLS diagnostics.

Let us turn now to portfolio construction after the risk forecast. I know of no widely used approach for monitoring the effectiveness of actively managed portfolio construction *per se*, though Michaud's book might suggest such a scheme.[2] However, one may suggest heuristic approaches to this end. I developed one such for my own use, christened the *poor man's optimizer*, which can be used to provide a baseline result against which the results of Markowitz optimization may be compared *ex post*.

The *poor man's* approach takes the universe of stocks ranked by forecast return as given. The bottom quartile is eliminated. The remaining stocks are given market capitalization weight to start. The eliminated capitalization weight of the bottom quartile is then allocated either equally or on a capitalization-weighted basis as additional weight for the stocks in the top quartile. This procedure assures a realistically moderate dose of return expectations will be embedded in the portfolio, as well as a good degree of diversification. The risk and return of the sequence of one's Markowitz-optimized portfolios may then be compared to the risk and return of the poor man's optimizer.

MEASURING TRADING PERFORMANCE

In Chapter 10 we discussed trading costs in the broadest possible sense. Easily measured direct commissions, and even the bid-ask spread, are often a small part of total trading costs. To be useful, the measurement and control of trading costs must at least include price impact, the fact that one's trades affect the price of the transaction. How should one measure it? It is first necessary to record the time of purchase and estimate the expected price that would have obtained if you had not been trading. Then one can subtract this market price from what was actually paid to estimate trading cost. It is necessary to average a large number of such measurements to get a reliable estimate, because individual transactions vary widely in their apparent costs.

---

[2] Richard O. Michaud, *Efficient Asset Management* (Cambridge, MA: Harvard Business School Press, 1998).

For large investors, the most commonly used estimates of the undisturbed market price for smaller stocks are inadequate. They do not take into account that large transactions can affect prices for several days or even weeks. Typically, even moderately large transactions relative to average daily trading volume disturb the bid-ask spread. In consequence, commercial information vendors supplied weighted-average prices for the day, against which one can compare. However, a better approach is to average the market prices over several days, beginning perhaps a day before the trade and extending for several days thereafter. This approach is further improved by adjusting prices from different periods by the market index movement (or even narrower indices) relative to the time of the trade. Closing prices may be adequate for assessing undisturbed prices, but only if averaged over many trades.

It is also possible to discern the overall time distribution of the price impact. If the single-day price estimates, adjusted for market movements, are aggregated across many trades, say at least 200, one may estimate an average price impact time distribution. Depending on whether one is buying or selling, it looks like either a pimple or a dimple.

How should we measure trading costs when trades not completed because the price gets away from us turn out to be profitable? This is likely to be very important if limit orders are used. To measure this opportunity cost, one must keep a record of all trades proposed. As pointed out by Perold, an appropriate way to capture all such costs in aggregate is to maintain a paper portfolio.[3] Apart from the additional record-keeping, which is daunting to most investors, this exercise will not provide feedback on particular securities or sub-classes of the portfolio. In addition, the paper portfolio would likely drift far from the actual portfolio. Nonetheless, it is an intriguing idea, though, regrettably, I have no experience to share concerning the result. As an alternative, one can record in detail the proposed trades that did not get executed, and calculate an opportunity cost over a compromise truncated time horizon, such as 30 days. At least one commercial vendor of trading cost measurements provides such a service.

COUPLING FORECASTING, PORTFOLIO CONSTRUCTION, AND TRADING

Portfolio construction balances the possibility of achieving forecast excess returns against many other factors — transaction costs, expected risk, and position constraints, not least the typical prohibition against short sales. The investor may arbitrarily set some of these factors less than optimally in the portfolio construction problem. For example, one may set too-conservative maximum active weights out of unquantified fear that the risk assessment will prove wrong. One

---

[3] Andre F. Perold, "The Implementation Shortfall: Paper versus Reality," *Journal of Portfolio Management* (April 1998).

may set tight turnover constraints that do not recognize that valid predictive information may be sporadic, and so on.

Let us assume the case of pure stock selection. How well does our forecasting model fit our portfolio construction approach, and vice versa?

A very simple heuristic for indicating the compatibility of the forecast with portfolio construction is to look at the autocorrelation of the forecast. If this period's forecast has a low cross-sectional correlation with last-period's forecast, portfolio construction is likely to miss a good part of the signal because it will be filtered out by transaction cost considerations. The danger zone where forecast persistence is too low may be determined very roughly by experience. For example, for a value-oriented investor, such a correlation below 0.9 might be a yellow warning light to slow down.

A more comprehensive indicator, but one requiring equally heuristic benchmarking, is the cross-sectional correlation between forecast return and active positions for any one month. Active positions are measured as the difference between the percentage weight given to each stock and its percentage weight in the benchmark.

An excellent but quite laborious assessment of the impact of mis-matches between forecast and portfolio construction may be gotten through simulating the portfolio with various degrees of structure in the portfolio construction optimization. For example, first measure the risk and return performance of the minimum risk portfolio with a full set of constraints and trading costs. Then allow the risk you would actually tolerate. Then free up turnover constraints, then long-weight constraints, then short-weight constraints, and finally allow trading costs of zero. The successive improvements as each hindrance is released give its cost in a return metric.

It is often worth sacrificing forecast R-squared to achieve more implementability. Here are two common examples and their treatment. If you have been forecasting monthly returns well, but based on very short-term signals, try smoothing the independent variables used in deriving the forecast. If releasing the constraint against short-sales triples the performance of the portfolio, your forecast model may be too slanted toward small stocks. Try re-estimating your forecast model giving more weight to observations of larger stocks.

The third element in the investment process, trading, may also be poorly coupled to earlier steps in the process. This can easily happen if assumed trading costs are not equal to actual trading costs or if they are amortized over too short or too long a period.

I have found that one can get a very useful measure of overall coupling success through the following innovation. Monitor and record period-by-period the cross-sectional correlation between *forecast returns* and *actual returns*. Then measure the usually much lower cross-sectional correlation between *active positions* and *actual returns*. The ratio of the latter correlation to that of the former is the desired ratio. For example, suppose the average monthly correlation between forecast and actual return is 0.09, a respectable forecast for stock selection. One will often find that portfolios are so constructed and traded that the correlation between active positions and actual return is 0.03 or even less. Would the reader grant me a small vanity? The "Wilcox ratio" in this case is 33%. That is, only one-third of the original forecast signal is getting through to the portfolio's active positions. Recording this signal degradation is a critical step in investment performance assessment because it often suggests easy ways to improve the total process.

PERFORMANCE MEASUREMENT IN THE LARGE

Of course, the justly famous performance ratio is the Sharpe ratio, the ratio of average excess returns to their standard deviation, usually on an annual basis. The original meaning was in terms of excess returns over cash, but later it was extended to excess returns relative to benchmark returns. The Sharpe ratio is a useful stimulant to thinking about norms of risk-to-reward. However, it has given rise to the misleading idea that it is characteristic of an investment process independent of the risk taken.[4]

Despite this defect, the Sharpe ratio is far superior to what most investors do. Even quantitative investors tend to focus most attention on 3- or 5-year return relative to competitors. The comparison may be with a universe of other investment managers or mutual funds, or with market indices such as the S&P 500. This activity, regrettably the most prominent part of decisions by investment consultants and clients to hire and fire investment managers, has minimal effectiveness for improving fund results. This becomes obvious, for example, in the near zero correlation between past 5-year performance and future 5-year performance of mutual funds. Its biggest defect may not even be ignoring risk taken, though that is clear. The problem is that there is a great deal of random content in the results, combined with an unstable process, making it statistically almost impossible to predict manager skill based on these aggregate data.

It is possible to get more insight by comparing a manager to a more narrowly defined standard. For example, one can relate performance to style benchmarks or prior asset mix replications to see if a manager's results are the consequence of an overall tilt or of short-term value-added. However, even these approaches suffer from lack of the high-frequency and more process-oriented observations that the investment manager is in a better position to collect internally.

In philosophy, the Deming approach to eternal process improvement through the cooperative use of statistical quality control tools is very appealing. One should embrace it not so much to see whether performance had been good recently. One should do so recognizing that the keys to non-random investment

---

[4] Note that the Sharpe ratio, since it is based on standard deviation and not on variance, is not independent of investor risk tolerance. It makes most sense if the CAPM is an accurate empirical predictor of available passive returns.

results are the abilities to learn in a rapid, sustainable fashion and to implement that knowledge with the precision that comes from a process under control.

As a quantitative investor, the most important task in investing may well be to learn how your decisions react to events, rather than the other way round. The tools in this chapter can help you do that.

Chapter 17

U.S. Stocks

The business of America is business.
Calvin Coolidge, *Speech, January 17, 1925, to the Society of American Newspaper Editors*

Some otherwise sophisticated quantitative investors think that, while there may be large market inefficiencies in the rest of the world, the U.S. stock market has matured and is largely efficient. Their argument goes as follows. Yes, contrary to the random walk theory, there *were* large inefficiencies signaled by small market capitalization and low price-to-book ratios. However, these have now been mostly exploited and remaining return premia are offset by real risk and cost differences. Yes, there *was* available information in changes in consensus analyst earnings estimates, but now this source of advantage has been over-exploited. They conclude that, perhaps, in the United States one should invest primarily in index funds.

It is true that the S&P 500 has been hard to beat as the U.S. stock market has risen to over four times book value. Still, this does not imply that there are no opportunities for the quantitative investor. In the land of the blind, the one-eyed man is king. Neither is it obvious that the U.S. stock market is in a state of near-equilibrium, with small disturbances quickly offset by vigilant arbitrage. The true picture is more complicated, with some aspects tightly arbitraged and others running riotously free. I believe that, whatever today's appearance of efficiency and equilibrium, it is a false one created by our preconceptions.[1] The kind of equilibrium that is the basis for modern financial theory is all too easily disturbed by new investor recruiting and changing rules of behavior. In its place we see waves of speculative delusion, sometimes followed by catastrophe. How could this be?

Consider the following logic. Suppose the world is exactly as postulated by Markowitz, but that (1) risk tolerance is a function of wealth, and (2) stock market holdings are a large portion of the wealth of active investors. Then it will be easy for natural business cycle fluctuations to drive much larger fluctuations in stock market pricing than can be justified by changing conditions in the real economy. The mechanism is a single implied positive feedback loop. An initial increase in earnings produces a higher-priced market, higher wealth, greater tolerance for risk, and a still higher stock market. When the underlying economy has a downward movement, the same mechanism works to amplify the downward price movement.

There are many more positive feedback loops in operation, each increasing the potential for extended excursions away from market equilibrium. Suppose that

---

[1] This has been the message of George Soros over the last decade, as he has moved from successful speculator to statesman. George Soros, *The Alchemy of Finance* (New York: Simon and Schuster, 1987).

overall perceived wealth based on stock market values is allowed to affect the attitude of bankers toward risk. In response to higher stock prices, they lend money at a rate that creates additional real business prosperity, although it may be of a temporary kind, because the loans may go to unsound enterprises. This additional credit expansion feedback further amplifies long-term fluctuations in stock market pricing.

Here is a positive feedback even more immediate. Within the market there are momentum investors. Under the conditions of high-amplitude, long-term cycles, momentum investing profitability is enhanced. The myths that evolve to support higher prices are unimportant — the essence is that one believes in the future of the thing that has enjoyed increased success. New investors are recruited to this kind of rule, rather than to value investing. Then, as we saw in Chapter 4, the system becomes yet more unstable. Completing the circle, still more momentum investors are recruited.

There has also been a *structural change* that weakens the potential for the market to correct itself before fluctuations get out of hand. This takes two forms. First, the rise of professional investment managers measured against competitors over relatively short terms promotes a fundamental shift in risk avoidance behavior. It is a shift away from avoiding total risk toward accepting it while showing less tolerance to deviation from competitive indices. This is the curse of undue attention to tracking error, whether with respect to a competitive universe or to a market index. No matter how silly the valuations of the S&P 500, managers cannot afford to deviate very far from it. Second, of course, capitalization-weighted *index fund* investing is totally price insensitive. Its spread has further weakened the potential for the early negative feedback inherent in value-oriented investing.

All these positive feedbacks produce extremes that do eventually attract corrective forces. At odd intervals, bitter doses of underlying economic reality combine with natural exhaustion of momentum to produce turning points, but their arrival will be very difficult to predict. At these turning points, the remaining value investors have their day in the sun. *However, there will be little correlation between past performance and future performance.* The lack of performance predictability would also be implied by perfect efficiency in incorporating new fundamental information into market pricing. Thus, this lack of correlation seems to support conventional equilibrium theory. I believe, however, that it has two causes. The first is, yes, a fair degree of market efficiency. The second is an equally impressive chaos arising from internal market dynamics created by shifting decision rules and the recruitment of inexperienced investors. This chaos disguises the residual inefficiencies.

Except for wealth effects, what has been said so far concerning the market as a whole also applies to cross-market comparisons. There are positive feedbacks concerning company prosperity and stock prices that create both fashion-wave investing opportunities and exploitable arbitrages. No additional principles seem to be involved. However, the scope for instability shrinks as one progresses from arbitrage between distantly related securities such as stocks and bonds to close relationships such as those between two competitors in the same industry.

The U.S. stock market, the largest and most thoroughly researched in the world, is still immature and inefficient. It is inefficient not so much in that some of us do so very much better as investors than others. Rather, it is inefficient because collectively we do a still primitive job of assimilating information into valid prices. Not only are we as its participants subject to emotion and cognitive biases, but there is simply not enough variety in our thinking to provide effective arbitrage across all the relevant dimensions. The U.S. market thus remains a stage on which many of our collective hopes and fears are dramatized.

In this chapter we apply three heuristics for identifying investment opportunities in the supposedly mature and efficient U.S. stock market.

First, begin with a plausible basic model of stock valuation, looking for opportunities in its residuals. I use the PB-ROE model as my first tool of analysis.

Second, expect to find increasing openings for contrary thinking and longer-term arbitrage as you move upward in generality from stocks to industries. (Global investors and asset allocators, of course, can move even further up the ladder.) As we move to more distant comparisons, simple models capture less of the relevant information; at the same time, consensus thinking can move further from equilibrium.

Third, try to discover when and where apparent inefficiencies are likely to be most available. The effort will lead to greater understanding of their basic causes, and in turn lead to perceiving new opportunities.

STRUCTURE THROUGH PB-ROE RESIDUALS

There are many rules of thumb in the market involving simple ratios or spreads. I have found most useful the model described in Chapter 12. In its simplest form it is just a comparison of price-to-book ratios. Better is PB-ROE, a straight line connecting log P/B with expected return on equity. In fuller forms, it encompasses interest rate expectations, time horizon, and dividend policy. It often provides enough fit to suggest opportunities within the remaining residual.

Here we will first use P/B as an a way to gain a quick broad understanding of the valuation of the U.S. stock market. Then we take a step toward refinement by adjusting for differences in return on equity. The sample is for stocks covered by Value Line. The stocks have been grouped by industry, and only the 24 industries with 10 or more Value Line companies are analyzed. (This excludes many interesting industries and companies, such as autos and Coca Cola, but the broad picture is unaffected.) The accounting data are as of December 1995. Prices are as of June 1996.

Exhibit 1 is a special kind of bar chart, with each bar representing one of these 24 key industries. The industries are sorted from left to right in order of increasing P/B. The width of the bar is proportional to the book value, or accounting equity, of each industry. The height of each bar represents the industry's P/B ratio, calculated as the sum of component company market values divided by the sum of their book values. The area of each bar represents the market value of the industry.

Exhibit 1: U.S. Key Industry Capitalization, June 1996

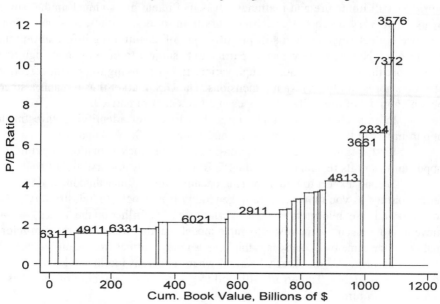

To reduce clutter, Exhibit 1 shows the SIC codes of only some of the industries. These codes, as well as those of the remaining key industries, are listed in Exhibit 2. Industry names, the name of the largest included company, industry P/B, equity book value, and return on equity are also contained in the exhibit. The industries are sorted by P/B so that you can identify Exhibit 1's unmarked industries. (If you draw a chart like Exhibit 1 by hand, you can write in more meaningful labels for each industry. You also will have space to include more industries. Note that the same kind of chart could also be a useful way for you to visualize individual stocks within an industry.)

One sees in Exhibit 1 that the market capitalization of the economy is very unevenly distributed, both by industry asset size and by the price accorded to those assets. If you looked at a series of such charts separated by 5-year intervals you would see a natural progression of these inequalities. Innovative new fields are at first not designated as separate industries. As they increase in importance they get their own designation and begin on the right half of the chart with high valuation and a narrow asset base. Then as they mature, the valuation shrinks, but the asset base increases. Finally, the industry fades away in importance. This life cycle is punctuated by occasional bursts of speculative valuation.

For example, in 1996 the highest flying industries charted are 3576, computer network and related companies such as Cisco Systems, and 7372, computer software companies such as Microsoft. They each have price-to-book ratios of 10 times or greater. If we were to draw the chart in 1998, Internet related companies engaged in electronic commerce might top the chart at the right. When I first drew this chart in 1980, the equivalent high fliers were oil field equipment manufacturers. Today, this group is no longer one of our key industries with 10 or more participants in Value Line's survey.

At the left in Exhibit 1, the mature, poorly-valued industries are 4911, electric utilities, and 6311, life insurance. In 1980, the railroad industry could have been found there. It is striking to note that in 15 years, computer systems have replaced oilfield equipment, and life insurance has replaced railroads. What will one see 15 years from now?

Such charts are useful because they lend perspective to counteract the short-term tunnel-vision encouraged by mass communication of optimistic ideas and by narrow circles of similar thinking. It is inevitable that in time the high fliers will decline in valuation. The question is whether their asset base will broaden at a rapid enough rate to offset this decline and produce healthy total returns. This does not imply that the companies in their industries will not be profitable, but that investors who buy for the long-term at such high prices may be disappointed.

Exhibit 2: U.S. Industries with 10 or More VL Stocks, June 1996

SIC_Code	Industry	Largest Company	P/B	ROE	Book (B's of $)
3576	Computer Systems	Cisco Systems	12.08	0.233	7.48
7372	Software	Microsoft Corp.	10.06	0.211	18.44
2834	Pharmaceuticals	Merck & CO.	6.65	0.275	68.24
3661	Telephone Equipment	Northern Telecom	6.00	0.139	7.93
4813	Telephone Utility	AT&T Corp.	4.23	0.196	109.68
5812	Eating Places	McDonald's Corp.	3.76	0.152	16.49
2890	Misc. Chemicals	Hercules Inc.	3.70	0.260	6.69
5411	Grocery Stores	Albertson's, Inc.	3.66	0.180	11.92
3674	Semiconductors	Intel Corp.	3.63	0.242	30.62
2711	Publishing	Gannett Co.	3.32	0.102	11.93
1311	Oil & Gas	Occidental Petrol	3.31	0.111	14.04
3714	Auto Parts	Alliedsignal Inc.	3.20	0.206	12.70
3571	Electronic Computers	Compaq Computer	2.82	0.153	15.57
5311	Department Stores	Sears, Roebuck	2.77	0.147	23.48
2911	Oil Refining	Exxon Corp.	2.54	0.136	164.62
3312	Steel Mills	Nucor Corp.	2.27	0.236	7.70
6021	National Banks	Citicorp	2.10	0.160	184.49
2621	Paper Mills	Kimberly-Clark	2.10	0.191	27.82
4924	Natural Gas Distributor	Pacific Enterpris	1.85	0.136	7.37
6022	Other Banks	Morgan (J.P.) & Co.	1.78	0.132	47.50
6331	Property & Casualty Ins.	Amer. Int'l Group	1.63	0.127	104.88
4911	Electric Utility	Southern Co.	1.54	0.117	107.44
4931	Electric & Gas	Consol. Edison	1.46	0.117	52.27
6311	Life Insurance	AmerGeneral Cor	1.33	0.103	28.38

Exhibit 3: U.S. Key Industry P/B-ROE, June 1996

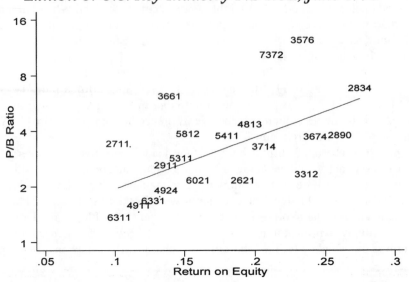

Another kind of perspective comes by looking at the big book value industries on the chart. A surprisingly large part of the asset base lies within financial companies: banks, led by Citicorp and J.P. Morgan, property and casualty insurance, led by American International Group, and life insurance, led by American General Corp. Both banks and insurance seem likely targets of coming radical change: distribution over the Internet. This is likely to create massive dislocations, opportunities for some, failure for others. To a fundamental analyst, specialization in this field might be very rewarding.

Now let us move beyond the long-term implications of P/B to assessing whether its level is justified over just the next few years. Exhibit 3 plots our key industries on a chart of log P/B versus recent return on equity, with a best-fit line regression drawn as the diagonal. This chart works because current ROE is a good indicator of expected ROE. This is in contrast to measures such as earnings growth rate, which have little or no autocorrelation.

We see things through a different lens when we can adjust P/B comparisons for differences in return on equity. The pharmaceutical drug industry, 2834, led by Merck, which looked a bit high-priced with a P/B of over 6 times in Exhibit 1, is seen to be well-supported by return on equity of 27%. On the other hand, the high valuation given computer-related systems and software is not well-supported by recent profitability. The other dangerously high-valued industries relative to their profitability are 3661, telephone equipment, and 2711, publishing. Can we predict that their ROE will increase? At the opposite end of the residual scale, 3312, steel mills, and 2621, paper mills, look interesting. The trick here is to decide how far relative profitability is likely to fall from cyclical peaks in prosperity.

Exhibit 4: Valuation of Value Line Stocks

In looking at such a chart, the straight-line diagonal should be considered to be a fair-value P/B adjusted for current levels of return on equity. If future relative return on equity for the industry is expected to increase, a position above the line is justified. If future relative profitability is expected to decrease, this justifies a position below the line.

OPPORTUNITIES THROUGH
MORE DISTANT COMPARISONS

Twice in a dozen years my barber, who is a savvy entrepreneur but not an expert investor, has told me that he was buying stocks. The first time was in the summer of 1987, shortly before a major crash. The next time was in the spring of this year, 1998. He seems an extreme case — one of the last investors recruited to a bubble. However, there were many investment professionals already recruited, because it is apparently very difficult to arbitrage between stocks, bonds, and cash in a dynamic economy.

In early 1998 the price-to-book ratio of the U.S. stock market was well over 4. (At 4.6 times according to MSCI, it almost equaled the 5 times book reached in Tokyo just before the great Japanese bubble burst a few years earlier.) In few other fields, grocery shopping, for example, would one rush to buy when prices had gone up a great deal. Yet that is apparently the case with the U.S. stock market. Let us see if we can understand this phenomenon better. I have ready at hand a database from a study done in early 1997. Nothing will be lost if we use it for an example of how good things can look before we find out that economic reality will not support our fantasy. Exhibit 4 charts the aggregate price-to-book ratio as defined in the preceding section, but over all stocks in the Value Line database rather than a single industry, as of February 1997. The rapidly increasing apparent wealth in the chart gives some indication of the forces that motivate recruits to the stock market scene.

We are used to seeing growth lines. Consider how fantastic that the growth line is not of assets but of the valuation given a dollar of equity assets, and that it applies to a broad market, not to a single exceptional company.

As a first approximation, we may model the log of P/B as a linear function of the product of an investment time horizon and the difference between expected return on equity and expected interest rates. That is,

$$P/B = e^{(r-k)T}$$ (1)

where r is expected ROE, k is a discount rate, and T is the investment horizon over which r is expected to maintain this value different from k. Perhaps we can use this approximation to better understand why P/B had risen so steadily from the early 1980s.

Again, I have at hand a history of U.S. short-term (90-day) interest rates. The appropriate interest rate to use in discounting, say 5 years ahead, undoubtedly behaves in a slightly smoother fashion than this rate. Still, it will be good enough for the kind of back-of-the-envelope insight we are trying to get from the model. Exhibit 5 shows a history comparing aggregate return on equity with these interest rates.

Remember that in 1980 inflation and inflation expectations were at a peak. Perhaps the first thing one notices from Exhibit 5 is that the short-term interest rate, the lighter of the two lines in the exhibit, has enjoyed a long-term secular decline from that peak. Second, return on equity seems to have had relatively little secular decline. Thus, the gap, or surplus, between the two series has widened immensely. (You might also note that there is a fair degree of correlation in the cyclicality of the two series overlying the disparity in secular trends, but that is not central to this story.)

There you have it. The increasing gap between profitability and interest rates is a perfectly reasonable explanation for the growth in valuations. Or is it? I will put aside the question as to whether these two series are comparable. It is true that interest rates have a clear inflation component, while the impact of inflation on ROE is more complicated. Also, there is the previously mentioned issue of whether short-term rates are more volatile than the discount rate employed by market participants. I put these aside because they are not the heart of the matter.

We can perform a more quantitative check of the logic behind expanding valuations using our P/B-ROE model. Looking back at equation (1), we expect that the log of P/B would be strongly and approximately linearly related to the expected surplus between return on equity and interest rates. The slope of the line should give the investment horizon in years. When we did this regression across industries in the last section we got an investment horizon measure of about 3 to 4 years.

Exhibit 5: History of Profitability and Short Interest Rates

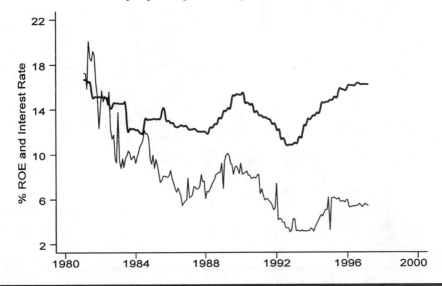

In this case, we look over time, including the varying interest rate. The resulting regression equation between log P/B and profit surplus follows.

```
. regress pbln surplus, robust;
Regression with robust standard errors          Number of obs  =       193
                                                F(1, 191)      =    397.42
                                                Prob > F       =    0.0000
                                                R-squared      =    0.7946
                                                Root MSE       =    0.12327
```

pbln	Coef.	Robust Std. Err.	t	P>|t|	[95% Conf. Interval]	
surplus	7.233182	0.36283	19.935	0.000	6.517513	7.94885
_cons	0.2599866	0.0264488	9.830	0.000	0.2078174	0.3121558

We have over 190 monthly observations. We have an R-squared of 0.79. The measured average time horizon is about 7 years. This is rather longer than the similar cross-sectional slope we obtained in the last section — about twice as long.

I do not take the extreme niceness of the fit nor the t-statistic of 19 too seriously. There are several statistical problems lurking here. The data are strongly trending, making the errors autocorrelated. At the same time, both P/B and ROE have the same variable in the denominator. This tends to create a positive relationship between independent and dependent variable beyond that implied by causality from one to the other. However, there is no doubt that there is a strong positive relationship.

Exhibit 6: Valuation and Excess Profitability

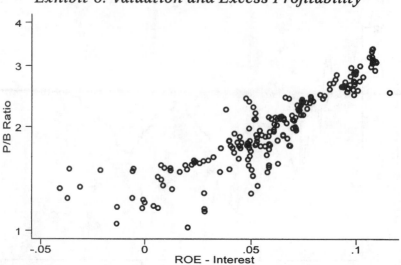

We may learn a little more by looking at the scatter chart to which the preceding regression is fit. This is shown as Exhibit 6. Note the flat area at the left. Valuation does not decline further even though profitability net of interest rates reaches ever lower levels. This reminds us that the linear model's variables are expectations, while the regression must make do with historical data. Very low profitability is not expected to last, so does not get the valuation discount it would otherwise deserve. Yet this thought raises an awkward point. Why is not very high profit surplus also perceived as more temporary than the implied 7-year horizon? Why should investors give more credence to the long life of differences between return on equity and interest rate, and shorter life to the differences in expected return on equity among different industries?

My interpretation is that the market is quite imperfect in its ability to recognize that extremely large profit surpluses are not sustainable. In 1996 there was a gap of over 10% between profitability and interest rates. This creates overwhelming corrective forces that operate with a delay of several years. For example, businesses will typically tend to add capacity at a rapid rate, creating overcapacity and a subsequent rapid decline in profitability. The expansion leading to lower profitability was clearly happening in the field of semiconductors by 1997 and the consequent overcapacity is leading to plant closures as I write in the fall of 1998. At the same time, increased borrowing for expansion will tend to raise real interest rates. While it is possible for a single company or even a small industry to maintain such differentials over long periods by restraining capacity, it is not likely for an economy as a whole. There is no competitive restraint discipline for the economy as a whole, and the parallel impact on interest rates is intrinsic to economic action on a large scale.

We will not pursue this larger imperfection extending through real business conditions, which takes several years to reveal itself. We can more easily demonstrate some good evidence, though not an airtight case, of another substantial inefficiency. It is contained entirely within the stock/fixed-income arbitrage centered on our model's relationships, operating within a space of a few months!

Remember from the preceding section that our variables are well within the information set, since both book value and ROE are measured with a 6-month lag. We can ameliorate earlier-noted econometric difficulties by transforming our relationship to focus on innovations, changes rather than levels. We will construct a relationship that could be used to earn additional returns. In doing so, we are questioning the efficiency of the market in arbitraging between stocks and fixed-income securities.

We will look at the 12-month change in log P/B, or *dpbln12*, and at the same comparison for the surplus ROE net of interest, or *dsurp12*, as predictors of next month's average stock return. We use equal-weighted returns, in part for convenience and in part to illustrate the practice of trying to look at the data in a way different from our competitor investors. The consequence is that implementation must consider at least additional small-stock exposure beyond that in the S&P 500. However, we do not exclude the possibility that a similar relationship predicts that index's returns.

We hypothesize that, in an imperfect market, if prices get too high relative to the arbitrage implied by a relationship between log P/B and profitability surplus, succeeding returns will be low. At the same time, if profitability increases relative to interest rates, succeeding returns will be high.

Here is our regression for predicting next month's percentage average stock returns. Note that the second coefficient is about 7.6 times the first, very close to the investment horizon of 7.2 years measured earlier.

```
. regress ifrtn dpbln12 dsurp12, robust
```

Regression with robust standard errors		Number of obs	=	180
		F(2, 177)	=	2.41
		Prob > F	=	0.0929
		R-squared	=	0.0523
		Root MSE	=	4.533

ifrtn	Coef.	Robust Std. Err.	t	P>|t|	[95% Conf. Interval]	
dpbln12	−5.953126	3.234766	−1.840	0.067	−12.3368	0.4305458
dsurp12	46.99406	22.9625	2.047	0.042	1.678552	92.30956
_cons	1.853674	0.4166928	4.449	0.000	1.031348	2.675999

This time, you may indeed take seriously the regression's R-squared and t-statistics. Why did I say earlier that this was not yet an airtight case for market inefficiency? To make the case tighter, one would show the same relationship predictive of the difference in returns between stocks and cash, and show also that the excess return does not imply offsetting extra risk. I leave this as an exercise for the ambitious reader.

UNDERSTANDING WHERE AND WHEN

In a market as mature as the U.S. stock market, one cannot hope to steadily add value using any rule consistently. If we could learn where and when different investment styles were most likely to pay off, we could be selective about our battles and improve our average return. This is exactly like learning not to bet on every race at the horsetrack. You can either be there for excitement or the profit, but not both.

The following conclusions on timing and focus within the U.S. stock market, presented without supporting evidence, are based on investment research I have carried out personally. You should take them as informed judgments rather than as scientifically proven. I have found that others often do not share them, which gives both caution and the hope that if correct they will be profitable for you, the reader. See if they make sense given what we have discussed in earlier chapters.

1. More variables are statistically meaningful predictors of return among smaller capitalization stocks. A model constructed on a thousand stocks may be very poor in predicting the behavior of the largest 300 stocks.

2. Relative market capitalization (say among the S&P 500) is not consistently, nor on average, an *ex ante* simple predictor of relative returns. It may, however, condition other predictors, and it may in turn be conditioned by cyclical factors.

3. The impact of market capitalization is correlated with several macro-economic variables. In the last cycles these included average return on equity and consumer confidence. When times are relatively good, large-capitalization stocks tend to outperform small company stocks. This implies they will also outperform in the early stages of a general decline.

4. Low P/B works better for small stocks, although it is not useless among large stocks. However, among large stocks its impact is rather cyclical.

5. The application of low P/B is more successful when the economy is just beginning to recover. Growth in the index of leading indicators is a helpful timing tool not often used by others.

6. The timing of the application of low P/B through accelerating economic growth can be further refined by industry. For example, there is no growth timing effect within the utility industry. This makes sense if low P/B is a quality indicator since quality spread narrowing because of a better economy would have little effect within the utility industry.

7. The most typical return autocorrelation pattern alternates reversals and trends at different time horizons. These patterns seem to evolve only slowly with time. However, they are sensitive to whether we are looking

at industry aggregate data or individual stock data. For example, both intermediate-term trending and long-term reversals have about twice the impact on forecast return in comparing industries as opposed to comparing stocks within an industry.

8. At all time horizons, momentum factors are much more positive when growth stocks are doing well. If we take the data at face value, we would use short-term reversals most when we also think we are in a value phase. We would use intermediate momentum more when we think we are in a growth phase.

Consider Conclusions 1, 2 and 3. Small stock effects in isolation occur when stocks are less liquid or have limited information available. Once companies reach several billion dollars in market capitalization, they are too liquid and well-known for still larger size to be meaningful. There is one group for whom still larger size is meaningful, however, the late recruits to market booms, uninformed investors who buy household names. They do so when business is good and they have both money and confidence. Remember also that a good part of the capitalization size measurement is really P/B in disguise, and should be considered as follows.

Consider Conclusions 4, 5 and 6. Low P/B shares some features with small capitalization because it is a major component of small capitalization. We also expect a less efficient market among small stocks. The main point is that low P/B stocks possess three properties described in earlier theoretical chapters.

First, they are low quality stocks and therefore deserve a premium for being poor hedges against possible future disasters. Large stocks that happen to have low P/B are higher quality and get less premium.

Second, low P/B stocks create social aversion because people confuse a bad company with a bad stock. This is more likely among small stocks, because people give status to size.

Third, when you buy low P/B and sell high P/B your active policy as the stock changes its price has an option equivalent. That equivalent is shorting both a put and a call, collecting an option premium in return. Of course, if the price goes up further after you sell it or down further after you buy it, you will discover the offset to the premium.

Consider Conclusions 7 and 8. Momentum effects occur when there are not enough informed or value-oriented investors to conduct the necessary arbitrage to correct them. Comparisons are more difficult across industries and thus momentum excursions can both trend further and need to reverse further. Finally, the existence of momentum implies trending. We have described a value-oriented style of investing as like selling both a put and a call. It will be unsuccessful when long trends take place and make excellent profits when prices move up and down within some identifiable range. To some extent, growth styles are the opposite of value styles. Their adherents may not purposely seek high P/B, but by not resisting it and by buying into success, they imitate the returns of a policy of purchasing a combined put and call. They will do well when there is large-scale trending, as will momentum investors.

Chapter 18
International Diversification

The gentle reader will never, never know what a consummate ass he can become, until he goes abroad.
Mark Twain, *The Innocents Abroad (1869)*

International investing is rewarding. Once you have tried it, it is difficult to confine yourself to a single country, even one as rich in possibility as the United States. We will devote three chapters to it. Even so, we can do little more than scratch the surface of the practical issues to be faced by the quantitative global investor. This chapter discusses developed-country international investing. The following two chapters deal with emerging markets and currency, which require more specialized knowledge.

THE INTERNATIONAL INVESTMENT MOVEMENT FROM A U.S. PERSPECTIVE

In the early 1980s, about 1% of U.S. pension fund assets were invested outside the United States. Starting from this small base, U.S. institutions have increased their foreign diversification at a very healthy percentage growth rate. At the end of 1995, Intersec Research Corporation estimated that 9% of U.S. pension assets were invested abroad, and this figure is rapidly increasing. For large, non-taxable institutions, the chief remaining barrier is a typical 15% dividend withholding tax on which they cannot get a refund. Taxable investors do not have this problem, because they can offset foreign taxes, but of course retail investors still face a lack of convenient institutional arrangements for individual accounts. Consider that about two-thirds of the world equity market lies outside the United States. Does it not seem likely that the eventual share of U.S. savings invested outside this country will be on the order of 30% to 50%? This growing penetration will ensure above-average growth in international investing for many years to come.

The United States is not alone in its increasing awareness of international investment alternatives starting from relative isolation. While the United Kingdom has been a significant international investor for many years, other large economies such as Japan and Germany have relatively small percentages of their savings invested abroad.

In the 1980s, it was widely believed that international returns were substantially greater than those in the United States. This enthusiasm for things international was reinforced by the acceptance of Markowitz portfolio theory and its demonstration of the superior diversification provided by global investing. Once investment consultants had internalized these ideas and promulgated them to pension funds and other institutional investors, diversification momentum built further. With increasing U.S. investor interest, additional informational infrastructure developed, reinforcing this movement. Diversification abroad has continued to increase year by year, despite a historic U.S. bull market in stocks.

However, in the period since 1990, there have been inferior overall international returns as indicated by the MSCI Europe, Australia and Far East Index (EAFE). A good part of this was simply based on the collapse of the Japanese bubble, Japan being at one point 60% of the index. In any case, this lesser return has raised doubts in some minds whether international diversification outside the United States is worthwhile.

Self-satisfaction with local investing results reminds me of two earlier incidents. In the late 1980s I used to listen to Japanese analysts describing the Nikkei index of Japanese stocks as soon going above 40,000. They sincerely felt that Japan's economy had superior growth prospects for decades to come. However, as I write in 1998 the Nikkei is at 13,000.

In 1994, I knew Swiss asset managers who complained that their U.S. diversification was of little value because the Swiss franc would always be much stronger than the dollar. Since then, the dollar has not declined relative to the Swiss franc and the U.S. stock market has surged relative to that in Zurich.

In both cases, investors confused looking backward over relatively few years with looking forward. The same thing is very likely true for some U.S. investors today who have enjoyed a period of relative success at home and may see less need to diversify abroad. Exhibit 1 shows a 5-year rolling average of monthly percentage returns for the United States, shown as the dark line, versus EAFE, shown by the lighter line. The data come from MSCI indices of total return net of dividend withholding. It is easy to see why U.S. investors might feel smug today. In 1988 it would have been just the opposite.

We cannot measure expected returns very accurately using past returns over periods even as long as 20 years. We also find it difficult to estimate the extent of one-time effects yet to come. We do better in estimating pure variance reduction from diversification. Since a key ingredient in this is lower return correlations across country boundaries than within country boundaries, the investment literature has emphasized the question of whether cross-border return correlations are increasing. However, correlations are not the only factor, and may even give the wrong signal.

Diversification reduces portfolio return variance. However, if there is not much variance in its component returns, then there cannot be much absolute improvement from putting these components together in a more diversified portfolio. Exhibit 2 shows a history of 5-year rolling monthly return standard deviation for both the United States and EAFE. Again, the dark line represents U.S. risk, the light line EAFE.

Exhibit 1: Rolling 60-Month Average Returns
U.S. versus EAFE

Exhibit 2: Rolling 60-Month Standard Deviation of Returns
U.S. versus EAFE

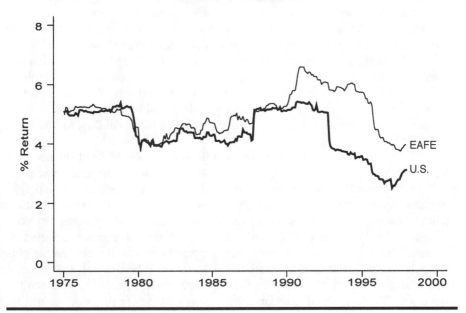

Exhibit 3: Rolling 60-Month Correlation of Returns U.S. versus EAFE

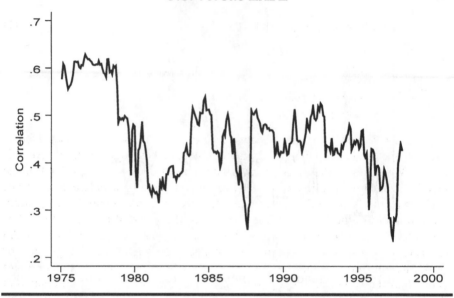

After about 1991, *ex post* risk declined to historically low levels for the United States, again reinforcing U.S.-centric thinking. But the key point of Exhibit 2 is that *ex-post* risk in *both* the U.S. and EAFE regions has declined sharply. Expected risk, *ex ante* risk, may or may not have declined. However, if it has, and if risk aversion did not increase and correlations did not decline, this trend would point to a decline in the risk reduction benefit of global diversification.

Contrary to the general opinion, U.S. and EAFE return correlation has indeed declined rather than stayed constant or increased. Exhibit 3 shows rolling 5-year correlations between U.S. and EAFE monthly returns. The U.S. business cycle has gotten particularly out of phase with those in Europe and Japan. A more compelling fact, however, is a decline in common factor variability, to which we will refer later.

To make a quantitative assessment of the net portfolio effect of simultaneous declines in correlation and in component risk, we need a more rigorous approach.

The benefit from incremental diversification is a complicated function of expected covariances, returns, risk attitudes, and constraints. Still, we can quickly gain insight into the key relationships that govern the size of the benefit by considering a simple two-asset case in which both the expected returns and variances are equal. In this case, the minimum variance will be achieved when the weights are each one-half. The resulting variance reduction will be one-half the variance times the difference between 1 and the expected return correlation between the two assets. Further, the impact on the investor's objective function, or utility, scaled to expected return dimensions, is given by multiplying by lambda, the risk aversion parameter, times the variance reduction.

$$\Delta\text{Utility} = (\lambda)\left(\frac{\sigma^2}{2}\right)(1-\rho) \tag{1}$$

where

λ = risk aversion parameter
σ^2 = expected return variance
ρ = return correlation

EAFE and the United States do have similar portfolio risks. Consequently, one can use equation (1) to approximate the potential benefit of diversification. We estimate the value of diversification as one-half the product of the monthly standard deviation of the U.S. return, the monthly standard deviation of EAFE's return, and the difference between unity and their monthly correlation. Exhibit 4 shows the 5-year rolling average of the value of diversification. For example, the value in November 1997 was 3.5%-squared, equal to 0.00035. An estimate of annual benefit, ignoring any change in correlation, is 12 times that, or .0042. Remembering from Markowitz that the gain in expected compound return is one-half the variance, this would translate into a return of 0.21%. If applied to the incremental diversification, it is equivalent to getting 0.21%/0.5, or 0.42% incremental return on the assets diversified out of the United States.

Exhibit 4: Rolling 60-Month Value of Diversification U.S. versus EAFE

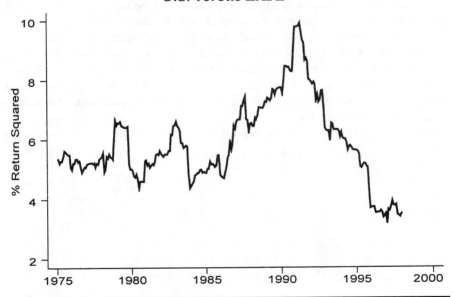

Taking into account the combined effects of falling risk and falling correlation, it is apparent that diversification benefit has been declining over the last six years analyzed. This brief analysis clears up two correlation-based arguments against U.S. investor's diversifying internationally.

First, there is the argument that overall correlations are increasing. While this is certainly true within Europe, we have seen that it is not true for the U.S. investor interested in international investing. On the other hand, when we look at a more inclusive formula for diversification benefit we find that the total benefit has declined. But it has done so for the very different reason that overall risk has declined. Whether the benefit of diversification will be larger in the future depends mainly on whether we think normal future volatility levels will return to their more typically higher levels.

Second, several studies of financial crises such as that experienced in October 1987 have shown greatly increased correlation among world markets for a few days during that period. This is only to be expected. Suppose for simplicity that returns have only a common global component and a specific local component. When there is extreme global risk, the common factor will dominate, causing total correlation to increase. But this does not imply that there is any less benefit from diversifying the specific risk.

This common-factor explanation also clarifies the earlier observation that over a longer period monthly correlations had declined at the same time as volatility had decreased for both the United States and EAFE. Both facts are consequences of reducing global common factor variation over the period. However, during this time, specific risk also declined, reducing the total value of diversification.

One should not conclude from the observed spikes in correlation during global crises that international diversification is not there when you need it. The reason is that at such times the overall variance increases to offset the increase in correlation. If the specific risk remains constant, the diversification benefit remains constant.

Over the period covered by the preceding exhibits, the correlations of the 60-month U.S.-EAFE correlation coefficient with the corresponding U.S. standard deviation and EAFE standard deviation were 0.63 and 0.42 respectively. That is, when correlations rose, the risk rose as well. The combined diversification benefit was essentially uncorrelated (0.04) with the correlation coefficient. (Note, however, that the true correlations are highly uncertain. If we were to restrict ourselves to non-overlapping periods, we would have only 4 five-year observations.)

```
. corr usmean eafemean usdev eafedev usefcorr divalue
(obs=275)
```

	usmean	eafemean	usdev	eafedev	usefcorr	divalue
usmean	1.0000					
eafemean	0.5968	1.0000				
usdev	−0.3338	0.2549	1.0000			
eafedev	−0.0582	−0.0675	0.5060	1.0000		
usefcorr	−0.6434	−0.3053	0.6297	0.4206	1.0000	
divalue	0.2109	0.4163	0.6712	0.7372	0.0421	1.0000

Some have said that the expected return for international stocks is not impressive. This is the assertion made by Rex Sinquefield in 1996.[1] He suggested that if we ignore the weakness in the dollar over an extended historical period, the non-currency returns of the EAFE index do not look much different than those of the United States. He cites the 1970-1994 compound return of the United States (10.97%) versus EAFE (13.21%) of which (2.37%) is based on currency, as evidence for skepticism on international returns. I would agree that in any case the difference in realized returns is not very significant on statistical grounds. However, his reasoning that we should ignore what evidence is available is quite misleading.

His explicit premise is that currency returns are less predictable than differences in local stock returns. There is little real basis for this thesis. Return differences among different equities are notoriously unstable. It would be hard to demonstrate statistically that they show more autocorrelation, especially over long intervals, than do currency returns. In fact, there has been a tendency for equity return differentials to reverse themselves over intervals of four to five years. At the same time, both currency returns show strong positive autocorrelation not only over short intervals but over very long time horizons. That is, stocks show some tendency toward long-term mean reversion, while currencies show a pronounced tendency to trends. [2]

Sinquefield's implicit premise is that currency returns are independent of local stock returns. This is very nearly correct on a monthly basis. However, as the time horizon is increased to a scale of years, the correlation becomes quite negative. For example, the 10-year MSCI EAFE-member country index returns of local stock returns and currency returns for the U.S. investor for the decade ending in mid-1986 have a −0.49 correlation. The 10-year returns ending in mid-1996 show a correlation between local stock returns and their currencies of −0.28.

The mechanism underlying this negative correlation between local stock returns and currency returns is the cumulative impact of even modest differentials between different countries' rates of inflation. To see why this is true, consider Brazil in its years of hyperinflation. If the local stock market had not gone up in nominal terms in near proportion to the decline in currency, one could have bought the entire country for a song. Even if international returns do come partly as currency returns, over the long-term this represents an offset to inflation-influenced foreign nominal returns. In the case of the United States versus EAFE, remember that Japan has formed a major part of EAFE for many years. The Japanese yen has enjoyed a long-term rise versus the dollar at the same time that Japanese inflation has been much lower than that in the United States. To exclude these currency returns is to blind oneself to the loss in value of the dollar.

These observations bring us back to our main topic — the movement of U.S. investors toward global asset allocation. This trend has been in place for at

---

[1] Rex A. Sinquefield, "Where Are the Gains from International Diversification?" *Financial Analysts Journal* (January/February 1996), pp 8-14.

[2] Glyn A. Holton, "Time: The Second Dimension of Risk," *Financial Analysts Journal* (November/December 1992), pp. 38-45.

least 15 years and shows every sign of continuing for at least another several decades. The skeptics have had no discernible influence thus far beyond the normal cultural lag for innovations of this magnitude. Nor do I expect their arguments to become more persuasive.

PASSIVE INTERNATIONAL DIVERSIFICATION

The essence of investing globally rather than just within the United States is the challenge of *segmented* markets, segmented both at the level of their underlying real economies and at the level of investor diversification. As we discussed in Chapter 6, diversification not only reduces risk but can also increase expected compound return. Since developed markets have only moderate individual risk, the gain in expected compound return is modest, but worth noting. There may be additional increases in expected return on a one-time basis as markets become less segmented through globalization and as sophisticated active investment techniques are applied in less-developed markets.

Let us consider the benefit to the passive investor.[3] First, as we have already concluded, diversification from the United States to a mix of the United States and EAFE is desirable for a minimum risk equity portfolio. Depending on what assumes for mean return, this conclusion is likely to hold for a wide variety of risk tolerances.

We can tell whether small amounts of a foreign country's equity will reduce the risk of a U.S. equity portfolio by calculating that market's "beta" to the United States. This is the product of the correlation with the United States times the ratio of the foreign risk to the U.S. risk. If it is less than one, the country has some diversification value. Though we do not support this assertion here, you may take it as a given that each of the developed countries in EAFE satisfies this constraint. This implies that each of the developed countries, considered in small proportions, would have had the effect of lowering total portfolio risk for a U.S. investor.

The possibility of country allocation raises several issues all at once. First, if we attempt a Markowitz optimization to determine a passive minimum risk diversification, we may forget that the correlations we begin with, as well as the associated variances, are mere statistical estimates. The result can be a portfolio that is both poorly allocated by country and subject to high turnover. On the other hand, if we apply the recommendations of Chapter 15, this need not be much of a problem.

Second, we may feel the need to come up with a scheme to determine passive expected return differentials. The CAPM might suggest basing expected

---

[3] An excellent review of international investing with many useful facts and charts along these lines has recently been published by Stephen Gorman under the auspices of the ICFA. See Stephen A. Gorman, *The International Equity Commitment* (Charlottesville, VA: The Research Foundation of The Institute of Chartered Financial Analysts, 1998).

return on beta versus a world index. Yet we know two things. Beta is not very well associated with expected return even within the United States. And international markets, almost by definition segmented, cannot be expected to conform to the CAPM in any case. I have sometimes resorted to the crude heuristic of making passive expected return a weighted function of total variance and world beta. In doing so, I have used a scaling of 6% mean return per 20% of standard deviation of return. The results have been satisfactory, but probably owing mainly to coincidence. As one attempts to make this formula more realistic, inevitably one enters a gray zone of semi-active management. For example, one could decide to apply one-quarter of the Fama and French P/B and small cap premiums, and so on.

Third, suppose we retreat from the problem of Markowitz allocation, and take the simpler approach of index investing. What is the appropriate index for a segmented market? It was probably not the cap-weighted EAFE index when Japan was 60% of the market. Further, no amount of rationalization that Japan was a special case because of inter-company shareholdings could have obscured that EAFE has not been as well-diversified as a suitably optimized portfolio. *Ex post,* it has not been demonstrably better than a portfolio equal-weighted by individual country index.

The individual MSCI country indices are approximately capitalization-weighted within country, and I have no direct evidence of their individual inefficiency relative to alternate diversified portfolios of stocks within each country. However, this does not imply that the country indices are even close to efficient at the stock level in the context of a global portfolio.

That brings up the fourth issue. Why should we use countries as our unit of analysis? Why not use a mix of countries and industry sectors, or even go down to the individual stock level in making our passive allocation? We may have been influenced to use countries in part because the number of countries is small, and the pertinent return data are easily available through MSCI. The truth is that stock variability is a mixture of country, industry, and specific-company effects. When we first allocate by country and then make decisions within the country as to stocks, we produce a convenient but less than optimal answer. We know that small stocks in one country have a lower correlation with small stocks in another country than do their respective large-capitalization stocks. A global passive portfolio somewhat tilted toward small stocks could be substantially more efficient in the Markowitz sense than any portfolio composed of MSCI country indices. To Sinquefield's credit, this is a major point of his 1996 article.

In general, the developed international markets provide an investment environment intermediate between the United States and emerging markets. The benefits of appropriate passive management in emerging markets are far greater. Consequently, we will defer a concrete asset allocation example to Chapter 19, which takes up emerging markets.

The existence of currency effects raises additional problems and opportunities for passive global investors. We will come back to this topic in Chapter 20 as we treat currencies.

ACTIVE INTERNATIONAL DIVERSIFICATION

International investing offers many promising avenues to the active investor, and equally many pitfalls. I can discuss some practical guidelines, but unfortunately cannot go into much detail without impairing proprietary techniques.

The most useful, yet hardest to implement, recommendation I have ever made regarding international investing is to pay less attention to residual risk and more attention to absolute risk in constructing international portfolios.[4] It is hard to implement because current practice is dominated by benchmarks. There is enormous agent risk in arguing that one should pay less attention to benchmarks. Fortunately, that is not required. Rather, one should pay less attention to *residual* risk as defined by the benchmark, and more attention to comparing your portfolio to the benchmark in terms of both return and *absolute* risk. Consider the following.

There are many quite different diversified international portfolios that are at least equal to EAFE in Markowitz risk-return terms. This means that a passive departure from this most widely accepted international benchmark, assuming a healthy degree of diversification, will be no worse in Markowitzian terms and often will be an improvement. Second, *for the active investor with skill, any passive benchmark is inferior to the available efficient frontier.* Residual risk-driven searches for efficient active portfolios will not locate any of the portfolios on this efficient frontier that have less absolute risk than your benchmark, even if they are superior in expected return! Richard Roll provides a rigorous explanation of why this is so.[5] This argument applies in every investing situation, but it is particularly important for global investing with its greater variety of potential portfolios than in the U.S. market.

Well then. You have decided to invest internationally using active investing approaches. Also, you have wisely chosen to construct your portfolio using a mixture of both tracking error and absolute risk to allow superior lower-risk portfolios to be constructed. What will you find for expected returns?

The simplest active return benefit to global investing arises from the mere increase in the number of investable securities. A typical large U.S. investor may select from among 300 to 1,500 securities, depending on investigational resources, liquidity requirements, and type of expertise. The expansion into international developed markets roughly doubles the number of opportunities.

Suppose that the institutional investor needs a portfolio of 50 stocks to provide sufficient diversification and liquidity. The investor can identify stocks that can earn an extra 3% annually after trading costs, but only under special circumstances. Suppose he or she can identify these excellent opportunities only if they are at least two standard deviations better than the average composite of identifying characteristics. If the characteristics are normally distributed, 2.3% of available

---

[4] Jarrod Wilcox, "EAFE is for Wimps," *Journal of Portfolio Management* (Spring 1994), pp. 68-75.
[5] Richard Roll, "A Mean/Variance Analysis of Tracking Error," *Journal of Portfolio Management* (Summer, 1992), pp. 13-22.

companies will meet this screen. Suppose there are 1,000 companies of sufficient liquidity available in the United States. On average, 23 U.S. companies will meet the screen. If the investor limits the portfolio to U.S. companies, then slightly less than half of its 50 stocks will be excellent opportunities and the rest will be average. Portfolio return will be better than average by a little less than 1.5%. On the other hand, if the investor can double his or her universe by searching globally, the pool will be 2,000 stocks. Then on average 46 stocks will be excellent, forming nearly the whole portfolio, which will have a value-added of nearly 3%.

We discussed in an earlier chapter the benefits that accrue to a global investor from diversifying across segmented markets on a passive basis. We will come back to this topic with regard to emerging markets. What about further active stock selection returns, beyond that obtainable from a simple increase in universe size?

Perhaps the local investors do not have access to the same investment sophistication? This is a dangerous assumption. I have usually found locals to be very well informed indeed. However, there does seem to be something to the argument that efficient stock markets become so through infrastructure and the training of different types of investors. If the U.S. market is the largest and deepest, then possibly some U.S. investors can migrate to greener pastures where there are fewer competitors of their particular persuasion and toolset. There is also a progression in terms of information resources and appropriate regulation and institutions. If a country has recently improved its infrastructure, a global investor experienced in the new opportunities might have an advantage for that reason as well.

Consider the example of the Japanese stock market. When I first began investing in it there were stocks whose prices were set precisely by banks. Other stock prices appeared to vary mostly in tune with coordinated retail broker communication programs. One would suppose foreigners to be at a great disadvantage in such an environment. Yet, I believe, the Japanese market was for many years a goldmine for global quantitative investors who played the role of the missing value-oriented investors.

There is an ample literature on the presence in foreign markets of both the value-oriented small cap and price/book anomalies and the price and earnings estimate momentum factors cited in earlier chapters.[6] However, one should note additional complexities involved in assessing international markets.

There are accounting differences among countries that lead to less comparability than one might like on certain measures. For example, book/price appears less important in Germany because of the widespread use of accounting reserves that make true book value difficult to determine.

If you wish to construct a global PB-ROE model you will have to take into account local differences in interest rates. That is, log P/B is a linear function both of ROE and of interest rate.

---

[6] One example is Louis K. C. Chan, Yasushi Hamao, and Josef Lakonishok. "Can Fundamentals Predict Japanese Stock Returns?" *Financial Analysts Journal* (July/August 1993), pp. 63-69.

Unlike in the United States, quarterly earnings reports are not typically available and data may be reported irregularly and according to different accounting standards. There may be a real payoff to the hard work necessary to bring accounting statements into greater comparability. The quantitative investor should resist skimping here.

Finally, there is the occasional problem of serious political risk, even within the EAFE countries. Malaysia is a good example. There are now political risk services that offer useful ratings by country. One approach to their incorporation might be to amplify expected volatility risk based on such ratings. On the other hand, it is probably a mistake to downgrade expected return because of higher risk — the evidence that exists is in the opposite direction.

It is often said that such differences in data and risk from U.S. standards make international investing unsuitable for the quantitative investor. I believe that this is missing the point. As one mountain camper said to another when confronted by a grizzly bear — "I don't have to run faster than the grizzly. I just have to run faster than you!"

Chapter 19

Emerging Markets

It was the best of times, it was the worst of times, it was the age of wisdom, it was the age of foolishness, it was the epoch of belief, it was the epoch of incredulity, it was the season of Light, it was the season of Darkness, it was the spring of hope, it was the winter of despair, we had every-thing before us, we had nothing before us....
Charles Dickens, *A Tale of Two Cities (1859)*

Emerging markets are a hope and a curse for the global investor. They are a hope for higher returns, akin to venture capital. They are a curse because new entrants into these markets are too often drawn by the favorable publicity that comes with peaks of speculation, to be followed by disaster.

Most investors, perhaps even many otherwise sophisticated investors, would be better off investing in emerging markets through a strategy with strong passive elements, for two reasons. First, the benefits to an intelligently structured passive strategy in emerging markets are large. Second, the siren-call of specula-tive fever for emerging markets can overwhelm the judgment of even some of the world's most sophisticated active investors.

Emerging markets range from those in moderately developed countries like Greece, Mexico, and Taiwan to the lawlessness of the economic frontier. But even in the more advanced of these markets, there are frequent huge changes up and down in market values. This chapter is intended to do two things. First, we show how to encapsulate this variety and return volatility into a more attractive passive package than the conventional capitalization-weighted indices. We dem-onstrate this with a portfolio annually equal-weighted by country. Second, we will show how to improve on an equal-weighted portfolio in keeping risk under con-trol through Markowitz optimization.

EQUAL-WEIGHTING EMERGING MARKETS

It is a remarkable fact that there is a naive equal-weighting strategy that has out-performed not only global emerging market capitalization-weighted indices but also, insofar as I can tell, the bulk of active managers.[1] The strategy is this. Each December 31, invest in a portfolio consisting of equal weights of the International

---

[1] Jarrod W. Wilcox, "Better Emerging Market Portfolios," *Emerging Markets Quarterly* (Summer 1997), pp. 5-16.

Finance Corporation country indices for those countries then in the IFC Composite Index.

Each IFC country index is a capitalization-weighted index of the stocks in that country. The annualized return for the strategy of equal-weighting these country indices over the life of the IFC Composite, 1984-1997, has been 29.6%. The annualized return for the IFC Composite Index, which is capitalization-weighted by country, has over the same period been 11.1%.[2] Since the turnover difference is less than 20% per year, this mean return difference is overwhelming even adjusting very conservatively for trading costs. This difference in mean return is not based on higher portfolio risk. The standard deviation of calendar year returns for the equal-weighted-by-country strategy over these 13 years has been slightly less than for the IFC Composite, 29.2% versus 30.6%.

We alluded to the reasons one should expect superiority of the equal-weighted index in this context in earlier chapters. One factor is that during downturns the equal-weighted average seems to have offered better diversification of risks. I stressed these advantages of diversification for multiple-period returns, noted in Chapter 6, in my earlier research in this area. However, when 1997 data are included it is apparent that the overwhelming reason for the superior performance of equal-weighting has been the higher average single-period return of smaller market capitalization countries. This in turn seems to be based on a combination of market segmentation and behavioral factors. Before exploring these in more detail, let us review the facts.[3]

The calendar year total returns by country since the inception of true real-time country indices by the International Finance Corporation in December 1984 are given in Exhibit 1. Note the huge individual gains and losses, as well as how independently they seem to be distributed across countries.

Exhibit 2 compares the results obtained by equal-weighted averages for each annual column with those of the capitalization-weighted IFC Composite Index. Exhibit 3 graphs this comparison with wealth indices. Not only was the equal-weighted index superior in the early years when emerging market investing began to be popular globally, but a strong difference persists a dozen years later. The outperformance continued in the unsettled conditions of 1997, the most recent year in our sample, providing a data point unavailable at the time I wrote my first article on this topic.

Note in Exhibit 3 again that not only is the cumulative return line from equal-weighting much steeper than the capitalization-weighted official index, the ride has even been a bit smoother. This is more apparent by looking at the relative mildness of the downturns than the standard deviation figure cited earlier, drawn around a much higher mean, would imply.

---

[2] It should be understood that this strategy could only be approximated by large institutional investors because of restrictions on foreign investment and lack of liquidity in some countries.

[3] Jarrod W. Wilcox, "Investing at the Edge," *Journal of Portfolio Management* (Spring 1998), pp. 9-21.

Exhibit 1: Emerging Market Returns (Dollar-Based)

Country	1985	1986	1987	1988	1989	1990	1991	1992	1993	1994	1995	1996	1997
Argentina	74.94	-26.47	9.79	38.80	175.87	-36.55	396.92	-26.49	72.74	-23.25	12.69	22.32	1.49
Brazil	94.17	-24.59	-63.07	125.59	39.93	-65.68	170.39	0.32	99.42	69.83	-20.24	34.45	4.41
Chile	49.26	154.79	30.15	37.07	51.22	40.44	98.06	16.18	34.60	44.99	0.58	-14.33	-16.97
China												91.51	24.20
Colombia	-11.25	150.04	78.56	-12.29	12.17	37.46	191.32	39.11	34.71	28.90	-23.77	8.05	8.61
Czech Rep.													-37.29
Egypt													-8.21
Greece	3.39	52.23	152.21	-37.60	80.21	104.15	-19.25	-26.97	21.93	2.03	10.30	5.06	7.64
Hungary											-27.14	97.87	17.83
India	105.10	-2.89	-15.59	37.31	4.26	18.77	18.41	22.89	18.76	7.44	-34.20	-2.13	-10.42
Indonesia						-0.57	-42.29	2.88	113.42	-19.32	11.97	19.85	-84.25
Jordan	48.41	-3.53	-4.56	-10.14	-1.10	4.25	15.13	24.73	24.18	-9.75	12.66	-1.28	14.12
Korea	38.07	85.87	36.48	112.79	7.00	-25.35	-15.87	3.56	20.93	19.05	-6.86	-38.18	-49.77
Malaysia	-14.25	11.93	0.91	27.72	44.04	-11.20	12.08	27.94	102.86	-21.50	3.56	24.52	-75.01
Mexico	18.35	97.20	-4.75	108.30	73.35	29.69	106.76	21.18	49.90	-40.64	-25.98	17.83	17.70
Morocco													32.21
Nigeria	4.98	-56.73	-13.23	7.05	21.14	40.55	37.81	-34.93	-11.56	190.91	-20.89	63.03	-8.95
Pakistan	18.33	20.75	6.68	13.78	6.41	11.09	172.09	-18.41	56.18	-8.51	-31.14	-19.57	0.39
Peru											11.04	3.12	-2.71
Philippines	46.50	382.60	52.29	38.06	59.53	-53.87	58.91	18.31	134.90	-0.60	-14.09	20.35	-66.09
Poland											-6.95	74.22	-21.61
Portugal			224.11	-28.31	40.09	-29.81	1.72	-19.42	38.07	20.08	-1.14	29.46	52.74
Russia													23.31
South Africa												-17.07	-8.98
Sri Lanka											-37.96	-11.21	1.13
Taiwan	10.43	49.33	120.79	93.26	99.96	-50.91	-0.60	-26.63	89.02	22.47	-30.66	37.36	-16.22
Thai.land	0.06	74.75	37.48	40.71	100.82	-20.74	19.21	40.29	103.00	-11.30	-1.43	-36.59	-71.16
Turkey			262.15	-61.08	502.36	-2.78	-41.78	-52.76	234.33	-40.75	-10.59	48.98	31.00
Venezuela	-26.61	57.38	52.58	-24.16	-33.09	601.62	44.63	-42.29	-6.94	-25.67	-29.47	138.58	7.64
Zimbabwe	153.83	18.37	94.66	24.99	40.76	94.94	-52.33	-59.76	143.80	28.27	16.67	66.60	-54.49

Exhibit 2: IFC Percent Returns

	Equal-Wtd	Cap-Wtd
1985	36.10	27.74
1986	61.24	12.81
1987	55.67	13.55
1988	27.99	58.24
1989	69.73	54.69
1990	34.27	−29.87
1991	58.57	17.60
1992	−4.51	0.33
1993	68.71	67.50
1994	11.63	−0.53
1995	−10.13	−12.32
1996	25.49	7.90
1997	−9.59	−24.50

Exhibit 3: Superiority of Equal-Weighting Emerging Markets

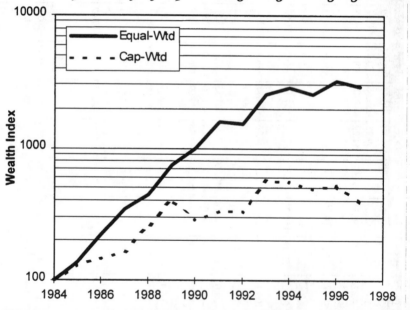

Now let us pursue the reasons for this dramatic difference. In earlier research I have noted that total variance is comparable between the returns of the typical large country and small country. However, a higher proportion of the risk of the small countries is uncorrelated with the co-movement of the group as a whole, or, indeed, with the EAFE index of developed countries. This suggests greater market segmentation and greater rewards for investing within segmented markets for the smaller countries. Such special characteristics of a small-capitalization country do not derive simply from market capitalization. Otherwise a large country could change its characteristics simply by dividing itself. What is the difference in valuation associated with low capitalization and what does it forecast about returns?

In Chapter 14 we noted that log market capitalization may be partitioned as the sum of log book value and the log of the price-to-book ratio. We can use this fact to further analyze the superior realized return of small-capitalization countries.

The following study includes all years and IFC Composite Index countries for which P/B is available the preceding December, beginning with December 1986.[4] There were 240 observations of annual returns for particular emerging markets. The means for each year were subtracted from both the dependent and independent variables, and the resulting data pooled. The excess annual percentage return was associated with prior excess log price/book and log book value as follows.

. regress xrtn12 xpblnz xlnbookz

Source	SS	df	MS
Model	133529.892	2	66764.9459
Residual	1056063.31	237	4455.96335
Total	1189593.21	239	4977.37743

Number of obs = 240
$F(2, 237)$ = 14.98
Prob > F = 0.0000
R-squared = 0.1122
Adj R-squared = 0.1048
Root MSE = 66.753

xrtn12	Coef.	Std. Err.	t	P>|t|	[95% Conf. Interval]	
xpblnz	−38.20004	7.121008	−5.364	0.000	−52.2286	−24.17149
xlnbookz	−6.333723	2.984414	−2.122	0.035	−12.21309	−0.4543561
_cons	−2.788243	4.308888	−0.647	0.518	−11.27685	5.70037

Market value variations stemming from differences in book value were bigger than variations stemming from differences in price-to-book ratio. That is, the standard deviation of excess log P/B was 0.6 as opposed to 1.4 for excess log book value. However, if you multiply these independent variable standard deviations times their regression coefficients, you will see that the absolute size of the P/B association's profit potential is about three times larger than for book value. It is also more reliable, as we see from a much bigger t-statistic.

I will note without presenting the evidence that the book value effect is entirely accounted for by differences in profitability. A regression including ROE would obliterate the significance of the book value t-statistic. That is, markets that turned out to have higher returns began not only with lower price/book but also with higher profitability.

We will leave it to others to find further explanations for this apparent market inefficiency and leave it to the reader to find ways to exploit it. Now we will use the same return data as an example for addressing the problem of risk estimation.

---

[4] However, June 1996 fundamentals were used rather than December 1996 fundamentals as predictors for 1997 returns to avoid having to re-gather fundamental data put together for a previous study. For the same reason of ease in data-gathering, the Czech Republic, Egypt, Morocco, and Russia were excluded even though their returns for 1997 were available.

Exhibit 4: Country Risk 1985-1990 Monthly Returns

Country	Monthly % Std Dev
Argentina	34.93
Brazil	22.03
Chile	8.01
Columbia	6.30
Greece	14.27
India	9.13
Jordan	5.31
Korea	8.69
Malaysia	8.40
Mexico	14.98
Nigeria	10.43
Pakistan	3.01
Philippines	11.78
Taiwan	16.61
Thailand	8.83
Venezuela	14.09
Zimbabwe	8.09

PRACTICAL HEURISTICS FOR
ESTIMATING COVARIANCE RISK

Equal weighting helps us in two ways. It puts more emphasis on countries with lower price-to-book ratios, countries whose valuations have not yet been inflated by speculation. It also gives us a well-diversified allocation that will both assist expected compound return and is highly tolerant of our uncertainty, uncertainty not only of return but also of risk.

In this section we focus on the advantage of equal-weighting for portfolio risk control. The technique for illustrating this benefit is to use six years of monthly returns to form a minimum variance portfolio which is then tested over the next six years. We compare three cases:

1. an optimal portfolio based on unadjusted historical return covariances (history)
2. an equal-weighted portfolio with risk estimate based on history (equal)
3. an optimal portfolio based on a simple shrinkage estimator (shrinkage).

The standard deviations of monthly returns in U.S. dollars for the 17 countries with full 72 month 1985-1990 histories are given in Exhibit 4. Note the modest risk indicated for Pakistan, and the enormous risk for Argentina and Brazil. Exhibit 5 gives the correlations for monthly returns over the same 72 months.

Exhibit 5: Monthly Return Correlations
1985-1990 Monthly Returns

Country	Argentina	Brazil	Chile	Columbia	Greece	India	Jordan	Korea	Malaysia	Mexico	Nigeria	Pakistan	Philippines	Taiwan	Thailand	Venezuela	Zimbabwe
Argentina	1.00																
Brazil	-0.06	1.00															
Chile	-0.10	0.07	1.00														
Columbia	-0.14	-0.03	0.35	1.00													
Greece	0.09	-0.02	0.14	0.34	1.00												
India	0.21	-0.01	-0.10	-0.10	-0.05	1.00											
Jordan	-0.05	0.00	-0.06	-0.01	0.05	0.13	1.00										
Korea	-0.14	0.06	0.09	0.06	-0.23	-0.10	-0.18	1.00									
Malaysia	-0.06	0.07	0.26	-0.03	0.03	-0.07	0.02	0.10	1.00								
Mexico	0.13	-0.06	0.32	0.10	0.16	-0.01	-0.04	0.18	0.40	1.00							
Nigeria	0.09	0.04	0.02	0.07	0.12	0.04	-0.06	0.02	-0.20	-0.12	1.00						
Pakistan	-0.02	-0.03	0.10	0.16	-0.09	0.23	0.14	0.13	-0.11	0.05	0.02	1.00					
Philippines	-0.11	0.10	0.26	0.09	0.05	-0.12	0.06	0.22	0.28	0.07	0.06	0.00	1.00				
Taiwan	-0.01	0.07	0.36	0.15	0.04	-0.17	0.04	-0.01	0.21	0.38	-0.23	0.01	0.02	1.00			
Thailand	0.02	0.04	0.26	0.17	0.25	0.00	0.13	-0.02	0.53	0.43	-0.10	0.13	0.21	0.040	1.00		
Venezuela	0.04	-0.23	-0.20	-0.10	-0.07	0.12	-0.01	-0.21	-0.03	-0.05	0.01	0.08	-0.21	-0.26	-0.14	1.00	
Zimbabwe	-0.26	-0.01	0.06	0.01	0.01	0.15	0.12	-0.22	0.02	-0.13	-0.01	0.22	0.05	-0.11	-0.05	0.07	1.00

Exhibit 6: Weights for Minimum Variance Portfolio

	History	Equal	Shrinkage
Argentina	1.19	5.88	1.74
Brazil	1.30	5.88	3.30
Chile	0.78	5.88	5.55
Columbia	6.90	5.88	7.12
Greece	2.23	5.88	4.19
India	1.46	5.88	7.09
Jordan	14.79	5.88	9.01
Korea	8.75	5.89	8.85
Malaysia	7.31	5.88	5.85
Mexico	0.00	5.88	1.78
Nigeria	4.98	5.88	7.00
Pakistan	38.32	5.89	9.20
Philippines	0.22	5.88	4.69
Taiwan	2.03	5.88	4.16
Thailand	0.00	5.88	4.42
Venezuela	4.15	5.89	7.75
Zimbabwe	5.58	5.89	8.29

When the inputs from Exhibits 4 and 5 are run through a Markowitz optimizer, the portfolio with least risk appears as in the leftmost column of Exhibit 6, the "history" column. If we assume the past is a good estimator of the future, this portfolio has an estimated standard deviation of return equal to 2.14% per month. The low portfolio risk is based on both the low correlation among many of the country return components and the heavy use of apparently low individual risk countries such as Pakistan.

On the other hand, countries with higher individual historical risk are excluded or given minimal positions, allocating two-thirds of the portfolio into only four countries.

In contrast, the equal-weighted portfolio would be the minimum variance portfolio if we assume that historical statistics are worthless — all countries are equally risky and equally correlated with all the others. However, we have instead generated it using the historical covariance matrix plus equal position constraints to see what the estimated risk would be based on the historical covariance matrix.

Finally, the shrinkage estimator is also the result of optimizing weights for minimum variance. However, it assumes a covariance matrix that is the weighted sum of the historical covariance matrix, implied by Exhibits 4 and 5, and a Bayesian prior covariance matrix. The Bayesian prior assumes all variances equal to the average variance, and all covariances equal to the average covariance, of the historical covariance matrix. In this case we give a weight of 0.5 to history and 0.5 to the Bayesian prior. Note that the allocation extremes of the "history" column are greatly toned down. For example, the lowest risk country in the history period, Pakistan, is given a 9% weight rather than the 38% weight obtained by taking historical statistics at face value. Overall, the low risk countries are given modest overweights and the high risk countries modest underweights, reflecting an assumption of some degree of information about the future. Exhibit 7 compares the expected risk from the Markowitz optimizations that created these portfolios with the actual risk during the subsequent 72 months ending December 1996. The expected risk for the history and equal weighted portfolios is derived from historical data. The expected risk for the shrinkage portfolio is derived from the modified covariance matrix. For reference, the realized risk of the capitalization-weighted index of these 17 countries is also provided.

The portfolio optimized around historical risks has the least forecast risk at just over 2% per month, but the highest of our minimum variance portfolios' realized risks, at over 5% per month. The equal-weighted portfolio cannot incorporate any data mining, and we see that indeed its expected risk of 3.81% comes the closest to an accurate estimate of future risk. It yielded a realized risk of 4.35%.

The shrinkage estimator gave an even lower realized risk, only 4.21%. It should be noted that we did not search for the best weight to give to the Bayesian prior covariance matrix; we simply split the difference at 0.5. There is no data mining in the result, and considerable possibilities for legitimate improvement had we the inclination.

The 5.41% risk of the capitalization-weighted index is shown as a baseline. This m onthly risk could have been reduced by 39 basis points by historical optimization, by 106 basis points through equal weighting, and by 120 basis points using our heuristic shrinkage estimator.

To conclude, I believe that for most investors in the frontier atmosphere of emerging markets, including many quantitative investors, a strategy with strong passive elements will produce better results. Equal-weighting by country may continue to be productive for many years. This is not to say that more complicated quantitative or qualitative strategies might not do even better. But the benefit of staying near equal-weighting is that you will certainly avoid the danger noted at the beginning of the chapter. This peril is the likelihood that you will be drawn by the hopeful fantasies characteristic of emerging markets to invest near peaks of speculative activity where markets are wildly overvalued.

Exhibit 7: Ex Ante and Ex Post Risk

| | Standard Deviation of Monthly Returns (%) | |
	Forecast	Realized
History	2.14	5.02
Equal	3.81	4.35
Shrinkage	3.44	4.21
Continuously Cap-Weighted		5.41

Chapter 20

Currency, The Hidden Side of Equity

Put not your trust in money, but put your money in trust.
Oliver Wendell Holmes Sr., *The Autocrat of the Breakfast Table (1858)*

International diversification of stocks is greatly advantaged by at least a rudimentary knowledge of currency. Many investment managers feel relatively comfortable in translating their knowledge of how to invest in stocks in their own home country to investing in stocks in other countries. But they feel uncomfortable with the currency portion of their investment. This chapter introduces basic currency ideas that can provide a solid foundation for the reader's future experience with international investments.

Currency return is the percentage change in the *spot* exchange rate. For example, if the price of a dollar quoted in yen rate moves from 100 to 120 as the yen weakens, one calculates the dollar currency return as 20%. (The yen currency return is −16.67%.) There is also a *forward* rate for delivery of currency at a time a few months in the future. If you own a foreign security, you could imagine hedging against changes in its currency by selling short an amount of currency equivalent to the security's current value. In practice, this is done by entering into a contract to sell the foreign currency at a fixed rate in terms of the home currency at some definite point in the future. There is an active futures market for currency; however, most hedging transactions are done with bank counterparties.

It is usually not possible to precisely offset currency returns by hedging. Instead, one receives a hedging return that reflects the difference between the current forward rate, say 90 days out, and the future spot rate. Arbitrage with short-term interest rates makes this the percentage change in the spot rate plus the interest-rate differential in favor of the home country. Thus, an accurate measure of the performance of currency management must be based on hedging return rather than on currency return. Assume you are a U.S. investor in Japanese securities for a year and U.S. interest rates were 4% higher than Japanese rates. Then a move in the yen from 100 to 120 would create a hedging return of approximately 24%.

Suppose one hedges all foreign currency exposure. The return that results is the total foreign return including currency, plus the hedging return. The currency return cancels out, and one is left with the home country interest rate plus the excess of the foreign stock return over the foreign interest rate.

Exhibit 1: Value of U.S. Dollar

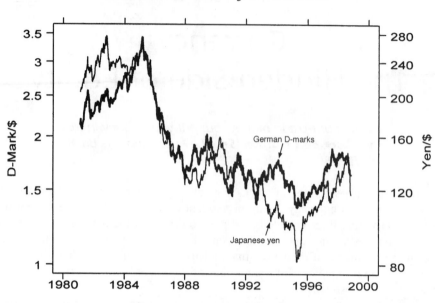

Currency volatility is often a significant part of foreign equity investment returns. Exhibit 1 shows a history of the dollar priced in Japanese yen (lighter line) and German D-marks (darker line). The price changes have been significant, both up and down.

Some in the investment community assume that growing globalization is making currency less important. That is, as nations come closer together, the volatility based on currency movements should decline. For example, consider the advent of the European Currency Union and its common currency, the Euro. Exhibit 2 plots weekly standard deviation of currency hedging returns as seen by the U.S. investor across two groups: 21 currencies in the EAFE index plus Canada (darker line), and the subset of those countries joining the European Currency Union, commonly known as Euroland (lighter line). This perspective excludes entirely the volatility of the U.S. dollar with respect to these baskets of currencies. It measures only the within-basket return dispersion. Note that while the volatility within the Euroland group has declined to essentially zero, the overall volatility of the larger currency basket has actually increased. If currency volatility is going away, this is not yet apparent.[1]

---

[1] Exhibit 2 was drawn using the STATA package with a Lowess smoother applied to each of the two very noisy series of weekly cross-sectional standard deviations. This technique is worthy of note because it is so broadly useful for spotting overall tendencies within noisy data.

Exhibit 2: Convergence of Weekly Hedging Returns
EAFE Plus Canada versus Euroland Countries

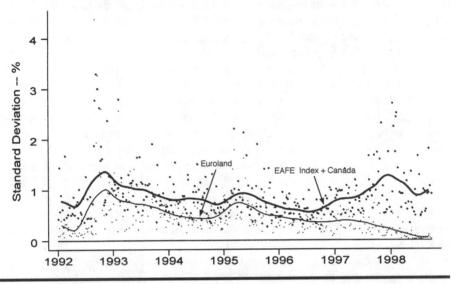

Having established that currency is important, let us go over what the investor needs to know to deal with it. In the remainder of the chapter we will discuss the following topics:

1. the source of currency hedging returns
2. typical strategic mistakes
3. currency return statistical characteristics
4. optimally hedged asset allocation
5. ideas for active currency management

THE SOURCE OF CURRENCY HEDGING RETURNS

Currency returns are fundamentally different from either stock or bond returns. Stock and bond returns each relate to a single economic unit. Currency returns, on the other hand, relate to the differential performance of two entities, the differential value between the script of two governments.

Let us relate to something more familiar. Suppose shares in Microsoft were your currency. You could spend it on real things, or exchange it for shares in Intel. The rate of exchange between Microsoft shares and Intel shares fluctuates every day. Assume the exchange ratio begins at 1 Intel/Microsoft. Over a period of time it may fall to 0.1 or rise to 10.0. On the other hand, if both companies do equally well, there will be no movement in their exchange rate. Suppose someone were to agree with you to exchange Intel shares for Microsoft shares at a fixed rate 90 days in the future. Consider how the value of that contract would vary over the next three months. Its expected return would be zero. Its standard deviation of returns would be different from that of the return of either Microsoft or Intel. The risk of the differential would be lower than the average of their individual risks if the correlation of their returns were more than one-half.

Now let us come back to the currency impact of buying a foreign stock and not hedging. You give up possession of your own currency, an obligation of your government, and take possession of a foreign currency, an obligation of a foreign government. If you intend eventually to sell the stock and convert the proceeds back to your home currency, and do not hedge, it is as though you borrowed money from your own government and lent it to a foreign government.

Even if there should be no difference in interest rate, you will still take a credit risk on the loan. Suppose the foreign government returns you a depreciated currency because it has created too much money during the period of the investment. This is analogous to a partial default on a loan. Consequently, you ought to think like a banker. You should be concerned about the borrower's ability and motivation to repay.

In practice, things are more complicated because each government that sponsors a currency stimulates conditions that create international interest rate differentials. The forward exchange rate will approximate the current spot rate adjusted for these interest rate differentials. Otherwise there would be profitable riskless arbitrage as follows. Borrow money in the low interest rate country, exchange it at the spot rate, lend it in the other country, and buy a forward contract entitling you to convert it back to the original currency.

Factoring in interest rate differentials, you should think like a very good banker. You must balance the excess interest rate paid by the foreign government against the excess credit risk of the foreign government over your own government. Note that this can work in either direction, because the foreign currency may be either a better or a worse deal than your own home currency in terms of future ability to buy real goods.

Suppose, on the other hand, that you are considering hedging. The decision to hedge will reflect the same ingredients, but with reversed signs. That is, you should hedge if the excess credit risk of the foreign government's script over-balances whatever excess exists in interest rates.

Hedging profits come when the market recognizes that the foreign country is falling in creditworthiness or your home country is rising in creditworthiness. They also come when your home interest rate rises, resulting in a higher current value of your home currency so that it can be expected to depreciate, or when the foreign interest rate falls. Although there are many individual sources of differential demand and supply for currency pairs, arbitrage with short-term interest rates means that the key uncertainty is market's perception of creditworthiness — the ability to repay.

TYPICAL STRATEGIC MISTAKES

In my experience as a currency manager I have found that currency is little understood and that investors frequently make strategic mistakes in dealing with it.

Inadequate International Diversification

The usual practice is to decide on how much foreign investment you want, and only later decide how much of it should be hedged against foreign currency risk. Two different securities will always have equal or higher optimal allocation than one of them individually. The choice of hedging a foreign holding creates a second security. Consequently, the optimal degree of foreign diversification would generally be larger if the option to hedge were considered from the beginning.

The sub-optimality that thus results from sequential rather than simultaneous asset allocation has modest consequence for U.S. investors. However, it overlooks a major opportunity for investors whose home countries are a smaller part of the global market and who thereby derive greater benefit from international diversification. The benefit of a proper Markowitz asset allocation study incorporating currency from the beginning can be quite large and economically significant for an investor from a smaller country.[2]

Inappropriate Passive Hedging Benchmarks

The best way to derive long-term strategic hedging ratios is to conduct a Markowitz optimal asset allocation in which both hedged and unhedged assets are represented. This should be done separately for stocks and bonds. For the typical U.S. investor in stocks with 20% of his or her portfolio placed outside the United States, the resulting stock hedging ratio is likely to be between 20% and 50%. (However, in practice one often sees 0% or 100% hedging ratios.) The consequent risk reduction through a passive hedging policy may be translated to equivalent return enhancement units by taking into account the investor's implied risk tolerance or *lambda*.

Note that one might rationally set different hedging ratios for stocks in different countries, although the further potential value-added is sometimes small and the risk of data-mining very large.

Beyond passive benefits, a partially hedged benchmark adds significantly to opportunities for active management results, as will be detailed shortly.

Over-Attention to Short-Term Downside Protection

Given a concern with currency risk, isn't downside protection what we should be interested in? If by that one means protection over periods such as a few months, the answer is "probably not." Since the pursuit of short-term downside protection

---

[2] Jarrod Wilcox and Stefano Cavaglia, "International Investing, The Dutch Investor's Perspective," *Journal of Investing* (Fall 1997), pp. 46-55.

has been a large part of currency overlay management practice in the last few years, we now take an extended look at the phenomenon of disappearing downside protection with longer time horizons.

A popular approach to currency risk protection involves the purchase of puts against currency futures, or the replication of option results through dynamic hedging or equivalents. Such methods attempt to alter the statistical distribution of returns so as to prevent large losses in a single period. While this can be a valuable short-term exercise, it is not generally understood that the resulting skewness does not carry over to the distribution of returns over multiple periods.

The most famous theorem of statistics is the Central Limit Theorem. It states that the sum of independent random variables tends with increasing numbers of variables to be distributed as a normal distribution. This is true no matter what the probability distributions of the variables being added, so long as they have finite variances. The normal distribution is bell-shaped and symmetrical.

To construct an example, since we are concerned with compound returns, we put returns into log form. (If we wanted to analyze percentage returns, there would automatically be downside protection for losses greater than 100%, but this would provide no comfort to the investor.) Each period's log return has a probability distribution which with downside protection will be skewed so that large losses are prevented.

The returns in successive periods are close to being independent. What is the average log return over multiple periods? It is the sum of these log returns, divided by the number of periods. As the number of periods increases, the mean log return becomes distributed more similarly to a normal distribution, with less and less downside protection.

Exhibit 3 shows a beginning distribution of monthly returns representing a simulated program of monthly downside risk protection applied to currency returns. (It is the result of 12,000 drawings from a non-central chi-square distribution.) The exhibit is a histogram showing what fraction of the outcomes falls within equally-spaced bins. The mean of the sample distribution is adjusted to be zero, and the standard deviation adjusted to within a plausible range of currency volatility. With downside protection, losses are limited to less than −2%, the median is a small loss of 0.2%, and there are some large gains of up to about 8%.

Exhibit 3 might appeal to some institutional investors. However, that is not what will be received over longer periods. Exhibit 4 shows the distribution of the cumulative log over non-overlapping 12-month periods. Because it contains only 1,000 observations, the sample distribution is not as smooth as in Exhibit 3. However, it is obviously much more symmetric. It shows almost as much "protection" against upside results as downside results. And whereas there was only a 1% chance of a 1-month result worse than −0.016, there is a 10% chance of a 12-month result worse than −0.046. Short-term downside protection does not defend against the accumulation of small losses into substantial ones over longer periods.

Exhibit 3: Monte Carlo Simulation — 1 Month

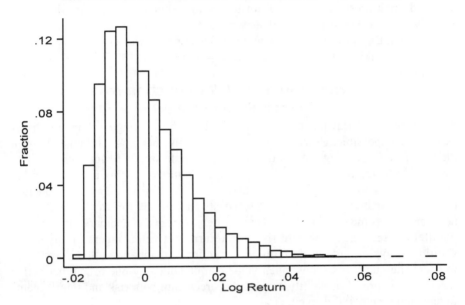

Exhibit 4: Monte Carlo Simulation — 12 Months

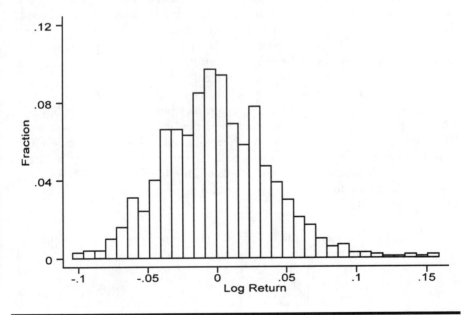

At normal risk levels, there is little long-term impact from short-term downside risk protection. This is not to say that short-term benefits should be entirely disregarded, especially if they come for free as part of return enhancement efforts. But they do not provide downside currency risk protection over normal institutional investment horizons.

Separating Active Risk Reduction from Return Enhancement

Some currency overlay managers have argued that forecasting currency returns is essentially impossible. However, they advocate active hedging through a program that involves forecasting risk. At times of higher risk, simply hedge more.

Although forecasting currency hedging returns is highly uncertain, in my experience it is no more so than is forecasting stock returns. As for the distinction between active bets based on return forecasts and on risk forecasts, there is less here than meets the eye. Once you actively depart from a benchmark there will be parallel consequences for both risk and return. Active managers of any stripe should always be judged on both active return enhancement and active risk impact. The question of how much value can be added by one or another active investment approach is strictly empirical. Forecasting both risk and return seems to have more potential than either alone.

Linking Currency Decisions Too Closely To Asset Exposures

Institutional investors come to currency from the viewpoint of hedging the risk of currency fluctuations as they affect investments in international stocks and bonds. The currency position is seen as an adjunct to the underlying foreign security rather than as a portfolio in its own right. The tighter this linkage, the narrower the perspective within which the currency portfolio can be managed. As compared to the Markowitz optimal portfolio, the problem is overconstrained.

In the evolution toward more sophisticated active currency management, most institutional investors retain single currency position constraints based on whatever they happened to have invested in particular country's stocks and bonds. They do not take a portfolio viewpoint. Keep in mind that active currency returns reflect two main components that may be differentially constrained. The first is position in the home currency versus a basket of foreign currencies. The second is the position of each foreign currency exposure relative to that basket. Three realistic examples follow.

1. The benchmark is 100% hedged. (This sometimes comes about because an institutional investor is attempting to reduce management fees by putting only a fraction of their international assets into a hedging program, rather than truly choosing 100% hedged as their passive strategy allocation.) Within this mandate, the currency overlay manager may only choose not to hedge, creating a currency position in each country of

between 0% and 100%. Any manager skill in forecasting degrees of above-average home-currency strength will be lost, and since there is no cross-hedging, much of the ability to forecast relative strength among different foreign currencies will also be lost. (Cross hedging is selling one foreign currency and buying another.)

2. The benchmark is 50% hedged, but cross-hedging is still not allowed. This is better than 100% hedged because the manager can exploit skill in forecasting the home currency in either direction. There is also less stress likely to result from incurring tracking error. On the other hand, since there is no cross-hedging, exploitation of skillful forecasts of the relative strength of foreign currencies will still be inhibited.

3. The benchmark is 0% hedged, but unlike the first case, cross-hedging is allowed. However, the total of active positions must be such that the portfolio is never short in the home currency. This alternative permits a reasonable degree of exploitation of skill in forecasting relative strength among a larger number of currencies. However, it is like the 100% benchmark in that skill in forecasting the home currency will be used over only half its range because of the restriction against a net short position in the home currency.

Note that for all three cases, the ability to exploit information regarding weak foreign currencies is especially restricted in the case of small countries. Suppose Singapore is 1% of the equity portfolio. Then conventionally one can only short Singapore dollars by 1%. However, a larger amount might be optimal in the sense of efficiency in achieving the least portfolio risk for a given level of expected portfolio return.

I recognize and respect the organizational realities that bring about such mandated constraints. Paradoxically, however, constraints on individual currencies tied to underlying assets, imposed to reduce currency risk, may actually hamper currency risk diversification at a given level of expected return.

CURRENCY RETURN STATISTICAL CHARACTERISTICS

The first statistical property we illustrate is that of dispersion of currency returns, examining them for non-normality. We will examine, not spot returns, but hedging returns. Exhibit 5 compares to a normal distribution the distribution of weekly log hedging returns into the U.S. dollar for each of the 21 currencies represented in the EAFE Index plus Canada over the period 1981-1997. Over 20,000 observations are summarized.

The exhibit shows two major departures from a normal statistical distribution. The first is an excessive fraction of returns near zero. It is as though exchange rates were sticky with respect to small changes. This is not the result of artificial restriction in prices, such as we find in stocks that are quoted in eighths — exchange rates are quoted with far greater precision. The second departure is the existence of a fair number of returns that are from five to eight standard deviations from the mean. These would be almost impossible to observe if the distribution were truly normal.

Exhibit 6 explores these events in the tails of the distribution in more detail. Each small circle represents the weekly hedging return for a particular currency in a particular week. Since over 20,000 observations are represented on the chart, only the widely separated extreme cases show up as separate events on the exhibit. For each circle, the vertical scale shows the actual hedging return, while the horizontal scale shows the return that would have occurred if the return fractile (quantile) were drawn from a normal distribution with the same mean and standard deviation as the actual distribution. The straight line represents that set of values mapped to the vertical axis.

The peak near zero seen in Exhibit 5 shows up as a small flat area in the center of the curve of the distribution in Exhibit 6. What is better revealed are the points in the tails — those with more than a 4% weekly currency movement that would come as a surprise to any investor projecting normality on future currency returns.

Both the stickiness of small movements and the occasional appearance of surprisingly large movements would be characteristic of a system in which governments resist and then capitulate to economic change. The dam breaks and the accumulated economic problems flood out to be incorporated in a new price.

Exhibit 5: Histogram of Weekly Hedging Returns

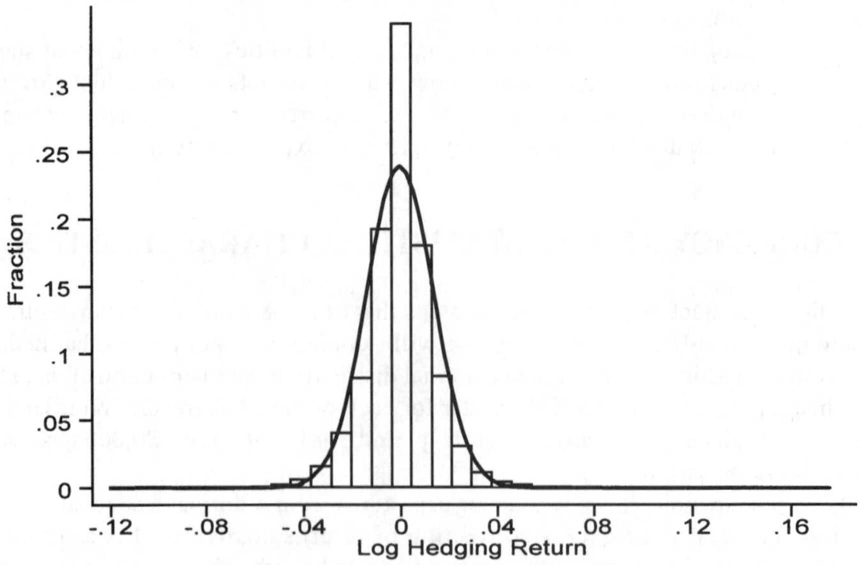

Exhibit 6: Hedging Returns versus Normal Distribution

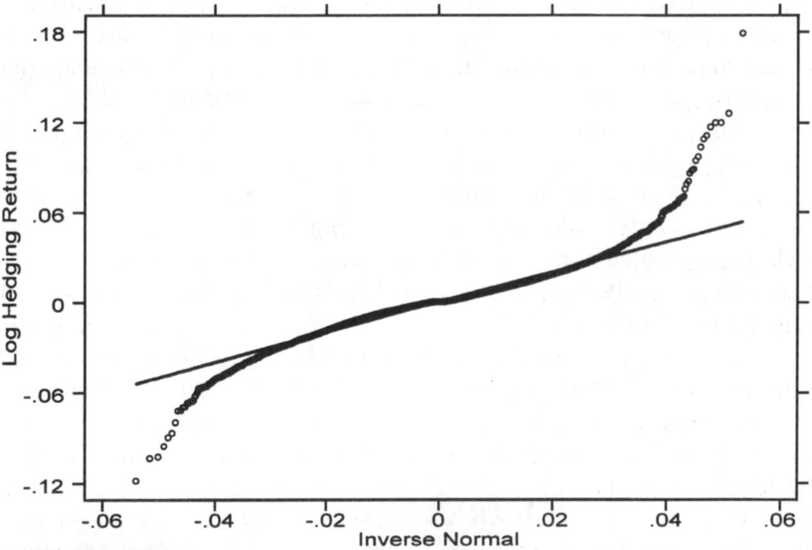

The second major property of currency hedging returns is the existence of more trends than could be accounted for if successive returns were precisely independent. To demonstrate this property, we first do a sequence of 25 regressions, each based on the more than 20,000 weekly currency hedging return observations previously collected. The first regression forecasts next week's returns against last week's returns. The second forecasts next week's returns based on the average weekly return over the past two weeks. The twenty-fifth regression forecasts next week's return based on the average weekly return over the past 25 weeks.

Exhibit 7 charts the successive regression coefficients of the 25 best fits over weekly lags from 1 to 25. An additional point is placed at the origin to make clear the cumulative nature of the coefficient as we take more and more information into account.

A Lowess smooth line is drawn through the points to show the overall tendency. The function appears to rise rather steadily, although at a declining rate, through the first 10 weeks or so, and then to level off. Those with a good imagination may see somewhat more structure, possibly an overshoot near the 15th week, but that is not our point. The key fact is that returns up to about 10 weeks old seem to positively affect the subsequent return. The market, at least in an overall sense, seems to only gradually adjust to new information.

Showing in a rigorous way that this effect is statistically significant is more subtle than it looks, not only because of correlated residuals within the same time period, but because we extend the effect through successive regressions. If we look at any single regression in the range between 3 and 16 weeks and also take the extraordinarily conservative assumption that we have only one degree of freedom at each time period because of cross-sectionally correlated returns, the effect is significant at between the 2% and 10% levels. For 8 of the first 10 lags, the coefficient on the average prior return increases as each lag's effect is added. This gives us evidence not on a single regression, but on the overall pattern. The binomial probability of 8 out of 10 increases if there were no overall lag structure would be 0.05. For a more conservative interpretation, since the 11th coefficient did not increase, the chance of 8 out of 11 if the true probability were one-half is 0.11.

While it is possible that the tendencies toward currency trending arise from speculative dynamics, the relatively long delay and the lack of a greater overshoot suggest adaptive sluggishness caused by governments resisting economic change already signaled to the market. Taken together, Exhibits 5,6, and 7 reinforce that picture.

The existence of fat-tails tells us that risk control should be conservative relative to the evidence of recent periods. The existence of trends tells us that technical models are likely to be helpful.

CURRENCY CYCLES?

An inspection of Exhibit 1 suggests a degree of cyclicality. To the statistically unaided eye, it certainly looks as though there might be a roughly 8-year cycle in the yen/$ hedging relationship. However, we should keep in mind that random noise can look like cycles, and that real cycles can be irregular in length and look random. We need some sort of statistical investigation to aid intuition here.

Exhibit 7: Influence of Prior Hedging Returns

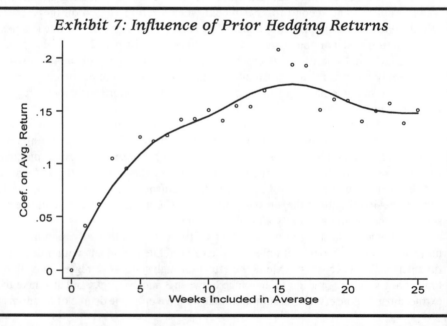

Based on Exhibit 7 there are no cycles with time periods on the order of 3 to 15 weeks. In my work, I have not been able to find any statistically significant longer period cyclicality. Unfortunately, though there is a suggestion of cyclicality at periods on the order of 8 years, my 17 years of data are not enough to discriminate its statistical significance.

For the reader interested in pursuing this topic further, I recommend the study of a tool called "rescaled range analysis," used for spotting structure in chaotic data.[3]

Keep in mind, however, that currency hedging profits, being functions of differentials, will often not have recognizable cyclicality even if each of their component currencies are driven by somewhat cyclical forces. For example, sometimes the business cycles of Europe and the United States are in phase, and sometimes out of phase. If the former case, one might expect small, random-appearing excursions of exchange rates between them; in the latter case, large excursions reflect the business cycle's influence on interest rates.

OPTIMALLY HEDGED ASSET ALLOCATION

One should determine an optimal passive hedge policy as part of an overall asset allocation study. In doing so, it is important to consider the total portfolio including both domestic bonds and stocks. This is because currency-hedged assets may have return correlations with these other assets that differ asset by asset from those of the unhedged foreign securities.

Let us go through a simple example, in which all foreign stocks will be aggregated as the MSCI EAFE Index. For the purpose of estimating risk, we will approximate the risk of hedged EAFE as though it were EAFE in local currency terms. This is a good estimate since short-term interest rate volatility is quite small compared to stock volatility.

The risk and correlation statistics shown in Exhibit 8 are for quarterly returns for the 55 calendar quarters beginning in 1982 and running through 1995. The risk standard deviations have been doubled to annualize them on a familiar scale. However, we should note that this analysis is proper only for a quarterly horizon, since correlations at quarterly intervals may differ noticeably from those measured annually. Cash and U.S. bonds have been added to the asset menu.

We will use our own *a priori* estimates for expected return based loosely on long-term history. The difference between expected hedged returns and unhedged returns reflects an estimated annual cost of 40 basis points for hedging in terms of frictional costs and fees. These priors, though plausible, are given simply for illustration.

---

[3] A good explanation of rescaled range analysis can be found in Edgar E. Peters, *Fractal Market Analysis* (New York: John Wiley & Sons, 1994). A precise academic presentation is contained in Andrew Lo, "Long-Term Memory in Stock Market Prices," Working Paper No. 2984, National Bureau of Economic Research, 1989.

Exhibit 8: Optimal Allocation Input

	EXP RTN	EXP Risk	Correlations			
Cash	5.0	0.0	1			
SP500	11.0	14.7	0	1		
EAFE	12.0	18.9	0	0.53	1	
Hedge EAFE	11.6	17.2	0	0.66	0.82	1
US Bond	7.0	9.7	0	0.37	0.27	0.19

Exhibit 9: Efficient Frontier without Hedging

Expected Return	9.0	9.5	10.0	10.5	11.0	11.5
Expected Risk	8.9	10.0	11.2	12.3	13.4	14.7
Cash	30.8	22.2	13.6	4.9	0.0	0.0
SP500	37.7	42.4	42.3	47.1	57.5	50.0
EAFE	22.2	25.0	27.7	30.5	34.0	50.0
Hedge EAFE	0.0	0.0	0.0	0.0	0.0	0.0
US Bond	9.3	10.4	16.4	17.5	8.5	0.0
Foreign Equity Ratio	0.37	0.37	0.40	0.39	0.37	0.50
Hedge Ratio	0.00	0.00	0.00	0.00	0.00	0.00
Stock Allocation	0.60	0.67	0.70	0.78	0.92	1.00

Exhibit 9 shows the resulting efficient frontier if no hedging is allowed. The rows labeled Cash, SP500, and so on show the percentage of total assets allocated to that asset at points of increasing risk and return on the frontier as one moves rightward. Since we have used a historical correlation of only 0.53 between U.S. and foreign stocks, diversification benefits cause large fractions of non-U.S. stocks to be allocated at every risk level, upwards of 37%. This effective risk diversification also allows large amounts of stock to be used for quite conservative portfolios.

When in Exhibit 10 we add the opportunity to hedge the currency exposure, we see very little change in the overall efficient frontier for a U.S. investor. (The standard deviation in the middle of the frontier is reduced only from 11.2% to 11.1%. Again, however, the improvement can be much larger in smaller countries.) However, the optimal composition in terms of assets is noticeably altered. This form of analysis allows us to see immediately the best hedging ratios as well as the additional foreign exposure that is optimum.

In this case, the optimal foreign exposure is increased from 37% to 43% across most of the frontier. The optimal hedging ratio varies depending on risk tolerance, but is in the range of 30% for all but the highest risk portfolios.

The apparent improvement in the efficient frontier possible through currency hedging may or may not increase materially as one divides assets into more and more categories. However, one should not do such an analysis without using some of the shrinkage estimators described earlier to limit the potential negative impact of data-mining.

Exhibit 10: Efficient Frontier with Hedging

Expected Return	9.0	9.5	10.0	10.5	11.0	11.5
Expected Risk	8.9	10.0	11.2	12.3	13.4	14.7
Cash	29.6	20.8	12.0	3.2	0.0	0.0
SP500	33.8	38.1	42.3	46.5	52.9	46.1
EAFE	16.7	18.8	20.9	23.0	27.3	44.1
Hedge EAFE	8.8	9.8	10.9	12.0	11.3	9.8
US Bond	11.1	12.5	13.9	15.3	8.5	0.0
Foreign Equity Ratio	0.43	0.43	0.43	0.43	0.42	0.54
Hedge Ratio	0.35	0.34	0.34	0.34	0.29	0.18
Stock Allocation	0.59	0.67	0.74	0.82	0.92	1.00

IDEAS FOR ACTIVE CURRENCY MANAGEMENT

Currency management efforts can usefully be split into better return enhancement and better risk control. An effective process will do both.

Return Enhancement

In contrast to the literature on stocks, much less has been written about currency market efficiency and inefficiency. It is my experience that the quantitative investor interested in currency management is in the enviable position of working in a field where the prevailing views are largely pre-scientific. As a practical proposition, it seems to me that one can add value best through a combination of technical and fundamental analysis.

As we have already seen, on average and over a long period of time, cumulative hedging returns have followed trends. The problem for the currency manager is that these trends are highly clustered both by currency pair and by time period. For example, in recent years the British pound and the U.S. dollar have moved more or less together relative to continental Europe and to the Japanese yen. To the extent that the British government makes an effort to maintain a stable dollar/pound relationship, one will observe more counter-trending, or reversion to the mean, than trending. The challenge is to discriminate when trends are most likely. This circumstance will reflect both any government intervention that may cause under-reaction to news, and the extent to which speculators have already built into the current price an expectation of trend continuance.

If the essence of hedging is a decision not to lend, then relative interest rates and relative creditworthiness are the factors of most interest. (Trade-related indicators such as purchasing power parity, the ability to buy the same goods at the same real cost in different countries, are also of some importance. But these can be viewed as additional ingredients in the ability to repay.)

Relative interest rates are critical but tend to be impounded in prices very quickly indeed, especially for major currencies. The better opportunity for most active investors is to become specialists in discerning changes in perceived creditworthiness, and, better, to forecast these changes. In my experience, the key ingredients are of two kinds — economic expansion and recession on the one hand, and accumulated government mistakes or deliberate inflationary tactics on the other. The classic currency deterioration comes when economic recession exposes an accumulation of economic problems. The government comes under pressure to lower interest rates or otherwise devalue the currency in order to satisfy domestic political needs.

Conventional measures of accumulating problems include a poor current account balance, but better active returns are likely to come from unconventional measures. For example, one might note the extent to which government or international agencies have subsidized the economy. Another important source of information is the stock market, which can reveal information about coming recessions far ahead of actual events.

Risk Control

Currency risk is best controlled at the portfolio level — otherwise too many diversification benefits are left untapped. The key challenge here is to prevent the kinds of problems described in Chapter 15. The arsenal of choice is the collection of Bayes-Stein estimators. I showed a simple heuristic for achieving a substantial portion of the benefits of a formal Stein estimator with the covariance shrinkage estimator introduced in Chapter 19.

Currency covariance elements may also be modeled more dynamically. A typical device is to make next-period risk a function of the most recently observed risks. Although sound in theory, it should be remembered that the more complex the analytical assumptions, the more fragile is the estimation system in the face of changes in the environment. Rather than presenting an inadequate introduction to GARCH, etc., it seems better to leave such topics for another author with more relevant experience. I have done some work in this area with the Kalman filter technique which I hope to report in some later publication.

Currency risks can be converted into new forms through the use of options, as described in Chapter 7. Bets on exchange rate levels are transformed into bets on relative volatility. Here again, my experience is limited, and similarly to the use of stock options, I leave exposition of this topic to others.

Assuming sufficient expertise with shrinkage estimators, I recommend Markowitz optimization as the main tool for managing currency risk. The final remaining caution is one he expressed. Do not go too far with opposing long and short positions, because risk of the resulting portfolio is highly sensitive to assumed correlations. In practice, this means position limits for attempts to exploit cross-hedging skills.

With that, we conclude the "best current practice" part of this book. However, I have one more topic that deserves serious discussion for the aspiring quantitative investor. In the future, we may have to take more analytic risks, and learn new ways of modeling, to go beyond the crowd. The final chapter of this book introduces the techniques of *genetic algorithms* and *neural nets*.

Chapter 21

Neural Nets and Genetic Algorithms

It's the same each time with progress. First they ignore you, then they say you're mad, then dangerous, then there's a pause and then you can't find anyone who disagrees with you.
Tony Benn, *British Labour politician. Quoted in: Observer (London, October 6, 1991)*

Why would any quantitative investor want to leave the well-ordered realm of econometrics to travel out to the lawless frontier of genetic algorithms and neural nets? Interesting computer simulations of neural nets have been around since at least the 1960s, and genetic algorithms at least since the 1970s. Each has had one or more periods of early hyperbole about the possibilities they offered for building models more like the "real world," only to be followed by periods of disappointment. They are undoubtedly subject to misuse by the gold-rush pioneers who may reach new depths of data-mining. But as we discussed at the beginning of this book, quantitative tools in investing are themselves subject to the iron laws of fashion. Successful innovation is followed by destructive imitation. If we want to keep ahead of the pack, we must be alert for possible new approaches.

In this chapter I will briefly examine two examples of non-linear modeling that seem to have future potential for investment work. For most of us, non-linear forecasting tools are not yet practical. Appropriate standardized software for the serious non-specialist is not available. Second, successful use of these methods requires significantly more data and computer processing time than conventional linear ordinary least squares (OLS). Yet software continues to get better, computer power grows greater, and the high-frequency data that provide sufficient degrees of freedom become more available. Consequently, we need to prepare ourselves to take advantage of these techniques now.

Nature is endlessly resourceful and yet she did not build organisms that were limited to learning through OLS regression. Facing a complex, non-linear, and unstable environment, Nature built species of organisms through a process of survival of the fittest genes within a carrier population. This genetic coding is transformed generation-by-generation through reproduction modified by mutation and sexual recombination. There may be something useful about generational learning at a population level that we can apply to investing. This is the domain of genetic algorithms.

329

When ecological niches developed that rewarded rapid adaptive behavior, Nature developed a system of computation through networks of neurons that could reinforce different successful behaviors in different situations. This learning at the individual organism level operates throughout the animal kingdom. Its structure is capable of adapting to an amazing variety of circumstances. Consequently, it would not be surprising if it, too, could be put to use by investors. This is the domain of artificial neural nets.

Neither genetic algorithms (GAs) nor artificial neural nets (ANNs) have yet been as thoroughly understood as conventional statistical tools such as ordinary least squares regression. Still, they share many of the same properties and require some of the same disciplines in their use.

Consider that OLS can be viewed as a searching device that finds good model solutions in the form of best-fit lines relating different types of measured variables. Think of a space in which the regression coefficient given for each independent variable represents a different dimension, with an additional dimension that measures model error over a set of observations. In this case, model error is the sum of squares of the differences between actual and predicted dependent variables. The observations of the independent and dependent variables specify a surface in this space. For an OLS problem, the surface is bowl-shaped, with a unique minimum. That is the location of the best-fit line we hope to discover.

It is only the simplicity of the functional form and the simplicity of assumed underlying stochastic process of the OLS problem that allows one to calculate a unique solution quickly. However, the same best-fit line may be found by a general-purpose hill-climbing (or, in this case, bowl-descending) algorithm. OLS is used because it makes use of specialized knowledge about the problem rather than relying on less efficient but more generalized procedures.[1]

Like OLS, genetic algorithms and artificial neural nets are also searching devices. They are capable of solving more difficult problems in which the topology of the problem surface may look more like the Dakota badlands than the Hollywood bowl. Genetic algorithms and neural nets are also very well adapted to on-line forecasting. This is practical forecasting where the best-fit solution adapts to a changing stochastic structure. In contrast, off-line work assumes an unchanging model for a long sequence of observations.

All learning is subject to a tension between adapting to the data already observed and generalizing to the data yet to be observed. Statistical methods such as linear OLS, genetic algorithms, and neural nets all are subject to a common problem. This is deciding between additional customization to the observations at hand versus greater parsimony and thus more generalizability to other datasets. However, by their nature, non-linear models are less-parsimonious and require much bigger observational samples to attain reliability for generalization to new data.

---

[1] There are less widely-used statistical modeling methods that are more general-purpose than OLS, including maximum-likelihood methods for modeling non-linear relationships and Kalman filters for modeling on-line change processes. I view them as half-way houses between the OLS and the GA, ANN ends of the modeling spectrum.

Consequently, even more than for conventional linear regression, GA's and ANN's should be employed in a way that conforms to the cycle of splitting observations into model-estimation and model-testing subsamples. Indeed, a third dataset is usually employed for additional validity testing with ANN's. Just as in conventional econometrics, it is necessary to limit the complexity of the model if we are to have a good chance of the model standing up in a validation sample. Unfortunately, with such general purpose non-linear methods we will generally not have the comfort of familiar t-statistics to guide us regarding model parsimony.

One offsetting advantage is greater flexibility in optimization criteria. Results for forecasting actual returns may, if we choose, be evaluated with respect to R-squared. However, since these models do not depend on specialized formulae for their solution, one is free to use a wider range of fitness optimization targets. For example, one may set them to work to minimize absolute value of the errors, or to maximize trading-oriented fitness criteria such as percentage of times the direction of the forecast is right.

With both genetic algorithms and artificial neural nets we can limit the list of variables which are inputs to the model as well as constrain the model's overall complexity. However, the greatest accommodation one must make for these biologically oriented methods is loss of control. With large neural nets, there may even be loss of detailed understanding of how the model works. This is a very serious deficiency. It means that it is difficult for us to guide the learning process with the theory and intuition that we can add to help reach properly parsimonious and generalizable models even with limited data.

Again, there are offsets. We get more precision in representing complicated problems. Also, allowing a degree of self-organization gives us increased opportunity for more creative and innovative model-building. Once a particular high-order relationship among a set of variables is discovered, it may be understood and tested in a more familiar setting. This can be done by reformulating non-linearities and interactions among independent variables as additional terms within a linear OLS model.

The plan of the chapter is as follows:

1. introduction to genetic algorithms
2. introduction to neural nets
3. a cautionary example.

INTRODUCTION TO GENETIC ALGORITHMS

The idea of solving problems by simulating the natural process of evolution through random mutation and testing of an *individual* solution had been circulating for some time. However, genetic algorithms (GA's), which solve problems with a *population* of potential solutions, sprang almost fully born from the brow of

John Holland in the 1960s.[2] The distinguishing feature of his contribution was the evolution of a population of potential solutions that could exploit parallel search through a *crossover* operation between strings of DNA-like symbols representing individuals. There is now a large literature on GA studies and applications.[3]

Holland's exact scheme has since been improved as genetic algorithms have been pressed to solve increasingly difficult problems, but the essential GA structure includes the following three steps, which we apply to our regression example.

> *Step 1:* Create an encoding scheme that translates a problem solution into a string of symbols. The classic GA uses only a binary alphabet of 0's and 1's, employed in a string of fixed length. These symbols are the "genes." Although we would not in practice choose to use a GA to solve a linear regression in one variable, we could do so as follows. Represent real numbers at the precision offered by binary string of length 32 positions or bits (4 bytes). Then the genotype of the solution is a string of 64 bits, with the first 32 representing the regression constant and the next 32 representing the regression coefficient.

> *Step 2:* Generate a population of random binary strings of length 64. These are genotypes. The best-fit lines into which each is converted are the phenotypes, in biological parlance. A typical population might be 50.

> *Step 3:* Iterate until the average fitness of the population can no longer be improved or until a fixed limit of generations has been reached. As each individual is created with new genes, a population of phenotype lines moves around until most or all of its individuals have optimal fitness as estimates. In this case, fitness is maximized when in the context of a set of observations the sum of the squared errors is minimized. The search is conducted using the following scheme:

> > *Selection:* Test to see if finished. If not, evaluate the fitness of each individual in the population. Using one of several possible schemes, generate a subset of individuals worthy of reproduction based on fitness. (The original scheme set probabilities of being selected based on the ratio of the individual fitness score to the population average fitness score.) Then randomly divide this group into pairs for mating. The remaining individuals are discarded.

> > *Crossover:* Create replacement individuals as follows. For a fraction of the pairs chosen randomly, say 30%, retain the parents as members

---

[2] John H. Holland, *Adaptation in Natural and Artificial Systems* (Ann Arbor, MI: University of Michigan Press, 1975). (The second edition: Cambridge, MA: MIT Press, 1992.)

[3] Melanie Mitchell, *An Introduction to Genetic Algorithms* (Cambridge, MA: MIT Press, 1996). See also David E. Goldberg, *Genetic Algorithms in Search, Optimization, and Machine Learning* (New York, NY: Addison-Wesley, 1989).

of the next generation of individuals. The remaining parents, say 70%, will be discarded after children are created. The genotypes for the two children are created as follows. Line up the binary strings side-by-side in the same direction. Randomly select a position on the string. Swap the portions of the strings beyond this position between the two parents. The resulting strings are the genotypes of the two new individuals.

Mutation: There will now be a new population of the same number as before selection. For each individual and for each position on their genotype, with a low probability, flip the code. For example, with probability 0.001 change a "0" to a "1" and vice versa. Now return to the *selection step.*

This process is not guaranteed to find the optimum of every possible problem in a finite number of steps. However, it will reasonably quickly discover surprisingly good solutions, which may then be typically improved with increased investment in generations. It is also extraordinarily robust in the face of different types of complex problems that would stump typical optimization routines that rely on all the good answers being close to one another. How does it work?

There are three learning processes at work. First, the *selection step* acts to move the population as a whole toward areas of solution space with higher average fitness. By operating to cause the increase in the proportion of "good" genes in the population as a whole, it behaves much as fashion does. It works through a process of imitation of the successful models. Second, the *crossover step* allows complementary partial solutions to find each other. For example, the correct regression constant can be crossed to the same string as the correct regression coefficient. By allowing sexual reproduction this step allows different individuals within the population to transmit their partial knowledge of the fitness landscape. Third, the *mutation step* allows exploration of new genes, or previously lost genes, that may not be in the repertoire of any individual in the current population.

The early experiments with genetic algorithms had many successes but also notable failures. Sometimes, on particularly deceptive problems, the GA never finds an isolated peak in the fitness landscape. Sometimes it converges too slowly because crossover breaks up useful combinations of genes too quickly. Sometimes it converges too quickly to a second-best solution. This happens when poor individual genes happen to be in proximity on the genotype to genes that offered such powerful fitness advantages that their entire strings are quickly multiplied throughout the population.

These problems have been dealt with reasonably effectively with slight variations in the method. For example, one may invent coding schemes between genotype and phenotype that better ensure that important groups of genes are closer in position and therefore less likely to be broken by crossover. One may select mating populations through tournaments within randomly chosen pairs, with the fitter individual winning with a specified probability, to better control the speed of convergence. And one can conduct crossover so that it occurs with higher probability at positions between, rather than within, important gene clusters. These examples are only representative. Many other constructive variations can be found in the footnoted references.

There is an analogy between two survival processes. The first is the operation of a GA on a population of investment rules that forecast stock returns based on characteristics like price-to-book and recent price and earnings movements. The second is the operation of the stock market itself on a population of investors. Though more complex rules are involved, investors are still subject to the mechanisms of selection, crossover of ideas, and random mutation through happenstance. The operation of a GA is not unlike the waves of fashion that sweep through the real stock market. However, it has the advantage over the stock market of not costing us much money to learn whatever lessons it has to offer.

My experimentation with GA's has been limited but interesting. I attempted to forecast corporate bond ratings from a list of accounting variables. This was a problem with which I had already some familiarity because of my experience in forecasting bankruptcy.[4] Thinking that I should get out to the very edge of GA practice, I constructed a generalized coding in which the strings represented a flexible assortment of ingredients to "if-then" rules. The "then" represented a particular bond rating, such as AAA or B. The "if" condition had a multiple-part template. It included possibilities for constants, independent variables scaled to fit compact binary representations, and logical relations like "less than," "greater than," AND, OR and NOT. I constructed fitness implicitly as "food." This must be shared by individuals that correctly or nearly correctly guessed the rating of the same particular bond, and allowed mating with higher probability among similar individuals who had amassed sufficient food. Food was used up with time and with incorrect guesses, and when it reached a low level, the individual would "die."

This scheme did indeed produce a population of modestly successful specialists at predicting various bond ratings. Still, I had substantial problems with crossover interrupting useful rules. In hindsight, I should have expected this and more closely restricted mating pairs given the diversity of population I was seeking. Eventually, however, I stabilized the parameters sufficiently to produce interesting results at quasi-equilibrium. (Of course, given the food sharing and assortive mating structure, the system would never converge to a population of identical individuals, and low-probability crossover kept producing divergent types.)

I found that the emergent rules for high bond ratings such as AA's did not look like the opposite of the rules for predicting low ratings such as B's. However, both extremes did make sense. This finding of non-symmetry would probably not have happened if I had stuck with linear regression.

A second success was the discovery that I could harness a diverse population cooperatively. I constructed a composite bond rating forecast to reflect the

---

[4] My first publication was Jarrod Wilcox, "A Gambler's Ruin Prediction of Business Failure Using Accounting Data," *Sloan Management Review* (Spring 1971), pp. 1-10.

median of the outputs of several different types of rules activated for any particular instance. These complementary rules even included different conditions predicting the same rating. This cooperative result allowed more complicated reasoning to be employed than could have been derived from a conventional GA without making the individual strings extremely long and therefore slow to converge. (Such a conventional structure would have individuals coded as rules for producing not a rating but a score that could rate any bond.)

My result was respectable in terms of R-squared between predicted and actual ratings. However, it was not better than I could achieve simply by using linear regression on the variables I already knew to be relevant. And that is where my GA experience stands for now.

At this stage in their theoretical development, the many choices in structuring GA's to be effective for solving particular problems are not well understood or standardized. Popular general purpose GA tools have not yet been commercialized. However, GA's have been applied by some pioneers for prediction of financial returns. They have also been used to increase the effectiveness of artificial neural nets. This is done by using a GA to design a customized artificial neural net for a particular problem. That is, the phenotype produced by the GA is a neural net. This net is then further trained to optimize predictions within a set of observations. Such a two-step product has been commercialized in a form suitable for experimentation by the ambitious quantitative investor.

INTRODUCTION TO NEURAL NETS

The idea of imitating the brain's functions through computer simulation dates from the aftermath of World War II. It was not many years before simple models of neurons began to be put together in networks and used to simulate pattern recognition. The *perceptron* is an abstract model of a single neuron. It includes several inputs and a single output. When the sum of the inputs crosses a threshold, the neuron "fires." A single perceptron can learn by varying the weights by which it multiplies these inputs before summing up to see if the threshold has been breached. Besides responding to a single stimulus, such an arrangement can easily perform logical linkages. For example, if the threshold is set high, we have AND. If it is set so low that any one input can trigger a response, we have OR. If we allow a stimulus with an inhibitory effect, that is, a negative weight, we get a NOT.

My apartment-mate in graduate school at MIT in the late 1960s was deeply involved in artificial intelligence work. (He was William Martin, later to earn a place as a member of the faculty working on MIT's famous Project MAC.) I was exposed to frequent war stories of progress and set-backs. The head of the Artificial Intelligence Laboratory at MIT was Marvin Minsky. He was known for his prediction that the next step in life's evolution would be from man to machines; another leading light, though from a more humanistic tradition, was his colleague Seymour Papert. Annoyed by the early overblown claims for the computational ability of networks of perceptrons, they proved that there were broad classes of problems for which a class of such networks was helpless.[5]

Minsky was not unaware of the merits of neural nets as general purpose finite-state machines, capable of being elaborated with feedback to solve a very broad class of problems. Despite this, his critique was harsh and all-inclusive. It had an extraordinarily chilling effect on neural net research. Unfortunately, they overlooked the possibility of connecting simple feed-forward networks into more layers, the so-called hidden layers. Such nets could discover solutions to the kinds of pattern recognition problems requiring global knowledge cited by Minsky and Papert.

It was nearly 20 years before neural nets re-emerged from the wilderness.[6] This time, the beneficial impact of additional hidden layers of neurons between inputs and outputs was recognized. The early neuron models had been on-off switches, firing either not at all or completely when a threshold had been just reached. It was now noted that artificial neurons could just as well be given a smooth S-shaped function to govern their output. The most typical activation function for smoothing this step-function was the logistic function, $y = e^x/(1+e^x)$, where x is the excess of the sum of inputs over a threshold, and y is the output. This function is asymptotic to 0 for large negative inputs and to 1 for large positive inputs.

The first benefit of such a firing rule was easy representation of real number outputs. The second was a smooth derivative that could be used as the basis for updating the weights given to each input stimulus. The slope of the output as a function of the weights could be calculated so as to allow trial solutions to follow downward along the gradient of the neural net's error from desired output. This made possible the *back-propagation* algorithm, which in turn created a widely understood basis for neural net computer programming and application.

That is, the new research first established that even simply structured feed-forward neural nets with no feedback from output to inputs could represent the solution to an extremely broad class of problems. For example, if enough neurons were put into a hidden layer, a neural net could closely approximate even very oddly behaved functions of an arbitrary number of inputs.

Second, the research provided a practical, easy to understand algorithm that allowed somewhat efficient search for that set of proper weights. In back-propagation, one calculates the slope of the error with respect to each of the weights, and then adjusts each weight by a small step based on that calculation. This happens after each evaluation so as to reduce the error slightly if the same instance should be presented again. Progress can be slow. Still, with a suitable number of neurons and hidden layers and a large enough number of training

---

[5] Marvin Minsky and Seymour Papert, *Perceptrons* (Cambridge, MA: MIT Press, 1969). An earlier, more favorable treatment of neural nets is given in Marvin Minsky, *Computation: Finite and Infinite Machines* (Englewood Cliffs, NJ: Prentice-Hall, 1967).

[6] David E. Rumelhart and James L. McClelland (eds.), *Parallel Distributing Processing* (Cambridge, MA: MIT Press, 1986).

instances, one can usually train an artificial neural net to the same or better level of accuracy as achieved through any conventional statistical technique.

If the defined error is the sum of squared residuals between a forecast and actual variable over some dataset, the eventual result of neural net training is a conventional best-fit or forecast function. Some people think of neural nets as "just" a kind of non-linear regression. Neural nets are able to self-organize to represent complex logical conditions and relationships without requiring recoding of various logical conditions on independent variables as new inputs. They are thus a good deal more capable than most of us would infer from the mere word "nonlinear."

During the last decade various improvements have been made to neural net modeling. These can speed up the convergence to a stable vector of weights, resist becoming stuck on a local optimum or in an oscillation, and at least partly overcome the traditional ANN problem of over-fitting (data-mining). The plain-vanilla back-propagation algorithm has become passé. However, these improvements are mostly incremental rather than revolutionary. They do not change the basic intuition that can be gained from practice with a simple network structure and the error back-propagation search algorithm. That intuition is a sensitivity to the enormously greater need for data and repeated validation testing as compared to linear models.

For concreteness, Exhibit 1 portrays a very simple neural network with five neurons. The top two, A and B, accept input regarding two different attributes. They simply scale inputs to the range 0 to 1 using the logistic function. They each have two outputs, one to each of the two neurons in the hidden layer, C and D, but with different weights to each. Finally, C and D have outputs transmitted to a final output neuron E that combines these signals again and further transforms the original input. If desired, the output may be subsequently re-scaled from the 0,1 interval to any interval on the real numbers.

In Exhibit 1, the bias units are not visible. One can think of these as additional inputs of a positive or negative constant. If negative, bias inputs may be viewed as thresholds. Each of the arrows represents a neuron's output signal multiplied by a weight, which may be positive or negative. For example, these include W_{AC}, W_{AD}, W_{BC}, W_{BD}, W_{CD}, W_{CE}, W_{DE} and possibly another below Output E. At each downstream neuron, the sum of the weights times their signals, plus any bias constant, is then transformed by an S-shaped function. This function, often the logistic curve, produces each neuron's output.

Of course this diagram is simpler than neural nets often found in practice. In general there may be more than one output, more inputs, and more hidden layers. The more complicated the shape of a function to be derived between inputs and outputs, the more neurons will be needed in the middle layer or layers.

If you want to go beyond this sketchy introduction, consider the book by Kingdon and Mannion.[7] At this point, we turn to an example.

---

[7] Jason Kingdon and C.L. Mannion (eds.), *Intelligent Systems and Financial Forecasting* (Springer-Verlag, 1997).

Exhibit 1: Simple Neural Net

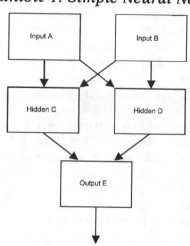

A CAUTIONARY CASE STUDY

In this final section we will apply a neural net analysis to an example, the market timing problem from Chapter 17. Here is the equation with which we had ended.

. regress ifrtn dpbln12 dsurp12, robust

Regression with robust standard errors

Number of obs	=	180
F(2,177)	=	2.41
Prob > F	=	0.0929
R-squared	=	0.0523
Root MSE	=	4.533

ifrtn	Coef.	Robust Std. Err.	t	P>|t|	[95% Conf. Interval]	
dpbln12	−5.953126	3.234766	−1.840	0.067	−12.3368	0.4305458
dsurp12	46.99406	22.9625	2.047	0.042	1.678552	92.30956
_cons	1.853674	0.4166928	4.449	0.000	1.031348	2.675999

This OLS model predicts an equal-weighted monthly return from a large sample of stocks over a 15-year period. It is based on two variables, the 12-month change in average log price-to-book and the 12-month change in average surplus return on equity over an interest rate. You may remember that this model was formulated after experimenting with a model based on *levels* of log P/B and surplus of ROE over interest rate. The change to 12-month differences was based on the judgment that a model forecasting market return based on time-differences in the input variables would have fewer econometric problems. However, the earlier levels-based version in Chapter 17 had a better fit in-sample. Keep in mind that this level of judgmental override will not be available to a neural net.

What I will do here is to compare OLS and a neural net package in their ability to forecast half of this sample based on models estimated from the other half. To put the two approaches on the same footing, we will use stepwise regression among a larger list of variables for the OLS entry in the contest. The odd months will be used as a model estimation sample and the even months as a validation sample. The neural net estimation will proceed using a further split of the odd months into training and testing samples, but iterate this process many times.

The use of such a small sample of observations puts neural nets to a severe disadvantage. However, a small-sample case has two advantages. First, overfitting neural net models to small datasets is the most typical mistake in their use. This way, you can see the tangible result. Second, though a problem with 100,000 observations would show neural net results to better advantage, it would require very extensive processing time. It is not unusual that, even on a fast personal computer, such problems can take days to compute.

I chose as a platform for this example the only moderately-priced software package I could find with some hope of successful use by the casual experimenter. The package consists of the companion programs Neuro-Genetic Optimizer and ExamiNeur, both supplied by BioComp Systems, Inc.[8] The programs are disadvantaged by providing no easily-available output to the user as to the weights incorporated in the neutral net after training, and they are not free from bugs. However, with some practice, they can provide interesting insights to the quantitative investor. The model building proceeds by training a population of different neural nets on a dataset, and then using a genetic algorithm at a higher level to evolve the population toward fitter neural nets. Flexibility extends to allowing for different kinds of threshold output functions, including not only the logistic function but also the arc-tangent and linear functions.

The user may set many different parameters. In the example I stuck to simple back propagation, with rather conventional choices, except to use an available fitness function option to combine R-squared and a bias toward nets of fewer neurons. The number of instances for training each net was selected by the program using default criteria.

Again, the odd month model-estimation subsample was divided into two further subsamples, one for training and one for testing. The fitness of individual ANN's was based on a combination of success in each sub-sample, but the training of the net was based entirely on the training sub-sample. I allowed the neural nets to be constructed from up to five inputs — log price-to-book, return on equity, the surplus of ROE over interest, and the aforementioned 12-month changes in log P/B and surplus.

Remember that the package had only 45 observations for net training and 46 observations for net testing to use in constructing a model to forecast equal-weighted stock market returns. To train the net, one presents the data many times.

---

[8] As of December 22, 1998, the Internet Worldwide Web address of BioComp is www.bio-comp.com.

Here is what the genetic algorithm selected as the best ANN after 10 generations with a population of 30 nets. The input variables were pared from five to only three: *pbln*, *surplus*, and *dsurp12*. This showed some judgment in rejecting *ROE* in favor of the *surplus* of ROE over interest rates, which contained similar but superior information.

The structure did not seem too complicated. With a choice of up to two hidden layers, the model selected one hidden layer with only two neurons. However, these had different forms: one was a logistic and the other a linear output. Also, the final single output neuron was given an arc-tangent function (tanh), which is essentially a logistic transformed so that its output ranges from -1 to 1 rather than 0 to 1, before final scaling. The actual weights of the inter-neuron connections were not reported.

Using Examineur, I found that the sensitivity of the standardized output to changes in the standardized inputs are approximately equal for *pbln* and *surplus*, and less than one-fifth as large for 12-month change in surplus, *dsurp12*. I could also see the shape of the output response surface as a function of two input dimensions at a time. The surface flattened where both primary inputs were extremely favorable or extremely unfavorable, and did not flatten where only one was favorable. This seemed to indicate an interaction effect, although it cannot be a very trustworthy one given the limited number of observations.

Compare the R-squared achieved by this net in the three different samples:

Training Sample: n = 45,   R-squared = 0.47
Testing Sample: n = 46,   R-squared = 0.11
Validation Sample: n = 90,   R-squared = 0.0022.

Of course by its nature we would expect the training sample to have the highest apparent fitness. But the falloff when we go to a hold-back sample is drastic.

Now let us put a step-wise regression to work with the same model estimation sample (n = 91), with access to all five input variables seen by the neural net.

. sw regress ifrtn pbln roe surplus dpbln12 dsurp12 if odd, forward pe(.4) pr(.> 5)

```
                     begin with empty model
p = 0.0222 <   0.4000    adding    dsurp12
p = 0.0079 <   0.4000    adding    dpbln12
p = 0.2228 <   0.4000    adding    pbln
p = 0.0016 <   0.4000    adding    surplus
p = 0.5433 >=  0.5000    removing dsurp12
```

Source	SS	df	MS
Model	533.193804	3	177.731268
Residual	1721.37791	87	19.785953
Total	2254.57172	90	25.0507969

Number of obs	=	91
$F(3, 87)$	=	8.98
Prob > F	=	0.0000
R-squared	=	0.2365
Adj R-squared	=	0.2102
Root MSE	=	4.4481

ifrtn	Coef.	Std. Err.	t	P>|t|	[95% Conf. Interval]	
surplus	180.3015	41.71575	4.322	0.000	97.38696	263.2161
dpbln12	−4.227664	3.634186	−1.163	0.248	−11.451	2.995673
pbln	−21.28845	4.499692	−4.731	0.000	−30.23207	−12.34482
_cons	5.802526	1.373752	4.224	0.000	3.072045	8.533008

We see that a regression equation with three variables was chosen, each with a t-statistic greater than 1. Two of them, *pbln* and *surplus*, are the same as chosen by the GA-ANN process. The third is different, but as with the neural net the third variable has far less weight, as indicated by its lower t-statistic.

The results for the stepwise regression approach were:

Estimation Sample: n = 91,   R-squared = 0.24

Validation Sample: n = 90,   R-squared = 0.0057.

That is, the hold-out sample had twice the R-squared as for the neural net. In both cases, there is a drastic reduction in R-squared as we move to fresh data.

It may be argued that with a different combination of fitness weights or sample sizes for training and testing the neural net could have done better than we saw here. Of course that is true, but one wonders where to stop in such a searching process. Perhaps there are better heuristics to use in setting the parameters of the process, so that the result will generalize better. But I do not know them, and I suspect they will take some years yet for their full development. Meanwhile the non-linear approach must compete with linear methods that have amassed both theory and lore to give guidance to the model-builder.

It is illuminating to try to translate the degrees of freedom concept to a non-linear model. Although the analogy is very rough, suppose that each connection weight uses a degree of freedom. How many potential connections are there with five inputs and, let us say, up to four neurons in the hidden layer and another as output? There are 5 times 4 plus 4, or 24. Now consider the curved responses produced by each neuron. Suppose we approximated each of these by piecewise linear regression with five line-segments. Now we have 24 plus 5 × 10, or 74 analogies to degrees of freedom used up. But we tried to train our net on only the equivalent of between 45 and 91 observations. The wonder is not that the net gave such poor performance out-of-sample but that it showed any promise at all.

Described this way, our example was doomed from the beginning. Yet this kind of overfitting is relatively common in the initial stages of learning about neural nets, or indeed, any non-linear procedure. In theory, we can approximate any non-linear structure with a linear equation whose ingredients are various powers and products of the inputs. If we imagine how many additional terms this will take, we can get some indication of the number of independent observations we are going to need to build a reliable model of a given complexity.

In the market-timing case given here, and being satisfied with limited non-linearity, I would want several thousand observations to work with before considering using the results. And even then, I would use the analysis primarily as a source of insight to construct a better OLS regression model. This would incorporate suggested interaction terms and functional transformations of my original independent variables. The OLS shadow model would allow me to better understand the ANN, to use t-statistics to make it more parsimonious, and to communicate more easily to others.

As with genetic algorithms, neural nets are interesting, worth time and trouble to explore, but are not yet superior to conventional model-building incorporating noisy observations in the hundreds or low thousands. But for problems with more frequent observations, for example daily trading data, or very large stock selection databases, they may prove themselves worth all the effort. For some, they may have already done so.

A FINAL WORD

This is the end of the book. For the reader who has made it all the way from Chapter 1 to 21, thank you for your attention. It has been my pleasure. Good fortune to you!

Index

A

A priori estimates, 323
Accounting variances, 261
Active currency management, 313
  ideas, 325–327
Active funds. See Closely controlled
  active funds.
Active international diversification,
  298–300
Active investing, 9–10, 45
Active investors, 4, 106, 175, 275,
  298
Active portfolio, 140
Active positions, 271
Active risk reduction, return
  enhancement separation, 318
Actual returns, 162, 271
Adjustment, 148–149
After-tax returns, 3, 35. See also
  Long-term after-tax returns.
  maximization, 168
Agent investors, 251
Agents. See Living agents; Non-liv-
  ing agents.
  risk, 143
Aggregate market feedback struc-
  ture, 52–59
Aggregation, global level, 25
Alexander, Gordon J., 13
American call, 110
American put, 110, 118
American-style investing tools, 6
AMEX, 237
Amortization. See Trading cost.
  period, 82
Anchoring, 148–149, 151
ANNs. See Artificial neural nets.
Annualized risk, 265
Anomalies, 11. See also Publicly
  revealed anomalies.
APT. See Arbitrage Pricing Theory.
Arbitrage, 170, 186, 187, 275, 276.
  See also Company arbitrage;
  Fixed-income arbitrage.
Arbitrage Pricing Theory (APT),
  126, 130–136
Arthur, W.Brian, 42, 177, 178
Artificial-agent simulations. See
  Markets.
Artificial agents, usage. See Stock
  market.
Artificial Intelligence Laboratory,
  335
Artificial neural nets (ANNs), 330,
  331, 337, 339–342
Artificial stock market, 41–44
Asset allocation, 120. See also
  Long-term asset allocation; Opti-
  mally hedged asset allocation;
  Tactical asset allocation.
  decision, 263

B

Asset allocators, 277
Asset base, 278, 280
Asset class, 185
  level, 25
Asset exposures, currency decisions
  linking, 318–319
Asset type, 250
Assets to equity ratio, 237
Astronomical Cycles, 206
Attribute combinations, 43
Auto-regressive scheme, 42
Autocorrelation, 267, 295. See also
  Returns.
Availability, 148, 151
Axtell, Robert, 39

B/M. See Book value to market
  value ratio.
B/P ratio, 169
Back-propagation algorithm, 336,
  337
Bailey, Jeffery V., 13
Balance sheets, 12
  variables, 238
Banking crisis, 251
Bankruptcy, 129, 139
Bard College, 41
BARRA, Inc., 134, 141
Base case, equilibrium characteris-
  tics, 59–67
Batterymarch Financial Manage-
  ment, 127
Bayes-Stein estimation, 88
Bayes-Stein estimators, 326
Bayesian prior, 256, 308
  covariance matrix, 257, 309
Behavioral finance, 145, 205
  principles, application, 151–153
Benchmark, 30, 78, 141, 252, 319.
  See also Capitalization-weighted
  benchmarks; Cash benchmark;
  Equity; International benchmark;
  Market-index benchmark.
  return, 86, 263, 272
  risk, 142
  tracking, 251
Best-practice example, 250
Beta, 126, 130, 133, 237, 238, 296
Bid-ask spread, 81, 159, 269
Binomial probability distributions,
  116
Binomial trees, option value, 116–
  118
Black, Fischer, 112, 120, 125
Black-Scholes-Merton continuous
  model, implications, 118–120
Black-Scholes-Merton option value
  model, 4
Black-Scholes option pricing model,
  107, 111-116, 119

C

Blazenko, G., 105
Bond returns, 224
Bond security allocations, 260
Book-to-market factor return, 241
Book-to-market ratios, 241
Book-to-price ratio, 17, 128, 237
Book-to-price returns, 139–140
Book value, 275, 305
Book value/market capitalization,
  239
Book value to market value ratio (B/
  M), 237, 238, 241
Book values, 194, 198
Booth, David G., 96
Boston Consulting Group, 178, 194
Boundary condition, 113. See also
  Terminal value.
Bounded knowledge, 33–34
Bounded rationality, 39
Brazil fund, 81
Brokerage commission, 159
Brownian model, 109
Brownian motion, 108–109, 113,
  114, 118
Brownian noise, 112
Business cycles, 323
  fluctuations, 275
Buying power, 206

Calendar effects, 6
Campbell, John Y., 132, 153, 220,
  242, 243, 245
Campbell/Stiller, research, 242–246
Capital asset pricing equilibrium,
  128
Capital Asset Pricing Model
  (CAPM), 4, 5, 38, 39, 43, 45, 60,
  78, 91, 98, 101, 105, 115, 133,
  137–139, 145, 166, 238, 240,
  296, 297. See also Equilibrium-
  based capital asset pricing model.
  assumptions, 48, 136
  contribution, 140
  descendants, 125
  empirical tests, 127–128
  formulation, 146
  model. See Sharpe-Lintner-Black
  CAPM model.
  postulated linear relationship, 47
Capital gains, 169
Capital gains taxes, 5, 167
  effects, 159
Capital volatility, 207
Capitalization effect. See Time-interacted small capitalization effect.
Capitalization-weighted basis, 269
Capitalization-weighted benchmarks,
  219, 259
Capitalization-weighted index, 46,
  141, 309

343

Capitalization-weighted index fund, 276
Capitalization-weighted official index, 302
CAPM. See Capital Asset Pricing Model.
Carrying capacity, 119
Cash benchmark, 213
Cash flow, 74, 137, 182, 193
Cash returns, 192
Cauchy, 255
Cavaglia, Stefano, 315
CCAPM, 126
Central Limit Theorem, 97, 100
Chan, Louis K.C., 152, 240, 242, 299
Chan/Jegadeesh/Lakonishok, research, 240–242
Changing preferences, role, 40
Chen, N., 134
Clarkson, Geoffrey, 153
Clean surplus accounting, 196
Closed-end emerging market funds, 81
Closely controlled active funds, 78
Cluster analysis, 135
Cognitive dissonance, 149–150
reduction, 149
Coleman, Kay A., 13
Collins, B.M., 161
Commissions, 269
Common factors, 132
Company arbitrage, 191
Complex feedback system, 52
Complexity theory, 175–180
Component analysis, 133
Component risk, 292
Composite bond rating forecast, 334
Compustat database, 237
Computational capacity, 33–34
Conditional CAPM, 126, 129
Confidence intervals, 259
Constant Proportion Portfolio Insurance (CPPI), 120–124, 203, 214
Constantinides, George M., 162, 166–168, 172
Construction performance, measurement. See Portfolio construction.
Continuous adaptation, 179
Contrarian investor, 182
Cootner, Paul H., 1, 46, 107–109
Corporate control, 57
Correlation-based arguments, 294
Correlation coefficients, 227, 253, 294. See also Cross-sectional correlation; Out-of-sample correlation coefficient.
Correlation structures, 219
Cost accounting. See Standard cost accounting.
Cost-of-risk lambdas, 143
Counter-trending, 325
Country selection, 263
Covariance matrix, 14, 84, 86, 252, 254, 308. See also Bayesian prior; Forecast.

Covariance risk estimation, heuristics usage, 306–309
Covariances, 78, 81, 84, 252, 253
Cox, John, 112, 126
Cox Ross Rubinstein (CRR), 116–118
CPPI. See Constant Proportion Portfolio Insurance.
Credit risk. See Excess credit risk.
Creditworthiness, 314
Cross-hedging skills, 326
Cross-market comparisons, 276
Cross-sectional analysis, 246
Cross-sectional comparisons, 202
Cross-sectional correlation, 271
coefficients, time-series sequence, 267
Cross-sectional differences, 256
Cross-sectional effects, 190, 201, 202
Cross-sectional means, 224, 339, 240
Cross-sectional regression coefficients, 238
Cross-stock decision-making, 45
Crossover, 332–333
step, 333
CRR. See Cox Ross Rubinstein.
CRSP, 237
Currency, 184, 295, 311. See also Home currencies.
baskets, 312
cycles, 322–323
decisions, linking. See Asset exposures.
manager, 315
strategic mistakes, 315–319
trading. See Short-term currency trading.
volatility, 312
Currency hedging returns, 321
source, 313–314
Currency management
ideas. See Active currency management.
performance, 311
Currency-related barriers, 24
Currency returns, 295, 320
statistical characteristics, 319–322
Currency risk, 315
protection. See Downside currency risk protection.
Cyclicality, 282, 322

D

Damped oscillations, 49, 50
Data, winsorization, 226
Data conditioning, 223–227
Data mining, 222, 229, 234, 236–238, 243, 256, 266, 329
error, 148
Day-trader, 34
De Long, Jay Bradford, 48
DeBondt, Werber, 152
Debt leverage. See Long-term debt leverage.

Decay, 164
value strategy, 164
Decision assumptions, measurement method, 153–157
Decision-maker, 32, 153, 186
Decision-making, 10. See also Cross-stock decision-making.
Demand equilibrium theories, 126
Deming, W. Edwards, 261, 272
Derivative security, 113
Differential equations, 182, 195. See also Time differential equation.
Dinardo, John, 190
Dissonance. See Cognitive dissonance.
reduction, 151
Diversification, 92, 95, 97, 141, 290. See also Active international diversification; Efficient diversification; Global diversification; International diversification; Investors; Passive international diversification.
analysis. See Markowitz diversification analysis.
Dividend interest arbitrage, 56
Dividend per share (DPS), 54–56, 224
Dividend yields, 17, 56, 64, 65, 67, 167, 243, 246. See also Long-term dividend.
smoothing, 62
Dividends, 46, 53, 68, 69, 72, 197
disturbances, 43, 61, 65
flow, 60
growth, 245
payments, 118
policy, 199, 277
projections, 193
DNA, 180
DNA-like symbols, 332
Dow Jones Industrial index, 149
Dow Theory, 16
Down event, 117
Down return, 117
Downside currency risk protection, 318
Downside protection, 316. See Short-term downside protection.
DPS. See Dividend per share.
Drew, Garfield Albee, 16, 206
Drift, 115
component, 112
Drop dead requirements, 104
DSLookup table function, 62
Duke University, 41
Dummy variable, 233, 234
Durlauf, S.N., 42, 178
Dynamic disequilibrium, 45
Dynamic economy, 281
Dynamic hedging, 104, 124
Dynamic market. See Individuals.

E

E/P. See Earnings to price variable.

EAFE, 290, 292, 294, 296
  countries, 300
  index, 295, 297, 304, 312, 319, 323
  return, 293
EAFE benchmark, 263
EAFE capitalization-weighted index, 141
Earning profits, 43
Earnings, 187
  announcements, abnormal return, 240
  growth, 193
  surprise, 240
Earnings estimates, 165
  revision, 163, 240
Earnings to price variable (E/P), 237, 238
Eastern Europe Fund, 81
Ecology, 175, 180–182
Econometric analysis. See Market inefficiencies.
Econometric modeling, 219
  techniques, 11
Econometric research, 220
  examples, 237–246
Econometric techniques and tools, 205, 219
Economic disturbances, 73
Economic events, 67
Economic growth, 286
Economic prosperity, 44
Edge investing, 79
Efficient diversification, 9, 12–16
Efficient frontier, 12, 37, 258, 324. See also Markowitz efficient frontier.
Efficient markets, 108–109
Efficient portfolio, 12
Eigenvalues, 134, 135, 156
Elder, Alexander, 206
Electronic trading exchanges, 161
Elliot Wave Theory, 206
Emergent phenomena, 176
Emerging markets, 299, 301. See also Equal-weighting emerging markets.
End-of-period wealth, 33
Endogenous variables, 52
Eng, William F., 206
Epstein, Joshua M., 39
Equal-weighted-by-country strategy, 302
Equal-weighted monthly return, 338
Equal-weighted portfolios, 240, 301, 308
Equal-weighting emerging markets, 301–306
Equal-weighting strategy, 301
Equilibrium, 47, 75. See also Capital asset pricing equilibrium; Dynamic disequilibrium; Market. characteristics. See Base case.
  point, 59
  price, 40, 61

return, 60
  theories, Demand equilibrium theories.
Equilibrium-based capital asset pricing model, 4
Equity, 311
  benchmark, 265
  managers. See Quantitative equity managers.
Error back-propagation search algorithm, 337
Error-generating process, 88
Estimates, dispersion, 77
Estimation error, 88
Euro, 24
Euroland group, 312
European call, 110, 114, 118
  option, 114
European Currency Union, 184, 312
European monetary integration, 23
European Monetary Union, 20
European put, 110
  payoff function, 121
Event risk, 251
Event studies, 152
Ex ante risk, 292
Ex post, 269
  risk, 292
  terms, 34
Examineur, 340
Excel (software), 13, 111
  hill-climbing facility, 164
Excess credit risk, 314
Excess returns
  forecast, 224
  standard deviation, 140
Excess risk, 140
Exchange rate levels, 326
Exercise price, 111
Exogenous disturbance, 54
Exogenous utility function. See Fixed exogenous utility function; Nonevolving exogenous utility function.
Exogenous variables, 52
Expected return, 138
Expected risk, 136
Expected utility, 146
Experience curve, 178

F

F-statistic, 18
Fabozzi, Frank J., 161
Factor analysis, 132, 133, 135, 252, 257
  usage, 254–255
Factor structure, 255
Fair value, 194. See also Stock market.
Fair-value P/B, 281
Fama, Eugene F., 17, 96, 125, 127, 137, 139, 152, 193, 220, 225, 239, 241
Fama/French, research, 237–240
Fama-MacBeth procedure, 238, 240

Fama-Macbeth regressions, 241
Fat-tailed distributions, 97, 104, 225, 250, 255
Feed-forward networks, 336
Feedback, 63, 179, 270, 336. See also Negative feedback; Positive feedback.
  structure. See Aggregate market feedback structure.
  systems, 49, 176, 177. See also Complex feedback system; Linear feedback system; Nonlinear feedback system.
Feedback loops, 51, 52. See also Negative feedback; Positive feedback.
Feedback structure, 45
Festinger, Leon A., 149
Financial risk premium, 130
Finney, Ross L., 112, 163
First-order approximation, 159
First-order term, 96
First-out delay, 61
Fixed effects regression, 190, 201
Fixed exogenous utility function, 39
Fixed-income arbitrage, 285
Forced liquidations, 171
Forecast, 269
  covariance matrix, 268
  errors, 266
  quality, 268
  returns, 271
Forecasting, 220. See also On-line forecasting; Risk.
  capability, 259
  coupling, 270–272
  performance, measurement. See Return forecasting.
Foreign currencies, 208, 319
  exposure, 318
Foreign diversification, 315
Foreign exchange bonds, 166
Foreign interest rate, 311, 314
Foreign investors, 187
Foreign taxes, 289
Forrester, Jay W., 49
Forward rate, 311
Fractal calculus, 112–114
Fractals, 108
Free-form judgmental analysis, 22
French, Kenneth R., 17, 127, 139, 193, 220, 239, 241
Frequency-based probabilities, 31
Frictional costs/fees, 323
Friedman, Milton, 89
Frontier-like economies, 21
Full-sample average, 243
Fundamental analysts, 63, 65, 73, 74, 183, 185
Fundamental attributes, 42
Fundamental factors, 85
Fundamental investors, addition, 63–67
Fundamental weights, 70
Future, 110

G

GA-ANN, 341
Gambler's ruin, problem, 80
Gann Analysis, 206
GARCH, 326
GAs. See Genetic algorithms.
Genetic algorithms (GAs), 7, 327, 329
   introduction, 331–335
Genetic coding, 329
Global databases, development, 12
Global diversification, 292
Global equity fund, 263
Global investors, 25, 277
Global markets, 184
Global portfolio, 297
Global risk, 294
Goldberg, David E., 332
Gorman, Stephen, 296
Government-backed bank interest, 186
Group influence, 149–150, 152
Growth, 67–72, 85, 157. See also Dividends; Earnings; Economic growth; Long-term growth.
   investors, 68, 71, 72, 74
   rate, 193, 196
   stocks, 29, 287
Growth-optimum model, 101

H

Hakansson, Nils H., 91, 92, 97–101, 207, 251
Hamao, Yasushi, 299
Harman, Harry, 132
Harvard Business School, 151
Harvey, Andrew C., 246
Hedged asset allocation. See Optimally hedged asset allocation.
Hedging. See Dynamic hedging; Inter-temporal hedging.
   benchmarks. See Passive hedging benchmarks.
   ratios, 315
   returns. See Currency hedging returns.
Hedging returns, 267
   source. See Currency.
Heterogeneity problem, 45, 49
Heteroscedasticity, 230, 245, 268
Heuristics, 147, 149, 208, 222. See also Technical heuristics.
   usage. See Covariance risk estimation.
Hidden layers, 336, 337
Hierarchical relationships, 135
High bandwidth Internet access, 21
High-beta stocks, 231
Hill-climbing algorithms, 82
Hill-climbing facility. See Excel.
Histogram, 316
Historical risk, 308
Hold-out sample, 340, 341
Holland, John H., 42, 175, 176, 332
Holton, Glyn A., 295

Home country interest rate, 311
Home currencies, 136
Horizon, 245
   model, 197
Huber, Audrey, 13
Huber-White sandwich estimator, 230
Hull, John C., 108
Hyperinflation, 295
Hypothesis testing, 259

I

IBES database, 241
IBES information, 240
IBM. See International Business Machines.
ICAPM, 126, 130
IFC. See International Finance Corporation.
Implementation difficulty, 164
Implementation shortfall, 160
   reduction, 161–162
Implementation shortfall trading costs, 160
In-sample fit, 244
In-sample returns, 246
In-the-money asymptote, 112
In-the-money calls, 112
Income statements, 12
   variables, 238
Index funds, 39, 275. See also Capitalization-weighted index fund.
Index investing, 297
Indexers, 4
Indexing, 45
Individual behavior, sum. See Market.
Individual judgment, 146–149
Individual Retirement Account (IRA), 3
Individual solutions, 331
Individuals, dynamic market, 175
Industry stratification, 250
Industry-wide problems, 138
Inefficiencies. See Market inefficiencies; Short-term inefficiencies.
Inflation, 195, 233. See also Hyperinflation.
Information
   ratio, 260
   transformations, 51
Infrastructure, 299
Ingersoll, Jonathan, 126
Innovation, 25
Input error, sensitivity, 252–253
Inputs, statistical estimates usage, 86–89
Inseparability. See Related decisions.
   utility, combination, 36
Insider-trading regulations, 178
Instability, 66, 256
Institutional environment, 183–184

Institutional investors, 139, 251, 298
Institutional portfolio, 83
Insurance. See Portfolio.
Int CAPM, 126
Inter-group correlations, 257
Inter-temporal hedging, 127–130
Inter-temporal risk premia, 130
Inter-temporal risks, 139
Interaction effects, 242
Intercorrelation, 252
Interest-bearing asset. See Riskless interest-bearing asset.
Interest-rate bonds, 130
Interest rates, 110, 192, 284, 326. See also Foreign interest rate; Home country interest rate; Risk-free interest rate; U.S. short-term interest rates.
   differentials, 314
Intermediate-term trending, 287
International benchmark, 298
International Business Machines (IBM), 46
International diversification, 289, 290, 294, 315. See also Active international diversification; Passive international diversification.
International equity investing, 263
International Finance Corporation (IFC)
   Composite Index, 302, 305
   country indices, 301–302
International investing, 289
International investment movement, U.S. perspective, 289–296
International markets, 297
Internet access. See High bandwidth Internet access.
Intersec Research Corporation, 289
Investing. See Active investing; Edge investing; Judgmental investing; Many-period investing; Momentum; Quantitative investing; Saint Markowitz investing; Single-period investing.
   plan, 1, 3–7
   purpose, 1, 2
   scope, 1, 3
   tools. See American-style investing tools.
Investment
   analysts, 30
   behavior, 99
   horizon, 170, 201, 282
   literature, 237–246
   managers, 82
   movement, U.S. perspective. See International investment movement.
   pool. See Riskless investment pool.
   principles. See Technical heuristics.
   research, 286
   returns, 26

risks, 24
strategies, 11, 83
styles, 63, 162
theory, 158
Investors, 186, 210. See also Active
    investors; Contrarian investor;
    Foreign investors; Growth; Long-
    term dividend; Markowitz inves-
    tor; Momentum; Quantitative
    investors; Rational investor;
    Value investors.
    addition. See Fundamental inves-
        tors.
    behavior modeling, 153
    diversification, 296
    theoretical finance comparison,
        31–36
    types, homogeneity, 36
IRA. See Individual Retirement
    Account.
Ito process, 113
Ito's lemma. See Lemma.

J

Jagannathan, Ravi, 129
January effect, 220–236, 238, 239
    study, 239
January enhancement, 235, 236
Jegadeesh, 240
Johnston, Jack, 190
Jorion, Philippe, 88
Judgmental analysis, 24. See also
    Free-form judgmental analysis;
    Strategic judgmental analysis.
Judgmental analysts, 22
Judgmental investing, 20–24
    example, 22–24

K

Kahneman, Daniel, 145–151
Kalman filter, 246, 326
Kingdon, Jason, 337
Kurtosis, 79, 97, 103, 104, 108, 214,
    225–227, 238, 251

L

Lakonishok, Josef, 240, 299
Lambda, 57, 315. See also Cost-of-
    risk lambdas; Markowitz lambda.
Lane, D., 42, 178
Large-scale trending, 288
Lattice Trading, 162
LDCs. See Less-developed coun-
    tries.
Least-cost policy, 162
Least-squares estimates, 18
Least-squares regression. See Multi-
    variate least-squares regression.
LeBaron, B., 42
LeBaron, Dean, 3, 127
Ledoit, Oliver, 257
Lefevre, Edwin, 9
Leland, Hayne, 119
Lemma (Ito), 113, 114

Less-developed countries (LDCs), 6
Less-developed markets, 296
Leverage, 81, 120, 122, 170, 237,
    250. See also Long-term debt
    leverage.
    cap, 121
Linear equality constraint, 86
Linear estimator, 18
Linear feedback system, 51
Linear regression, 267, 341
Lintner, John, 125, 136, 137
Liquidation, 173. See also Forced
    liquidations.
    value, 169
Liquidity, 35, 109
Living agents, 41
Lo, Andrew W., 132, 153, 220, 323
Lock-in effect, 178
Log book value, 239
Log-linear relationship, 194
Log market capitalizations, 227,
    228, 234
Log-normal distribution, 225, 251
Log-normal return, 246
Log P/B, 285
Log returns, 98, 213, 245
    mean-variance framework, 105
Long-short portfolios, 87
Long-term after-tax returns, 168–
    170
Long-term asset allocation, 78
Long-term bonds, 129
Long-term debt leverage, 129
Long-term dividend
    investor, 68
    yield, 56
Long-term equity return expecta-
    tions, 45
Long-term fluctuations, 276
Long-term growth, 91
Long-term portfolios, 168
Long-term returns, 4, 127, 172
Long-term risk premia, 134
Long-term unrealized gains, 30
Long-term wealth, 92. See also
    Mean long-term wealth.
Look-ahead bias, 244, 246
Loops, gain, 51
Lotka-Volterra predator-prey equa-
    tions, 182
Low-beta stocks, 231
Lowness smooth line, 321
Luce, R. Duncan, 32

M

Maastricht Treaty, 23
MacKinlay, A. Craig, 132, 153, 220
MacLean, L.C., 105
Macro-economic factors, 85, 134
Magill, Michael, 162
Mandelbrot, Benoit, 108, 109, 175,
    212, 225, 250
Mannion, C.L., 337
Many-period investing, 91
Market capitalization, 18, 20, 127,

128, 227, 228, 237. See also Log
    market capitalization; Relative
    market capitalization.
    impact, 286
    non-linear effect, 232
Market environment, 178
    consequences, 73–75
Market equilibrium, 46–49, 275
Market factor, 137
Market funds. See Closed-end
    emerging market funds.
Market impact transaction costs,
    160
Market index. See Capitalization-
    weighted market index.
    movement, 270
Market-index benchmark, 125
Market inefficiencies, 12
    econometric analysis, 9
    identification, 16–20
Market portfolio, 126, 167
    return, 131
    risk, 131
Market prices, 36, 136
    long-term increases, 167
Market technicians, 211
Market value variations, 305
Markets, 175. See also Emerging
    markets; Equal-weighting emerg-
    ing markets; Individuals; Interna-
    tional markets; Trending markets.
    artificial-agent simulations, 4
    components, 48
    feedback structure. See Aggre-
        gate market feedback structure.
    imperfections, 219
    individual behavior, sum, 145–146
    risk, 37
    segmentation, 127, 136–139
    structure, 30. See also Trading
        cost.
    taxes, impact, 166–168
    theoretical finance comparison,
        36–39
Markowitz, Harry M., 4, 12, 33, 34,
    38, 77, 79, 84–86, 88, 89, 91–93,
    96, 250, 253. See also Multi-
    period return.
Markowitz allocation, 297
Markowitz analysis, 82, 85. See also
    Single-period Markowitz analysis.
Markowitz diversification analysis,
    16
Markowitz efficiency, 125
Markowitz efficient frontier, 126, 140
Markowitz framework, 34, 35, 98
Markowitz investor, 57, 75, 138
Markowitz lambda, 102, 103
Markowitz mean-variance
    analysis, 141
    framework, 126
    optimization, 36
Markowitz objective function, 79
Markowitz optimal portfolio selec-
    tion, 158

Markowitz optimizations, 86, 250–252, 309, 326
Markowitz-optimized portfolios, 269
Markowitz optimizers, 143, 308
technique, 249
Markowitz portfolio theory, 289
Markowitz single-period analysis, 36
Martin, William, 335
Martingale, 108
Massachusetts Institute of Technology (MIT), 2, 3, 98, 107, 261, 335
McClelland, James L., 336
MDS. See Multidimensional Scaling.
Mean long-term wealth, 92
Mean-residual variance framework, 142
Mean-variance formulations, 99
Mean-variance framework. See Log returns.
Mean-variance optimization. See Markowitz mean-variance optimization.
Merton, Robert C., 92, 98–101, 107, 112, 114, 126, 128–131, 137
Merton-Samuelson critique, aftermath, 105
Mexico Fund, 81
Michaud, Richard O., 88, 97, 253, 257, 269
Micro-economists, 31, 45
Microeconomics, 31, 132
Mid-month transactions, 263
Minsky, Marvin, 335, 336
Mitchell, Melanie, 332
Model-builder, 341
Model-estimation, 331
subsample, 331, 339
Model structure, 223–227
Modigliani, Franco, 1
Momentum, 85, 157, 276
addition, 63–67
factors, 287
investing, 212
investors, 64, 67, 72, 74, 83, 119, 123
loop. See Positive momentum loop.
process, 165
strategies, 128, 213
thinking, 182
weights, 70
Momentum-based strategies, 120
Momentum-type strategies, 166
Money managers, 30
Monotonic transformations, 97
Monte Carlo analysis, 246, 251
Monte Carlo simulation, 110, 114, 121, 134, 156, 168, 212, 243, 250, 252, 257, 260
results, averaging, 253–254
usage. See Option valuation.
Morgan Stanley, 242
Morgan Stanley Capital International Perspective, 187
Morgenstern, Oskar, 31, 100
Mossin, 125

Moving average, 206, 209
MSCI, 281, 290, 295, 323
country indices, 297
MSCI indices, 263, 290
data, 242
Multi-period models, 131
Multi-period return (Markowitz), extending, 95–97
Multi-prey predators, 182
Multicollinearity, 232, 239
Multidimensional Scaling (MDS), 155
Multivariate least-squares regression, 86
Municipal bonds, 166
Mutation, 333
step, 333
Mutual Fund Theorem, 100
Mutual funds, 99, 152

N

NASDAQ, 237
Near-term risk, 12
Negative feedback, 49–52, 176
loop, 49, 50, 56, 65
Net capital, growth rate, 251
Network structure, 337
Neural net analysis, case study, 338–342
Neural nets, 7, 327, 329. See also Artificial neural nets.
introduction, 335–338
New York Stock Exchange (NYSE), 159, 237
NYSE-traded stocks, 98
Next-period risk, 326
Nikkei, 290
No-market timing solution, 45
Non-intuitive solutions, changes, 257
Non-linear complexity, 158
Non-linear derivatives, 250
Non-linear model, 236
Non-linear regression, 337
Non-linear relationships, 135
Non-linearities, 177, 233
Non-living agents, 41
Non-negativity constraints, 79–81, 86, 257
Non-negativity financing constraints, 81
Non-overlapping, 316
Non-quants, 80
Non-symmetry, 334
Non-taxable shareholders, 167
Non-U.S. stocks, 324
Nonevolving exogenous utility function, 39
Nonlinear complex systems, 52
Nonlinear feedback system, 52
Nonlinear networks, 179
Null hypothesis, 267
NYSE. See New York Stock Exchange.

O

Objective probabilities, 146
October 1987 crash, 12, 216
Odd-day sample, 215
Odd-lot trades, 211
Off-line work, 330
Ohlson, James A., 193
OLS. See Ordinary Least-Squares.
On-Balance Volume, 206
On-line forecasting, 330
On-line trading, 183
One-way trading cost, 229
Opportunities. See U.S. stocks.
Opportunity costs, 160
Optimal holding period, analytic determination, 82
Optimally hedged asset allocation, 323–325
Optimization, 253, 258. See also Markowitz optimizations; Single-period optimization.
sensitivity, 252
Optimizer, 80, 85. See also Markowitz optimizers; Poor man's optimizer.
building, 13
constraints, 257–258
issues/solutions, 257–260
multiple levels, 259–260
problems, 249
Option models, 110
Option portfolios, 120
Option position, 124
Option premium, 203
Option-selling payoff pattern, 212
Option theory, applicability, 212–214
Option valuation, Monte Carlo simulation usage, 110–114
Option value. See Binomial trees; Closed-form option value.
tree, 118
Options, dynamic equivalents, 107
Ordinary Least-Squares (OLS), 232, 267, 329, 330, 339
assumptions, 18, 231. See also Residual errors.
diagnostics, 269
model, 19, 234, 246, 331, 338
re-running, 233
shadow model, 342
Ordinary Least-Squares (OLS) regression, 17, 18, 26, 27, 226, 232, 242, 329
model, 342
structure, 234
Oscillations, 49, 52, 61, 66, 177. See also Damped oscillations.
period, 50
Oscillators, 206, 211
Out-of-sample correlation coefficient, 244
Out-of-the-money puts, 119
Over-fitting error, 148
Owner-investor utility, 31

P

P/B. See Price to book ratio.
Palmer, R., 42
Papert, Seymour, 336
Passive benchmark, 298
Passive hedging benchmarks, 315
Passive international diversification, 296–297
Passive investor, 161
Passive strategy, 301
Path dependence, 214
Payoff
  functions, 122
  patterns, 124. See also Option-selling payoff pattern.
PB-ROE, 187, 194, 277
  analysis, example, 198–203
  model, 193–198, 282, 299
  residuals, structure, 277–281
Penetration, logistic curve, 25
Percentage R, 206
Perceptron, 335
Performance
  analysis, 261
  correlation, 276
  measurement, 272–273. See also Portfolio construction; Return forecasting performance; Trading.
Performance drag, 160
  minimization, 162–166
Perold, Andre F., 84, 120, 160, 270
Peters, Edgar E., 323
Phase shift, 50
Phenotype, 335
Physical securities, 161
Point and Figure, 206
Poor man's optimizer, 269
Portfolio construction, 19, 35, 249, 257, 261, 266
  coupling, 270–272
  multiple elements, simultaneous estimation, 256–257
  optimization, 271
  performance, measurement, 268–269
Portfolio manager, 250
Portfolio optimization, 257
Portfolio returns, 33, 77, 79
  risk, 134
  variance, 290
Portfolio risk, 33, 34, 77, 134, 251, 293, 319
Portfolio selection, 145
  methods, 86
  problem, 101
Portfolios. See Active portfolio; Equal-weighted portfolios; Global portfolio; Institutional portfolios; Market portfolio; Risk; Stock portfolios.
  allocation methods, 88
  arithmetic return, variance, 251
  estimated risk, 14

holdings, 258
insurance, 104, 120. See also Constant proportion portfolio insurance.
  level, 86
  theory, 33. See also Markowitz portfolio theory.
  turnover rate, 82
Position constraints, 258, 308
Positive feedback, 49–52, 176, 178
  loop, 49, 275
Positive momentum loop, 65
Potential solutions, population, 331
Pre-tax returns, 167, 169
Predator-prey equations. See Lotka-Volterra predator-prey equations.
Predator-prey relationships, 181
Predictive relationships, estimation, 227–229
Price/book anomalies, 299
Price/book ratios, 17
Price-book/return on equity valuation model, 5
Price-earnings-multiple stocks, 192
Price-earnings portfolio, 127
Price-earnings ratio, 17, 127, 186
Price momentum, 240, 241
Price movement, 122
Price returns, 224
Price signal, 209
Price-to-book effect, 19, 20
Price to book ratio (P/B), 18, 127, 186, 190, 192–197, 199, 275, 277, 278, 280, 287, 297, 305, 306, 338. See also Fair-value P/B; Log P/B.
  criterion, 202, 203
  quartile, 190, 191
Price-to-book ratios, 17, 83, 139, 141
Price trajectories, 108
Price trends, 203
Price volatility, 43
Probabilities, 31. See also Frequency-based probabilities; Objective probabilities; Subjective probabilities.
Probability distributions, 316
Process-oriented observations, 272
Production
  amplification, 50
  capacity, 177
Productivity, 176
Profit opportunity, 214
Profit surplus, 284
Project MAC, 335
Publicly revealed anomalies, 11
Purchasing power parity, 325

Q

Quadratic programming, 78, 83
  problem, 85
Qualitative analysis, 198
Quality control, 261, 266
Quantitative analysis, 21, 198
Quantitative equity managers, 78

Quantitative investing, 9
Quantitative investors, 1, 130, 185, 207, 211, 237, 249, 255, 275
  reasons, 9–20
Quantitative model, 192
Quants, 5. See also Non-quants.

R

Raiffa, Howard, 32
Random error, 88
Random numbers, 16
Random walk, 53
Rational investor, 73
Rationality, Savage model, 147
Rationalization, 297
Real world scenario, 29–30
Recessions, 130
Regression, 189, 197, 259, 305, 321. See also Fixed effects regression; Non-linear regression; Ordinary Least-Squares; Step-wise regression.
  coefficients, 26, 192, 230, 232, 234, 238, 266, 332. See also Cross-sectional regression coefficients.
  models, 154
Related decisions, inseparability, 34–35
Relative market capitalization, 286
Relative strength, 206
Relative volatility, 326
Representative investor, 178
Representativeness, 147–148, 151
Rescaled range analysis, 323
Reserve levels, 104
  variation, 102
Residual errors, OLS assumptions, 229–231
Residual returns, 252
Residual risk, 219, 250, 298
  management, critique, 127, 140–143
Residual variance, 133
Residuals, 237
  structure. See PB-ROE.
Return distribution, 109, 255
Return enhancement, 325–326
  separation. See Active risk reduction.
Return forecasting, 261
  performance, measurement, 266–268
Return intervals, 254
Return on Equity (ROE), 191, 193, 278, 280, 282, 283, 285, 305, 338, 340. See also PB-ROE.
  surplus, 339
Return predictability, 243
Return statistical characteristics. See Currency.
Returns. See Actual returns; Forecast returns.
  autocorrelation, 152

correlation, 314
variance, 137
Reversals, 217
predictive power, 215
Reward to risk ratio, 265
Risk. See Agents; Annualized risk;
Benchmark; Component risk;
Expected risk; Global risk;
Investment; Market portfolio;
Markets; Near-term risk; Portfolio returns; Portfolios; Volatility.
characteristics, 250
control, 151, 207, 326–327
discomfort, 139
estimation. See Covariance risk
estimation.
factor, 254, 255
forecasting, 42, 249, 251–257
linearity, 131
management, 249
portfolio, 15, 324
premium, 192
reduction, 292. See also Active
risk reduction.
single elements estimation, 255–
256
tolerance, 138, 275
variance, 60, 79
Risk assessment, 249
multiple elements, simultaneous
estimation, 256–257
Risk aversion, 99
reconciling, 101–105
Risk-free asset, 126
Risk-free interest rate, 38, 115- 117,
126, 131, 137
Risk-free returns, 103, 105
Risk management
critique. See Residual risk man-
agement.
philosophy, 249–251
Risk premium, 60
Risk-return terms, 298
Risk-taking, propensities, 102
Risk-taking species, 181
Risk-tolerance spectrum, 15
Riskless interest-bearing asset, 37
Riskless investment pool, 59
ROE. See Return on Equity.
Role Repertory Test, 154
Roll, Richard, 92, 98–101, 126, 131,
134, 141, 298
Rosenberg, Barr, 140, 141
Ross, Stephen, 112, 126, 130-132,
134
Row vector, 14
Rubinstein, Mark, 112, 119
Rule dominance cascading, 43
Rumelhart, David E., 336
Runyon, Richard P., 13

S

S-shaped function, 336
Samuelson, Paul A., 92, 98–101,
108

Santa Fe experiments, 78
Santa Fe group, 180
Santa Fe Institute (SFI), 4, 41
economics efforts, 177
experiments, 29, 44, 78, 158
Satisficing, 145, 151
Savage, L.J., 31
model. See Rationality.
Scholes, Myron, 107, 112
Schulman, Evan, 162
Schumpeter, Joseph, 179
Schwager, Jack D., 2, 206
Scientific method, advantage, 11–12
Search algorithm. See Error back-
propagation search algorithm.
Securities, 79. See also Physical
securities.
quantity, 84–86
return, statistical structure, 175
Segmentation, 140. See also Market.
Selection, 332
step, 333
Selling power, 206
Selling pressure, 206
Semi-variance, 79
Separation Theorem, 100
SFI. See Santa Fe Institute.
Sharpe, William F., 13, 140
Sharpe, William S., 36, 137
Sharpe-Lintner-Black CAPM
model, 237
Sharpe-Lintner model, 101
Sharpe ratio, 272
Sherif, M., 150
Shiller, Robert J., 220, 242, 243,
245
Shleifer, Andrei, 48
Short sales, 81, 87, 242, 270, 271
Short-selling errors, 88
Short-term average return, 4
Short-term bonds, 208
Short-term currency trading, 2
Short-term downside protection,
315–318
Short-term equilibrium, 36
Short-term inefficiencies, 161
Short-term interest rates, 323. See
also U.S. short-term interest rates.
Short-term mean dividends, 53
Short-term prices, jumps, 109
Short-term rates, 282
Short-term reversals, 128, 152
Short-term trading strategies, 183
Short-term treasury bills, 186
Shortfall, reduction. See Implemen-
tation shortfall.
Shrinkage estimators, 326
SIC codes, 278
Simulations, 39–40. See also Stock
market.
capability, 260
controls, 53
Simultaneous estimation. See Port-
folio construction; Risk assess-
ment.

Single-period analysis, 91. See also
Markowitz single-period analysis.
Single-period investing, 77
Single-period Markowitzian frame-
work, 80, 104
Single-period optimization, 89
Single-period returns, 15, 91, 97
Single-period thinking, 129
Sinquefield, Rex A., 295
Situational framing, 148
Skewness, 108, 123, 124, 207, 251
Sloan School, 107, 108
Slovic, Paul, 146, 153
Small-cap effect, 236
Small-capitalization country, 304
Small-capitalization stocks, 139, 161
Small-stock effect, 16
Small-stock fund manager, 35
Small stock returns, 139–140
Small stocks return premiums, 221–
236
sample selection, 221–223
structural issues, 231–234
unstable processes, 234–236
validation sample, 236
Smith, Adam, 5, 158
Smoothing delay, 67
Smoothing price, 68
Social science, 39–40
Solnik, Bruno H., 136
Solutions. See Potential solutions.;
Individual solutions
Soros, George, 275
South Sea Bubble, 66
Specialization, 180
Speculative dynamics, 322
Speculative valuation, 278
Spot exchange rate, 311
SRETDAY, 215
Standard & Poor's 500, 46, 135,
214, 272, 275, 276, 285, 286, 324
futures, 104, 216
Index, 214, 242
returns, 215
Standard cost accounting, 261–266
framework, 266
STATA, 132, 230
code, 224
manuals, 190
statement format, 223
statistics program, 187
Static relationships, 22
Statistical distribution, 97
Statistical estimates, 79
usage. See Inputs.
Statistical techniques, 151
Stein estimators, 257
Step-function disturbance, 56
Step-wise regression, 340
Stochastic calculus, 112–114
Stochastic process, 192
Stochastics, 206
Stock-bond combinations, 260
Stock market, 10, 26, 48, 60, 151,
175, 179. See also Artificial stock

market; U.S. stock market.
fair value, 186–192
simulations, artificial agents
usage, 39–44
Stock portfolios, 135
Stock prices, 209
Stock returns, 202, 242, 295
Stock selection, 263
Stock superiority, 221
Stock-to-stock comparisons, 196
Stock valuation model, 193
Stocks. See U.S. stocks.
cross-sectional relative returns, 47
fraction, 66
Strategic judgmental analysis, 23
Structural change, 276
Structural representations, 179
Subjective probabilities, 31
Summers, Lawrence H., 48
Survivor bias, 202, 235, 236
Survivorship bias, 20
Synthesis, 24–27
System structure, 64
Systematic risk, 47, 130, 237

T

Tactical allocation. See Two-asset
tactical allocation.
Tactical asset allocation, 208
Tax-deferred savings, 3
Tax-free asset, 170
Tax option, 170–172
Tax option value, 169
arrangement, 172–173
Tax returns. See Long-term after-tax
returns.
maximization. See After-tax
returns.
Taxable shareholders, 167
Taxes, 159. See also Foreign taxes.
environment, 166
impact. See Market.
liability, 168
reduction, 172
Tayler, R., 42
Taylor series, 96
Technical analysis, 205, 209
Technical attributes, 42
Technical heuristics, 205
investment principles, 207–212
Technical rules, study, 214–218
Terminal value, 95
boundary condition, 196
Terminal wealth, 93, 94
Thaler, Richard, 152
Theoretical finance
comparison. See Investors; Mar-
ket.
sub-field, 45
Theories. See Complexity theory;
Investment; Portfolio.
usefulness/purpose, 30–31
Theory
applicability. See Option theory.
Thermodynamics, Second Law, 180

Thomas, Jr., George B., 112, 163
Thorp, Edward O., 105
Threshold effects, 190, 200, 233
Threshold output functions, 339
Tic Volume, 206
Time differential equation, 196
Time horizons, 193, 246, 282, 283,
287
Time integration, 55
Time-interacted small capitaliza-
tion effect, 235
Time-interacted variables, 240
Time interval, 112
variance proportion, 109
Time modeling, 153
Time scales, 177
Time sensitivity, 25
Time-series approaches, 246
Time-series effects, 190, 202
Time-series forecasts, 224
Time-series regressions, 241
Time-series sequence. See Cross-
sectional correlation.
Time-series variances, 256
Tobin, 125
Tracking error, 78, 319
Trading, 261
capital, 208
coupling, 270–272
data, 342
performance, measurement, 269–
270
process, management, 259
ranges, 250
strategies. See Short-term trading
strategies.
volume, 43
Trading cost, 81, 159, 165, 172,
257, 263, 270. See also Implementation shortfall trading costs;
One-way trading cost.
amortization, 83, 259
environment, 159–160
market structure, 160–161
problem, 83
Transaction costs, 79, 81–83, 123,
170, 172, 190, 195. See also Market impact transaction costs.
considerations, 271
Transaction taxes, 159
Trend extrapolation, 64
Trend-following strategy, 213
Trending. See Intermediate-term
trending; Large-scale trending.
Trending markets, 206
Treynor, 125
Tulip Mania, 66
Turning points, indicators, 212
Turnover, 166, 254, 296
constraint, 258
rate, 82. See also Portfolios.
Tversky, Amos, 145–151
Two-asset case, 292
Two-asset tactical allocation, 78
Two-parameter model, 92

U

Uncertainty, 146–149
Heisenberg Principle, 6
University of Michigan, 41
University of Wisconsin, 41
Up-front costs, 124
U.S.-EAFE correlation coefficient,
294
U.S. short-term interest rates, 282
U.S. stock market, 29, 38, 40, 57,
187, 214, 250, 275, 277, 286, 290
U.S. stocks, 30, 132, 236, 263, 275.
See also Non-U.S. stocks.
comparisons, 281–285
opportunities, 281–285
understanding, 286–288
Utility
combination. See Inseparability.
framework, adequacy, 35
functions, 98
industry, 286
model, 145
Utility-based theories, 91

V

Validation samples, 222, 237
Valuation
discount, 284
Valuation models, 185, 203. See
also Stock valuation models.
Valuation theories, 125
Value-added curve, 82
Value-added process, 266
Value at Risk (VAR), 250, 251, 260
Value fund, 89
Value investors, 67–72, 74
Value Line, 198, 200, 221, 237, 277
database, 223, 282
Survey, 18, 279
Value-oriented anomalies, 127
Value-oriented criteria, 17
Value-oriented investors, 271, 287
Value-oriented managers, 141
VAR. See Value at Risk.
Variables, 286. See also Balance
sheets; Dummy variable; Income
statements; Time-interacted vari-
ables.
intercorrelation, 231
Variance, 57, 97, 103, 108, 114,
124, 256, 265. See also Portfolio
returns; Residual variance;
Returns; Risk; Semi-variance;
Time-series variances.
framework. See Mean-residual
variance framework.
portfolio, 306
risk-related limitations, 79–80
sequence, 262
stock, 171
Vector product, 252
Vensim, 53
format, 58
Volatility, 43, 44, 268. See also Cap-

ital volatility; Currency; Price
volatility; Relative volatility.
information, 212
risk, 300
von Neumann, John, 31, 100
von Neumann-Morgenstern estimated utilities, 158
von Neumann-Morgenstern rational
investor, 99
von Neumann-Morgenstern utility
calculation, 146
maximizer, 126
theory, 99, 145

W

Waldman, Robert J., 48
Walton, Mary, 261
Wang, Zhenyu, 129
Wealth, 95, 99, 121, 138, 276. See
also Terminal wealth.
denominator, 103
fraction, 58
index, 46
Wilcox, Jarrod W., 82, 95, 141, 153,
160, 165, 166, 194, 207, 298,
301, 302, 315, 334
Wilcox ratio, 272
Wild-card randomization, 122
World War II, 23, 31, 335

Z

Zannetos, Zenon, 261
Zero-mean annual return, 243
Ziemba, W.T., 105